THE
MEN
WHO
KILLED
THE
NEWS

ERIC BEECHER

THE MEN WHO KILLED THE NEWS

**The Inside Story of how Media Moguls
Abused their Power, Manipulated
the Truth and Distorted Democracy**

SCRIBNER

First published in Australia in 2024 by Scribner,
an imprint of Simon & Schuster (Australia) Pty Limited
Suite 19A, Level 1, Building C, 450 Miller Street, Cammeray, NSW 2062

Simon & Schuster: Celebrating 100 Years of Publishing in 2024.
Sydney New York London Toronto New Delhi
Visit our website at www.simonandschuster.com.au

10 9 8 7 6 5 4 3 2 1

A catalogue record for this
book is available from the
National Library of Australia

9781761631658 (UK edition)
9781761428050 (ebook)

Cover design by John Canty
Cover photos via Getty Images: Georges De Keerle (Robert Maxwell);
Keystone/Stringer (Lord Beaverbrook); Brian Dowling (Elon Musk);
James Devaney (Rupert & Lachlan Murdoch)
Typeset by Midland Typesetters in Adobe Caslon Pro 11.5/16
Printed and bound by CPI (UK) Ltd, Croydon CR0 4YY

Contents

MALFEASANCE

THE FUTURE

Why this Book?

The abuse of journalism by media moguls isn't a new story. The shelves are lined with their biographies. But it's clear to me, after a lifetime spent inside the media ecosystem, that not even a library of biographies and histories can begin to explain the *cumulative* damage inflicted on liberal democracies by owners of journalism who place profits and power ahead of civic responsibility and decency.

I have written this book to try to describe how abuse of media power works, its impact on society, and the ways in which its perpetrators get away with it. We think we know this story because we see so much evidence of it – misinformation, concoction of facts, invasion of personal privacy, maligning of public figures, weaponising of reckless opinions, the normalising of sensationalism.

But this isn't a story that can be told simply through a catalogue of bad, or even dangerous, journalism. Media power is built on the gigantic loophole in democracy that protects the freedom of the press without requiring any ethical, moral or societal responsibility from its owners. Media power sits at the centre of a *system*.

Despite its obvious flaws, this system has functioned for more than a hundred and fifty years as the least-worst way of safeguarding journalism's paramount role: holding power to account. The First Amendment to the US Constitution, and similar laws or conventions in other countries, are the protective mechanisms underpinning this system. They provide the legal architecture that supports the foundational precept of journalism's place in democracy, summed up in Thomas Jefferson's famous contention: 'Our liberty depends on the freedom of the press, and that cannot be limited without being lost.'[1]

Many media owners *do* live up to their ethical responsibilities. They are able to balance the tensions between journalism and commerce; to stay afloat without bending the truth for profits; to recognise that idealism and serious journalism mostly don't pay the bills but can be subsidised by other, more commercial activities. The others – the moguls, magnates and charlatans who have exploited journalism to accumulate money and power – are the main subject of this book. For them, democracy's loophole has been the source of a suite of formidable operating levers: *access* (almost every door in society opens privately to those media owners and their underlings), *information* (intelligence gathered inside their doors becomes a tradeable, often lethal, commodity), and *fear* (the motivation that explains why most powerful people never pick a fight with someone who, as the saying goes, 'buys ink by the barrel').

When I first became a journalist in my twenties I was highly motivated, like most of my peers, by its mission to report the facts and uncover important things that people don't want aired in public; to be society's watchdog. Over the years, as I graduated from reporter to newspaper editor and finally to media owner (not on a mogul scale), I began thinking less about the obvious virtues of journalism and more about the exploitation of journalism by its owners and their enablers. I know why it happens – human nature and greed – but I remain perplexed as to why most people working inside the media almost never talk about their power or make themselves accountable for it.

It's even worse than that. Most media proprietors, editors and journalists minimise the extent of their influence, or pretend it doesn't exist, because they know it's unregulated, unaccountable and usually invisible. But there is nothing invisible about its impact, even when it is applied positively. Anyone who has run a newsroom understands the frisson generated by creating a big, impactful story. We all know our power; we just don't want to talk about it.

Today, mistrust of the media is growing rapidly. Misinformation is festering, partisanship is booming, social media is a global menace, and the business model supporting journalism is unravelling. Yet not only does media exploitation continue to proliferate, there are even greater financial incentives in an era of shrinking advertising revenues and profits for owners to deceive and sensationalise. Two giant plat-forms, Fox News and Twitter/X, disseminate more false 'news' than any outlet in any previous era. Billionaires are buying up cheap media assets. And dictators and totalitarian regimes are increasingly stran-gling freedom of the press.

Media power lurks in the shadows like a prowler. For Hearst, Pulitzer, Northcliffe, Rothermere, Beaverbrook, Murdoch, Berlus-coni, Musk, and history's other media moguls and magnates, that's where the strings are pulled and the fortunes are made.

It's time that story was told, in all its unsavoury detail.

THE MOGULS

Joseph Pulitzer World's first media mogul. Invented populist mass-market journalism. Created the Pulitzer Prizes. Went blind. Died on his boat.

William Randolph Hearst Prototype mogul. Inspired *Citizen Kane*. Built a newspaper empire. Regarded facts as inconvenient. Lived extravagantly.

Alfred Harmsworth (Viscount Northcliffe) Originator of British popular journalism. Founded the *Daily Mail*. Flaunted power. Launched family dynasty.

Harold Harmsworth (Viscount Rothermere) Succeeded his brother Alfred. Built a massive publishing kingdom. Right-wing elitist who supported Hitler.

Max Aitken (Lord Beaverbrook) Nickname 'The Beaver'. Newspaper magnate. Political schemer. Powerbroker. Cabinet minister. Womaniser. Loved gossip. Churchill supporter.

Henry Luce Created the *Time*, *Life* and *Fortune* magazine empire. Purveyor of mass quality journalism. Sweeping worldview. Expansive vision for America.

Rupert Murdoch Restless empire builder. Political meddler. Obsessively dynastical. Feared and widely despised. Gaudy private life. The mogul's mogul.

Roy Thomson (Lord Thomson) Serious-minded Canadian/British newspaper magnate. Presided over best days of *The Times* and *Sunday Times*.

Robert Maxwell Czech war refugee. Built and financially destroyed a British media conglomerate. Overbearing bully. Died suspiciously at sea.

Conrad Black (Baron Black) Canadian publisher. Controlled global quality newspapers. Pompous and verbose. Author. Stole from his company. Jailed.

Silvio Berlusconi Former prime minister of Italy, its biggest media owner and richest man. All at the same time. Playboy. Full of bluster. Life of conflicts of interests.

Mark Zuckerberg Facebook founder and controller. Social media pioneer. Arbiter of privacy and media surveillance. Philanthropist. Multi-billionaire.

Elon Musk Owner of Twitter/X. Eccentric and unpredictable.

THE B-LIST

Walter family World's first media dynasty, creators of *The Times* of London.

Adolph Ochs Built *The New York Times* into a great world newspaper.

James Gordon Bennett Founder, editor, publisher of *The New York Herald*.

Colonel Robert McCormick Press freedom fighter. *Chicago Tribune* owner.

Keith Murdoch First-generation initiator of the Murdoch dynasty.

Sam Newhouse Founder of an American newspaper and magazine empire.

Otis Chandler Built the *Los Angeles Times* into a powerhouse, last of a dynasty.

Kerry Packer Australian TV and magazine magnate with forceful personality.

Matthias Döpfner A German, and increasingly global, journalism czar.

Bernard Arnault World's richest man, powerful French media owner.

Vincent Bolloré Built France's 'Fox News' into influential political force.

Gautham Adani Indian billionaire industrialist with media properties.

Jain family Influential Indian media dynasty, owner of *The Times of India*.

Introduction

When Rupert Murdoch lured me away from my job as editor of *The Sydney Morning Herald*, then arguably the best newspaper in Australia, I was thirty-six and loved being a serious journalist.

It was 1987. Murdoch wasn't the international ogre he later became (this was pre-phone-hacking, pre-Fox News), but like many journalists in the Anglosphere, I felt apprehensive about his editorial values, his voracious commerciality, and the methods he used to dispense power.

I decided to accept his offer to become editor-in-chief of his Melbourne newspaper group because it was an exquisite challenge, or so I told myself, and because I didn't lack ambition. Murdoch had just acquired Australia's largest stable of newspapers, which included the Melbourne *Herald*, flagship of his father's publishing empire. It was a paper struggling to survive after losing half its circulation of 437,000 in the previous decade. My challenge – and the reason Murdoch hired me – was to attempt to revive the *Herald* as a quality afternoon newspaper, as his father Keith Murdoch had done sixty-six years earlier when he became its editor.

My flirtation with Murdoch lasted two years. I resigned when my moral compass became dysfunctional. He implored me to stay, telling me with uncharacteristic emotion as we sat together alone on a leather couch in his father's old office, weeks before I finally quit, that he thought 'we'd be working together all our lives'. But I found myself incapable of navigating the ethical hurdles that litter the path of a Murdoch editor. Also, I didn't know how to be suitably obsequious; he told me I was 'aloof'.

On many days during those two years, I felt like an infiltrator operating behind enemy lines. From the outside, and to its faithful employees, News Corporation is a respectable company that deploys journalism to challenge and scrutinise the pillars of the establishment. Behind this facade, I discovered, was a kind of medieval fiefdom where we all lived in the shadow of a proprietor whose predilections – commercial, editorial, ideological, personal, political, economic, philosophical, racial, sociological – were insinuated into every important decision and direction we took. Harold Evans, who edited the London *Times* before he became another former Murdoch editor (there have been hundreds of us), identified this process as 'charismatic authority', the phrase used by the German sociologist Max Weber to describe how a leader's courtiers are 'forever attempting to win favor by guessing what the boss wanted or might applaud but might well not have asked for'.

The *Herald* was my first exposure to the subterranean world of media moguldom. As a newspaper insider, I was hardly surprised by Murdoch's ambitiousness or ruthlessness, or by the compliant culture that permeated his kingdom, or even by his indifference to the concept of serious journalism. But what really disconcerted me during my time at News Corp, and has ever since, was the lurking presence of his *power*.

A few months after I started at the paper, Murdoch flew in from America for an Australian federal election campaign. This gave me an intimate view of a hands-on, behind-closed-doors media machinator at work, as he massaged the politicians, directed his editors, and worked over their editorials. 'A propaganda sausage factory,' I wrote in my diary notes, 'with Murdoch seeing and vetting no less than eight or nine election endorsement editorials, all faxed by editors to him in Sydney.'

Observing him dealing personally with political leaders, and watching him networking, I began to realise there was almost no-one anywhere who wouldn't take his call or didn't want to impress him. One day in Melbourne, after the prime minister Bob Hawke had been leaving messages for him, Murdoch asked me, 'Do I really need to talk to Hawke?' As the election drew near I was present for drinks in the office with the opposition leader John Howard, where Murdoch took him aside to inform him, as a courtesy, that News Corp would be endorsing his opponent, Hawke, in the upcoming election. (Howard's party went on to lose badly.) I assumed this was Murdoch's way of leaving the door open for future collaboration with no hard feelings. If so, it worked. Howard later became a long-serving Australian prime minister, enthusiastically supported by News Corp, and still remains one of Murdoch's most effusive public spruikers.

Howard was adhering to the unwritten rules of engagement between senior politicians and the Murdoch empire, rules that operate on the sidelines of democracy, out of sight. One of Howard's successors, John Hewson, discovered those rules a few years later when he became leader of Australia's federal opposition. 'I approached all the major editors at the time for a discussion,' Hewson explained. 'The editor at *The Australian* told me, in no uncertain terms, that I needed to understand they had their agendas, so if I advanced ideas consistent with those agendas, I may – it was emphasised, just may – expect positive coverage. But if I advocated against those agendas then I could be guaranteed that I would be attacked accordingly.'

When the global share market collapsed in late 1987, I watched Murdoch work the phone from a gloomy office inside the grey newspaper empire fortress built by his father in Melbourne in the 1920s. A few days into the crisis, after taking a call from Ronald Reagan, Murdoch told some of us he had advised the president to ensure that his government and the Federal Reserve held their nerve through the economic upheaval. Meanwhile, he instructed his editors and executives to provide vigorous support during the crisis for the capitalist system in the company's newspapers.

Exercising power was a routine part of his life. This became amusingly evident at a lunch I convened with Murdoch and a group of senior editors in a private room at The Society, a courtly Italian restaurant that had served Melbourne's establishment since his father's era. It was a week or so after he had bought yet another newspaper, a London daily called *Today*. 'Why did you buy *Today?*' asked a junior editor with a gravelly voice. Murdoch seemed puzzled. 'I didn't buy anything *today*,' he replied, then realised he had misheard the question. A smile crept over his face as respectful laughter rippled across the table.

A Murdoch editor, I realised, is a footman dispensing media power on behalf of a single family. In two years at News Corp I never heard an editor or executive attempt to discuss, navigate or even acknowledge the existence of moral ambiguity, the subject that was so memorably decoded by the writer Janet Malcolm in one memorable paragraph: 'Every journalist who is not too stupid or too full of himself to notice what is going on knows that what he does is morally indefensible. He is a kind of confidence man, preying on people's vanity, ignorance, or loneliness, gaining their trust and betraying them without remorse.'

As I watched the sausages being made inside News Corp it was obvious that morally indefensible journalism is an inevitable outcome in a news organisation that lacks an ethical compass. Journalism, by its nature, is an exercise in manipulation. If you aren't prepared to recognise that occupational reality – even in seemingly benign choices such as who to interview or ignore, or what facts to include or leave out – how can you expect to practise your craft in good conscience?

Rupert Murdoch wasn't the first media proprietor to capitalise on the loophole in democracy that legitimises the worst excesses of journalism. Nor did he invent the magic formula that emerged in the late 1800s when Joseph Pulitzer acquired *The World* in New York, and Alfred Harmsworth launched the *Daily Mail* in London: *titillating journalism = mass audiences = abundant advertising revenue = vast profits = political power*. This is the formula, in its raw simplicity, that empowered a coterie of moguls to exploit journalism to both uphold *and* pollute civil society, with Murdoch as its greatest exponent.

Until I joined News Corp, I'd never had to think about what ethicists describe as 'moral fading', the self-deception created by behaving unethically while maintaining the appearance of being good and moral. My only previous professional experience had been in a media organisation where the journalism was disconnected, structurally and culturally, from the business side of the business. In the Murdoch universe, where no such structural separation exists, they don't talk about ethics and moral behaviour because such a discussion would inevitably collide with the company's true mission: to make money at all costs.

I have often wondered what goes through the minds and consciences of otherwise dedicated professionals who find themselves inhabiting a news organisation that engages in amoral or immoral journalism. What were the private thoughts of journalists at News Corp after learning that their co-workers had spent two decades hacking into personal voicemails? Or Fox News employees on discovering, via court documents, that their colleagues and owners had promoted election denial and riots at the US Capitol to ensure viewers didn't defect to another network? Or those at the London *Sun* on reading an op-ed in late 2022, written by columnist Jeremy Clarkson, describing his 'cellular level' loathing of the Duchess of Sussex, Meghan Markle, and 'dreaming of the day when she is made to parade naked through the streets of every town in Britain while the crowds chant, "Shame!" and throw lumps of excrement at her'?

For a media mogul and his underlings, flexing power without responsibility is as natural as stretching any other body muscle. I recall a meeting with my *Herald* editors, attended by Murdoch, where we were tossing around ideas for a public campaign to draw attention to the new look of the paper. What were the big issues in Melbourne right now, Murdoch asked the group. Someone mentioned a controversy involving teenagers jumping onto moving trains to deface the carriages with graffiti. Murdoch lit up. That's the perfect subject for a newspaper crusade, he said. As we workshopped ideas for policies we could advocate to deter graffitists, Murdoch had a suggestion: 'Capital punishment.' The room fell silent. I said we would look into it.

The kind of abuse of power that's at the heart of this book's subject matter is hard to see, easy to conceal, almost always denied by its perpetrators, and even glamorised in TV shows like *Succession*, where stereotypes of rich, flamboyant moguls are portrayed as dare-devils and swashbucklers. It is an insidious editorial power that has hardly changed in style or substance in the hundred years since Vern Whaley, an editor on William Randolph Hearst's *Los Angeles Herald Examiner*, tripped over a dirty little secret of the newsroom: 'We had a crime story that was going to be featured in a 96-point headline on page one. When I found the address that was in the story, that address was a vacant lot. So I hollered over at the rewrite desk, I said, "You got the wrong address in this story. This is a vacant lot." The copy chief that night was a guy named Vic Barnes. And he says, "Sit down, Vern." He says, "The whole story's a fake."'[1]

As Vern Whaley discovered that day in Los Angeles, the exercise of media power is, by its nature, subtle and covert. Sometimes, though, it rears its head very publicly, as I discovered in 2022 when my journey through the world of journalism and publishing was disrupted – again – by a Murdoch.

MOGULDOM

An Encounter with Lachlan Murdoch

In late August 2022 an unusual ad appeared in *The New York Times*:

An open letter to Lachlan Murdoch, co-chairman of News Corporation and executive chairman of Fox Corporation

Dear Lachlan,

As you know, nearly two months ago *Crikey* published a piece of commentary about the sorry state of US politics, and the January 6 insurrection, that mentioned the Murdoch family name twice.

You responded through your lawyer with a series of letters in which you accused us of defaming you personally in that story.

Crikey is an independent Australian news website, launched in 2000, covering politics, media and public issues. We at *Crikey* strongly support freedom of opinion and public interest journalism. We are concerned that Australia's defamation laws are too restrictive.

Today in *Crikey*, we are publishing all the legal demands and accusations from your lawyer, and the replies from our lawyers, in full, so people can judge your allegations for themselves.

We want to defend those allegations in court. You have made it clear in your lawyer's letters you intend to take court action to resolve this alleged defamation.

We await your writ so that we can test this important issue of freedom of public interest journalism in a courtroom.

Yours sincerely,
Eric Beecher
Chairman, Private Media

Peter Fray
Managing Editor, Private Media
Editor-in-Chief, *Crikey*

On the same day we placed that ad, I wrote a piece in *Crikey* explaining what was going on:

Crikey has decided to lift the veil and reveal how abuse of media power in Australia really works. Today we're publishing a series of lengthy legal demands sent to us over the past two months by Lachlan Murdoch, the billionaire chairman of News Corp and Fox Corporation, as well as our lawyers' replies to those demands.

Murdoch's lawyer believes an article in late June by *Crikey*'s politics editor Bernard Keane was an 'unwarranted attack on my client, without any notice and in complete disregard to the facts' and 'is malicious and aggravates the harm to my client'.

The article in question was commentary about Donald Trump's involvement in the January 6 insurrection attempt at the US Capitol. The article briefly refers to the role of Fox News in these events, and doesn't mention Lachlan Murdoch by name. The headline – 'Trump is a confirmed unhinged traitor. And Murdoch is his unindicted co-conspirator' – clearly refers to Rupert Murdoch, the only 'Murdoch' used as shorthand by the media and the rest of the world. The only other reference to the Murdoch family in the entire story is in the final paragraph: 'The Murdochs and their slew of poisonous Fox News commentators are the unindicted co-conspirators of this continuing crisis.' The rest of the article is about Trump's role on January 6 and the state of US politics.[1]

Based on that headline and one sentence, Lachlan Murdoch's lawyer began sending us long legal letters of demand, threatening litigation and accusing *Crikey* of making outrageous suggestions that his client 'illegally conspired with Donald Trump to overturn the 2020 presidential election', 'illegally conspired with Donald Trump to incite a mob with murderous intent to march on the Capitol', 'knowingly entered into a criminal conspiracy with Donald Trump to overturn the 2020 presidential election result', and 'engaged in treachery and violent intent together with Donald Trump to overturn the 2020 presidential election result' – among 14 alleged defamatory imputations in total.

Absent any feelings about the Murdochs, their ethics or their role in the media, think about this: A small Australian news website publishes an opinion piece about the Trump presidency and the US Select Committee investigation into the January 6 riot, briefly (and critically) including the key role of Fox News. The article is not dissimilar to thousands of stories published in the US media about the complicity of Fox News in the Trump presidency and January 6 riots – many of those stories far more accusatory than ours. Indeed, Lachlan Murdoch described the role of Fox News after the 2020 presidential election as 'the loyal opposition ... that's what our job is now with the Biden administration'.[2]

The Murdochs haven't taken legal action in the US (where Fox News operates) because they are public figures and can't successfully sue for defamation over a matter of public interest under US law, where the constitution protects freedom of the media. Instead, the head of Fox News attempts to use Australian defamation law against a small Australian publication – *Crikey* – including a claim that 'persons have approached members of Mr Murdoch's family, staff and his friends about the allegations in the article, *Crikey* tweet and *Crikey* Facebook post that he is an unindicted co-conspirator with Donald Trump, and have specifically queried whether he was the subject of evidence before the House Select Committee'.[3]

We are publishing these letters because we believe they expose the normally concealed world of Australian media power, in its most bullying form. Lachlan Murdoch and his father run two of the Western world's biggest and most powerful media organisations, with a combined market capitalisation in the tens of billions. Our company, Private Media, is valued at less than $20 million.*

Murdoch, his father and their companies are strong public advocates of media freedom. Their string of newspapers, websites and TV networks expose hypocrisy and publish controversial (sometimes incendiary) opinions on an almost daily basis. In Australia, News Corp is the biggest player in commercial journalism and is regularly attacked for its market dominance.

We know it's unusual to publish correspondence of this type, but confidentiality can't be imposed unilaterally by a lawyer, only by a court or government. Besides, we're just following Rupert Murdoch's own playbook. In the 1950s, as the fledgling owner of the small Adelaide tabloid *The News*, he responded to a threat from his large competitor, *The Advertiser*, to drive him out of business if he didn't sell out to them, by printing their threatening letter on the front page.

Like the Murdochs, we believe in the public's right to know. Exposing this legal assault is the only way we believe we can

---

* *With the exception of quoted material, all dollar amounts in this book refer to US dollars unless otherwise stated.*

shine light on the actions of a powerful media owner (and therefore a competitor of ours) to silence a small publisher by resorting to Australia's defamation laws – laws that News Corp itself constantly argues should give the media more freedom to fulfill its mandated role.

At Private Media, we're proud of our moral compass and our editorial mission. Sure, we're small, but if publishers like us didn't exist in Australia, the Murdochs would be even more powerful and politically influential.

Ironically, News Corp, Fox News and Crikey do the same thing – journalism. We may do it in different ways, but we share a desire to reveal truth and expose hypocrisy. As Lachlan Murdoch argued in a lecture to the Institute of Public Affairs a few months ago, 'we should reject every effort, and there are many, to limit points of view, to obstruct a diversity of opinions, and to enforce a singular world view. Those efforts are fundamentally anti-Australian.'

We didn't start this senseless altercation with Lachlan Murdoch. We may not be as big, rich, powerful or important as him, but we have one common interest: we're a news company that believes in publishing, not suppressing, public interest journalism. That's why we're looking forward to meeting Lachlan Murdoch in court, as he has foreshadowed, to test the defamation laws he and his editors constantly complain about. And to hear him express his views to a judge about the purpose of journalism, as he articulated so cogently in his 2014 Keith Murdoch Oration at the State Library of Victoria:

> Censorship should be resisted in all its insidious forms. We should be vigilant of the gradual erosion of our freedom to know, to be informed and make reasoned decisions in our society and in our democracy. We must all take notice and, like Sir Keith, have the courage to act when those freedoms are threatened.

The next night, a couple of hours into my birthday dinner, came a flurry of calls, emails and text messages. Lawyers acting for Lachlan Murdoch had just served a defamation writ in the Australian Federal Court against *Crikey*, its editor and politics editor. The news was jarring but not unexpected. We could hardly complain after placing an ad in the pages of a globally reputable newspaper *asking* to be sued.

But it still felt surreal. We were being litigated for allegedly defaming a billionaire media mogul's son in a mildly provocative opinion piece about a subject of huge international interest in which he wasn't named. The article was so routine that the editor hadn't even referred it to our lawyers before publication, the normal process for anything legally contentious. When the Monty Pythonesque statement of claim arrived, I was reminded of a colleague's amusing adage: 'If you stand on a street corner with your mouth open long enough, a Peking Duck will fly in.' Increasingly, I felt, this was our Peking Duck moment.

According to the writ, there were *fourteen* 'defamatory imputations' conveyed against Lachlan resulting from a single headline and paragraph in our story:

- He illegally conspired with Donald Trump to overturn the 2020 presidential election result;
- He illegally conspired with Donald Trump to incite an armed mob to march on the Capitol to physically prevent confirmation of the outcome of the 2020 presidential election;
- He illegally conspired with Donald Trump to incite a mob with murderous intent to march on the Capitol;
- He illegally conspired with Donald Trump to break the laws of the United States of America in relation to the 2020 presidential election result;
- He knowingly entered into a criminal conspiracy with Donald Trump to overturn the 2020 presidential election result;
- He knowingly entered into a criminal conspiracy with Donald

Trump and a large number of Fox News commentators to overturn the 2020 election result;

- He engaged in treachery and violent intent together with Donald Trump to overturn the 2020 presidential election result;

- He was aware of how heavily armed many of the attendees of the planned rally and march on the Capitol building were on January 6 before it occurred;

- He was a co-conspirator in a plot with Donald Trump to overturn the 2020 election result which cost people their lives;

- He conspired with Donald Trump to commit the offense of treason against the United States of America to overturn the 2020 election outcome;

- He conspired with Donald Trump to commit the offense of being a traitor to the United States of America to overturn the 2020 election outcome;

- He should be indicted with conspiracy to commit the offense of being a traitor to the United States of America to overturn the 2020 election outcome;

- He should be indicted with the offense of being a traitor to the United States of America to overturn the 2020 election outcome;

- He conspired with Donald Trump to lead an armed mob on Congress to overturn the 2020 election outcome.

The writ attracted global commentary ranging from bemusement to incredulousness. Clay Calvert, an expert on media law at the University of Florida, told *The Washington Post* that the phrases 'unhinged traitor' and 'unindicted co-conspirator' were obviously used in a loose, figurative sense – 'no reasonable reader would take them as assertions of literal facts regarding criminal activity'. At *The Guardian*, legal writer Richard Ackland described Murdoch as 'someone whose own very skewed and shouty media organization can dish it out with impunity, but he can't take it if a minnow does the same'. And Ackland raised the issue we discussed frequently with our lawyers: would Murdoch have the guts to appear on the witness stand in front of the world's media? If he did, speculated Ackland, 'it will be interesting to see how the applicant, hypersensitive as he appears to be, fares under sustained cross-examination'.

On the US industry website *Techdirt*, Mike Masnick raised another issue that seemed to defy logic: 'At some point, did anyone bother to remind Lachlan Murdoch that he, too, is in the news business and subject to defamation law? You'd think at some point, it would get through Lachlan's apparently thick skull, that maybe having stronger defamation laws protects him and his employees from lawsuits as well.'[4]

Crikey's position was neatly summed up by my hometown Melbourne newspaper, *The Age*: 'This is as gobsmacking an example of an attempt to stomp on free speech as can be imagined. In this case, we're with the little guy.'[5]

But in the bitchy media world, the case also created an opening for rival journalists to slag off a competitor. 'We all like watching the little guy stick it to the man,' wrote Chip Le Grand, chief reporter at *The Age*, before twisting the knife. 'If you look a little deeper, this episode is less about lofty principles than towering egos and cold commercial interests. If the three central protagonists – Beecher, Murdoch and Crikey editor-in-chief Peter Fray – ever found them-selves in the same room, they would each be convinced they were the smartest person there.' Then he got even more personal. 'Although Beecher, a former editor of both Fairfax and News Corp publica-tions, holds genuine, long-standing concerns that the Murdoch media interests exert a disproportionate and corrosive influence over Australian public life, he also understands that slotting the Murdoch name into a headline gets clicks.'[6]

So why *did* Murdoch sue? Was it thin skin, hubris, or something more consequential? 'It is one thing for a news website to stand by its journalism, but repeatedly publicly daring a billionaire to sue is like stomping barefoot on a bullant's nest: eventually you'll get stung,' wrote media lawyer Sam White in *The Sydney Morning Herald*.

'The ads were so prominent and continuous that Murdoch felt he had no alternative but to sue.'[7]

Or was it some form of retribution? According to Joe Pompeo in *Vanity Fair*, Murdoch believed *Crikey* had a 'preoccupation' with him and his family, and was 'more attuned to what's being written about him now that his kids are back at school in Australia'.[8] The *Daily Beast*'s Lachlan Cartwright went even further, claiming that Murdoch had been in touch with other prominent Australians 'who have had issues' with *Crikey*. If he was to 'take *Crikey* out, that would be a good outcome for him', claimed Cartwright.[9]

For me, Murdoch's writ was an abuse of media power that was both *institutional* and *personal*. I'm one of a handful of Rupert Murdoch's editors who resigned voluntarily, and in the decades since, I have publicly expressed my deep concern about the pervasive power of News Corp. It was also personal between Lachlan Murdoch and me. In 2000, when I delivered the Andrew Olle Media Lecture – a somewhat pompous annual Australian black-tie dinner address – I discussed the differences between commercial and serious media. Most serious journalism in Australia, I argued, has more in common with the charity industry, because it is subsidised by classified ads or government funding. Two years later, in *his* Andrew Olle Lecture, Murdoch attacked my lecture.[10] 'The industry is littered with self-styled purists who believe the business of media – the requirement to make a profit – somehow corrupts the craft,' he told the audience. 'The self-anointed media elite among us believe, somewhat self-servingly, that not only the act, or process of making a profit is positively sinister, but also that the very desire to do so is,' he said, concluding with a slap: 'Well, this bloke couldn't have been more wrong.' He'd refused to even mention my name.

———

Back in the Federal Court, the legal contretemps quickly ramped up. We launched a crowd-funding campaign to help pay some of our legal costs, raising AUD$285,065 in the first four days (and later

reaching almost AUD$500,000). Two former Australian prime minis-
ters, Malcolm Turnbull and Kevin Rudd, each tipped in AUD$5,000.
'Lachlan Murdoch owns boats that are worth more than *Crikey*,'
Turnbull noted in a comment he added to his donation.

The case was assigned to Justice Michael Wigney, a seasoned
defamation judge who three years earlier had delivered a blistering
verdict against the Murdochs' Sydney *Daily Telegraph*. In that splashy
case, at the height of the Me Too movement, Wigney described *Telegraph* articles that portrayed the actor Geoffrey Rush as a pervert
and sexual predator as 'recklessly irresponsible pieces of sensationalist
journalism of the very worst kind'.

Leading our courtroom team was Michael Hodge, an accom-
plished barrister in his early forties, once described by *The Australian
Financial Review* as 'bespectacled and famously baby-faced ...
studious and a little shy'. Representing Lachlan was a formidable
defamation specialist, Sue Chrysanthou, who had comprehensively
won Rush's case against Murdoch's tabloid in front of Justice Wigney.
Her reputation as a feisty courtroom combatant with, ironically, a
predilection for hyperbole, was immediately obvious during the
early case hearings. Even at her most preposterous, she was always
entertaining.

As the case hearings began in September, ahead of a trial scheduled for the following March, we found it hard to constrain our
bewilderment at Lachlan's real motives. Early on, Michael Hodge
(whom I was by now calling the 'silent assassin') drew attention to
one of the absurdities of the case. 'As presently pleaded,' he told the
court, 'Lachlan Murdoch denies that Joseph Biden won the 2020
presidential election, and that Donald Trump lost it.' But Lachlan
never changed his plea and refused to publicly acknowledge that
Biden was the president. Our incredulity increased a month later
when the judge himself ruled that Lachlan would have to explain his
own view of who won the 2020 election. His *view*?

More absurdity followed when Murdoch's lawyers questioned
whether the allegedly defamatory article – a story about a sitting

president denying the result of a presidential election *and* a bloody attack on the seat of US democracy – was *in the public interest.* Justice Wigney was having none of it: 'It would perhaps not be unfair to characterize some of the submissions that were advanced on Mr Murdoch's behalf in respect of the objection to *Crikey's* public interest defense as being, to put it colloquially, rather high, wide and handsome,' he told the court.

Just before Christmas, with their arguments faltering under the weight of their own incomprehensibility, Murdoch's lawyers pressed the panic button. Not with a tweak, but by rebooting their entire case. Instead of suing us just for the offending article, which had been taken down the day after publication, they now included the republication of the same article two months later. This meant that as well as suing us for defamation, they were making the even shakier allegation that our CEO Will Hayward and our chairman (me) were responsible for 'a scheme to improperly use the complaint by Murdoch about the article to generate subscriptions to *Crikey* and thus income to Private Media under the guise of defending public interest journalism ... We say Beecher and Hayward are the relevant guiding minds of Private Media and I should say, your Honor, surprisingly so. We cannot think of any case in this country where management interferes in the editorial decision-making of a media company ... it did not enter our minds that the suits, the businessmen, the non-journalists, would have been part of that editorial decision-making.'

This startling discovery – that publishers were *publishers* – was based on their interpretation of internal company documents procured from us during the legal discovery process. And now, after not publishing a word about the case since it had started five months earlier, Murdoch's newspapers finally began to cover it. 'Crikey "begged" to be sued by News Corp chair to drive subscriptions', was the headline over a story in News Corp's flagship *The Australian* that claimed we had used the defamation case 'to sell subscriptions worth $500,000, promote an online fundraising campaign and sell merchandise'. His lawyers accused us of hiring a political strategy firm 'to engineer a "David and Goliath" style public relations campaign around being sued by a billionaire'.[11] This elaborate scheme, according to Chrysanthou, killed our public interest defence – 'How can a person with a straight face claim a public interest journalism defence in these circumstances for an article that wasn't even . . . newsworthy?'

The decision by Lachlan's lawyers to re-plead their case handed us a series of legal gifts we unwrapped like kids on Christmas Day. First, it presented us with the opportunity to add another potent argument – abuse of media power – to our existing defences of public interest and qualified privilege. But an even bigger gift was the new evidence that became available because the trial date was pushed out by eight months by the new plea – a trove of internal texts, emails and witness testimonies in Fox's $1.6 billion defamation battle with Dominion Voting Systems that had cascaded into public view in the US.

These documents proved beyond doubt that the Murdochs and their Fox News functionaries were complicit in fuelling election denial conspiracies, and had acted in their own commercial self-interest, not the public interest. What's more, the bombshell US documents blew apart Lachlan's case in Australia by exposing hundreds of examples of the Murdochs and their henchmen interfering in editorial decision-making at Fox News, making a mockery of his proposition that 'the suits' don't get involved in editorial matters.

The cache of information from the US case also allowed us to add yet another defence to our growing menu: the one known as contextual truth. This is how our solicitor Michael Bradley explained the concept: 'Say *Crikey* had written that Murdoch was a serial killer who underpaid his taxes. He might sue for the defamatory slur that he was a tax cheat, in which case *Crikey* could plead in defence that the more damaging imputation – that he was a serial killer – was true. That's the contextual imputation; if it is true and it overwhelms the imputations being complained about, even if the latter are lies, then there's a complete defence.'

Our lawyers wrapped up the contextual truth argument with two powerful propositions in our defence statement filed with the court in April:

A. Lachlan Murdoch is morally and ethically culpable for the illegal January 6 Attack because Fox News, under his control and management, promoted and peddled Trump's lie of the stolen election despite Lachlan Murdoch knowing it was false (Contextual Imputation 1);

B. Lachlan Murdoch's unethical and reprehensible conduct in allowing Fox News to promote and peddle Trump's lie of the stolen election, despite Lachlan Murdoch knowing it was false, makes him morally and ethically culpable for the illegal January 6 Attack (Contextual Imputation 2).

Put all this together, we argued, and anything Murdoch believed was defamatory in Keane's article would 'not further harm the reputation of the applicant'. Or as our barrister Michael Hodge told the court, 'The applicant could have stopped Fox News channel from promoting the lie.'

By now, Justice Wigney was getting tetchy. As the new claims and defences threatened to extend the court date yet again, he proposed a further round of mediation. 'It seems to me that both parties . . . could take stock at what's turning into a scorched earth policy,' he told the court. 'There does seem to be a hint that this case is being driven more by, and I say this with the greatest respect, ego and hubris and ideology than anything else.'

By mid-April, the judge didn't have to worry about presiding over an ego-fuelled trial because Fox News finally caved in under the huge embarrassment generated by the release of the court documents in the US, and agreed to pay Dominion nearly $800 million to avert a trial that would have exposed their lies about the 2020 presidential election. And a day later – eight months after launching his misguided legal action – Lachlan Murdoch hoisted the white flag in

Sydney with a single line filed in the Federal Court: 'Pursuant to rule 26.12(2)(a)(ii) LACHLAN KEITH MURDOCH, the Applicant, discontinues the whole of the proceedings.'

It was what the legal trade referred to as, our lawyer Michael Bradley quipped, an unconditional surrender. But even in surrender there was churlishness from our billionaire opponent. 'Mr Murdoch remains confident that the court would ultimately find in his favor,' declared his lawyer, 'however he does not wish to further enable *Crikey*'s use of the court to litigate a case from another jurisdiction that has already been settled and facilitate a marketing campaign designed to attract subscribers and boost their profits.'

That subterfuge fooled no-one. 'After hundreds of hours spent in preliminary court battles and thousands of pages of discovery, he simply dropped his case,' wrote Amanda Meade in *The Guardian*. 'Behind the scenes his lawyers made several offers to bring the case to an end as early as January. But *Crikey*, the little mouse that roared, refused to back down and apologize – or remove the piece . . . it was quite the backflip by the 50-year-old media mogul whose legal case has played out in lurid media headlines for eight months.'[12]

Later that day, the irreverent Australian satirical website *The Chaser* (motto: 'Striving for mediocrity in a world of excellence') published its own summary of the case:

Hi everyone! It's me, Lachlan Murdoch!

Dear Readers,

It's your favorite billionaire heir here. Yeah – the real Lachlan Murdoch. I'm writing a guest piece for The Chaser newsletter because I've been trying to improve my public image lately, and thought that writing a guest piece for a small, satirical newsletter would be a good way to show off my funny and relatable side.

But mainly I'm writing because I'd like to address a few misconceptions about the fact that I dropped my defamation case against Crikey this morning.

First of all, it doesn't mean that I lose. At best [it] is a tie. I basically won except for the money or being vindicated. I have a team of the best lawyers my dad's money can buy, and we simply made the difficult decision that they would be unable to defend my honor and reputation.

And the reason why is ridiculous. Get this. It turns out that in this country, to be able to sue someone for defamation, I would need to have honor and reputation to defend in the first place! That is a ridiculously high bar to have to pass, and shows you why Australia's defamation laws are in urgent need of reform.

Second of all, could everyone please stop saying on Twitter, and Facebook, and HBO, that I have unresolved daddy issues? My father is a great man, and I'm just following in his footsteps by trying to be the most successful and powerful person in the world using the tried and tested method of suing email newsletters.

In conclusion, I just want to remind everyone to tune into my network and enjoy the incredible content we provide. And if anyone out there has something negative to say about me, just remember: I have a team of lawyers who are ready to sue you into a position where you're only left with [a] massively increased subscriber-base and an expanded global profile.

Best regards,
Lachlan Murdoch
Unindicted Co-conspirator to the January 6th Capitol Riot
(and no relation to Kendall Roy)[13]

Gutenberg to Zuckerberg

Thomas Jefferson, third president of the United States, died almost a century before the first media moguls barged onto the public stage to meddle with democracy. But his pronouncement in 1786 – that liberty depended on a free press – legitimised their existence, anointed journalism as the protected species of democracy, and created the loophole that has empowered a handful of tycoons to manipulate journalism with impunity for nearly a hundred and fifty years.

This is the paradox at the heart of the free press. The custodians of journalism are entrusted to protect it, yet incentivised to exploit it. News moguls have been both the watchdogs *and* the rottweilers of democracy. Using their privileged status, they have intimidated governments, invaded personal privacy, peddled mistruths, stirred up sensationalism, dispensed patronage, denigrated their enemies, twisted social values, and in the process accumulated obscene fortunes.

Time magazine's founder Henry Luce addressed the inherent conflict between profits and conscience in a letter to US president Herbert Hoover in 1937: 'How are you going to regulate a free press? And if you don't regulate it, I can see nothing to rely on except private conscience. And if you will rely to some extent on the private conscience of editor-publishers (hoping that the conscience of an Ochs will prevail over the conscience of a Hearst) why not rely also on the private conscience of bankers, manufacturers, educators, etc?'[1]

Hoover and other national leaders in Western democracies have largely resisted the temptation to regulate journalism because they recognise its crucial role. But unlike Jefferson, they knew who and what they were protecting. 'I sometimes think that Hearst has done more harm to the cause of democracy and civilization in America than any three other contemporaries put together,' wrote US president Franklin Roosevelt.[2] 'The only evil man I ever met,' said British prime minister Clement Atlee about Lord Beaverbrook.[3] 'The most dangerous man in the world,' was US president Joe Biden's description of Rupert Murdoch.[4]

Comments like these, while scathing, also normalise the status of media owners, and their subordinates, as *participants* in the system of governing. That uncomfortable reality was starkly acknowledged by former British prime minister Tony Blair in a landmark speech delivered just before he left office in 2007, describing a media that hunts in a pack 'like a feral beast, just tearing people and reputations to bits, but no one dares miss out.' Blair continued: 'I am going to say something that few people in public life will say, but most know is absolutely true: a vast aspect of our jobs today – outside of the really major decisions, as big as anything else – is coping with the media, its sheer scale, weight and constant hyperactivity. At points, it literally overwhelms. Talk to senior people in virtually any walk of life today – business, military, public services, sport, even charities and voluntary organizations and they will tell you the same.'[5]

An owner of a journalism enterprise in a Western democracy operates under constitutional, legal and societal protection. He (they are almost always a *he*) can present his own version of the news, his own opinions, and more or less anything that isn't defamatory or obscene, no matter how outrageous. Freedom of the press, noted Luce, includes the freedom to publish 'yards and yards of mediocrity, acres of bad fiction and triviality, square miles of journalistic tripe.'[6] The only people with the power to constrain these excesses are readers or viewers – yet they're usually the most avid consumers of the excesses. 'I operate in a world so free that its only explicit law is that there shall be no law,' said Luce. 'Ours is the only business in America whose behavior the Senate of the United States would not dare to investigate.'

These were the freedoms ratified by the US Supreme Court in 1971 when it upheld the right of *The New York Times* to publish secret government documents known as the Pentagon Papers. The function of the First Amendment, ruled the court, is to 'serve the governed, not the governors' and to give the press 'the protection it must have to fulfill its essential role in our democracy'.[7]

Media freedom is also protected constitutionally in France, Canada, Germany, Spain and Italy. In Britain and Australia it is implied but not legally mandated. All these countries effectively operate within the spirit of Jefferson's other great axiom about journalism: 'Were it left to me to decide whether we should have a government without newspapers, or newspapers without a government, I should not hesitate a moment to prefer the latter.'[8]

Yet Jefferson wasn't naive. He fully recognised the difference between the *role* of the press and the *behaviour* of its owners. Newspapers, he wrote to a friend in 1807, are 'an evil for which there is no remedy'.[9] This view was shared by many thinkers of his era. Journalism, declared the nineteenth-century philosopher John Stuart Mill, is 'the vilest and most degrading of all trades because more affectation and hypocrisy and more subservience to the baser feelings of others are necessary for carrying it on than for any other trade from that of brothel-keeper upwards'.[10]

Two centuries later, journalism is still deeply mistrusted by the public, yet remains a cornerstone of democracy. And although most of the old-style moguls have disappeared, apart from the Murdoch, Sulzberger and Northcliffe families, they have been superseded by a new breed of tech titans who control an even more powerful tool to mess with facts, taste, privacy and civility – social media. Enter Mark Zuckerberg and Elon Musk, who own no newspapers or TV stations, employ no reporters or editors, and publish no original journalism. Even though they don't cook up their own stories to intimidate governments, Twitter/X and Facebook disseminate more false, incendiary, hateful, racist and sexist content than any publisher, ever.

'In the end journalism is an act of character,' wrote Bill Kovach and Tom Rosenstiel in *The Elements of Journalism*, because there are no laws of journalism, no regulations, no licensing, and no formal self-policing. 'And since journalism by its nature can be exploitative, a heavy burden rests on the ethics and judgment of the individual journalist and the individual organization where he or she works.' This, they argue, would pose a challenge in any profession, but for news practitioners there is also the 'tension between the public service role of the journalist – the aspect of the work that justifies its intrusiveness – and the business function that finances the work'.[11]

———

Media owners as a species began to emerge in the late 1700s as newspapers transitioned from coffee house pamphlets into consequential publishing enterprises. In Britain, this created a new institutional pillar known as the fourth estate, sitting alongside the government, the monarchy and the Church. For the first time in history, ordinary people were given access to society's news, an idea never previously contemplated by the three governing estates, which had run England for centuries by keeping the most important information to themselves.

Like the founders of Google and Facebook two hundred years later, the early press barons worked through a fog of trial and error as they forged a full-blown communications revolution. Two centuries apart, the parallels between the media entrepreneurs of the 1800s and the 2000s are striking. In each era they pioneered radical technology, distributed content at scale, basked in a gush of advertising revenue, occupied a legal and regulatory vacuum, and created havoc inside the governing classes by delivering previously inaccessible information to mass audiences.

London was the Silicon Valley of the first media revolution. John Walter, a prosperous coal merchant, became a printer and launched

The Times in 1788 from a disused printworks near the River Thames, as the world's first serious commercial journalism business. By the mid-1800s, with a daily circulation of around 40,000, the paper's influence was undisputed. 'The degree of information possessed by *The Times* with regard to the most secret affairs of State is mortifying, humiliating, and incomprehensible,' the Whig statesman Lord John Russell wrote to Queen Victoria.[12]

The business of news soon began to attract the attention of entrepreneurs. One of those was Joseph Pulitzer, a penniless Hungarian refugee who arrived as a teenager in Missouri in the late nineteenth century to start an American life. Pulitzer was the first publisher to sense the opportunity to *humanise* newspapers. After jobs as a waiter and a railway clerk, the 31-year-old Pulitzer scraped together enough money to buy the *St. Louis Dispatch*, a small, bankrupt newspaper that he merged with the opposition *St. Louis Evening Post* in 1878, to create a paper for the 'common man', as he described the new *Post-Dispatch*.

Pulitzer spent five years honing his formula in St. Louis before taking it to the epicentre of America culture and media, New York. 'There is room in this great and growing city,' he wrote in a manifesto published on the first day of his ownership of the New York *World*, 'for a journal that is not only cheap, but bright, not only bright but large, not only large but truly democratic, dedicated to the cause of the people rather than that of purse-potentates, devoted more to the news of the New than the Old World ... that will expose all fraud and sham, fight all public evils and abuses ... that will serve and battle for the people with earnest sincerity.'[13]

Determined to create serious accountability journalism that was also popular, Pulitzer's *World* served up a daily smorgasbord of sensational crime stories, investigations into local corruption, pages of comic strips, soap opera tales about colourful New York characters, and a new journalistic technique known as 'the interview'. *The World* soon became the most influential, imitated newspaper of its era, and its owner one of the richest, most powerful men in America. 'I can never be president because I am a foreigner,' he once told a friend, 'but some day I am going to elect a president.'[14]

Watching Pulitzer's success from the other side of the continent was William Randolph Hearst, the 24-year-old playboy heir to a Californian mining fortune. After Hearst had been expelled from Harvard University for unruly behaviour, his father gifted him the *San Francisco Examiner*, the family's struggling newspaper. Willy Hearst wasted no time. Within weeks he had relaunched the *Examiner* as a clearing house of scandal and crime that he pledged would 'startle, amaze and stupefy the world'.[15] And it did. An early front-page story – under the headline 'THUGS! ... A Band of Murderers Discovered in San Francisco ... Killing Men to Collect Their Insurance' – claimed to expose 'the most frightful conspiracy in the modern criminal annals of the civilized world'. The *Examiner* was the birthplace of modern sensationalist journalism, a publishing laboratory where Hearst cooked up the editorial techniques and fabrications that would stretch the limits of American public taste for another six decades.[16]

Hearst soon followed the trail of his hero, Pulitzer, by acquiring the *New York Journal* as the platform to launch a ferocious commercial war against none other than *The World*. He poached Pulitzer's staff, imitated his tricks, out-promoted his promotions. Within a year, the *Journal* had almost overtaken *The World*'s daily circulation of 750,000, in a costly battle that at its peak was losing Hearst $100,000 a month (around $3.7 million today) – 'the most enormous deficit ever seen in journalism', according to one observer. 'It was war between the strapping 32-year-old interloper and the 48-year-old "half blind nervous wreck",' wrote W.A. Swanberg, the biographer of both moguls. 'There was about Hearst the air of a precocious, unpredictable, slightly raffish adolescent taking the measure of an aging and ailing rival.'[17]

In a strict sense, Hearst's papers weren't newspapers at all. 'They were printed entertainment and excitement, the equivalent in newsprint of bombs exploding, bands blaring, firecrackers popping, victims screaming, flags waving, cannons roaring, houris dancing, and smoke rising from the singed flesh of executed criminals,' according to Swanberg.[18] This was the gaudy recipe Hearst used to build an empire of papers and magazines that at its height in the 1930s attracted 30 million readers. Even after he expanded into broadcasting, movies and magazines with a worldwide audience, his regional American newspapers remained the fulcrum of Hearst's power – and he used them to pull strings relentlessly. During the 1920s and 1930s his columnists included Winston Churchill, David Lloyd George, Benito Mussolini, Adolf Hitler and Hermann Göring.

In 1896 another upstart entered the frenzied newspaper marketplace dominated by Hearst and Pulitzer. An unprepossessing 38-year-old Cincinnati-born son of German immigrants, Adolph Ochs purchased and relaunched *The New York Times* with a novel proposition: unbiased, quality journalism. Ochs published his editorial principles in the *Times* under the heading 'BUSINESS ANNOUNCEMENT', promising to 'give the news impartially, without fear or favor, regardless of party, sect, or interests involved; to make the columns of THE NEW-YORK TIMES a forum for the consideration of all questions of public importance, and to that end to invite intelligent discussion from all shades of opinion'.[19] It was an ambitious pledge because, like most American newspapers during much of the nineteenth century, the *Times* that Ochs acquired was hardly known for its editorial impartiality; its founder, Henry Raymond, was one of the founders of the Republican Party and during the 1850s was described as the party's 'godfather'.

Ochs's commitment to impartiality was to be severely tested over the coming decades. The paper's coverage of the Russian Revolution was motivated by a desire to see the Bolshevik regime collapse, 'a case of seeing not what was, but what men wished to see', according to the admired newspaper commentator Walter Lippmann and his co-author Charles Merz in their long-form report 'A Test of the News'. 'From the point of view of professional journalism, the reporting of the Russian Revolution is nothing short of a disaster.'[20] The *Times*'s

coverage of the Holocaust two decades later was another embarrassment, although it took sixty years before Laurel Leff's book *Buried
by The Times* lifted the lid, with a damning account of how the paper
effectively ignored the Nazi atrocities against Jews between September 1939 and May 1945. 'The story of the Holocaust – meaning articles
that focused on the discrimination, deportation, and destruction of
the Jews – made the *Times* front page just 26 times, and only in six of
those stories were Jews identified on the front as the primary victims,'
Leff wrote.[21]

One of those observing the editorial acrobatics of Pulitzer and
Hearst in the final decade of the nineteenth century was Alfred
Harmsworth, a resourceful Londoner who saw the opportunity to
adapt their methods for British audiences. In 1896 Harmsworth
launched the *Daily Mail* as a uniquely English popular newspaper,
a brew of human interest stories ('Was it Suicide or Apoplexy?',
'Another Battersea Scandal'), women's features and local crime
('Bones in Bishopsgate', 'Killed by a Grindstone'). A banner headline
draped across its entire front page made the subdued, single-column
headlines in other newspapers look like tadpoles in a shark tank.
Naturally, the *Mail* created ructions (that was the point). Although
it was dismissed by Britain's Conservative prime minister Lord
Salisbury as a paper run by office boys for office boys, its exploding
circulation figures suggested otherwise.[22]

By the 1920s, Harmsworth (later elevated to become Viscount
Northcliffe) and his brother Harold (later Viscount Rothermere)
had built a national newspaper empire – *The Times*, *The Observer*,
Daily Mirror, *The Evening News*, and their flagship *Daily Mail* – that
meddled relentlessly in British affairs for most of the first half of
the twentieth century. No-one had ever assembled non-State power
on this scale. In the House of Commons the prime minister, Lloyd
George, attacked Northcliffe as a victim of 'diseased vanity', sarcastic-
ally tapping the side of his head with his finger.[23]

Northcliffe flaunted his power shamelessly. He never tried to
hide his right-wing views, actively supporting the rise of the Nazis

throughout the 1930s, regularly meeting and corresponding with Hitler, publishing pro-Nazi propaganda columns in the *Mail* under his own byline, and endorsing the fascist British Blackshirts movement led by Oswald Mosely. In 1934, a year after the Nazis introduced an Editors Law mandating that only 'racially pure' non-Jewish editors and journalists could be employed by German newspapers, Northcliffe wrote a column arguing that the Nazis needed to control the 'alien elements and Israelites of international attachments who were insinuating themselves into the German state'.[24] It was only when the reality of the Nazi nightmare became too obvious to ignore, and the drums of war started beating, that he finally swung his papers' support behind his own country.

While newspaper proprietors like Hearst, Pulitzer and the Harmsworths regarded political influence as a perk of ownership, the next emerging mogul, Max Aitken – later elevated to become Lord Beaverbrook – viewed power as his motivator-in-chief. Beaverbrook is a case study in upward mobility. Starting life in rural Canada, the son of a Scottish-born Presbyterian minister, he moved to Montreal at the age of thirty-one to launch a weekly magazine; he invested in the city's oldest daily newspaper then briskly departed for London. Within a year he was a British parliamentarian and a shareholder in the *Daily Express* – a fact he kept secret for several years in order to pull political strings without complications. When Beaverbrook bought into the *Express* in 1916 it was selling 40,000 copies a day; by the mid-1940s he was in full control of a hugely successful and genuinely interesting popular newspaper with a circulation of 3.7 million.

Beaverbrook was one of the world's great schemers. He orchestrated plots, manipulated politics, peddled rumours. He was shamelessly conflicted, sitting inside the British cabinet while in control of the *Express*, and writing critical editorials about his own government's performance. 'I claim the right to criticize the Coalition leaders in their public capacity in the columns of a daily newspaper,' he wrote to Winston Churchill in 1918. 'You are a friend of mine. But surely you do not expect that fact to make a vital difference in any public comment I made on your policy in affairs of state?'[25]

Beaverbrook ran the *Express* 'purely for the purpose of making propaganda, and with no other motive', he told the 1947 Royal Commission on the Press. When asked what happened when his editors disagreed with his view he said, 'I talked them out of it.'[26]

———

Almost surreptitiously, another news empire was rising quietly at the bottom of the world. Keith Murdoch, the son of a Scottish Presbyterian vicar (like Beaverbrook), started his working life as a reporter covering local events in the middle-class suburbs of Melbourne. He then moved to London to launch a spectacular career that combined journalism with influence-peddling, culminating in a brazen exposé of the ill-fated World War One Gallipoli campaign that forced the withdrawal of Allied troops and, in its wake, raised many questions about Murdoch's motives and ethical behaviour.

In 1921, aged thirty-six, he returned home and became chief editor of the Melbourne *Herald*, the afternoon paper that dominated Australia's second-largest city. He quickly became a rising star in a frontier country that offered rich opportunities for a parvenu with a skill for making connections. 'Murdoch had one very simple idea,' observed former premier of New South Wales Jack Lang. 'He wanted to be the most powerful man in the Commonwealth [of Australia]. If he could make the Prime Minister and then boss him around, he was the Big Boss. It was as simple as that.'[27]

It wasn't long before Murdoch was fast-tracked from the editor's office to the managing director's suite. This made him the Big Boss of daily newspapers across most capital cities, a formidable presence and political kingmaker in Australia's small, clubby business community. In 1931, after concluding that his country needed a new prime minister, he successfully threw his papers behind the election of Joe Lyons, a politician who had deserted the ruling Labor Party to establish a new party.[28] Lyons was the man 'whom we chose and made',

Murdoch later wrote to one of his executives. A scene in Murdoch's office in the 1930s was witnessed and later described by a former *Herald* copy boy who served his boss tea: 'Murdoch was still shouting and JA Lyons was standing before the desk. I put the tea down on the big desk and went out through the door. As I went through it I turned and there, with his hat in his hand, like a man seeking a job, stood the Prime Minister before Murdoch's desk. As I shut the door, I heard the leader of the nation say: "Yes, sir."'[29]

Keith Murdoch had a preternatural flair for cultivating relationships with people in high places. One was Lord Northcliffe, who actively encouraged the ambitions of his Antipodean protégé. In 1921, Murdoch cabled Northcliffe with an opportunity to co-invest in Sydney's *Evening News*. 'Feeling this is my big chance,' Murdoch informed Northcliffe, inviting the press lord to 'join financially with a few thousands'. Northcliffe replied positively: 'Gladlyest invest five thousand as encouragement to others and proof [of] my complete confidence in you.' Within weeks, Murdoch was able to telegram 'My very dear Chief' confirming the *Evening News* deal was done.[30] He viewed Northcliffe as a father. 'You have been the biggest influence and the biggest force over me,' he once wrote to him. 'I often feel that your eye is on me, and that you insist on great work here.' The relationship between the Australian up-and-comer and the English press powerhouse twenty years his senior was encapsulated in Murdoch's popular nickname: Lord Southcliffe.[31]

When Keith Murdoch died unexpectedly of a heart attack in 1952, he bequeathed his son the Adelaide *News*, a minor afternoon newspaper in a backwater city of Australia. But 21-year-old Rupert, fresh out of Oxford University, inherited several other far more significant assets that weren't listed in his father's will: steely ambition, ruthless indifference, and an obsessive interest in making money. Those were the talents that built the global media salon of influence that so many Australian prime ministers, American presidents and British prime ministers have entered to pay obeisance to father, son and son.

Over the next seven decades, Rupert Murdoch assembled a journalism empire unprecedented in scale, profit and power. An empire which is, at its heart, a manufacturing business that churns out consumer products and sells eyeballs to advertisers. Civic responsibility isn't listed in its operating manual. 'My own view is that anybody who, within the law of the land, provides a service that the public wants at a price it can afford is providing a public service,' he once told News Corp executives.[32] And he has never disguised that view: 'There are two kinds of newspaper,' he explained. 'There are broadsheets and there are tabloids. Or, as some people say, there are the unpopular and the popular newspapers.'[33]

Building
the Empires

The foundations for each media empire were laid individually. But their architecture was remarkably similar: bullish young man buys/ inherits a struggling newspaper ... ignores convention by pushing the limits of accepted behaviour ... intuits/bulldozes his way to early success ... grows in self-belief/confidence ... accumulates more acquisitions/start-ups ... builds wealth/power ... develops hubris/ notoriety ... pursues an extravagant/hedonistic private life.

Many of these empires were assembled by dirt-poor bootstrappers, often immigrants making their way in a new country. But the world's two dominant moguls, Hearst and Murdoch, were handed their seed funding from wealthy, indulgent fathers. While that didn't guarantee success, it sure helped. As the overlord of the *Forbes* magazine empire, Malcolm Forbes, once acknowledged, his achievements were the result of 'sheer ability – spelled i-n-h-e-r-i-t-a-n-c-e'.[1] In another rich son's rare moment of self-deprecation, Rupert Murdoch recalled that one of his earliest hurdles was as a newspaper proprietor in Adelaide at the age of twenty-two, when he pulled his car into the company lot on his first day. 'Hey, sonny, you can't park here,' the garage attendant admonished him.[2]

William Randolph Hearst decided it would be fun to take over his family newspaper after he was expelled from Harvard for making chamber pots plastered with photographs of faculty members. 'If you should make over to me the *Examiner* – with enough money to carry out my schemes, I'll tell you what I would do,' the 23-year-old Hearst wrote to his father in 1885.[3]

What followed was the neophyte son's blueprint for revolutionising the *San Francisco Examiner*. 'In the first place, I would change the general appearance of the paper,' his letter continued. 'Secondly, it would be well to make the paper as far as possible original, to clip only some such leading journal as the New York *World* which is undoubtedly the best paper of that class to which the *Examiner* belongs – that class which appeals to the people and which depends for its success upon enterprise, energy and a certain startling originality and not upon the wisdom of political opinions or the lofty style of its editorials.'[4]

Young Willie then turned his attention to staffing: 'To accomplish this we must have – as the *World* has – active intelligent and energetic young men; we must have men who come out west in the hopeful buoyancy of youth for the purpose of making their fortunes and not a worthless scum that has been carried there by the eddies of repeated failures.' Then followed 'a suggestion of great consequence . . . namely, that all these changes be made not by degrees but at once so that the improvement will be very marked and noticeable and will attract universal attention and comment'.[5]

George Hearst, a rich miner turned US senator, agreed to his son's request. Another letter arrived. 'I have all my pipes laid, and it only remains to turn on the gas,' wrote Willy a few days before he installed himself as 'Proprietor and Editor'. 'One year from the day I take hold of the thing our circulation will have increased ten thousand . . . and in five years it will be the biggest paper on the Pacific slope.'[6]

———

The early days of the expanding media empires were heady. If the entrepreneurial up-and-comers worried about financial or reputational risk as their businesses exploded, those thoughts didn't last long. The tailwinds seemed unstoppable.

The first issue of Britain's *Daily Mail* in 1896 sold almost 400,000 copies, against an expected 100,000. 'We've struck a goldmine,' wrote its founder Alfred Harmsworth in his diary. 'A big success, I think, bigger than we anticipated.'[7] Harmsworth's goldmine created history's most successful populist newspaper (and much later its most sensational mainstream website) and laid a pipeline of wealth and power for the next four Viscount Rothermeres, who have run it for more than a century.

The young entrepreneurs with their ambitious ideas invariably bumped up against entrenched competitors and detractors. When Joseph Pulitzer bought *The World* in 1883, his rival Charles Dana, owner of the New York *Sun*, offered this character assessment of the upstart: 'Mr Pulitzer possesses a quick and fluent mind with a good share of originality and brightness, but he has always seemed to us rather deficient in judgment and in staying power.'[8] Being under-estimated by rivals and critics turned out to be a crucial competitive advantage for almost every mogul.

In 1923, two brash 23-year-olds planted the seeds of another great media empire when they launched *Time*, America's first news magazine. College friends Henry Luce and Briton Hadden raised $86,000 (around $1.5 million today) to fund their ambitious concept of summarising and contextualising the news into a pacy weekly package. A key part of *Time*'s distinctiveness was its quirky form of editorial English – mockingly described as 'Time-ese' by its critics – that used inverted sentences like 'Up to the White House portico rolled a borrowed automobile', and adjectival contrivances like 'coffee-colored' and 'bandy-legged' to describe people in the news. When *The New Yorker* published a biting profile of Luce in 1936 it was written as a parody of Time-ese. 'Backward ran the sentences until reeled the mind,' wrote Wolcott Gibbs. 'Where it will all end, knows God!'[9]

Time transformed journalism throughout the twentieth century. Within four years it was selling more than 175,000 copies, and by the end of the century it had 4 million subscribers. As editor-in-chief, Hadden had only just begun his self-styled creative revolution when he became ill and soon died, in 1929, having 'drunk and partied his way to the deathbed', according to Isaiah Wilner's biography

The Man Time Forgot. Luce then took over the magazine and built it into an empire, without ever publicly acknowledging Hadden's role in the creation of *Time*.[10]

The Luce kingdom soon expanded beyond its only child when it launched *Fortune* in 1930 as a modern conception of the business magazine. Six years later Luce purchased *Life*, then a light entertainment magazine, and relaunched it as *LIFE*, America's great picture magazine.[11] Within four months its weekly circulation had surged from 380,000 copies to more than a million. Initially this created a problem because the magazine's low introductory advertising rates didn't cover its costs. The more copies they printed, the more money they lost – *LIFE* was 'dying of success', as one editor described it.[12] Once the advertising rates were lifted, the magazine eventually turned around, and by 1948 it was being read by 21 per cent of Americans aged over ten, and hauling in 19 per cent of every magazine advertising dollar spent in the US.

———

History's most expansive media empire, the hundred-year Murdoch dynasty, effectively started following the death of Keith Murdoch in 1952. But it really began, surreptitiously, three years earlier. Murdoch, then in his seventh year as chairman of the Herald and Weekly Times group, Australia's biggest newspaper publisher, convinced his fellow executives to allow him to buy a personal stake in one of the company's assets, the Adelaide *News*, which itself competed with another of the company's papers, the Adelaide *Advertiser*. He was 'cannibalizing the empire from within', wrote Walter Marsh in *Young Rupert*. It was 'skulduggery, absolute unblushing theft', his chief internal rival John Williams told colleagues following Murdoch's death.[13]

It was this shareholding in *The News* that materialised into Rupert Murdoch's primary inheritance from his father's estate, and became the springboard that created an empire. Rupert spent eight years in Adelaide developing his tabloid skills before moving to Sydney to acquire the struggling *Daily Mirror* for AUD$66 million (in today's dollars) from the patrician Fairfax publishing family, who also owned the *Mirror*'s dominant afternoon competitor, *The Sun*. 'Fairfax ran the *Mirror* down and tried to entice Rupert to buy it to put him out of business,' recalled the long-serving Australian journalist Eric Walsh. Murdoch reportedly danced a jig on the expensive tiles of the Fairfax executive floor after inking the deal, then had the last laugh (as usual) as his hyped-up *Mirror* overtook *The Sun* in circulation and profitability. 'Fairfax totally underestimated Rupert,' said Walsh. 'They thought they'd get rid of him easily.' Instead, they supplied him with a stepping stone to build a global empire.[14]

Murdoch found his next susceptible newspaper family in London in 1969. The Carrs, owners for eighty years of Britain's biggest-selling newspaper, the *News of the World*, were ready to cash out. Murdoch arrived from Australia to bid against another foreign mogul-in-waiting, Robert Maxwell, who was portrayed by the establishment as a crass Jewish Czech interloper attempting to grasp control of a tea-and-scones British institution. Murdoch worked his considerable charms on Sir William Carr by pledging not to take control of the company and promising that Carr could remain chairman and joint managing director. Both commitments were broken within months of completing a deal Murdoch later described as 'the biggest steal since the Great Train Robbery'.[15]

The battle for the *News of the World* launched a faux rivalry that lasted thirty years, in which Maxwell tried and failed to usurp Murdoch. 'Maxwell thought he had entered the ring with another boxer, but he hadn't,' said Harold Evans, one-time editor of *The Times* under Murdoch. 'In fact, he'd entered the ring with a jiu-jitsu artist who also happened to be carrying a stiletto.' Maxwell competed unsuccessfully with Murdoch to buy newspapers several more times. 'The more Murdoch thwarted him, the more determined he was to get his revenge,' wrote John Preston, author of *Fall: The Mystery of Robert Maxwell*. 'For his part, Murdoch insists he never regarded Maxwell as anything more than an irritant, albeit one he could never quite manage to shake off.'[16]

Acquiring the *News of the World* established a three-step Murdoch playbook – *overwhelm, overpromise, overpay* – that he repeated dozens of times over seven decades. When he sent two executives to San Antonio, Texas in 1973 to buy his first US newspaper from a local publisher, they returned without a deal because they thought the price was too high. 'I didn't send you to negotiate,' Murdoch reportedly told them, 'I sent you to buy the paper.'[17]

As commission-hungry investment advisers fed him with opportunities, Murdoch acquired media properties like other people ticked off items from a pantry shopping list. In 1976 he bought the *New York Post* for $32 million. ('I may have paid too much for it, but it was the chance of my lifetime.')[18] In 1977 he scooped up *New York* magazine and its iconic stablemate *Village Voice*, offending Manhattan liberal sensitivities and triggering a walkout of dozens of writers and editors in protest against his style of journalism.

In 1985 he paid an astonishing $1.05 billion for Metromedia's television stations in Los Angeles, Washington DC, Chicago, Houston and Dallas-Fort Worth. Then followed the *South China Morning Post* in Hong Kong for $284 million. A year later came the Herald and Weekly Times group, his father's old stable, in Australia's biggest-ever media takeover. ('It was a bloody bonanza. He was paying forty times earnings,' exclaimed the incumbent chief executive, who was swiftly and personally sacked by Murdoch.) Next cab off the rank was a deal that valued book publisher Harper & Row at fifty-five times earnings. ('If somebody offers you more money than you think you could ever make through earnings, you have to take it,' said the company's outgoing chairman.) Then Murdoch added his fifth national British newspaper, *Today*, paying £38 million for a masthead that was losing £30 million a year.[19] In between those deals through the 1980s, he stocked his larder with the London *Times* and *Sunday Times*, *Boston Herald*, *Chicago Sun-Times*, and the venerable 20th Century Fox movie studio.

In 1988 Murdoch transacted the most expensive publishing acquisition ever made at the time, paying $3 billion for *TV Guide*, then

America's biggest selling magazine (now defunct), and its stable-mates *Daily Racing Form* and *Seventeen* magazine. 'Those who follow Murdoch closely believe that he operates more like an inveterate deal maker than a global strategist,' reported the *Los Angeles Times* on the purchase. 'If somebody comes to him with a good deal, he will check his senses to see if the deal smells good, check his bankers to see if he has the money and then buy.'[20] Sometimes he didn't even bother to get his board's approval to buy a large asset. In 1993, after agreeing to pay $525 million for control of the Asian Star satellite system, he reportedly told his top executive Gus Fischer to 'call a couple of the directors and tell them'.[21]

I recall a discussion in Melbourne between Murdoch and my paper's business columnist, Terry McCrann, just after the *TV Guide* deal was announced. At the time, News Corp was carrying debt of around $5.6 billion, but Murdoch was nonchalant when Terry asked how the deal was financed. 'I'm not sure of the details, Dick's looking after that,' he said, referring to News Corp finance director, Richard Sarazen. When *TV Guide*'s owner, Walter Annenberg, was weighing Murdoch's offer, he reportedly asked the legendary investor Warren Buffett whether he should sell for that price. 'Run to the bank, Walter, run to the bank,' Buffett replied.[22] The Bancroft family received similar advice when Murdoch offered them $5 billion to acquire *The Wall Street Journal* in 2007. They had never seen 'such an overvalued offer', the advisers told their clients.[23] The family said yes.

Was Murdoch being reckless when he overpaid for a media asset? No. Did every acquisition pay off? No. Are many of the assets he has acquired over the past seven decades worth more now than their purchase price? Probably not. Are some worthless or not even in existence anymore? Yes. But none of that really matters to Rupert Murdoch and his family because they're much richer now than ever before, having built enough cash-generative businesses, and sold enough assets at high prices, to eclipse all the losses created by the sickly dogs that have passed through his media kennel.

The arrival of the internet in the early 2000s dislocated, and in many cases wrecked, almost every established media business. Like his peers and competitors, Murdoch took several years to fully comprehend the enormity, and dimensions, of the technology threat. Although he was sceptical about its potential throughout the internet's infant years, by the early twenty-first century he was ready to do what he always did: follow the money. 'The trends are against us,' Murdoch told the American Society of Newspaper Editors in Washington, DC in 2005. 'Unless we awaken to these changes, which are quite different than those five or six years ago, we will, as an industry, be relegated to the status of also-rans. We've been slow to react. We've sat by and watched.'[24]

His embrace of digital media, like many of Murdoch's hunches, wasn't seamless. Three months after his also-rans speech, News Corp paid $580 million for a two-year-old social networking platform called Myspace. By 2008 Myspace was generating $800 million in annual revenue, it had launched local editions in eleven countries, and was America's most visited website. The acquisition looked like a masterstroke. But a year later, Facebook overtook Myspace in traffic and from there it was all downhill. In 2011 News Corp offloaded Myspace for $35 million; it was an adventure that cost around $1.3 billion over six years (purchase price plus operating losses), according to the *Ars Technica* technology website.[25]

The following year, together with my business partners, I too became a beneficiary of Murdoch's acquisitiveness. News Corp paid AUD$30 million for our fledgling and unprofitable Australian online financial news venture, *Business Spectator*, whose revenues constituted barely a third of the purchase price. This mere blip on Murdoch's multi-billion-dollar radar was symptomatic of the mood of the times as the internet stalked traditional media like a predator. Our mini-deal was one of a series of small digital bets placed by Murdoch. Another was *The Daily*, a start-up touted as 'the world's first iPad-only news app', which lasted less than a year.

Murdoch's instincts about the direction, if not the velocity, of the media tailwinds have been wholly vindicated. News Corp is now effectively a digital media company. Its biggest profits are generated from online real estate, digital news subscriptions, pay TV, and electronic business information. By the end of 2023 all the company's newspapers across the world, apart from *The Wall Street Journal*, contributed just $52 million out of News Corp's quarterly profit of $473 million.

———

The pace of media empire-building throughout the twentieth century was frenetic. By the end of the 1920s, the Harmsworths had assembled five British newspapers selling more than 6 million copies a day in a country of 45 million people. In the same period, Hearst accumulated more than twenty newspapers across America's biggest cities, including New York, Boston, Chicago, Baltimore, San Francisco and Los Angeles. Roy (later Lord) Thomson built a newspaper conglomerate that started in provincial Canada and later incorporated three grand British mastheads, *The Times*, *The Sunday Times* and *The Scotsman*. Robert Maxwell, before his empire collapsed, turned the small scientific publisher Pergamon Press into a cash cow, then piled on debt to buy the UK *Daily Mirror*, the US book publisher Macmillan, *Official Airline Guides*, the New York *Daily News*, and a slew of magazine and printing businesses that were owned by a maze of 800 companies, many based in Liechtenstein to minimise tax.

By the middle of the twentieth century the newspaper business in most developed countries was booming. The end of World War Two created a strong appetite for news among an optimistic generation who were building new lives, and a desire by advertisers to promote the shiny products that were emerging in the burgeoning postwar economy. Most towns and cities in America had old, family-owned newspapers that now became attractive acquisition fodder for the handful of large operators like Edward Willis Scripps, a farm boy from Rushville, Illinois who bought or launched fifty-two dailies. Owning the dominant newspaper in a big city not only became a licence to print money, it provided local power and prestige for its proprietors and their families.

Otis Chandler, a fourth-generation family publisher, transformed the *Los Angeles Times* into one of America's best newspapers, whose prosperity tracked the growth of its remarkable city. In Chicago, Colonel Robert McCormick built the *Chicago Tribune* into a midwestern powerhouse described by *Time* as 'one of the last, anachronistic citadels of muscular personal journalism'.[26] In Louisville, Kentucky, the Binghams became almost regal (and very rich) through their civic-minded stewardship of *The Courier-Journal*.

The same potent cocktail of money, power and journalism was playing out across the Western world. In Australia it was the Fairfax and Packer families; in France, Robert Hersant spent four decades building an empire that owned almost 40 per cent of the national press, including the major dailies *Le Figaro* and *France-Soir*. Deeply conservative politically, Hersant was briefly jailed after collaborating with the Nazis in the 1940s. 'I'm neither Citizen Kane nor Randolph Hearst,' he once said. 'I own no mines, no factories, no oil companies. I am only a press baron.'[27] *Only*.

In Germany, Axel Springer, the son of a small-time printer, began building his newspaper empire in the aftermath of World War Two. Within a decade he owned two substantial national papers, the sensational mass-circulation tabloid *Bild* and the serious broadsheet *Die Welt*. After Springer's death in 1985, control passed to his fifth wife Friede, who began grooming one of the company's smartest journalists Mathias Döpfner, the editor-in-chief of *Die Welt*, as her successor. After initially selling him around 3 per cent of the shares in the company, she gifted him a further 19 per cent, worth more than $1 billion, giving him effective control. As CEO of Axel Springer SE, Döpfner has acquired two up-scale US digital publications, *Insider* and *Politico*, as he tries to build his company into a global media presence.[28]

Another collector of twentieth-century newspapers was Sam Newhouse, the eldest of eight children of poor Eastern European immigrants who arrived in New York. Newhouse was seventeen when he first learned the skills of newspaper micro-management, at the struggling New Jersey *Bayonne Times*. After leaving the paper, he began acquiring his own, first in New York and New Jersey through the 1920s, followed by bigger acquisitions in Portland, St. Louis, New Orleans and Cleveland, eventually building an empire of twenty dailies with a combined circulation of 5.7 million, plus magazines, television and cable businesses. Newhouse was described by *The New Yorker*'s A.J. Leibling as a 'journalistic chiffonnier' – the French word for 'ragpicker'.[29]

For Sam Newhouse, satisfaction was measured by accumulation. In 1959, when his wife Mitzi asked him to buy a copy of *Vogue*, he went out and bought Vogue the business (or so the story goes).[30] After purchasing the iconic *Times-Picayune* in 1962, he told a friend, 'I just bought New Orleans' – but his decision not to buy *The Jerusalem Post* deprived him of the opportunity to say, 'I just bought Jerusalem.' After his death, his son S.I. Newhouse (known as Si) expanded the business into one of the world's most respected magazine and book publishers, which still houses *Vogue*, *The New Yorker*, *Vanity Fair*, and much more.[31]

Like Sam Newhouse, Conrad Black started small. His original $500 investment in the *Knowlton Advertiser* in rural Quebec in 1966 launched a North American provincial newspaper fiefdom. Over thirty years Black and his business partner David Radler accumulated half of Canada's 105 daily papers, with a strategy euphemistically described as the three-man newsroom – 'one journalist and two advertising salesmen'. Radler was known to walk into a newly acquired newspaper with an instruction to 'count the chairs'.[32] Those were the chairs that built an empire that, before it collapsed ignominiously, encompassed the London *Daily Telegraph*, *Chicago Sun-Times*, *The Jerusalem Post*, Canada's *National Post*, *The Sydney Morning Herald* and the Melbourne *Age*.

Nicknamed 'Conrad the Barbarian' in Canada, Black was masterful at identifying opportunities lurking beneath the cobwebs of old newspaper families. After almost twenty years building a regional newspaper chain in Canada, he stumbled across the Berry family hibernating in Fleet Street behind the colonnade facade of Peterborough Court, the art deco building that housed the bastions of British conservative journalism, the *Daily* and *Sunday Telegraph*s.

Black met with the family's paterfamilias Lord Hartwell, chairman and editor-in-chief of the *Telegraph*s for thirty years. Described as 'the last of Britain's real press barons' by *The Guardian*, the shy, stuttering Hartwell presided over a crumbling business that by 1985 desperately needed cash to modernise its production capability after three-quarters of a century of mismanagement.[33] The scale of the juicy prize became clear to Black when he phoned *The Daily Telegraph*'s classified sales department from his London hotel room, asking to place an advertisement. The saleswoman who answered told Black the paper was full for several weeks, and advised him to try placing his ad in *The Guardian* or *The Times*.

Black's negotiations with Hartwell were colourfully chronicled in *Outrageous Fortune: The Rise and Ruin of Conrad and Lady Black*. Author Tom Bower describes how Black offered £10 million for 14 per cent of the *Telegraph*s' shares, on the proviso that, if Hartwell needed to raise more money, 'Black should have the first right of refusal, and that any investment would give Black a majority shareholding in the company . . . Hartwell replied without fully understanding the implications of Black's condition, "I don't think, Mr Black, we can resist that."'

When the banks refused to advance Hartwell more money two months later, Black offered £20 million for 50.1 per cent of the shares. After considerable dithering, Hartwell accepted. 'Black had won control for just 30m pounds,' Bower wrote. 'Overnight he had been transformed from a small-time publisher into an international star . . . "I've hit the jackpot," he laughed to a friend in a telephone conversation.'[34] Robert Maxwell echoed that sentiment soon after the deal had been consummated, when he told a gathering of the New York Society of Financial Analysts, 'Mr Black has landed history's largest fish with history's smallest hook.'[35]

When Black's empire subsequently toppled over, the next owners of the Telegraph group to pick up the pieces were Sir David and Sir Frederick Barclay, a pair of odd, reclusive, billionaire twin brothers who had built a successful property and hotel empire before buying into newspapers. Their acquisition of the *Daily* and Sunday *Telegraph*s and their sister magazine *The Spectator* in 2004 showcased Conrad Black at his most guileful. As his Hollinger Inc. was sinking, Black quickly offloaded the *Telegraph*s to the Barclays for the bargain-basement price of $346 million in order to raise desperately needed cash. When his shareholders discovered what he had done, they sued both buyer and seller, won in court, then proceeded to auction off the newspapers to the highest bidder – which turned out to be the Barclays – but this time for $1.2 billion (in cash).[36]

As powerful newspaper families began emerging in different countries, each business model was almost identical: heavy on local news and sports, a sprinkling of international and business coverage, dollops of lifestyle stories, comics and entertainment, one or two opinion pages, and as many classified ads as could be stuffed into a hefty bundle of newsprint. In India, though, the model contained another element – paid news. And no publisher has exploited this as profitably as the Jain family, owner of *The Times of India*, one of the biggest-selling English-language newspapers in the world, with a daily circulation of 1.8 million.

'We are not in the newspaper business,' Vineet Jain, who runs the organisation with his brother Samir, told Ken Auletta in *The New Yorker* in 2012. 'If 90 per cent of your revenues come from advertising, you are in the advertising business.'[37] But Jain isn't talking about conventional ads that sit separately from the editorial content, he's referring to the distinctive *Times of India* 'hard business sensibility', as the *Financial Times* once called it, which sells *editorial* space across its newspaper, including its entire front page if a client is prepared to pay enough. This paid content, written by the paper's journalists, is always favourable, and sits within a positive, optimistic editorial environment that downplays stories about crime and poverty. 'Nobody in the Indian media loves Samir Jain's business philosophy that treats journalism merely as a necessary nuisance and celebrates the advertiser as the real customer,' wrote R. Jagannathan in *Firstpost*. But paid news has been so successful since its introduction in the early 2000s that it has become a trademark feature of the Indian media.[38]

Succession

No-one becomes the ultimate boss of News Corporation, Hearst Communications, the New York Times Company, or Associated Newspapers unless they are a direct descendant of a Murdoch, a Hearst, an Ochs or a Harmsworth. There are plenty of career opportunities for successful midshipmen or first mates on those vessels, but the captain can only be someone from the founder's family.

When Elisabeth Murdoch established her own TV production outfit, called Shine, in 2001, her father's British TV company took a 5 per cent interest in the business. Ten years later, News Corp acquired the rest of Shine, 40 per cent of which went to Elisabeth. 'MURDOCH'S DAUGHTER TO GET £370M FROM DADDY', blared the front-page headline in the London *Evening Standard*.[1]

The deal shouldn't have surprised News Corp's shareholders because it was the second time Rupert Murdoch had used the public company, in which he was a minor shareholder, to give one of his children a corporate leg-up. Fifteen years earlier, News Corp bought and then shut down James Murdoch's hip-hop record company Rawkus after it ran into financial difficulties. That acquisition cleared the way for James to join the family company, where he quickly rose almost to the top before his role in the British phone-hacking scandal dismantled his corporate reputation.

'No matter how much you respect him, this all-in-the-family stuff just isn't right for a public firm,' wrote *Fortune* magazine senior editor

Allan Sloan after the Shine deal was announced. 'It's one thing to have News Corp employ family members. But it's a different thing to use assets of a company 88 per cent owned by the public to buy businesses owned by Murdoch children.'[2]

Sam Newhouse was another media overlord who made nepotism a distinguishing feature of his empire. Not only did sixty-four Newhouses work for his American newspaper and magazine business at one stage, he also encouraged his executives and editors to employ *their* family members. But he added a rule to balance this nepotism, wrote Carol Felsenthal in *Citizen Newhouse*: 'No family member would receive special treatment.' (Other than being employed in the first place, of course.)[3]

Nepotism in family-controlled media companies complicates life for ambitious and talented people with the wrong genes. Barry Diller, one of the smartest operators in American media, left his perch as chairman and chief executive of Murdoch's 20th Century Fox because he knew he could never rise any further. 'There is in this company only one principal,' he noted without apparent rancour on his way out the door.[4]

Family control, messy relationships, inheritance tensions, and the whole awkward business of succession are defining features of media dynasties. They are the juicy themes that underpin *Succession*, the highly popular HBO streaming series based on a Murdoch-styled family headed by Logan Roy, a despotic media dictator. At one crucial succession moment he says to his fawning son Kendall, 'The top job? Well, I dunno, maybe. You know, you're smart, you're good, but I just don't know. You're not a killer.'

What matters most in a media autocracy, way ahead of brains or grit, is *control*. The wife of the creator of the *Time* magazine empire, Clare Boothe Luce, once chastised her husband for tying up all his money in Time Inc. stock: 'You know, Harry, that's a terrible mistake, having all your eggs in one basket.' To which Luce replied, 'Not as long as it's my basket.'[5]

The family intrigues portrayed in *Succession* are technically fictitious, but in mogul world, life frequently imitates art. A good example can be found in the murky, secretive private lives of the eccentric Barclay twins. In 2021 Frederick Barclay sued his nephews for 'commercial espionage on a vast scale', alleging secret bugging of family members in the conservatory of London's Ritz Hotel, previously owned by the Barclays. The embarrassingly public case was eventually settled out of court.[6]

In 2023, 88-year-old David was sued for failing to pay about £245,000 he owed his ex-wife Hiroko Barclay. 'Over four days, the court would hear of the Barclay brothers' lifelong tax avoidance, a family now at loggerheads over succession, and finances so complex that even the beneficiaries claimed not to fully understand them,' wrote Jane Martinson in *You May Never See Us Again: The Barclay Dynasty*, her revelatory book about the twins. A once close family 'was now riven with division, with no love lost between husband and wife, but also between brothers, mother and daughter, uncles and nephews and cousins'.[7]

Within the Murdoch family, succession is a dish that never goes cold. Although elder son Lachlan has been installed as his father's heir, his longer-term future will be decided by his three siblings after Rupert's death. This is the result of a deal – struck as part of the divorce settlement with his second wife, Anna – that excludes his two younger daughters, from his next marriage to Wendi, from any entitlement to shares (although they will still get their pro rata cash from his estate). That may take a while, given that longevity is a family trait. Rupert's mother, Dame Elisabeth, lived actively until she was 103. When the Queen Mother died at the age of 101, the head of Fox News, Roger Ailes, remarked to his boss, 'She had a good run.' To which Murdoch replied, 'I'd call it an early death.' In 1999, after surviving a prostate cancer scare, he declared, apparently apocryphally, 'I'm now convinced of my own immortality.'[8]

When Murdoch does finally enter the great newsroom in the sky, Lachlan may find his position challenged by James, with the support of their sisters Elisabeth and Prudence. 'This brotherly rivalry will be bloody,' says former Murdoch editor Andrew Neil. 'The two have not spoken for five years. They refuse to be in the same room. Even meeting over Zoom on matters of mutual importance to both is near-impossible to arrange.'[9] According to another avid Murdoch-watcher, author Michael Wolff, James is on a 'mission to expel his brother'.[10]

Nepotistic succession within media dynasties is often a tightly choreographed charade acted out among family, executives, board directors and a retinue of sycophants, whose role is to maintain the fiction that offspring are selected for their talent, not their genes. Under this pretence, Jonathan Harmsworth would be running the *Daily Mail* even if his name was Jonathan Smith, and Lachlan Murdoch would still be running News Corp and Fox News if he was Lachlan Jones.

When James and Lachlan were appointed co-chairmen of 21st Century Fox in 2015, the company's lead director, Rod Eddington, announced without irony that 'the board has long been focused on succession and we're fortunate to have two very talented executives in Lachlan and James to take this company into the future'.[11] James shone light on how meritocracy works in a family company after he was appointed CEO of Star Television in Hong Kong in 2002. First came a phone conversation with his father, who said casually, 'Think about China.' A few days later father and son caught up. 'Do you like Chinese food?' Rupert asked James. 'And that was kind of it,' James told a *Time* magazine reporter. 'It had been decided.'[12]

Dynastic machinations within the Murdoch family have been grinding away since 1952, when Keith Murdoch died and bequeathed his son 28 per cent of the family holding company Cruden Investments, and 36 per cent of its voting rights.[13] Forty years later, on a luxury Alaskan ocean cruise with his then wife Anna, his three sisters and their husbands, Rupert negotiated his siblings' exit, paying them around $430 million to take full control of News Corp.[14]

Since then, money has flowed to Murdoch's six children on a grandiose scale. After each pocketing $150 million in cash and shares in 2007, their big payday arrived in 2019 when Murdoch, after a lifetime spent as a corporate predator, sold off slabs of his crown jewels: the 21st Century Fox movie studio, national and regional cable channels and networks, and his stake in Britain's Sky pay TV service.[15] The buyer was the Walt Disney Company. The price tag: $71 billion. 'Like King Lear confronting his mortality', *The New York Times* reported, the 86-year-old was dividing up a lifetime of spoils and 'throwing into confusion the line of succession and testing the ties that bind the family-run fief'.[16] As decoded by media analyst Laura Martin, 'He tried to buy, and when that didn't work, he doesn't sulk – he sells.'[17]

The Disney sale was a windfall for the Murdochs: Rupert pocketed $4 billion and his six children took home $2 billion apiece. But even that payday didn't leave the cupboard bare; they still sit on joint family ownership of News Corp and Fox News, and their dividends from their stake in Disney, as part of the mega-deal, plus their own companies, can reach around $200 million in a good year.

But not all the family cash has ended up with the Murdochs. Sizeable amounts have been pocketed by Rupert's four ex-wives, part of the cost of doing marital business for a mogul who has enthusiastically supported the institution of (not just one) marriage. His exes – flight attendant Patricia Booker (1956–67), journalist Anna Torv (1967–98), entrepreneur Wendi Deng (1999–2013) and model Jerry Hall (2016–22) – shared in the spoils over a period of sixty-two years.

The longest marriage, to Anna Torv, a former cadet journalist on his Sydney *Daily Mirror*, was the costliest and messiest. Under their divorce settlement in 1999, Anna reportedly received $1.6 billion in assets and $110 million in cash, following a 32-year marriage in which he was regarded as a model husband and father whose only mistress was his business. When Anna was removed as a News Corp director after the split, her ex-husband allegedly told her, 'You're an embarrassment to everyone else on the board.'[18]

Within a year, Murdoch had married wife #3, Wendi Deng. They divorced fourteen years later when she was forty-five and he was eighty-two. The break-up was tempestuous but swift, after evidence surfaced in internal News Corp emails that seemed to confirm a relationship between Deng and former British prime minister Tony Blair. According to *Vanity Fair*, Murdoch's sons handed a dossier on Wendi's extracurricular activities to their father. 'Of course she's cheating, Dad. Everyone knows that but you,' Lachlan allegedly told him.[19] Deng admitted as much in an email she wrote to herself that later emerged: 'Oh s***, oh s***. Whatever why I'm so so missing Tony. Because he is so charming and his clothes are so good . . . He has such a good body and he had his really, really good legs Butt [*sic*] . . . and he is slim tall and good skin. Pierce blue eyes which I love. Love his eyes. Also I love his power on the stage . . . and what else what else what else . . .'[20]

Murdoch pulled the plug on the marriage after discovering that Blair had stayed overnight with Deng at his California ranch, where they were seen by staff feeding each other and entering the same bedroom. Deng's divorce settlement included the couple's courtyard-style mansion in Beijing, near the Forbidden City, with its underground swimming pool and simulated golf driving range, as well as their three-level, $44 million Manhattan apartment.[21]

Three years later, Murdoch married the statuesque American model and actress Jerry Hall, former partner of Rolling Stones singer Mick Jagger. They met in Melbourne when Hall was playing Mrs Robinson in the stage version of *The Graduate*. 'He was an old-fashioned gentleman,' Hall told friends after their first date in New York. 'We laughed together nonstop.' That merger lasted only six years, yielding Hall a multi-million-pound settlement including an £11 million Oxfordshire mansion. According to *Vanity Fair*, Murdoch, then ninety-one, ended the marriage with an abrupt email: 'Jerry, sadly I've decided to call an end to our marriage . . . We have certainly had some good times, but I have much to do . . . My New York lawyer will be contacting yours immediately.'[22]

The ultimate arbiter of a mogul's succession – regardless of legal and estate planning – is his death. William Randolph Hearst began seeing Marion Davies, a Ziegfeld Follies dancer, when he was fifty-five and she was twenty-one. He left his wife Millicent and openly lived with Davies for the next twenty-six years. 'Pop was smitten with her and she became his sex kitten,' recalled William Randolph Hearst Jr.[23] Hearst's death in 1951 brought Davies into direct conflict with his sons and wife, when they discovered he had left all his Hearst Corporation preferred shares to his mistress. Moreover, he had constructed an agreement that combined his 170,000 shares with her pre-existing 30,000 to give her voting control over the business after his death – in other words, to be the boss. 'To suggest that my father actually wanted her to run the corporation was contrary to all his previous policy,' wrote Hearst Jnr in his memoir.[24]

After days of meetings between lawyers, Davies agreed to relinquish her voting rights and, in a face-saving move, became an 'advisor to management' at a salary of one dollar a year.[25] Hearst's wishes were overruled from the grave.

Decline and Fall

The decline of media empires and their emperors, like almost everything about them, has been erratic, spectacular, personal and businesslike. When Hearst died in the Los Angeles mansion of Marion Davies, the corporate transition was swift and ruthless. Twenty minutes after a brain haemorrhage ended the life of his boss, the president of Hearst Corporation, Richard Berlin, arrived at the house. 'You're all working for me now,' he told the assembled staff.[1]

Marion Davies was distraught. 'He was gone. I asked where he was and the nurse said he was dead. His body was gone, whoosh, like that. I didn't even know whether he was dead when they took him. Old W. R. was gone, the boys were gone. I was alone. They didn't even let me say good-bye. Do you realize what they did? They stole a possession of mine. He belonged to me. I loved him for thirty-two years and now he was gone. Yes, I couldn't even say good-bye.'[2]

By definition, and by nature, entrepreneurial media enterprises are vulnerable to risk and potential disaster. Business models disintegrate. Spectacular new technology appears. Economic cycles sweep away advertising revenues. Start-ups misfire. Hubristic owners overreach. Families squabble. Laws and regulations change. Founders die. Bad things happen.

As the Depression decimated the US economy in the 1930s, the Hearst conglomerate almost collapsed under the weight of its debt.

William Randolph Hearst lost financial control of his empire in 1937 when his long-time friend Judge Clarence Shearn was appointed by shareholders as the sole voting trustee of the corporate entity. Shearn slashed costs, sold assets, closed newspapers, retrenched staff, and cut Hearst's annual salary from $500k to a mere $100k (around $2.1 million today).

Rupert Murdoch barely survived a similar fate in 1990 when he came within days of losing control of News Corp to its banks. Lumbering under more than $700 million of debt funding from Citicorp, who needed to reduce its exposure, Murdoch pleaded with 146 other global bankers not to call in billions of dollars in short-term loans. He pitched his survival plan in roadshows in Sydney, London and New York, but it took three months for all of them to agree to freeze more than $6 billion in News Corp loans for three years. Murdoch's worst moment came when he was forced to place a phone call to the credit manager of a small bank in Pittsburgh to persuade him to roll over $10 million owed by News Corp. 'He was so vulnerable. One phone call could mean the end of his whole life's work,' Ann Lane, the commercial lawyer who coordinated the refinancing, told Murdoch biographer William Shawcross. 'He was visibly shaking, but he didn't go crazy. It is not a pretty sight to see a great man like that.'[3]

Nine months after Murdoch dragged his company back from the precipice, the naked body of another media mogul was plucked from the Atlantic Ocean near the Canary Islands, southwest of Spain. Sixty-eight-year-old Robert Maxwell had drowned after falling (or, more likely, jumping) off his yacht, the *Lady Ghislaine*, where he was cruising alone with a small crew. On the day before his body was retrieved from the sea, three major banks, Goldman Sachs, Lehman Brothers and Citibank, began calling in their loans. Maxwell was in deep financial trouble when he died; he was within days of defaulting on £50 million in loans, facing an investigation by the Bank of England, and about to be exposed by the *Financial Times*. And after his drowning it emerged that he had misappropriated hundreds of millions of pounds from his companies' pension funds to prop up his businesses.

In the aftermath of his death the banks called in their massive loans and his web of companies collapsed. His son Kevin, one of Maxwell's designated successors, was declared bankrupt with debts of £400 million. The official cause of death was a heart attack combined with accidental drowning, but Maxwell's life had turned so hellish that it was hard to avoid the conclusion reached by his long-time rival Rupert Murdoch. 'He knew the banks were closing in, he knew what he'd done and he jumped,' Murdoch told John Preston, author of *Fall: The Mystery of Robert Maxwell*.[4] 'He was a man who could not face the ignominy of jail, of being shown to be a liar and a thief,' concluded Roy Greenslade, former editor of Maxwell's *Daily Mirror*.[5] His company debts of £2.7 billion and his defrauding of pension funds resulted in an update of Maxwell's profile in the Oxford Dictionary of National Biography to 'publisher and swindler'.[6]

Robert Maxwell's life story reads like a morality tale turned parody. A destitute Czechoslovakian Jewish refugee (birth name Ján Hoch), he had escaped the Nazis and trekked alone across Europe as a teenager, before joining the British army in 1943. Two years later he won the Military Cross for 'storming a German machine-gun nest', then reinvented himself in postwar England as Robert Maxwell (renaming himself after the formal, British-sounding coffee brand Maxwell House), adopted a plummy BBC voice, and became a highly successful educational publisher and a Labour Party member of parliament.[7]

Maxwell failed in his first attempt to become a newspaper baron, in 1969, when he was underbidder to Rupert Murdoch for the *News of the World*, the hugely popular Sunday newspaper of the 'Vicar in Love Nest' genre owned by the establishment Carr family. Maxwell was outmanoeuvred by Murdoch in a corporate battle besmirched by anti-Semitism and British snootiness, culminating in a front-page opinion piece written by the paper's editor, Stafford Somerfield, opposing Maxwell's bid. 'This is a British paper, run by British people . . . as British as roast beef and Yorkshire pudding,' Somerfield fulminated. 'Let us keep it that way.'[8]

Fifteen years later, Maxwell finally achieved his press ownership ambitions when he acquired the mass-circulation, Labour-leaning *Daily Mirror*; Scotland's *Daily Record*; and *Sunday People*. But he was an erratic empire builder, piling up debt as he accumulated book and magazine publishing businesses, TV production companies, language schools, football clubs, and the New York *Daily News*. Dubbed the 'Bouncing Czech' by the satirical magazine *Private Eye*, Maxwell morphed into a grossly obese emperor strutting the world, over-paying for assets and spouting pompous pronouncements.

Like Maxwell, Conrad Black was scornful of corporate govern-ance. This proved to be an expensive oversight when, in 1997, he and his business partner David Radler began milking large sums of cash from Hollinger Inc., the media company they controlled but didn't fully own. Over the next six years they personally received $401 million in management fees – 95 per cent of Hollinger's total net income – for providing their services.[9]

Hollinger sued Black and a handful of associates in 2004 for $1.25 billion, charging them with committing 'unlawful acts' through a 'pattern of racketeering activity'. As the charges moved through the US courts, Black emailed two of his most trusted advisers in Toronto outlining his dilemma: 'There has not been an occasion for many months when I got on our plane without wondering whether it was really affordable. But I'm not prepared to reenact the French Revo-lutionary renunciation of the rights of nobility. We have to find a balance between an unfair taxation on the company and a reasona-ble treatment of the founder-builders-managers. We are proprietors, after all, beleaguered though we may be.'[10]

Radler pleaded guilty and gave evidence against his former business partner in court. In 2007 Black was convicted on four counts of felony fraud and obstruction of justice, later reduced to two charges. He served thirty-seven months in prison and his reputation was shredded. Later in 2007, Hollinger filed for bankruptcy protection in Canada and the US.[11]

In an inquiry conducted for Hollinger's shareholders, former U.S. Securities and Exchange Commission chairman Richard Breeden summarised the caper: 'This story is about how Hollinger was systematically manipulated and used by its controlling shareholders for their sole benefit, and in a manner that violated every concept of fiduciary duty. Not once or twice, but on dozens of occasions Hollinger was victimized by its controlling shareholders as they transferred to themselves and their affiliates more than $400m in the last seven years ... Behind a constant stream of bombast regarding their accomplishments as self-described "proprietors", Black and Radler made it their business to line their pockets at the expense of Hollinger almost every day, in almost every way they could devise ... The special committee knows of few parallels to Black and Radler's brand of self-righteous, and aggressive looting of Hollinger to the exclusion of all other concerns or interests, and irrespective of whether their actions were remotely fair to shareholders.'[12]

The summary was part of a 500-page report which also revealed that company funds were used to 'satisfy the liquidity needs arising for the personal lifestyle Black and his wife had chosen to lead'. These needs included purchasing or leasing two corporate jets; a $530,000 holiday in French Polynesia; a $2,463 handbag; Barbara's birthday party at La Grenouille restaurant in New York at a cost of $42,870; salary contributions for a chef, senior butler, guard and chauffeurs at their homes in London, New York and Florida; perfume; food; shopping trips; tips for the shopping trips; exercise equipment; opera tickets ...[13]

Even though he reached a voluntary settlement with the U.S. Securities and Exchange Commission, and accepted a permanent ban from acting as a director or officer of a public company, and paid a $4 million penalty, Black never acknowledged his guilt. 'Unlike the Milkens and Bernie Madoffs of the world, Black tenaciously fought the case against him every step of the way,' wrote Bryan Burrough in *Vanity Fair*, pointing out that Black's lawyers succeeded in having all but two of the seventeen charges brought against their client defeated, dismissed, overturned or dropped. 'They took his fight all the way to the Supreme Court, in fact, and actually won.'[14]

Black wrote his own version of his downfall in a 598-page memoir titled *A Matter of Principle*. 'My prison number, 18330-424, is stamped on my clothes and mandatory on all correspondence,' he began. 'I am sixty-five years old. I entered these walls a baron of the United Kingdom, Knight of the Holy See, Privy Councillor, and Officer of the Order of Canada, former publisher of some of the world's greatest newspapers, and author of some well-received non-fiction books ... I have gone through but survived straitened financial circumstances, have sold two of my homes, and am responding to and initiating endless civil litigation. For the last six and a half years I have been fighting for my financial life, physical freedom, and what remains of my reputation against the most powerful organization in the world, the U.S. government ...' He went on to blame the bankruptcy of his businesses on 'the dead weight of the incompetence and corruption of my enemies, who have hugely enriched themselves under the patronage of American and Canadian courts of law and equity ... For years I was widely reviled, defamed, and routinely referred to as "disgraced" or "shamed" and "convicted fraudster" ...'[15]

The signs pointing to Black's ultimate undoing had been lurking for decades. 'Greed has been severely underestimated and denigrated – unfairly so, in my opinion,' he told the Canadian writer Peter Newman in the 1980s. 'I mean, there is nothing wrong with avarice as a motive, as long as it doesn't lead to dishonest or anti-social conduct. I don't think greed, as such, is anything to be proud of, but a spirit of moderate acquisitiveness is not un-akin to a sense of self-preservation. It is a motive that has not failed to move me from time to time.'[16]

One empire that not only survived its existential crisis, but eventually thrived, was the Sulzberger family's *New York Times*. In the early 2000s, as the internet hijacked large slabs of advertising from once highly profitable newspapers, the *Times* started running out of cash. To survive, the Sulzbergers unloaded almost all their non-core assets between 2007 and 2013. They flogged off nine TV stations for $575 million, sixteen regional newspapers for $143 million, two radio stations for $45 million, *The Boston Globe* for $70 million (a $1.1 billion acquisition twenty years earlier), and suspended dividend payments to shareholders. Just to make sure the money didn't run out, they borrowed $250 million from the Mexican billionaire Carlos Slim at a 14 per cent interest rate.[17]

But the Sulzbergers didn't waste their crisis, they used it to wholly reinvent the business of *The New York Times*. In what has become a global case study in the successful commercialisation of quality journalism in the internet age, the *Times* recast itself as a digital subscriber business with a printed newspaper hanging off the side – an elegant example of a media-owning family asserting its commercial nous to create a positive outcome for society.

By 2020, the *Times* had fully recovered; it was sitting on $800 million in cash, carried no debt, had a $250 million credit line and full ownership of its glassy Manhattan headquarters.[18] Three years later it had more than 10 million online subscribers and was collecting vastly more revenue from digital than from print subscribers. It had also built a suite of specialist digital subscription businesses – recipes, games, consumer reviews and sports – that supported the core editorial mission (and profitability) of its flagship masthead. 'This is a stunning success for a business model pivot,' noted the respected industry watcher Brian Morrissey in *The Rebooting*. 'It's hard to remember now,' he said, referring to the desperate situation the *Times* had emerged from, 'but the smart money was on the *Times* as a legacy brand in terminal decline.'[19]

Sadly, *The New York Times* is not a replicable model for the future of commercial quality journalism. It's an outlier. Almost no other news business in the world has the scale, editorial muscle, market size or reputation to imitate the *Times* formula. It would be 'like trying to copy Harvard or trying to copy Google', says the American media commentator Clay Shirky.[20]

The revival of the *Times* is a striking example of autocratic media power exercised as a public good. Motivated by the Ochs mission to pursue truth through journalism, the Sulzbergers used their corporate control to make a big bet, unencumbered by the internal bureaucracy, equivocating shareholders or squeamishness that often prevents large organisations from acting decisively. Their resolve contrasts with the inaction of many of the towering twentieth-century media dynasties that failed to successfully transition from their analogue comfort zone, particularly after the deaths of their founders. It was proof that, whatever skills they may have possessed, their biggest asset was just being born at the right time in history.

Beaverbrook's stable of newspapers barely outlived his death in 1964. His son, Sir Max Aitken, declined to assume his father's lordship and put the *Daily* and *Sunday Express* up for sale in 1977. After offers from the Harmsworths and Rupert Murdoch, the successful buyer was the Trafalgar House investment group, owner of the *QE2* and London's Ritz Hotel.[21] The papers, now a shadow of their former glory, have changed hands three more times since then and no longer rattle the corridors of political power.

The sun set on the Pulitzer empire in 2005 when the founder's great-grandchildren sold the *St. Louis Post-Dispatch*, the paper that started it all, to a chain publisher. This was almost a century after Pulitzer died in 1911. Control of his proudest asset, the New York *World*, passed to his sons. But as its circulation diminished and its losses increased, his heirs sold it in 1931 to its competitor, *The New York Telegram*, whose owners merged it to create the *New York World-Telegram*, which itself shut down in 1966.

The magazine kingdom conceived by Henry Luce in 1922 was crafted so personally for an era and a founder that its ethos was never likely to extend too far beyond his death in 1967. In the booming magazine market of the late twentieth century, *Time* continued to sell millions of copies a week, *Fortune* and *Sports Illustrated* were tremendously profitable, and the company – now under managerial control that didn't involve Luce's heirs, after he'd left most of his $100 million fortune to the philanthropic Henry Luce Foundation – churned out more than a hundred glossy magazine brands, including *People, InStyle, Travel + Leisure, Food & Wine, Southern Living, Real Simple* and *Entertainment Weekly*. By 1990, the party was over. Time Inc. merged with Warner Communications to create Time Warner, and in 2018 it was acquired by magazine publisher Meredith for $2.8 billion. Now it's a shadow of its former self in a world where printed magazines, like newspapers, are becoming an anachronism.[22] Luce's empire today is a motley collection of spare parts: *Life* closed in 2012, *Time* was sold to software billionaire Marc Benioff, *Fortune* is owned by a Thai business tycoon, and *Sports Illustrated* is, sadly, in its final death throes.

The same Darwinian process has been playing out across hundreds of American towns and cities for decades. The Bingham family unloaded the Louisville *Courier-Journal* in 1986, *The Boston Globe* was sold by the Taylors in 1993, the Chandlers sold off the *Los Angeles Times* in 2000, and *The Washington Post* was acquired from the Graham family by Amazon billionaire Jeff Bezos in 2013.

Watching the demise of a great editorial enterprise is an excruciating experience. During my years as a young reporter through the 1970s and 1980s at the Melbourne *Age*, and later as editor of its stablemate *The Sydney Morning Herald*, my colleagues and I knew (or know now) that we were charmed participants in a golden age of journalism. We worked for iconic broadsheets that furnished our affluent communities with trusted news and commentary, underpinned financially by vast tracts of classified advertising known as 'rivers of gold'.

These were monopoly businesses surrounded by deep financial moats that generated overweight returns for their shareholders, and in the process underwrote our editorial mission. No-one from the executive floor ever tried to tell us what to write. Our owners, the Fairfax family, happily and honourably reinvested part of their newspaper fortune into quality journalism – a global example of a media owner who contributed to society while also benefiting from it.

The original John Fairfax was an insolvent printer who arrived from England in the nineteenth century with £5 in his pocket to make a new life in Australia. He acquired *The Sydney Morning Herald* in 1841, the crown jewel that launched a storied media company incorporating *The Age*, *The Australian Financial Review*, a national television and radio network, a fleet of magazines, and dozens of regional newspapers.[23]

It all imploded in 1990 when Warwick Fairfax – a shy, unconfident 29-year-old, sixth-generation Fairfax, with a Harvard MBA and no publishing experience – attempted to fast-track his ambitions by nabbing control of his family's grand company. 'Young Warwick', as he was uncharitably known, botched the takeover bid and sent the family dynasty into receivership, before it shuffled through two more owners.[24]

In 2004 Fairfax acquired the publishing business my colleagues and I had built over more than a decade, after we started taking big chunks out of its lucrative real estate advertising revenue. So Fairfax followed the playbook of other well-heeled media conglomerates during the golden era of newspapers and magazines by gobbling up a small competitor. (It was my second sale to a large media company, after the digital business publisher I co-owned with several partners was bought by News Corp.)

Now that I was no longer a competitor, one of the Fairfax board directors asked me if I would spend a few months scrutinising their entire business, to give a practitioner's view of its future. Like me, he was deeply concerned that without an internet strategy or any media experience on its board, Fairfax was sleepwalking towards a disaster that was camouflaged by its still-buoyant print revenues. At that time, its two flagship newspapers each carried around 200 broadsheet pages of classified advertising a week, generating combined annual profits of some AUD$200 million.

In my 37-page report for the Fairfax board, I raised the prospect of a 'catastrophe scenario' that could wipe out most of the company's profits as print classified ads inevitably migrated to the internet. 'Fairfax runs two businesses,' I wrote, 'a loss-making journalism/display advertising business, and a highly profitable classified advertising business.' Because these businesses had different readers and advertisers, their connection was 'largely an accident of history', I argued.

Fairfax was one of many old-economy companies and industries that failed to recognise or acknowledge the decline of their business model until it was too late. 'A mixture of human emotion, defensiveness, hubris, the defender's mindset and an inability to think like an "outsider" have contributed to these failures of recognition,' I wrote. 'But the truth is that great industries and products do fall; that daring new technologies do replace successful old ones; and that 170 years of success is no protection against a faster, cheaper, better interloper.'

I urged the board to act quickly to reinvent its business, offering a range of possible strategies that included establishing a gorilla 'attacker' digital operation to compete with the parent company, and launching niche publications and newsletters to broaden the audience and advertiser base. 'In my view, there is only one greater risk for the board,' I wrote, 'and that is doing nothing.'

After I finished presenting my findings to the full Fairfax board, a visibly agitated director strode to the head of the boardroom table, picked up a copy of one of the company's hefty broadsheets, bulging with classified ads, and dramatically held it aloft. Then he told his fellow directors that he never again wanted anyone coming into the boardroom suggesting that people would 'buy houses or cars or look for jobs without *this!*' as he dropped the lump of newsprint onto the boardroom table with a loud thud.

Fairfax was too slow and arrogant to address its existential challenge. *The Age* and *The Sydney Morning Herald* still exist in print, but hardly anyone buys them anymore. They have retrenched thousands of staff. Relative to the twentieth-century rivers of gold, the papers are barely profitable. After being sold off again in 2018, these once-storied independent newspapers are now a small division of a large entertainment company.

POWER

Editorial
Dictators

'What is the point in running a newspaper,' asked Conrad Black at the peak of his power, 'if you have absolutely no say?'[1] For most media moguls, a 'say' means issuing instructions to compliant editors, endorsing political parties, sacking recalcitrant employees, and generally acting like a dictator. But Black was different. He expressed his views by writing formal letters to his own newspaper for publication on the letters-to-the-editor page, signed 'Conrad Black, London N6'.

It was an approach he explained in his book *A Matter of Principle*: 'I asserted my views forcefully but have met the full range of editorial resistance tactics. Raising children is a good formation for dealing with editors and journalists. They are all fiendishly clever at promising compliance with the wishes of the owner, appearing to give superficial adherence while in fact continuing in their exceptionable practices. A cat-and-mouse game ensues, in which my refusal to be made a mockery of struggles for mastery with my desire not to have to micro-nanny every detail of the production of the newspaper and my concern not to be ground down by arguing endlessly with the editor and his entourage.'[2]

Before taking the job as Black's editor of *The Daily Telegraph* in 1986, Max Hastings flew from London to Toronto to meet his new boss. Clad in an ill-fitting double-breasted suit, Black steamed through the door 'not unlike a capital ship entering harbor', recalled Hastings in his memoir. When he outlined his own political preference – 'a left-of-center Tory' – Black replied, 'Any newspaper that attempted to impose my convictions on its readership would be in danger of possessing a circulation of one.' For Hastings this was 'an encouraging moment of self-deprecation'.[3]

And indeed, Black remained a largely passive proprietor even when his commercial interests were under threat. In 1994 his British magazine *The Spectator* produced a story under the headline 'Kings of the Deal' that investigated the 'increasing influence and success of Hollywood's new Jewish Establishment'. Black was assailed with angry complaints from Tom Cruise, Steven Spielberg, Barbra Streisand and Kevin Costner. Advertisers threatened to pull their ads across Black's empire. The story, with its anti-Semitic undertones, created a global controversy that reached Israel, where Black owned *The Jerusalem Post*. 'It was one of the few moments in my time with Conrad when I saw him look seriously rattled,' wrote Max Hastings. 'My entire interests in the United States and internationally could be seriously damaged by this,' Black told him.[4]

Henry Luce, by contrast, was an activist media proprietor with strong views who acted more like a monarch than a dictator. Luce dispatched dozens of daily memos to *Time*'s editors laying out his worldview. 'The chief editorial policymaker for Time Inc. is Henry R Luce, and that is no secret that we attempt to conceal from the outside world,' he once acknowledged. Luce was one of the first true national propagandists, wrote David Halberstam in *The Powers That Be* – 'he spoke to the whole nation on national issues, one man with one magazine speaking with one voice, and reaching the entire country'. Not everyone agreed, of course. 'Mister Henry Luce is like a shoe salesman,' sniped Earl Long, the folksy governor of Louisiana in the 1940s and '50s. 'All the other shoe-store owners stock all different sizes of shoes, but Mr Luce, he only sells shoes that fit hisself.'[5]

Like Luce, Beaverbrook's editorial control was ubiquitous. He dictated instructions into a device called a Soundscriber that created discs that were transcribed and distributed to his minions. 'He was capable of sending his editors 147 directives in a single day and delivering peremptory summonses to his secretaries while they were in the lavatory,' wrote Piers Brendon in *The Life & Death of Press Barons*. One underling was so exasperated, according to Brendon, that he bellowed at the butler through the door, 'Tell the Lord I'm having a shit, and I can only deal with one shit at a time.'[6]

The columnist Alan Brien described Beaverbrook as the only proprietor he had worked for 'whose eye I could feel burning along every line I ever wrote, however trivial, specialized or obscure the part of the paper in which they appeared'. And just when you thought you had disappeared, said Brien, 'there would come a message to you by name, sometimes handed down by proxy from above, sometimes delivered in person by telephone'.[7]

The Beaverbrook eyes darted across the spectrum of humanity. His files were sprinkled with notes, usually but not exclusively from women, asking – in some cases begging – him to keep their divorces out of his newspapers, according to Anne Chisholm and Michael Davie in *Beaverbrook: A Life*. 'He was on the whole sympathetic to such requests, an attitude he would justify by pointing out that to Presbyterians marriage is merely a contract, not a sacrament.'[8]

There were some instructions, however, that never needed to be issued inside the Beaverbrook bunker. 'At any time, Winston Churchill was beyond reproach in Lord Beaverbrook's papers,' recalled Arthur Christiansen, editor of the *Daily Express* from 1933 to 1957. 'It was axiomatic that if you wished to remain a Beaverbrook editor you did not permit any word of criticism to creep into the leading articles.'[9] On the other side of the coin, if you were a Beaverbrook enemy, the opprobrium could be ferocious. He weaponised his newspapers in a vendetta against prime minister Stanley Baldwin 'to stalk and seek to destroy a public man who would not bend to his will', according to former Fleet Street editorial guru Hugh Cudlipp.[10]

Hearst also ran his empire via instructions to his editors, like this telegram that landed on their desks in April 1950: 'THE CHIEF INSTRUCTS NOT, REPEAT NOT, TO PRESS THE CAMPAIGN AGAINST COMMUNISM ANY FURTHER. HE WISHES THE CAMPAIGN HELD BACK

FOR A WHILE. PARTICULARLY THE EDITORIALS. HE FEELS WE HAVE
BEEN PRESSING THE FIGHT TOO HARD FOR TOO LONG AND MIGHT BE
AROUSING WAR HYSTERIA.'[11]

Drafts of important editorials were sent by teletype machine to
Hearst in California, for vetting. After approval, or amendment,
they were stamped with the words: 'Following editorial is hereby
released by Chief for publication in all morning papers, and afternoon papers where no mornings.' Hearst set the topics, dictated the
tone, and directed many of the editorials in his papers – 'the major
ones he wrote himself and displayed prominently on his front pages;
he endorsed candidates for office and condemned them when they
betrayed their promises; he emblazoned his name on his magazines,
his newsreels, and his radio outlets,' noted David Nasaw in *The Chief*.[12]

Hearst's cables often framed words and phrases that were cut-
and-pasted directly into his papers' editorials. In August 1934, he sent
this instruction about Roosevelt's economic recovery program to
his minions: 'TELL ALL PAPERS MORNING EVENING KEEP FREE FROM
VIOLENT POLITICAL DISCUSSION OR EXTREME POLITICAL PARTISAN-
SHIP BUT TO GIVE MODERATE SUPPORT TO SOUND AND JUDICIOUS
CANDIDATES OF EITHER PARTY. RECOVERY IS BEING RETARDED BY
VISIONARY SCHEMES OF UNSOUND RADICALS. EVEN AMERICAN INSTI-
TUTIONS ARE ENDANGERED. PATRIOTIC CONSERVATISM REGARDLESS
OF PARTY SHOULD BE APPROVED AND SUPPORTED.'[13]

Northcliffe was another micromanaging magnate. He would wake
around 5.30am, read all the rival newspapers, use coloured pencils
kept by his bedside to scribble notes over the pages of his own newspapers, then phone his editors with positive or negative feedback (or
both), sometimes criticising the paper page by page, according to
Andrew Roberts in *The Chief*. Then his views, ranging over 'every detail
in every department', were telegraphed to staff. 'He would warn us
with equal seriousness to "watch" Ireland, or the divorce courts, or the
comic animals in our children's features,' according to a senior editor.

In the manner of Northcliffe, his mentor, Keith Murdoch sent
senior executives his 'Managing Editor's Notes', printed on quality

quarto notepaper, early each morning. According to historian Michael Cannon, the Notes were written 'in crisp, direct language and short, newspaper-like paragraphs, suggesting that Murdoch wished to identify himself with the men he was addressing and set them the more effective example of the virtues of clarity and precision that he preached'.[14]

His son Rupert has always favoured a blunt verbal style of editorial management. After acquiring the *News of the World* in 1969 he told a reporter, 'I did not come all this way from Australia not to interfere.'[15] He later described his method of managing editorial resistance to a biographer: 'When one of my editors tries to prevent me from exercising my rightful domain over a paper, he's gone.'[16]

Over time, as his empire grew and personal intervention became impractical, Murdoch achieved editorial compliance through a kind of osmosis. 'Throughout the 11 years that I was editor of *The Sunday Times*, I never got an instruction to take a particular line, I never got an instruction to put something on the front page and I do not think I even got an instruction not to do something, but I was never left in any doubt what he wanted,' Andrew Neil told the UK Parliament's Select Committee on Communications in 2008. 'On every major issue of the time and every major political personality or business personality, I knew what he thought and you knew, as an editor, that you did not have a freehold, you had a leasehold, as editor, and that leasehold depended on accommodating his views in most cases, not all cases, and there were sometimes quite serious disagreements we had and I still survived as editor.'[17]

The fact that Murdoch rarely issues direct instructions is the explanation proffered by his sycophants to prove he's not an interventionist proprietor. 'With a conspiracy-heavy culture there is no greater cult beloved of media polemicists and populist politicians than the spectre of Rupert Murdoch on the phone rapping out orders to hapless editors about his targets for the next day's front page,' contended one of his loyalists-in-chief, Paul Kelly, editor-at-large of Murdoch's Antipodean flagship *The Australian*. 'This notion persists in a form of myth as reality,' claimed Kelly.[18] But this 'myth' was punctured in broad daylight in 2023 when transcripts of Murdoch's emails to his Fox News executives emerged during the Dominion defamation case. They revealed an interventionist proprietor giving orders, directions and hints to support Trump's election denial gibberish, and never issuing the single instruction he alone could give: to cover Trump *truthfully*.

Kelly is technically correct: Murdoch doesn't issue 'daily orders' to editors. That's because, as Andrew Neil pointed out, he doesn't need to. News Corp's internal culture, honed over decades, means that editorial lieutenants always know, or can intuit, their proprietor's opinions, grievances, preferences and financial interests. Murdoch's wishes emanate 'rather like ectoplasm' to his subordinates, who anticipate his views because they are constantly anxious to please him, explained his biographer-admirer William Shawcross.[19]

After *The Wall Street Journal* was acquired by Murdoch in 2007, the staff created a phrase to describe the defensive posture needed to work under their new interventionist proprietor: 'pre-emptive capitulation'. It was like learning a foreign language for journalists accustomed to making their own professional decisions. The paper's editor, Marcus Brauchli, soon became 'exhausted by the need to anticipate everything Murdoch might expect', wrote Sarah Ellison in *Vanity Fair*, and his attempts to 'outsmart Murdoch's manipulation and maintain a sliver of independence' ended with his sacking.[20]

On the rare occasions that acculturated osmosis doesn't work, Murdoch leaves his underlings in no doubt as to what he *really* thinks. Kelvin MacKenzie, long-serving editor of the London *Sun*, recalled the day Murdoch called him, 'incandescent about the paper', from New York. 'I took it for about three or four minutes and then decided it would be fun (and give me a break) if I put the phone in my desk drawer. I walked slowly round the desk, pulled out the phone and he was still shouting,' he wrote in a column in *The Spectator*. But ever the loyalist, MacKenzie found a way to praise his boss for being obnoxious. 'Oddly, I admired him for that. He cared. There aren't enough bosses who really do.'[21]

Despite sacking its editor, however, Murdoch realised that *The Wall Street Journal*'s journalistic integrity was crucial to its financial performance – neither readers nor advertisers would retain trust in a business newspaper that was seen to be a proprietor's plaything – so he wisely adhered to the commitment he had pledged in an email to the editor Paul Steiger during the bidding process to buy the paper:

PERSONAL AND CONFIDENTIAL FROM RUPERT

Paul,

I thought it useful to write you a personal note, given that we are all about to be in the midst of a maelstrom of rumor and speculation. More than anything else, I wanted to assure you that the journalistic principles that you have embodied at The Wall Street Journal will remain sacrosanct. There are many good reasons for buying – or at least attempting to acquire – Dow Jones ... screwing up the Journal is not one of them.

1. I have absolutely no intention of sending in the bean counters. I believe in serious investment in serious journalism and that the global need for high quality journalism has never been greater – not more potentially lucrative.

2. There is no doubt that Marcus Brauchli is a worthy successor, though he has a hard act to follow. Robert Thomson, who has known Marcus for many years, speaks without reservation in his praise of Marcus's editorial ability and his integrity.

3. What is on the Opinion pages will never be allowed to flow into the news pages. The two must be kept distinct and while I sometimes find myself nodding in agreement with the comment and commentators, even I occasionally find the views a little too far to the right.

If there are serious concerns among the journalists about 'Rupert Murdoch,' then we should discuss how best to handle it.

Paul, I look forward to chatting at greater length at a time that is appropriate and convenient, either in New York or in LA.

Rupert[22]

But nothing, including assurances made to governments, stops Murdoch when he wants to interfere. In removing Harold Evans as editor of *The Times* he repudiated the formal guarantees he gave the British government before he bought the paper – that editors could only be appointed or removed by agreement of a majority of the independent national directors. 'In my year as editor of *The Times*, Murdoch broke all these guarantees,' Evans recalled. Murdoch's riposte, when later reminded of his undertakings to the Secretary of State, was succinct: 'They're not worth the paper they're written on.'[23]

Early in the 1997 election campaign that delivered Tony Blair the British prime-ministership, *The Sun*'s deputy editor Neil Wallis produced what he later described in a BBC documentary as a 'fairly standard' front page about the election. 'As soon as I set foot inside my office Mr Murdoch was on the phone and said hated your paper this morning, "you've got this all wrong, I'm coming down now". Two or three minutes later my door opens, Rupert comes up and says "you're getting this wrong. You've got this totally wrong. We are not just backing Tony Blair but we are going to back the Labour party and everything he does in this campaign 200%. You've got to get that right."' The result, soon after, was the memorable front-page screamer that left nothing to readers' imaginations: 'THE SUN BACKS BLAIR'.[24]

Life as a Murdoch editor, as Wallis realised, involves a lot of walking on eggshells. I remember sitting in my office one day when a call came through from News Corp's Australian managing director, Ken Cowley. He was in a rage over a news report on the front page of the Melbourne *Herald*, the paper I edited, about the crash of a jumbo jet in the Indian Ocean that had killed more than a hundred passengers. News Corp at that time was also co-owner of Ansett Airlines, Australia's second-largest domestic airline. 'Don't you know we own half an airline,' Cowley exploded. 'WE DON'T RUN STORIES ABOUT PLANE CRASHES ON THE FRONT PAGE!'

The ectoplasm clearly hadn't worked.

My way of dealing with demands and complaints from Murdoch and his sidekicks was to ignore them. I disregarded his relentless urging over many months to sack our newspaper's Washington reporter, Geoffrey Barker, a whip-smart liberal Australian journalist whose coverage of the Reagan administration was overly critical for a conservative, US-domiciled proprietor who doted on the president. Between Murdoch and his jockeying henchmen, it was a febrile environment, but I tried to protect my staff from News Corp's bullies and meddlers and I never told Barker that the owner wanted him removed.

When Murdoch applied pressure on me to support the conservative opposition Liberal Party in a Victorian state election, my editors and I resisted because we could see no compelling reasons for a change of government. A little while later, after the Liberals lost, I was chatting with Australian journalism luminary David McNicoll. He had just returned from a Commonwealth Press Union conference in Zimbabwe, also attended by Murdoch, who had complained to him bitterly that if it wasn't for the *Herald*, the Liberals would now be running Victoria.

The charade that media proprietors have no influence over the journalism they publish was elegantly exposed by Lord Robert Blake, the conservative British historian, in an account of a lunch at Beaverbrook's country estate, Cherkley Court, in 1951, also attended by Brendan Bracken, publisher of the *Financial Times*: 'The subject of the freedom of the press somehow came up, and the two potentates began a sort of cross-talk evidently for my benefit. Beaverbrook declared that it was essential to leave editors with complete freedom and never interfere. "I have no idea what is going to be in the *Sunday Express* tomorrow," he said. "It will be as entirely fresh to me as to any of the readers." "I entirely agree, Max," said Brendan Bracken. "I never interfere in the *Financial Times* [which he effectively controlled in those days]. The Editor must be free to make up his own mind."'

Sometime later, the butler entered carrying a silver salver on which sat a piece of ticker tape bearing the news that Aneurin Bevan and Harold Wilson had resigned from Clement Atlee's cabinet. 'Before I could draw breath,' wrote Blake, 'Beaverbrook was telephoning instructions on the treatment of this startling development to John Junor (now Sir John), the Political Correspondent of the *Sunday Express*, and Bracken was doing the same to a man called Grimes who, presumably, had a similar role on the *Financial Times*. When they had finished – and it took quite a time – they resumed their discussions of editorial freedom as if nothing at all had happened.'[25]

In that distant analog world, editorial dictatorship was conducted discreetly by press barons from behind closed doors or on the balconies of country estates. Today, the world's newest media mogul, Elon Musk, has elevated intervention to a whole new level of flagrance. After buying Twitter in 2022 and pledging to earn the public's trust by making it a non-partisan space for 'free speech', Musk transformed his media plaything into a platform which, as described by Charlie Warzel in *The Atlantic*, 'offers a haven to far-right influencers and advances the interests, prejudices, and conspiracy theories of the right wing of American politics'.[26] Musk has meddled in ways that Beaverbrook, Hearst and Murdoch could never contemplate. 'Unless the woke mind virus, which is fundamentally anti-science, anti-merit, and anti-human in general, is stopped, civilisation will never become multi-planetary,' Musk told his biographer Walter Isaacson in 2023.[27]

The idea that editorial freedom can operate uninhibited inside a media dictatorship is a mirage. In the arc from Northcliffe to Musk, the owner's power of veto over his company's journalism has been absolute, a reality encapsulated perfectly by the media critic A.J. Liebling. 'Freedom of the press,' he wrote in *The New Yorker* in 1960, 'is guaranteed only to those who own one.'[28] All that differs is the method of execution.

The Exercise
of Power

Henry Luce was once asked how he felt about president John F. Kennedy. 'He seduces me,' replied Luce. 'When I'm with him I feel like a whore.'[1]

There's a complicated dance that takes place between media magnates and political leaders. It's the kind of dance that was witnessed by the legendary London *Sunday Times* journalist Phillip Knightley early in his career as a reporter for Keith Murdoch's Melbourne *Herald* in the late 1940s. Knightley travelled with Murdoch on a visit to Australia's 'bush capital' Canberra, accompanied by a youthful Rupert who had just finished school. Knightley told the story in his memoir *A Hack's Progress*: 'Murdoch [senior] had lunch with the Prime Minister, Robert Menzies, and I went along to hand out the cigars and field telephone calls. Then he dictated a letter to his fellow newspaper proprietor Sir Lloyd Dumas, of Adelaide. It gave a summary of what had been discussed over luncheon, including four or five paragraphs on what the Prime Minister had said about the likelihood of an alteration in the currency exchange rate between Britain and Australia and advice on what Dumas should do to take advantage of the inside information.'[2]

The world 'is governed by go-betweens', according to Edmund Burke, the eighteenth-century statesman and philosopher. Lord Beaverbrook, one of history's great manipulators, memorised Burke's thesis and spent a professional lifetime applying it. Beaverbrook was obsessed with the exercise of political power. 'He has an artist's interest in it, in its use and transfer, the means by which men can be bent to its purpose, the subtle courses by which it can be directed in this way or that,' wrote the British editor and academic Francis Williams.[3]

In a remarkably frank speech in 1926, Beaverbrook described the power of the press as 'a flaming sword which will cut through any political armor ... [W]hen skillfully employed at the psychological moment no politician of any party can resist it'. He went on: 'That is not to say that any great newspaper or group of newspapers can enforce policies or make or unmake governments at will, just because it is a great newspaper. Many such newspapers are harmless because they do not know how to strike or when to strike. They are in themselves unloaded guns. But teach the man behind them how to load and what to shoot at, and they become deadly. It is only genius which can so load and point. The risks of its control are therefore limited, seeing that genius is rare. And this is as well, for so great is the potency of the weapon that if it ever fell into the hands of a thoroughly unscrupulous man of genius, there is no limit to the harm it might do.'[4]

Media dictators have been brandishing the flaming sword ever since Thomas Barnes, editor of *The Times* for twenty-four years during the nineteenth century, was described by Lord Lyndhurst, England's Lord High Chancellor as 'the most powerful man in the country'. 'Barnes was consulted about ministerial appointments. He was privy to official secrets. The proudest peer in England, Lord Durham, waited in the editor's outer room to intercede on behalf of a crowned head, King Leopold of the Belgians,' wrote Piers Brendon in *The Life and Death of the Press Barons*.[5]

The dance of the go-betweens is an exercise in mutual self-interest. Because political leaders in democracies are transfixed by media coverage, they are easy prey for moguls seeking inside information, favoured treatment, advantageous policy decisions, or all three. Rupert Murdoch wasn't born when Beaverbrook raised the spectre of a 'thoroughly unscrupulous man of genius' in control of newspapers. But little more than half a century later, British prime ministers, Tory and Labour alike, 'were so scared of blackmail by headline they gave him whatever he asked', observed former *Times* editor Harold Evans in 2011.[6]

Murdoch explained his approach to political supervision to his biographer Tom Kiernan in the mid-1980s: 'You tell these bloody politicians whatever they want to hear, and once the deal is done you don't worry about it. They're not going to chase after you later if they suddenly decide what you said was not what they wanted to hear. Otherwise they're made to look bad, and they can't abide that. So they just stick their heads up their asses and wait for the blow to pass.'[7]

Prominent British Labour politician Tom Watson, a member of the parliamentary committee that investigated News Corp's illegal phone hacking, told the House of Commons in 2010: 'The barons of the media, with their red-topped assassins, are the biggest beasts in the modern jungle. They have no predators. They are untouchable. They laugh at the law. They sneer at Parliament. They have the power to hurt us, and they do, with gusto and precision, with joy and criminality. Prime ministers quail before them, and that is how they like it. That indeed has become how they insist upon it, and we are powerless in the face of them. We are afraid. That is the tawdry secret that dare not speak its name.'[8]

Former Australian prime minister Kevin Rudd assiduously courted Murdoch while in power, but attacked him mercilessly after leaving politics. 'Everyone's frightened of Murdoch,' he told an Australian parliamentary inquiry into media ownership in early 2021. 'There's a culture of fear across the country. The truth is as prime minister I was still fearful of the Murdoch media beast. When did I stop being fearful? Probably when I walked out of the building in 2013.'[9] Rudd initiated a parliamentary petition in 2020 that called for a government inquiry into Australian media ownership and bias. It was signed by 501,876 people, the largest petition response ever recorded on the national parliament's website. Of course, there has been no inquiry because no Australian government in power would dare risk incurring the wrath of the country's most powerful family.

Of all the lethal instruments in a media owner's toolkit, the most effective one for managing politicians is *fear* – the emotion that 'preserves you by a dread of punishment which never fails', as described by Niccolò Machiavelli. And it was surely fear that was running through the minds of British politicians as they observed *The Sun* demolish Labour cabinet minister Clare Short in the mid-1980s after she criticised the paper's use of photographs of topless women to sell more copies. 'Killjoy Clare', 'Fat', 'Jealous', 'Ugly', 'Short on looks', 'Short on brains' were among *The Sun*'s headlines during its jihad, which included distributing free car stickers ('Stop Crazy Clare'), sending half-naked women to her home, and running a beauty contest asking readers whether they would prefer to see Short's face or the back of a bus.

Rupert Murdoch began playing the fear card from his earliest days as a media proprietor. In the 1960s, when he owned Western Australia's *Sunday Times*, and dabbled in other investments on the side, he met with the mining magnate Lang Hancock to discuss a joint purchase of mineral prospects in a remote Western Australian desert, a deal that was being blocked by the state government. Hancock's biographer Robert Duffield described how Murdoch dealt with the political roadblock. 'If I can get a certain politician to negotiate, will you sell me a piece of the cake?' Murdoch apparently asked Hancock. 'Yes, by all means,' replied the miner. At ten o'clock that night there was a knock on Hancock's door. It was Murdoch. 'You're in!' he told Hancock, who asked: 'How on earth did you manage that?' to which Murdoch replied: 'Simple . . . I told him: look you can have a headline a day or a bucket of shit every day. What's it to be?'[10]

Headlines-or-a-bucket-of-shit became standard Murdoch operating procedure. In 1992, the British prime minister John Major telephoned *The Sun* editor Kelvin MacKenzie to ask whether the paper would be supporting the government during a crisis over the European exchange rate mechanism. 'Well John, let me put it this way,' MacKenzie told the PM. 'I've got a large bucket of shit lying on my desk and tomorrow morning I'm going to pour it all over your head.'[11]

Abusing and haranguing prime ministers and presidents is business as usual for many media owners and their henchmen. When Lords Northcliffe and Rothermere owned the *Daily Mail*, they acted at times as though they also owned the British government. In 1918, when Northcliffe offered Prime Minister Lloyd George editorial support in the *Mail*'s overseas edition, which was widely read by soldiers returning from World War One, he added a condition: 'I do not propose to use my newspapers and personal influence unless I know definitely, and in writing, and can consciously approve, the personal constitution of the government.'[12] Lloyd George immediately turned him down, as he did the following year when Northcliffe demanded to be appointed to the British delegation to the Versailles Peace Conference.[13] When Lloyd George rejected that second diktat, Northcliffe's newspapers turned against the government mercilessly.

After Rothermere took over running the *Daily Mail* group, following his brother's death, he informed the opposition leader Stanley Baldwin that he wouldn't get his papers' support 'unless I am acquainted with the names of at least eight, or ten, of his most prominent colleagues in the next Ministry'. Baldwin was appalled, telling a special meeting of the Conservative Party that 'a more preposterous and insolent demand was never made on the leader of any political party'.[14]

Baldwin was also the object of a vendetta by Beaverbrook's newspapers, 'to stalk and seek to destroy a public man who would not bend to his will', wrote Hugh Cudlipp in *The Beaverbrook I Knew*.[15] Baldwin, Britain's post-World War One prime minister, described Beaverbrook as a man he would not have in his house. When the Conservative Party lost the 1929 general election, Beaverbrook was ecstatic. 'I rejoiced in Baldwin's downfall. I wanted the defeat of the government because I believed it was bad.'The year before he died in 1963, Beaverbrook told *Time* magazine, 'When a man hits me, I wait until he's not looking and then hit him twice.'[16]

The insidious power of the media is a permanent feature of political life in most Western democracies. When Israeli prime minister Benjamin Netanyahu was charged with bribery, fraud and breach of trust in 2019, it was in part because he allegedly met with media owners to trade favourable coverage in return for government assistance for their businesses. According to the charges laid by Israel's attorney-general, Netanyahu and Arnon Mozes, who controlled one of Israel's largest-selling newspapers *Yedioth Ahronoth*, discussed in a series of meetings 'the promotion of their common interests: improving the coverage that Mr Netanyahu received in the *Yedioth Ahronoth* media group' and the 'imposition of restrictions' by the government on Mozes's competitor *Israel Hayom*. Netanyahu was also charged with proposing a 'reciprocal arrangement' with the news website Walla to favourably cover his government in return for the prime minister using 'his powers and authorities as a public servant' to promote the business interests of its owner Bezeq, Israel's biggest telecommunications company.[17]

———

The day after Lachlan Murdoch issued a defamation writ against my company's publication *Crikey*, a large government car pulled up outside News Corp headquarters in Sydney. Its three passengers – Australia's prime minister, deputy prime minister and foreign minister – were there to meet Murdoch, the son who effectively runs News Corp. 'For those in power some rings still need to be kissed, it seems,' noted *The Sydney Morning Herald* two days later.[18]

When a country's three most senior politicians decide to meet with a media owner in *his* office, they are providing him with something that's inaccessible to 99.999 per cent of the rest of the population: *access to power*. For the Murdoch family, the availability of senior politicians to attend to their interests is a service as natural as domestic staff, private jets, expensive yachts, and all their other requisites of wealth and power.

One of Boris Johnson's first engagements as British prime minister, three days after winning the 2019 general election, was a private meeting with Rupert Murdoch. That was the first of forty meetings between Johnson and his ministers and Murdoch or his editors and executives in the first fourteen months of his government. After the next prime minister, Liz Truss, lasted just fifty days in office, Murdoch had five personal meetings with the subsequent PM, Rishi Sunak, in his first year in office, according to government records cited by *The Guardian*. It was the same access to Downing Street that had been at the disposal of Murdoch and his subordinates for the previous four decades. Murdoch always used to enter by the back door of Downing Street, revealed former Labour insider Chris Mullin in his published volume of diaries.[18]

Australian prime ministers don't unlock their back gates for a Murdoch, they go to *his* front door. After Keith Murdoch hand-picked and supported Joseph Lyons to head the federal government in the 1930s, the new prime minister frequently lunched at Murdoch's Melbourne office. Lyons' secretary once asked her boss why Murdoch didn't visit him – 'after all, you are the Prime Minister' – to which Lyons replied, 'It pleases him to see me in his office and it does me no harm to go there.' Thus began the pantomime of power that has required Australian prime ministers to pay an obligatory visit to the home or office of Keith's son whenever they visited New York, just as heads of State visit the Pope in Rome.[19]

When US Secretary of State Mike Pompeo and Defense Secretary Mark Esper arrived in Sydney in 2019 for ministerial meetings with their Australian counterparts, their first engagement was not with government officials, it was a private dinner and drinks at Le Manoir, the harbourside home of Lachlan and Sarah Murdoch. 'Guests were casually dressed and ate home-made pizza topped with fresh lobster caught by Lachlan's old friend Ian "Pucko" Puckeridge, an Australian spear-fishing champion who worked on the wharves at

Botany Bay and joined the feast,' according to Lachlan's biographer Paddy Manning in *The Successor*. A month later, when the Australian prime minister visited the US, Lachlan and Sarah sat at the head table at a White House State dinner, alongside President Trump and his wife Melania, as violins serenaded tables decorated with thousands of roses from California and wattle flowers from Australia.[20] And in late 2023, after Murdoch visited war-ravaged Ukraine, the president's office – using diplomatic language usually reserved for heads of State – announced on its website: 'The Head of State (Zelenskiy) thanked Lachlan Murdoch for his visit and emphasized that it is a very important signal of support at the time when the world's attention is blurred by other events.'

It was Keith Murdoch's relationship with 'Honest Joe' Lyons in the 1930s that effectively launched a hundred years of quid pro quo between the Murdochs and their political supplicants. A year after Lyons wrote to Murdoch thanking him for his support in winning the previous election, Murdoch complained about the law that restricted ownership of radio stations by newspaper companies. Two days later, new regulations were introduced in what became a tenet of Australian media policy – favourable coverage for the government, favourable treatment for the Murdochs.[21]

Improbably, I became caught up in this subversive process in 2017 when the Australian government decided to abolish the law that restricted ownership of analog media – newspapers, network television and radio – to just two of those forms. The government was under pressure from the country's biggest media companies to remove the constraints on buying or selling media properties so they could consolidate more of their businesses. It was an outmoded law in the digital age, but its abolition needed the support of minority party senators to pass through parliament.

The leader of one of the smaller parties began talking to independent media owners, including me, about voting to rescind the cross-media law on condition that the government agree to support independent news media by introducing an AUD$50 million innovation grants scheme to assist small and regional publishers. Our group of independent publishers supported the concept because we believed it would materially assist the growth and quality of our journalism.

Until then I had only ever been an *observer* of News Corp wielding its political power. But when I began navigating the details of the proposed legislation on behalf of independent publishers, I became a *participant* in the process. And that's when, to my astonishment, I found myself negotiating the fine details of the new law with News Corp's Group Executive of Corporate Affairs, Policy and Government Relations. It was he, not a politician, who effectively wielded the behind-the-scenes veto over the key terms of the grants scheme legislation. Once the minority senators agreed to *his* conditions, the law passed through parliament.

Deference by a politician towards a media mogul has rarely been as transparent as Donald Trump's transactional relationship with Rupert Murdoch. The two long-time residents of New York with a shared interest in power, money and gossip had known each other for decades before Trump launched his presidential aspirations. Trump had been milking the celebrity-infested Page Six of Murdoch's *New York Post* to promote himself ever since he became a real estate hustler in the 1970s.

Former Australian prime minister Malcolm Turnbull attempted to explain the contours of that relationship in an interview after he left office in 2021. According to Turnbull, access to presidential power is for Murdoch 'like sex, it's an urge ... so Murdoch went in boots and all to put Trump in the White House, and in return for that the deference Trump showed him was extraordinary'. Turnbull revealed that when he, as prime minister, and Trump were due to start their first one-on-one leader's meeting, Trump wanted Murdoch in the room with them. 'Oh no we can't do that,' Turnbull told Trump, 'but he really wanted him to be there.'[22]

Murdoch had initially been dismissive when Trump announced his decision to run for the presidency. 'When is Donald Trump going to stop embarrassing his friends, let alone the whole country?' Murdoch tweeted in 2015, describing Trump as a 'phony' and a 'fucking idiot', according to Michael Wolff in *Fire and Fury*.[23] But once Trump clinched the nomination and then the presidency, Murdoch and Fox News, ever the pragmatists, swung their support behind him. 'After decades of ups and downs, Mr. Trump now counts Mr. Murdoch as one of his closest confidants,' wrote Amy Chozick in *The New York Times* in 2017. 'The calls to the White House come at least once a week. "Murdoch here," the blunt, accented voice on the other end of the line says.'[24]

That rapport ended on the night of the 2020 election when the Fox News Decision Desk made an early prediction during its live broadcast that Trump had lost the state of Arizona, and therefore effectively the presidency. Trump was livid. He instructed his son-in-law and White House adviser Jared Kushner to call Murdoch and implore him to reverse the prediction. 'Sorry, Jared, there is nothing I can do,' said Murdoch, according to Kushner's memoir. 'The Fox News data authority says the numbers are ironclad – he says it won't be close.'[25]

After Trump refused to concede the election, Murdoch turned on him. When the *New York Post* called Trump a 'prisoner of his own ego' in mid-2022, his spruiker-in-chief Steve Bannon took to social media.[26] 'The Murdochs – Australians via England – not American, have never sacrificed anything for this Country – their entire media Empire has turned on Trump – Fox News, *Wall Street Journal*, *New York Post*, *Times* of London, *The Sun* etc etc etc – all lockstep against Trump,' he posted.[27] Trump's decision to run for the 2024 election was covered by the *New York Post* with a skimpy headline at the bottom of its front page – 'FLORIDA MAN MAKES ANNOUNCEMENT' – pointing to the story on page twenty-six. Murdoch told Trump his media outlets wouldn't support his return to the White House: 'We have been clear with Donald.'[28]

But by 2023, with Trump the emphatic Republican frontrunner, Fox News was under intense ratings pressure to support him, in deference to its largely MAGA (Make America Great Again) audience. 'Like a pair of powerful gangsters who quarrel over how to divide the spoils,' wrote Jack Shafer in *Politico*, 'Murdoch and Trump will reconcile if they determine it's in their mutual interests to reconcile.'[29]

———

Murdoch's first taste of hands-on political string-pulling on a big stage dates back to 1972, when he threw his support behind the election of Gough Whitlam to lead Australia's first non-conservative government in twenty-three years. The young media upstart viewed Whitlam as a reforming idealist who could take Australia into a fresh new era after decades of provincial, small-minded national governance.

Murdoch first met Whitlam and his wife in a private room at the Hungry Horse restaurant in Sydney's trendy Paddington, the year before the election. 'How do we get rid of this government at the next elections?' Murdoch reportedly asked his guests.[30] (*We!*) The two met several times over the following year – on a Sydney Harbour cruise, at Murdoch's sheep farm near Canberra, at his Essex country house in England, and in London and New York.

Once Murdoch had made up his mind to back Whitlam he not only hurled his newspapers at the task, he became a self-appointed policy adviser to the presumptive prime minister. He personally helped write Whitlam's speeches, assisted in the planning of Labor's advertising campaign, attended strategy meetings with party officials, recommended who should run government economic strategy, and advised on policies ranging from housing-interest tax breaks to a new national anthem. On one occasion he contributed to writing a press release announcing that Whitlam would abolish national service within a week of the election.[31]

As he pored over the results two days after Whitlam's election victory, Murdoch felt pride in his role in the success. 'How many seats do you think *we* won?' he asked his then Australian managing director John Menadue.[32] Murdoch hosted a swish celebratory dinner at a restaurant at the top of Sydney's tallest tower, attended by the Whitlams, the Australian governor-general and a visiting media VIP – Katharine Graham, publisher of the *Washington Post*. 'She would have been impressed at how Murdoch could whistle up a prime minister,' Menadue later wrote in his autobiography. 'Neither she nor Murdoch knew how difficult it had been to get Whitlam to turn up. "Comrade," he said, "I am not a national exhibit."'[33]

The Murdoch-Whitlam honeymoon barely lasted two years. As the inexperienced new government fumbled its political and economic management, Murdoch's support evaporated. Although he believed, inaccurately, that his newspapers had 'single-handedly put the present government in office', he was now telling colleagues that 'if they don't straighten up we'll bloody well get rid of them', just as his father had dealt with another Australian prime minister, Joe Lyons, decades earlier.[34] It was around that time that the US consul-general in Melbourne sent a cable to the State Department in Washington reporting that 'Rupert Murdoch has issued [a] confidential instruction to editors of newspapers he controls to "kill Whitlam" ... If Murdoch attack directed against Whitlam personally this could presage hard times for prime minister; but if against Labor government would be dire news for party.'[35]

Murdoch achieved his objective in 1975 when Whitlam was removed from office by the governor-general, a titular unelected role that represents the British Crown in Australia. Murdoch had turned *The Australian* into a blunt anti-Whitlam vehicle that aggressively supported the undemocratic sacking of the prime minister and endorsed the election of a conservative leader.

Outraged journalists at *The Australian* sent a collective letter to their proprietor condemning 'the deliberate or careless slanting of headlines, seemingly blatant imbalance in news presentation, political censorship and more occasionally distortion of copy from senior specialist journalists, the political management of news and features, the stifling of dissident and even unpalatably impartial opinion in the paper's columns'.[36] In the final week of the election campaign, 109 journalists at *The Australian* went on strike for two days in protest against their newspaper's coverage. 'Anyone who works for his papers knows how odious that control is and some of the journalists have found it very difficult to get their stories published,' claimed Whitlam.[37] The impact on *The Australian*'s credibility was severe: its circulation fell from 153,000 in late 1974 to 109,000 in 1978.[38]

Undermining Whitlam was the start of a fifty-year cavalcade of embracing, then rejecting, political leaders across the world. 'Murdoch has no friends. He has no loyalties. He has no principles. And never has,' claimed media commentator Jack Shafer in *Politico*. 'His support of politicians has always been transactional and extractive. Murdoch has always been a political cad, swooning and then dumping his political partners when a better-looking one comes along.'[39]

Murdoch's talent lies in detecting and then reinforcing public moods and trends, according to Menadue, who later became head of the Department of Prime Minister and Cabinet, and then Australian ambassador to Japan: 'He will back political winners who he thinks can be made kings. Whosoever wins, Murdoch is determined not to be a loser. It didn't need a king-maker to conclude that Whitlam would win in 1972, Fraser in 1975, Reagan in 1984, Thatcher in 1987 and Blair in 1997. Murdoch's political power is that politicians think he can make or break them and they are not prepared to chance their careers on a gamble to find out. The perception is enough.'[40]

Murdoch wasn't the first press baron to blur the lines between being an observer and a player in national politics. Twenty years earlier, Henry Luce made himself an active participant in the 1952 US presidential campaign when he threw *Time*'s muscle behind the election of Dwight Eisenhower. Luce co-opted two of his senior editors to write Eisenhower's speeches and oversaw a shamelessly pro-Eisenhower edition of *Time*, which his staff placed on the seat of every delegate at the Republican convention in Chicago. 'In the truest sense he was Ike's sponsor,' wrote David Halberstam in *The Powers That Be*.[41] And with his man sitting in the oval office, Luce advocated for the appointment of his ambitious wife, Clare, to a prestigious role in the new Eisenhower administration. The president first offered her the job of Secretary of Labor, but Clare declined because she didn't feel qualified. 'I'm not your man,' she told Ike with uncharacteristic 1950s irony, before accepting the role of US ambassador to Italy.[42]

Flattery can get you everywhere when it's dispensed by a president or prime minister to a media boss. Sam Newhouse, who was regarded as an apolitical publisher because he always put business first, was travelling in the presidential limousine with Lyndon Johnson a few months before the 1964 election when the president began pushing him for endorsements from *all* his twenty newspapers. 'The minute we got in the car, the president turned to Mr Newhouse and said, "I want both the Syracuse papers,"' recalled William Tolley, chancellor of Syracuse University, who was travelling with both men. '"You may have them," Newhouse replied, to which LBJ said: "I want the Harrisburg paper." "No problem," responded Newhouse. Johnson then started running down the list of more papers whose endorsements he wanted. Finally Newhouse stopped him and said: "I've given you enough. I don't need to give you any more."'[43]

———

No politician in history helped Rupert Murdoch as much, or for as long, as his conservative fellow traveller Margaret Thatcher. It was a mutual admiration society that operated for a decade, starting in 1981 when Thatcher intervened to help Murdoch buy *The Times* and *Sunday Times* without regulatory approval.[44] The fix was later revealed by Woodrow Wyatt, a Thatcher confidant who acted as her go-between with Murdoch. 'I had all the rules bent,' Wyatt wrote in his published journals. 'Through Margaret I got it arranged that the deal didn't go to the Monopolies and Mergers Commission which almost certainly would have blocked it.' A few years later the playbook was repeated when the Thatcher government green-lit Murdoch's purchase of *Today*, his fifth UK national newspaper, without scrutiny. 'We look like having another pro-Margaret newspaper,' Wyatt told Thatcher.[45]

By the mid-eighties, after cementing his alliance with Thatcher, Murdoch's influence over British politics was prodigious. 'Around here he's often jokingly referred to as "Mr Prime Minister", except that it's no longer that much of a joke,' said the editor of *The Times*, Charles Douglas-Home, in 1984. 'In many respects he *is* the phantom Prime Minister of the country.'[46]

Murdoch's final gift from Thatcher – approval for his Sky satellite TV to merge with its rival BSkyB – arrived a few days before she resigned as prime minister in 1990. It was rushed through days ahead of changes to independent broadcasting regulations, again without reference to the Monopolies and Mergers Commission. 'This gave Murdoch an unprecedentedly dominant position in the British media, greatly beyond anything Northcliffe had achieved,' wrote former BBC foreign correspondent John Simpson. 'Once more, the rules had been skilfully evaded.'[47]

While he was unwrapping this latest political gift, Murdoch was also trying to help keep Thatcher in office in the face of a leadership challenge from her one-time cabinet colleagues John Major and Michael Heseltine. When Heseltine declared his candidacy, Murdoch told his *Sunday Times* editor Andrew Neil, 'Heseltine would be disastrous. We owe Thatcher a lot as a company. Don't go overboard in your attacks on her.'[48]

They didn't, but Murdoch began to lose interest in Thatcher after she lost the prime-ministership. 'The man who had been able to see her or call her on the phone any time he wanted, who had been invited to spend Christmas with the Thatchers at Chequers several times, and who had attended various intimate family celebrations over the years in the position of a personal friend rather than a political ally, seems to have had little to do with her once she was out of power,' wrote Simpson. 'Mrs Thatcher replied to this coldness with a silence of her own. In her memoirs his name is not even mentioned once. She had delivered British journalism and the British media to him on a plate; yet only three years later she had completely written him out of her life.'[49]

Thatcher's successor, John Major, a quiet, proper Englishman, viewed Murdoch's muscularity with deep suspicion. The pair had a tepid relationship, meeting only three times during Major's seven-year prime-ministership. After winning the 1992 election, Major soon became the target of attacks in *The Sun*. 'Dithering Major', 'Pigmy PM', 'Not up to the job', '1,001 reasons why you are such a plonker John', 'A broken man', 'A discredited Prime Minister' were some of the headlines in 1993. Major discouraged his cabinet ministers from attending social events organised by Murdoch, and when the home secretary, Michael Howard, informed the PM he had accepted an invitation to one soiree, Downing Street advisers told Howard to 'catch a diplomatic cold'.[50]

Even though he was an Australian-turned-American, Murdoch was obsessive about limiting Britain's place in Europe. In a private meeting with Major three months before the 1997 election he demanded the government change its policy on strengthening ties with the European Union – 'if not, his papers could not and would not support the Conservative government', Major told the Leveson Inquiry into the phone hacking scandal in 2012. After resisting Murdoch's bullying, 'it came as no surprise' to Major when *The Sun* announced its support for Labour. It was at the same inquiry that a straight-faced Murdoch told Justice Leveson, 'I have never asked a prime minister for anything.'[51]

His next Downing Street supplicant, Tony Blair, began schmoozing Murdoch two years before he won the prime-ministership, with a gruelling fifty-hour return flight from London to a ritzy island resort in Queensland to address a News Corp executive conference. Before arriving, Blair asked then Australian prime minister Paul Keating for his insider's view on Murdoch. 'He's a big bad bastard, and the only way you can deal with him is to make sure he thinks you can be a big bad bastard too,' Keating told him. 'You can do deals with him, without ever saying a deal is done. But the only thing he cares about is his business and the only language he respects is strength.'[52]

Armed with Keating's advice, Blair unveiled his 'new moral purpose' to the assembled News Corp executives and editors, vowing to liberate media companies from 'heavy regulation'. Murdoch responded tentatively. 'If our flirtation is ever consummated, Tony, then I suspect we will end up making love like two porcupines. Very, very carefully,' he told Blair.[53] A few months later the Labour Party dropped its commitment to strengthen regulation of cross-media ownership, which could have required Murdoch to sell off some of his most profitable British newspapers, and announced its opposition to proposals for a privacy law. 'It is better to be riding the tiger's back than let it rip your throat out,' Blair later rationalised.[54]

Blair's payoff arrived six weeks before the 1997 British election with a banner headline splashed across the front page of *The Sun*:

THE SUN BACKS BLAIR

Historic announcement from Britain's No 1 newspaper

The people need a leader with vision, purpose and courage who can inspire them and fire their imaginations. The Sun believes that man is Tony Blair. He is the best man for the job, for our ten million readers and for the country.

Blair's victory not only delivered Murdoch friendly media policies, it also provided a binding commitment – written personally by the new PM in *The Sun* – that Britain would not adopt the euro. 'The price of Rupert Murdoch's support for Tony Blair was that Blair promised he would not take us into the European currency without first having a referendum,' former UK Independence Party leader Nigel Farage told a BBC documentary in 2020, 'and if Rupert Murdoch had not done that we would have joined the Euro in 1999 and I doubt Brexit would have happened.'[55]

After almost a decade of John Major, the marionette who wouldn't dance, Murdoch now had a wholly acquiescent government working under Blair's watchful eye. 'The line between church and state ... between press and state, became so blurred that at one stage it was quite hard to tell which was which,' *Sunday Times* editor Andrew Neil told the BBC.

The extent of Murdoch's influence on the new government was revealed by Blair's special adviser, Lance Price, in his 2010 book *Where Power Lies*: 'I have never met Mr Murdoch, but at times when I worked at Downing Street he seemed like the 24th member of the cabinet. His voice was rarely heard (but, then, the same could have been said of many of the other 23) but his presence was always felt. No big decision could ever be made inside No 10 without taking account of the likely reaction of three men – Gordon Brown, John Prescott and Rupert Murdoch. On all the really big decisions, anybody else could safely be ignored.'[56]

But in a strange personal twist, Tony Blair's post-prime-ministerial relations with Murdoch turned ice-cold when evidence emerged that Blair's alleged intimate relationship with Wendi Deng was the reason for her divorce from Murdoch. This came several years after it was revealed that Blair was godfather to the Murdochs' daughter Grace, and had attended her christening on the banks of the Jordan River. The whole event became a photo spread in *Hello!* magazine, its front cover displaying a smiling Murdoch in an open-necked shirt.

When Murdoch supports a favoured politician, it comes with all guns blazing, as well as bazookas and missiles, as Whitlam, Thatcher and Blair discovered to their benefit. 'Rupert used the editorial page and every other page necessary to elect Ronald Reagan president,' US congressman Jack Kemp told a 1981 dinner honouring Murdoch for his contribution to Reagan's success.[57] While *The New York Times* might endorse you in a column, three-term New York governor Mario Cuomo explained, 'with Rupert, he turns the whole paper over to you'.[58]

One of Murdoch's New York mayoral endorsements was Rudy Giuliani, who scraped into office thanks to the rousing support of the *New York Post*. Giuliani rewarded Murdoch with a $20 million tax break when News Corp moved into its Manhattan midtown head-quarters, along with a deal to air Fox News on a public-access channel when Time Warner tried to keep it out of the New York market in 1996 – a move blocked by a federal judge who accused the mayor of acting 'to reward a friend and to further a particular viewpoint'.[59]

————

In between whacking each other, moguls and political leaders also engage in a lot of mutual back-scratching. Murdoch is a master of the hard cop/soft cop routine, mingling threats and fear with invitations to politicians to attend his corporate retreats, suppress their embarrassing news, and publish their memoirs.

HarperCollins, his book publishing arm, handed a multi-million-dollar contract to Margaret Thatcher to write her memoirs, plus two more books, after she lost the Tory leadership. It has also published other well-known conservatives, including Ronald Reagan, John Major, former Australian prime ministers John Howard and Scott Morrison, former US vice-president Dan Quayle, Republican vice-presidential candidate Sarah Palin, and former US House speaker Newt Gingrich. In 1995, as Murdoch was desperate to make commercial inroads into China and impress its leadership, HarperCollins published the official biography of Deng Xiaoping, China's former leader, written by his daughter Deng Rong.

But the tactic backfired badly in 1997 when HarperCollins signed a book deal with Chris Patten, Hong Kong's last governor. Patten's unfiltered critique of China was bound to antagonise the leadership in Beijing, so when Murdoch heard about the project six months after Patten had signed a £125,000 advance, he ordered the Harper-Collins global CEO to 'kill the fucking book'.[60] It was a decision that created a damaging media storm as authors began to boycott the publisher. Eventually the company issued a grovelling apology and paid Patten a significant indemnity to avoid a legal conflagration. When another publisher, Macmillan, released the book in the US, it placed a sticker on the cover with the words 'The book that Rupert Murdoch tried to stop'.

Like other moguls, Beaverbrook worked most of his political relationships covertly. In the late 1930s, as Britain teetered on the edge of war, he developed a highly advantageous friendship with the home secretary, Sam Hoare, one of prime minister Neville Chamberlain's closest advisers. Hoare encouraged Beaverbrook to provide fulsome editorial support for Chamberlain's attempts to appease Hitler, culminating in the infamous *Daily Express* headline 'PEACE FOR OUR TIME' as Chamberlain flew to his final abortive meeting with Hitler, which failed to prevent World War Two. What no-one knew at the time was that Beaverbrook was secretly paying Hoare £2,000 a year (around $43,000 today) to supplement his government income after Hoare's wife, Lady Maud, approached Beaverbrook for financial support to allow her husband to continue in politics.[61]

Another favoured method used by politicians to kowtow to media owners is the conferring of official honours and blandishments on them. In post-World War One Britain – and virtually ever since – 'almost anyone who owned an important paper could take it for granted that they would be rewarded with a peerage from one party or the other', wrote Chisholm and Davie in *Beaverbrook: A Life*. When the *Daily Mail*'s founder Alfred Harmsworth wanted a lordship in 1903, he went straight to the king. Harmsworth, King Edward VII wrote to his prime minister Arthur Balfour, 'is a great power in the Press and strongly supports the government as well as Mr Chamberlain's policy. Should you wish to recommend his name to me, I will certainly give my consent.' Six months later Harmsworth became Lord Northcliffe, and the following year he was elevated to a peer of the realm. Rumours persisted that Harmsworth had bought his title for £100,000 after apparently joking that 'when I want a peerage I will buy one, like an honest man'.[62]

Conrad Black's successors at *The Daily Telegraph*, the twin Barclay brothers, were press proprietors of the old school. They were knighted together, kneeling before Queen Elizabeth in a so-called double dubbing. The Barclays were almost sycophantic in their embrace of the Conservative Party. In 2010, after dining with then British prime minister David Cameron, their chief executive sent a handwritten letter of thanks to Cameron, adding: 'We desperately want there to be a Conservative government and you to be our next Prime Minister. We'll do all we can to bring that about and to give you great support in the gruelling months ahead. And as we are no fair-weathered friend, we'll be there with you too when you're in Downing Street.'[63] Earlier, they had not only supported Margaret Thatcher politically, but after she lost the prime-ministership they financed her five-bedroom Georgian house in London's exclusive Belgravia, and later provided a suite at their Ritz Hotel in the final days of her life.[64]

Black himself was Northcliffian in his desire for honorifics. In 1990 the Canadian government awarded him its highest honour, the Order of Canada, for 'a lifetime of achievement'. In 2001 British prime minister Tony Blair handed him a lifetime peerage, along with a title befitting the pompous proprietor of an establishment news-paper: The Baron Black of Crossharbour.

Black's titled world fell apart after he was convicted and impris-oned in the US in 2007 for defrauding his own company. He was stripped of his Order of Canada by the country's governor-general and removed from the Queen's Privy Council. Although he didn't lose his British peerage, Black spent the next sixteen years in absentia from the House of Lords, in disgrace.

In 2019, after lobbying by former secretary of State Henry Kissinger, conservative talk-show host Rush Limbaugh and singer Sir Elton John, Black was pardoned by then US president Donald Trump. In a pardon that was widely interpreted as quid pro quo for Black's highly sympathetic biography *Donald J. Trump: A President Like No Other*, the White House cited his 'tremendous contributions to business, as well as to political and historical thought', and for his work in supporting fellow prisoners while in jail.[65]

———

I first met Rupert Murdoch when he invited me to his Sydney office for a private discussion to test my interest in running the newspaper once edited by his father. We were chatting away when his secretary quietly entered the room and handed him a folded piece of paper. As he read it, his bushy eyebrows raised and he looked at me. The note revealed that the little-known son of the proprietor of *The Sydney Morning Herald*, where I was then editor, had just acquired a large tranche of shares in his family's company. This was sensational information in the tight Australian media world, suggesting a takeover bid for the Fairfax company could be imminent.

When I returned to my office I asked the chief editorial executive, who was the management conduit to the Fairfax family, whether he was expecting a company announcement. He said he hadn't heard anything. Several hours later he called me in an agitated state. Get ready for a major Fairfax announcement, he told me. Of course I already knew its content, because our biggest competitor, Rupert Murdoch, had told me half a day earlier.

Covert media manoeuvring has a lot in common with the espionage business. Both involve a network of informants and sources who are mined for valuable intelligence that can become a tradeable commodity. Possession of private information about a public figure is a powerful tool in the hands of a media organisation. Tessa Jowell was the British cabinet minister responsible for government media policy when she became one of the victims of the *News of the World*'s phone hacking enterprise. Her voicemail, she was eventually informed by police, was hacked twenty-eight times. 'This amounted to industrial espionage,' according to *Daily Telegraph* journalist Peter Oborne in 2011. 'Could have some important detail or element of media policy been left on her voicemail? The media group can scarcely have avoided discovering commercially sensitive information, even though its primary purpose was to discover details about Ms Jowell's private life.'[66]

Much of the intelligence gathered from illegal phone hacking was sorted into dossiers by employees at Murdoch's UK arm, News International. Sometimes this information was published, sometimes not. 'The knowledge that News International held such destructive power must have been at the back of everyone's minds at the apparently cheerful social events where the company's executives mingled with their client politicians,' observed Oborne.[67]

Slabs of information gathered by voicemail intercepts became valuable raw material that could be used as a form of barter or blackmail. These illegally acquired tidbits would be taken by a reporter to a celebrity's agent as a bargaining chip: the unsavoury story would be suppressed in return for something just as juicy. As *News of the World* entertainment journalist Sean Hoare explained to *Vanity Fair* in 2011, 'You'd say, I've got this detail. I don't want to fuck over your client, but what do you have for me?' If the agent offered an alternative story, Hoare would back off, still with the initial piece of compromising information up his sleeve. 'It's not really about journalism,' he told *Vanity Fair*, 'it's negotiation.'[68] Glenn Mulcaire, who was sentenced to six months' jail for phone hacking, described information gathered from hacking as 'currency' that could either be published, traded for other information, or kept in the vault. 'If I could get any clinical information on a child abduction I would,' said Mulcaire. 'How that was used by the tasker, you know, the journo is up to him. They were the broker.'[69]

Several years ago I asked a senior Australian cabinet minister to explain the mechanics of so-called information harvesting between news organisations and politicians. He told me about a recent call he had received from the CEO of News Corp in Australia, informing him, in a friendly manner, that one of his editors possessed a confidential dossier, compiled by a reporter, on the personal life of one of the minister's cabinet colleagues. I'm calling to assure you, the CEO told the minister, that the editor is under instructions *never* to publish the information.

Everybody in the British power elite had heard the stories about safes in the offices of Murdoch editors filled with dossiers on the private lives of politicians and competing businessmen, according to Nick Davies in *Hack Attack*, and it was also known 'that Murdoch and his people agree to suppress these gross embarrassments in exchange for yet more favors'.[70] Chris Bryant, an openly gay British Labour member of parliament who received a £30,000 payout from the *News of the World* in 2012 after his phone was hacked, described the hovering threat of personal exposure as 'a kind of permanent blackmail'. Bryant recalled being greeted at the door of a News International party during the 2004 Labour Party conference by *Sun* editor Rebekah Brooks. 'Oh, Mr. Bryant, it's after dark – shouldn't you be at Clapham Common by now?' she asked, referring to a well-known gay meeting spot in London.[71]

Highly confidential information in the hands of an unscrupulous newspaper is the raw material that underpins a manoeuvre known as catch-and-kill. David Pecker, publisher of the mass-circulation US supermarket tabloid *National Enquirer*, was for decades the chief exponent of this scam, which involves paying a source for a story that is then buried as a favour to someone else.

Ahead of the 2016 presidential election, Pecker acquired exclusive rights to stories that would embarrass his friend Donald Trump (the 'catch'), in order to make sure they were never published (the 'kill'). Porn star Stormy Daniels was paid $130,000 and Playboy Playmate Karen McDougal $150,000 to keep quiet about their alleged affairs with Trump. According to 2018 court records, Pecker's role in assisting the presidential campaign was to 'deal with negative stories about [Trump's] relationships with women, by, among other things, assisting the campaign in identifying such stories so they could be purchased and their publication avoided'.[72] The *Enquirer* kept a safe containing documents on other catch-and-kill deals. 'We had stories and we bought them knowing full well they were never going to run,' Jerry George, a former *Enquirer* senior editor, told *The New Yorker*.[73] The convicted rapist and former Hollywood boss Harvey Weinstein, who was allegedly protected in this way by Pecker and the *National Enquirer*, became known in the tabloid industry as an untouchable 'F.O.P.', or 'friend of Pecker', according to *The New York Times*.[74]

Items of embarrassing private information are like bullets in a gun: they're benign until someone pulls the trigger. In 2009 the writer Michael Wolff found himself on the receiving end of a 'thorough monstering' by the *New York Post* while he was working on a biography of Rupert Murdoch, the paper's owner, Nick Davies revealed in *Hack Attack*. When typescript of the manuscript somehow reached Murdoch, Wolff was warned by a senior News Corp executive to make changes.

> 'What will you do if I don't?' Wolff asked.
> 'Then we will not support the book.'
> 'How bad is that?'
> 'It could be bad.'

And it was. The *New York Post* discovered that Wolff had been having an affair, and ran stories over seven days, including a secondary story that accused Wolff of evicting his mother-in-law from her apartment, as well as a cartoon of Wolff in bed with his lover, portraying the Jewish writer in a style which might reasonably be described as antisemitic.[75]

Another human casualty of information harvesting was a British government bureaucrat whose marital infidelity was exposed by the *News of the World*, effectively ending the career of a man described by Alan Rusbridger, former editor of *The Guardian*, as a 'courageous and decent figure who had devoted much of his life to public service'. The fact that one of the paper's reporters went to jail for his illegal methods can have been little comfort to his victim, who died a few years later. He said that reading the story was like 'reading your own obituary while you are still alive', reported Rusbridger.[76]

Collateral human damage almost always ricocheted beyond the lives of the public figures whose voicemails were hacked. After journalists at the *News of the World* listened in to hundreds of messages left by the then British home secretary David Blunkett, the government minister responsible for police and security services, the resulting front-page revelation of his relationship with a married woman was like shrapnel fired at his friends and family. 'I was in the public eye. And I was responsible for my behavior,' said Blunkett. 'But it's always the family of people that gets hurt.'[77]

Sycophants
and Sackings

A media monarch's castle is stocked with loyal henchmen who follow the principles of *Führerprinzip*, the Germanic concept of slavish loyalty to a leader who, alone, determines what is true and right. In return, these minions are handsomely rewarded, accorded status, and given intimate access to the leader and those around him. 'In all Murdoch's far-flung enterprises, the question is not whether this or that is a good idea,' explained Murdoch's former London *Times* editor Harold Evans, it is: "What will Rupert think?"'[1]

Gofers with fancy titles and big pay packets serve multifunctional roles in a media autocracy. They do the boss's dirty work, navigate the corridors of politics, keep watch for embarrassing landmines, prop up morale during difficult times, plant leaks to discredit internal and external enemies, spy on disloyal colleagues, and, always, praise the leader publicly and privately.

During my two years as a Murdoch editor I observed their handiwork with a mixture of bemusement and distaste. On one occasion I was shocked to find an unknown man sitting, uninvited, in my planning conference with editors. Having introduced himself as Arnold Earnshaw without explaining his role, he reappeared for several days. I suspected he was there to report back to Murdoch or some other senior executive on my work. After a few days of this, I told him to fuck off and never come back. Earnshaw was a forty-year News Corp veteran who, among his other shoe-leather assignments, compiled a private internal company newsletter that collated media, business and political gossip (often scurrilous or highly opinionated), which was faxed daily to Murdoch and other senior executives.

The *modus operandi sycophanta* inside News Corp was described by Andrew Neil, who edited the *Sunday Times* for Murdoch. 'You are not a director or a manager or an editor: you are a courtier at the court of the Sun King – rewarded with money and status by a grateful King as long as you serve his purpose, dismissed outright or demoted to a remote corner of the empire when you have ceased to please him or outlived your usefulness.' Courtiers, no matter how senior or talented, must always remember two things vital to survival, explained Neil in his memoir *Full Disclosure*. 'They must never dare to outshine the Sun King; and they must always show regular obeisance to him to prove beyond peradventure that, no matter how powerful or important they are, they know who is boss.'[2]

Obeisance starts at the top of the org chart of a media dictatorship. 'We have to be like Rupert. We have to institutionalize the imagination, nerve and vision he represents,' Peter Chernin, then head of Fox Group, told an executive retreat in 1998.[3] 'We at News Corp stand on the shoulders of a giant,' the company's global CEO Robert Thomson told a Melbourne Press Club dinner in 2014.[4] Nine years later, on the day Lachlan Murdoch ascended the corporate throne, Thomson again furnished the servility. 'His thoughtful engagement with our teams already enhances the business each working day and his passion for principled journalism is obvious to all who work with him,' he declared. 'There is no doubt that Lachlan's multidisciplinary expertise and his philosophical integrity will be invaluable as we continue to the next phase of our crucial journey.'[5] Not to be out-grovelled, the fifty-year News Corp veteran and former UK executive chairman Les Hinton described Murdoch as 'an authentic colossus and his own kind of revolutionary' in the *British Journalism Review*. 'One day, when his enemies have gone and taken away their wounds and blind fury, a new generation of chroniclers will come along to rethink his history,' he wrote.[6]

Most of Hearst's top executives were cowards, according to his trusted adviser John Francis Neylan (speaking after he had left the company, of course). 'They drew enormous salaries, bought homes on Park Avenue, then spread out to country places on Long Island, and before you knew it they became yes-men because they felt they had too much to lose to argue with Hearst.'[7] Northcliffe's underlings had to 'stand respectfully to attention when "The Chief" entered the room', former editor Hugh Cudlipp recounted. 'He humiliated senior staff before their subordinates. Telephone lines in the office were tapped by his spies.'[8]

Max Hastings, editor of Conrad Black's *Daily Telegraph* for ten years, described his role in Black's realm as 'the grand vizier to a medieval Turkish sultan'. Hastings was accorded considerable powers, 'but it would have been unwise to forget for a moment that few of one's peers retired by choice into a comfortable old age. The garrotte, the scimitar, the oubliette are domestic accessories of every newspaper proprietor. Risk, whim, hostile intrigue, the letter de cachet are occupational hazards for their servants.'[9]

When John F. Kennedy lunched with Henry Luce and the editors of *Time* and *Life* in New York in the 1960s, he praised Luce – 'he is like a cricket, always chirping away' – but not his sycophants. 'What I can't stand are all the people around Luce who automatically agree with everything he has to say,' said JFK.[10]

One important technique used by sidekicks and their masters is so-called wilful blindness – the art of carefully evading knowledge of a wrongful act that could create legal or other problems. 'Shortly after 1900 Hearst had initiated the policy of refusing to hear from his executives how his desires were achieved,' wrote Ferdinand Lundberg in *Imperial Hearst*. 'His lawyers had told him that many embarrassments would be averted if he pleaded ignorance of the deeds of his hirelings and merely fired them when their plans miscarried or became public.'[11]

In 2011 Rupert Murdoch denied he was aware that his British newspapers had been illegally hacking the voicemails of thousands of public figures for years: an all-knowing, all-seeing emperor disclaiming responsibility for a catastrophe that had been unfolding for decades within his empire. So who was responsible? 'The people that I trusted to run it and then maybe the people they trusted,' he told a UK parliamentary committee.[12]

The phone hacking debacle taught Murdoch an important lesson in the art of obfuscation, according to his former *Wall Street Journal* columnist Bret Stephens – 'Never put anything in an email.' Writing in *The New York Times* immediately after the Fox News–Dominion legal contretemps in 2023, Stephens recalled a conversation with Murdoch twelve years earlier. 'His private takeaway, it seemed, wasn't to require his companies to adhere to high ethical standards. It was to leave no trace that investigators might use for evidence against him, his family or his favorite lieutenants.'[13]

Inevitably, however, the day arrives when one of those loyal lieutenants must be flushed down the toilet. Rupert Murdoch began the occupational task of sacking editors and senior executives from his earliest days as a proprietor. In 1960 he removed Rohan Rivett, editor of *The News* in Adelaide, via a three-sentence letter. Rivett had just won an important seditious libel case, but Murdoch had tired of his editor's autonomous ways; they were upsetting the state government, which provided the fledgling proprietor with favourable commercial treatment. Rivett cleared out his desk within an hour.[14]

After acquiring the *News of the World* in 1970, Murdoch hastily removed its editor, Stafford Somerfield. 'I want your resignation,' he told Somerfield. 'I never resign,' replied the editor. Murdoch suggested he see a solicitor. 'Don't worry, I've seen a solicitor,' Somerfield said before walking out of his office. 'The whole episode had taken three minutes,' he recalled.[15]

In 1972 Murdoch dismissed the editorial director of News Limited, the distinguished Australian journalist Tom Fitzgerald. 'No-one working for Murdoch would have any editorial independence,' Fitzgerald later told a colleague. 'Not only did he interfere with the most senior executives, but he would humiliate them by

going to comparatively junior editorial executives and giving instructions.' In 1973, when Murdoch approached the brilliant editor of the
Melbourne *Age*, Graham Perkin, to become editor-in-chief of News
Corp's Australian newspapers, Perkin said, 'Why should I work for
you? Your career is littered with the carcasses of dead editors.'[16]

Murdoch sackings often became animated news events. When
he tired of Harold Evans, the super-talented editor of the London
Times, Murdoch told him, 'The place is in chaos. You can't see the
wood for the trees.' (This is a common Murdoch placeholder for
removing independent editors – during a critique session he once
told me my newspaper was 'an embarrassment'.) Evans was sacked
immediately after returning to the office from his father's funeral.
'Murdoch summoned me to his office. He leaned forward in his
chair, took off his glasses, and stared at me. "I want your resignation
today," he said. I was astonished at how calm I was: it was rather
like the out-of-body sensation I'd had at the time I was mugged in
New York,' wrote Evans in his memoir.[17]

Sometimes Murdoch preferred live executions. In 1987, after acquiring his father's old Herald and Weekly Times newspaper chain, he
instructed the unsuspecting incumbent chief executive to fly to London
from Melbourne. John D'Arcy was a stuffy, conservative former
accountant who was never going to fit into the unorthodox Murdoch
culture. But the style of his beheading was cruel: evening drinks at
Murdoch's St James Square apartment, followed by an offer to D'Arcy
to move from his high-profile CEO perch to become chairman of a
small regional newspaper in Queensland. 'What have I done wrong?'
D'Arcy asked. 'Nothing,' replied Murdoch. 'You have been very good.
But you don't like the way we do things.' D'Arcy found it hard to
believe what he was hearing, he later wrote in his brief memoir. 'I could
never have imagined a situation so lacking in truth or conscience.'[18]

When Murdoch decided to guillotine his former school chum
Richard Searby in 1992, he ended their five-decade association in
a fax message. Searby had spent fifteen years as chairman of News
Corporation and was regarded as one of Murdoch's few close friends.

They'd been students together at Geelong Grammar School, near Melbourne, and later at Oxford University. Searby was a smart, urbane lawyer who did much of Murdoch's early legal work and political fixing; he had a particular talent for negotiating cozy deals with the government of the day. He was responsible, with the assistance of then prime minister Malcolm Fraser (another Oxford graduate from Melbourne's patrician elite), for a change to Australia's broadcasting laws in 1981 – a modification that was described around Canberra as the 'Murdoch amendment' – to protect Murdoch's control over his TV licences.

After taking over *The Wall Street Journal*, Murdoch delegated the removal of the editor, Marcus Brauchli, to his henchman Les Hinton. 'There's no easy way to put this, but we want you to step down as managing editor,' Hinton told Brauchli. 'We don't think things are working out. We'd like to make a change.' The other News Corp executive present at the sacking, Robert Thomson, advised Brauchli not to worry because 'we can take care of you financially'.[19]

Even those who leave the Murdoch empire voluntarily continue to live under its shadow. Ken Cowley, who loyally ran News Corp's Australian operations for twenty seven-years, retired into obscurity in 2011. Three years later his name reappeared spectacularly in the pages of a Murdoch competitor, the *Financial Review*, Australia's daily business bible. In a tape-recorded interview published under the headline 'Elisabeth Should Be Running Murdoch Empire, Says Cowley', the former News Corp patriot was uncharacteristically, and undiplomatically, candid. 'Both James and Elisabeth are much smarter than [Lachlan] is,' claimed Cowley. 'I like Lachlan. He's a nice man, but he's not a great businessman. He's not a big and good decision-maker.' He went on: 'The problem is now Rupert doesn't have many people around him [who] tell him the things he doesn't want to hear.' Cowley then described the company's flagship news-paper, *The Australian*, as 'pathetic'.[20]

The response to this perfidy was swift. 'I'm sure my many former colleagues share with me in offering sympathy to someone so gripped by delusion,' Cowley's successor as News Corp CEO, John Hartigan, told *The Australian*.[21] The paper ran another story alleging that Cowley had asked the Murdochs to help fund his struggling business venture and Lachlan had turned him down.

In an attempt to clean up his self-inflicted mess, and avert becoming the target of a ferocious jihad from his former employer, Cowley claimed he was misquoted, even though it was an on-the-record taped interview with an experienced reporter. It was an unsubtle signal to other News Corp alumni: don't foul the nest, even after you've flown the coop.

Like his father, Lachlan Murdoch sacks underlings dispassionately. When he took over the family company's Australian operations early in his career, and began building his own team of loyal cadres, the body count mounted. His chairman was dispatched for an 'early retirement', and other editors and executives found themselves unemployed, prompting one to comment that 'it's hard when proprietors' sons turn up, clomping around in size-11 shoes and breaking all the porcelain'. The sacked editor of *The Australian*, Malcolm Schmidtke, recalled that Lachlan 'chatted about the football for 20 minutes before he got around to telling me I'd been replaced – I probably finished the sentence for him'.[22]

Sometimes the removal of a long-serving editor by a proprietor can be needlessly careless. After thirty-six years as editor of *Vogue*, Grace Mirabella heard about her dismissal on a TV news program. Her boss at Conde Nast, Si Newhouse, confirmed the report was true after she called him. 'I'm afraid it is,' he told her. He acknowledged that 'the way it was handled was graceless', without apparent irony.[23] Her sacking particularly upset Conde Nast president Bernie Leser, who was responsible for maintaining the company's creative culture, especially among editors. But Mirabella's callous removal didn't prepare Leser for his own. While on a business trip to Japan, he received a phone call from Newhouse, who was calling to discuss a story that had appeared in a trade paper predicting Leser was about to be replaced. 'Oh well, we've heard that before,' Leser replied.

'This time it's true,' his boss informed him. 'You shit!' said Leser as he slammed down the phone.[24]

Lord Beaverbrook removed his finest editor, Arthur Chistiansen, by stealth after Christiansen had spent twenty-four years running the *Daily Express*. First he appointed a replacement editor without telling Christiansen, followed by a bizarre period where both editors separately tried to run the paper. Then he demoted Christiansen to manage syndications on the *Evening Standard*, a humiliating putdown for a man described as 'one of the greatest newspaper technicians of all time' by the press historian Francis Williams. When Christiansen was finally invited to discuss his future with Beaverbrook, the two men had an emotional meeting. They both cried. Beaverbrook told his former editor he had always thought of him as a son. But there was to be no rapprochement. 'I'm sorry it's come to this, Chris, but it can't be helped,' he said as he guided Christiansen to the lift. As he closed the door, Beaverbrook leaned forward and said, 'Well, goodbye, Chris. Sorry to see you going down.'[25]

Northcliffe's style, on the other hand, was often peremptory and sometimes conducted by telephone.

'Who's that?'

'Editor, *Weekly Dispatch*, Chief.'

'You *were* the editor.'[26]

The Mogul
Politicians

For a media magnate armed with money, empire, influence, ego and a taste for power, there's an obvious attraction in wanting to play on the biggest stage of all, politics, instead of just jeering from the sidelines. But most forays into representative democracy have ended badly for media owners, who are not accustomed to kowtowing to ordinary people like voters. Steve Forbes, heir to the *Forbes* magazine dynasty, unsuccessfully sought the Republican nomination for US president in 1996 and again in 2000. Those presidential aspirations were described within the Forbes family as 'the $75 million sales call'.[1] When Alfred Harmsworth stood as the Conservative Party candidate for Portsmouth in 1895 he bought a local newspaper (the business, not just one copy) to assist his campaign. But he lost badly and never again attempted politics as a practitioner.

William Randolph Hearst's appetites were large in everything, including a desire to hold high public office. 'The over mastering want of his entire lifetime was the Presidency,' wrote his biographer W.A. Swanberg. 'He schemed, maneuvered, pulled strings, used the power of his newspapers as a bludgeon . . . in his own mind there was no doubt that he would make the greatest of Presidents.'[2]

Hearst was elected to Congress in 1902, representing New York's 11th District. Despite his seemingly confident rhetoric, he was an inconspicuous performer and often absent from the House. 'There has never been a case of a man of such slender intellectual equipment, absolutely without experience in office, impudently flaunting his wealth before the eyes of the people and saying "Make me President",' blared an editorial in the *New York Evening Post*, one of his competitors' papers.[3]

Despite his lacklustre debut, Hearst persisted with his political ambitions. In 1904, shamelessly supported by his eight newspapers across the country, he made an unsuccessful attempt to secure the Democratic presidential nomination. The *New York Evening Post* again offered commentary. Under the headline 'The Unthinkable Hearst', it described him as 'a low voluptuary trying to sting his jaded senses to a fresh thrill by turning from private to public corruption'. A year later he narrowly failed to become mayor of New York; his election, predicted *The New York Times* using words that resonated in Trump's America, 'would have sent a shiver of apprehension over the entire Union'.[4]

Having failed to succeed as a candidate for the two major parties, Hearst established his own, the Independence Party. In 1908 he ran for New York governor, viciously opposed by his arch enemy President Teddy Roosevelt. 'Hearst's private life has been disreputable,' wrote the president in a letter to an English editor. 'His wife was a chorus girl or something like that on the stage ... He is the most potent single influence for evil we have in our life.'[5] After a ferocious campaign, Hearst lost by a narrow 60,000 votes out of 1.5 million cast. His political career finally hit the rocks a year later when he ran third in a three-horse race for the New York mayoralty.

Hearst blatantly mobilised his media empire to support his political campaigns. 'Sometimes they took a man-on-the-street approach, like "BANK PRESIDENT TELLS WHY HE IS FOR HEARST"; other articles reported fervent expressions of public sentiment, such as "A HEARST VICTORY! CRY POLICEMEN'S WIVES",' explained University of Pennsylvania historian Jonathan Zimmerman.[6] Hearst's newspapers covered an election result involving their owner with as much spin as possible, without actually lying. On election night they printed two sets of papers – the first with the headline 'HEARST WINS', the other with 'FRAUD'. The appropriate version was distributed only after word came from head office.

Beaverbrook was a different breed of mogul politician. As a member of the British parliament before he became a newspaper tycoon, he knew how to read the political landscape. Because his life was an almost seamless conflation of pulling both levers of power – journalism and politics – he never lost the urge to barge his way into the cockpit of government. His political career reached glorious heights during World War Two when he became Churchill's minister of aircraft production, a role he later described as 'twenty-one months of high adventure, the like of which has never been known'. In that portfolio he masterminded the production and supply of the Spitfire and Hurricane aircraft that won the Battle of Britain. It was, according to Sir Archibald Rowlands, the chief civil servant running aircraft production, a battle the Royal Air Force would never have won 'but for the activities of one man – and that man was Lord Beaverbrook'.[7]

The only media mogul to actually reach the top of politics – which he did oafishly, decadently and unscrupulously – was Silvio Berlusconi. He spent nine years as Italy's prime minister, biggest media owner and richest man – all at the same time – while he was simultaneously under investigation for bribing judges, tax evasion, abuse of office, mafia collusion, and paying a seventeen-year-old for sex.

Berlusconi began his working life as a crooner singing Nat King Cole songs on a Mediterranean love boat. He then accumulated a real estate fortune by building vast concrete housing developments for thousands of residents, funded by what has been elliptically described as 'a mysterious Swiss finance company'.[8] All the sleazy showman's characteristics that would later project him onto Italy's biggest stage were formed in his thirties, but it was his next venture – acquiring several dozen local television stations and filling their airtime with imported American game shows and popular entertainment series like *Wheel of Fortune* and *Baywatch* – that made him a billionaire and paved his path to political power. But there was one problem for 'Mister TV', as Berlusconi was then known: under Italian law, private television stations could broadcast only locally, not nationally. When his competitors complained that Berlusconi had in effect created a national broadcasting network in defiance of the law, federal agents arrived at his TV stations to impound tapes and close down hundreds of his transmitters.

Berlusconi's response was to befriend and bribe the person best placed to change the law – Bettino Craxi, Italy's then prime minister and head of the Socialist Party, who soon became Berlusconi's *patrono*, best man at his second wedding and godfather to two of his children. Berlusconi's company Fininvest secretly channelled $17 million into Craxi's offshore bank account and – *presto!* – a decree was issued by the government that allowed Mister TV to transform his stations into Italy's first national commercial television network.[9]

This piece of political chicanery would have barely raised eyebrows at almost any other time in twentieth-century Italy, but it occurred just as one of the country's biggest corruption inquiries, Mani Pulite (Operation Clean Hands), was being launched in Milan. This exposed Craxi and Berlusconi to the zealous prosecutors targeting heads of companies, public-sector officials and high-ranking politicians in the country's $8 billion-a-year bribery industry, in which Craxi's Socialist Party was believed to be the biggest recipient.

As the investigators circled and Craxi fled into luxurious exile in Tunisia, Berlusconi played out his next brazen move. Just as Hearst had done eighty-five years earlier, he formed his own political party, which he named Forza Italia, the words screamed by Italians at soccer games (imagine a political party named 'Go America'). Almost overnight, Italian politics, business and media were melded together under the control of a super-salesman for whom the words *conflitto d'interesse* (conflict of interest) didn't compute. Berlusconi moved into politics with two objectives: to run the country and to divert enough attention from himself to avoid jail. 'I am forced to enter politics, otherwise they will put me in prison,' he brazenly told the journalists Indro Montanelli and Enzo Biagi at the time.[10]

Only months after the creation of Forza Italia in 1994, Berlusconi was elected prime minister of Italy. He did this by harnessing the resources of his media empire, enlisting dozens of his top ad salesmen to become parliamentary candidates, pumping out Forza Italia propaganda over his TV network, and instructing journalists at his newspaper, *Il Giornale*, that they needed to change their political views if they wanted to be better paid.

'I am an outsider, I created an empire for myself and I can do the same for you,' he declared in his stump speech. 'The politicians are corrupt and have betrayed you, and I am the man to lead the country.' It was a blurring of lines between money, media, law and politics on a scale never seen in the global history of democratic governance. 'Imagine if a real-estate mogul along the lines of Donald Trump also owned CBS, NBC, the Fox network, Paramount Pictures, *Newsweek*, Random House, Condé Nast, the *Los Angeles Times*, HBO, the Dallas Cowboys, Walmart stores, Aetna insurance, Loews Theaters and Fidelity Investments and had the political clout of Bill Clinton or Newt Gingrich, and you get an idea of the long shadow Mr. Berlusconi casts in Italian life,' wrote Alexander Stille in a 1996 profile of the mogul in the *The New York Times Magazine*.[11]

Berlusconi was a legal Houdini. He faced more than a dozen trials for fraud, false accounting or bribery, but avoided a four-year prison sentence for his only standing conviction, for tax fraud in 2013, because he was aged over seventy. In 2015 he was sentenced to three years' jail for offering a bribe of €3 million ($4.4 million) to a senator to switch political factions, but again escaped incarceration because a statute of limitations kicked in before an appeal could be held. He was convicted in several other trials that were also timed out by a statute of limitations – 'at least twice because Mr Berlusconi himself changed the law', as *The Economist* noted in its powerful 2011 cover story 'The Man who Screwed an Entire Country'.[12] In 2021, aged eighty-five, he was still fighting witnesses in a Milan courtroom over bribery charges from an earlier case in which he was accused of paying for sex with a Moroccan prostitute known as Ruby Rubacuori ('Ruby the Heartstealer'). He was acquitted in 2023, the year he died. 'Accusing me of corruption,' he once remarked without sarcasm, 'is like arresting Mother Teresa because a little girl under her care stole an apple.'[13]

During four terms as prime minister, Berlusconi controlled 90 per cent of all Italian national television broadcasting, through the stations he owned directly and the government stations where he could apply political influence. In 1990, when the Italian parliament banned individuals from owning both a national television network and a national newspaper, Berlusconi passed *Il Giornale* to his younger brother, Paolo, who was later sentenced to twenty-one months' jail and fined €49 million for fraud and corruption in a landfill scandal, and then jailed again years later for falsifying invoices.[14]

Berlusconi's prime-ministership was a bumbling mess marked by gaffes and embarrassments. In 2001, at a news conference in Berlin soon after the September 11 attacks in New York, he described Western civilisation as 'superior' to Islam. In the same year he told the European Union that Finland didn't deserve a food safety agency as 'Finns don't even know what prosciutto is'. Four years later he claimed to have used his 'playboy' charms on Finland's president after being forced to 'endure' Finnish food. In 2003, at the launch of Italy's presidency of the European Union, he suggested the German EU parliamentarian Martin Schulz should be cast as a Nazi concentration camp guard in a new Italian movie. In 2006 he claimed that communists in Mao's China had boiled babies for fertiliser. In 2010 he was caught on camera joking about a Jew who charged fellow Jews money to hide in his basement from the Nazis, without telling them the war was over.[15]

None of these follies were enough to bring him down, but his prime-ministership eventually ended in ignominy in 2011 as the Italian economy tanked, leading voters in local elections to overwhelmingly reject his incompetence and trigger his downfall. There was dancing in the streets outside the Quirinal Palace when he arrived to tender his resignation to the president. 'The Magic Flute is Broken', declared the headline on the front page of the left-leaning *La Repubblica*. Two years later Berlusconi was barred from serving in any legislative office for six years following his tax fraud conviction. But he remained irrepressible and in 2022 was back in the political mainstream as a minor coalition partner in the government of Italy's first female prime minister, Giorgia Meloni.

It would be wrong to think of Silvio Berlusconi as a media mogul in the Hearst-Beaverbrook-Murdoch sense. He was an *anti-media* mogul, a comic figure whose main interest in journalism was to suppress it. He was an utter bullshitter who made up quotes he attributed to famous personalities, like American tycoons. 'People are totally gullible,' he once told his executives, 'they drink up quotations!'[16]

Berlusconi regarded any scrutiny of his life with contempt. In 2010 *La Repubblica* published phone transcripts of him bawling out a commissioner at Italy's independent broadcast regulator, Agcom, over an upcoming program on the state broadcaster RAI examining corruption cases against him. 'What the fuck are you doing with all this?' he shouted over the phone at the commissioner, Giancarlo Innocenzi (a former journalist at Berlusconi's Mediaset network). In another call, he told Innocenzi to muzzle a show that investigated his alleged mafia links. 'It's obscene,' Berlusconi is reported as saying. 'Now you need to make a concerted effort to push RAI to say enough, we're shutting everything down.' In response, RAI suspended all political talk shows ahead of regional elections.[17]

Alexander Stille tells the story in *The Sack of Rome* of how investigative journalists Giovanni Ruggeri and Mario Guarino were taken to court by Berlusconi while they were working on a book about the mysterious origins of his fortune. When the popular newspaper *La Notte* published a long interview with the authors, Berlusconi called the paper's editor, Petro Gioigianni. 'Writing about that book, you have risked my goodwill,' he told the editor. 'I will reduce you to poverty.' To which Gioigianni replied, 'You can't, I'm already poor.'[18]

The *mogulissimo* died in 2023. 'It is now difficult to imagine an Italy without Berlusconi,' editorialised *La Repubblica*. 'In the last 50 years, there hasn't been a day in which his name hasn't been mentioned, on TV, in the newspapers, in parliament, in bars and at the stadium.' Mostly, they were negative or jocular stories about a man who was 'unfit to govern a democratic republic', as he was described by politics professor Maurizio Viroli, a biographer of Machiavelli.[19] The simple essence of the Berlusconi method was explained by Giuliano Ferrara, editor of the pro-Berlusconi newspaper *Il Foglio*, after the then prime minister was convicted in the Ruby Rubacuori under-age sex and bribery case. '*Siamo tutti puttane*,' he wrote. 'We are all whores.'[20]

The Madness
of Great Men

They inhabit a world of favours, deals and IOUs. They accumulate platoons of enemies as well as sycophants. They are feared. Everyone knows who they are. No-one wants to cross them. Unconstrained by society's rules and conventions, they select their delectables – desire, greed, hatred, power, sex, hubris, arrogance, selfishness, jealousy – from every shelf of human indulgence. Everything we know about the dictators who have run media empires since the late nineteenth century points to extreme narcissism as one of their defining features. 'When people feel powerful, they stop trying to "control themselves",' says Stanford University professor Deborah Gruenfeld, a social psychologist who focuses on the study of power. 'For most people, what we think of as "power plays" aren't calculated and Machiavellian – they happen at the subconscious level. Many of those internal regulators that hold most of us back from bold or bad behavior diminish or disappear.'[1]

For a highly visible media tycoon, it can be hard *not* to be narcissistic. Whose ego wouldn't feel stroked, for example, if they read this about themselves, as William Randolph Hearst did in October 1935 when he picked up *Fortune*, America's dominant business magazine: 'Mr. Hearst does not merely own newspapers. He owns magazines, radio stations, ranches and New York City hotels. He owns mines and a warehouse full of antiques. He hires 31,000 men and women for $57,000,000 a year and he has working for him nearly a hundred executives who earn $25,000 or more ... Living literally like a king, he has probably been the nation's No. 1 spender even surpassing Mr. Ford with his schoolhouses and Mr. Mellon with his paintings. He is certainly the world's No. 1 collector of objets d'art, specializing in armor, tapestry, and furniture of any period he fancies. At heart a medievalist, he keeps his ear to the ground in a hundred local political issues, in all the major national ones. His correspondents cover the earth; he has acquaintances everywhere and invites them wholesale to his palaces. And all this is his, and he runs it.'[2]

One of the biggest occupational hazards for the owners of big media, however, is acquiring enemies. For this, they need a thick skin. 'I am the loneliest man in the world,' Joseph Pulitzer once told Lord Northcliffe. 'I cannot afford to have friends. People who dine at my table one night find themselves arraigned in my newspaper the next morning.' Northcliffe concurred; the only way to run a newspaper, he said, was by being impersonal: 'Friendships become costly luxuries to a publisher.'[3]

Rupert Murdoch has constructed a cast iron detachment to manage nearly all his relationships, except those with selected members of his close family. 'Don't fall in love with Rupert,' advised Bruce Matthews, one of his top London executives, in 1987. 'He turns against lovers and chops them off.' Murdoch can't afford friends, said Gus Fischer, another of his former British executives. 'He has built his empire by using people, then discarding them when they have passed their expiration dates. It is not the sort of management style which lends itself to lasting friendships.'[4]

Decades of hostility have made Murdoch wary of almost everyone. When he was invited to a private dinner at London's Savoy Hotel in the early 1970s by the debonaire Gerald Long, then general manager of Reuters, it was arranged as a friendly occasion where several dozen media leaders and other influential people could meet the new mogul on the block. But when guests were asked to say something about Murdoch, eyes darted around the table. 'Nobody wanted to say what they thought, but nobody wanted to be heard saying what they didn't think,' one of the attendees, Anthony Smith, a BBC producer who became president of Magdalen College at Oxford University, later told *Vanity Fair*. As a way of starting the conversation, Long randomly picked a Canadian professor with expertise in British elections who was sitting three chairs from Murdoch. 'He opened his mouth,' recalled Smith, 'and told us how Murdoch had degraded the working-class papers, he had demeaned the dialogue in the country.'[5]

After seven decades of vitriol and abuse, Murdoch knows, more than anyone, that spite is a permanent feature of the territory inhabited by a media disrupter. As a result, he has been unflinching in deflecting or ignoring his critics, as though they don't exist.

———

There is almost nothing normal or conventional about the lives of the moguls. Everything is *big*. Almost everyone else is subservient. Alfred Harmsworth's grandiose office, known as Room One, contained a bust of Napoleon on the mantelpiece (Pulitzer also acquired a bust of Napoleon, and Black collected Napoleon's books and displayed his portrait in his London office) and coal fires at each end of the room. 'Big rooms for big ideas,' he was fond of saying. When he worked from his Broadstairs estate in Kent there was a telephone in every one of its forty-six rooms and a pair of Florida alligators slithering in mud inside a custom-built greenhouse.[6]

Beaverbrook's style was less ostentatious but no less domineering. 'He was demanding, exacting, tyrannous, vindictive and malicious, yet all or most of the excesses of the master journalist were forgiven by the men and women who worked for him because of the success of his publishing enterprise and his impish sense of fun,' observed Hugh Cudlipp in *The Beaverbrook I Knew*.[7] But everyone in the court of a mogul is paid to intuit the king's sensitivities. In Beaverbrook world, one topic never mentioned was the Orson Welles movie *Citizen Kane*. As Michael Foot, a Beaverbrook confidant, wrote, 'No one could deny it: there was just an element of Citizen Kane in him, and he could be furious with any reference which exposed it.'[8]

Hearst, by contrast, although he was the mogul who inspired the disagreeable Citizen Kane character, was disconcertingly mild in real life. He had a high voice, a limp handshake, dressed like an undertaker, rarely smiled and had steely cold blue eyes. 'He was an autocrat who couldn't fire anybody,' wrote his biographer David Nasaw, who noted that despite his enormous power, Hearst 'was shy, he was withdrawn, he was very difficult to talk to'.[9]

Management concepts like motivational leadership are not relevant in corporations run by newspaper barons. They were and are dictators, even when being polite. Hearst would summon executives to travel for meetings at San Simeon, his Californian castle, where he'd make them stew for up to a week in the grand surroundings before confronting them with his icy stare. It was his unnerving way of exerting power. The best response, his secretary Joseph Willicombe privately advised editors, was to stare right back.

Each mogul was eccentric or obsessive in his own way. Rupert Murdoch has been preoccupied with fitness and longevity since the 1980s, when he started his uber-health regimen, assisted by personal trainers, strenuous exercise and special diets. He once told his London butler, Philip Townsend, 'Phil, I'm into yin and yang and all that shit.'[10] In 2013 he revealed he was wearing a smart bracelet known as a 'Jawbone' which, he said, 'keeps track of how I sleep, move and eat – transmitting that information to the cloud'.[11]

Despite his determination to stave off the inevitability of aging, his health in recent years has been challenged by a series of accidents – a broken back, seizures, two bouts of pneumonia, atrial fibrillation, and a torn Achilles tendon, according to an unnamed source in *Vanity Fair*. In 2018, after reportedly falling down a step in the bathroom of Lachlan's boat *Sarissa* while cruising in the Caribbean, he was stretchered in James's private jet to a Los Angeles hospital in a critical condition. Doctors who examined him found previous fractured vertebrae – 'Murdoch explained it must have been from the time his ex-wife Deng pushed him into a piano during a fight, after which he spent weeks on the couch,' claimed *Vanity Fair*, whose reporting on modern moguls and their private lives has been heavily researched and is rarely challenged.[12]

Robert Maxwell, although aggressive and crude, was also clever, devious and paranoid. He spoke English as if he were an Englishman, French as if he were a Frenchman, and the same for German and Russian. He became so concerned about the loyalty of his employees that he bugged their offices to hear what they were saying; tapes of these conversations were uncovered in a suitcase of his former head of security, by a BBC production crew working on a 2007 biographical film.

Maxwell claimed the two things he hated most in life were taxes and Germans, and was once heard to describe a German contact as a 'fucking kraut'. He ate with his bare hands, like a glutton, and drank out of a huge cup displaying the words 'I Am a Very Important Person'. On one occasion, stuffing down food as he watched himself on the TV news, he instructed his secretary to unbutton his trousers to release his vast stomach. His wife Betty recalled the night he raided the pantry and ate 'a pound of cheese, a jar of peanut butter, two jars of caviar, a loaf of bread and a whole chicken in one go'. The word 'pig' was invented for Maxwell, said Terry Pattinson, a union leader at the *Daily Mirror*. 'One *Mirror* executive once approached me covered with crumbs, custard and what looked like vomit on the front of his executive suit. "Maxwell sneezed into my face," he told me. "His mouth was full of food at the time."'[13]

Betty Maxwell wrote to her husband in 1981 with her views about his grotesque behaviour: 'For years, I've accepted it all – a complete lack of love and consideration, derision, condescension. I've put up with your sermons, your unjustified reproaches, your sudden absurd anger, your murderous moods for the most trivial of reasons. Your latest mania is to dramatize everything: it's almost as if your anger can only be appeased by the weekly ritual of family catharsis. Like the Hydra of the ancients, you have to devour your victim, one of your own children, every week. You cannot live without your ration of Maxwellian drama, accompanied by exorcism, yelling, threats, tears, gnashing of teeth, repentance and contrition.'[14]

Conrad Black's style was classier than Maxwell's, but no less arrogant. 'Let us be completely frank,' he told an interviewer in the late 1980s, 'the deferences and preferments that this culture bestows upon the owners of great newspapers are satisfying ... [A]s the beneficiary of that system, it would certainly be hypocrisy for me to complain about it.' Black painted an imperious word picture of the study in his Kensington home in his book *A Matter of Principle*: 'All about me was the reassuring evidence of an active career and an eclectic range of interests. Shelves of leather-bound first editions ... Jules Mazarin and the esteemed diplomat Ercole Cardinal Consalvi, strikingly rendered, looked down impassively upon, among other things, a small bust of Palmerston, a fine crystal model of the Titanic ... and an iron copy of the death mask and hands of Stalin that I had bought from the estate of the great British maverick politi-cian Enoch Powell. Gifts: a shield from Chief Buthelezi of the Zulus, a naval painting from our directors in Australia, the extravagantly inscribed latest memoirs of Henry Kissinger and Margaret Thatcher, each evoking interesting times and powerful friends, historic figures who had helped me and whom I had helped.'[15]

Although Black's net worth was several noughts below those of Hearst, Murdoch and Zuckerberg, he and his four-times-married wife Barbara Amiel flaunted their lifestyle as if they were billion-aires. Barbara's 1986 article 'Why Women Marry Up' in the Canadian magazine *Chatelaine* set the tone, highlighted by her much-quoted boast, 'I have an extravagance that knows no bounds.' A few years later, Amiel invited a *Vogue* writer to inspect her London dressing suite, which included 'a fur closet, a sweater closet, a closet for shirts and T-shirts, and a closet so crammed with evening gowns that the overflow has to be kept in yet more closets downstairs'. Asked why Hollinger Inc. needed two private jets, Amiel explained it's always best because 'however well one plans ahead, one always finds one is on the wrong continent'.[16]

Black's admiration for the world of opulence was captured in a scene by Bryan Burrough in *Vanity Fair* in 2011. Peering into a storefront during his first days of living in Palm Beach, Florida in 1969, Black heard the sound of cars crashing behind him. He turned to see that a Rolls-Royce Silver Cloud had rammed a Rolls-Royce Phantom V, which had been rammed by another Rolls-Royce Phantom. 'That was the moment I knew I was where I belonged,' Black later told friends, according to Burrough.[17]

Before his downfall, Conrad Black owned a Park Avenue apartment in New York, a 17,000-square-foot British Colonial-style home in Palm Beach, an eleven-bedroom London townhouse with a giant portrait of Napoleon in the stairwell, and a gated mansion on Park Lane Circle in Toronto's exclusive Bridle Path neighbourhood, incorporating a three-storey elliptical library containing 15,000 books and a dome modelled on St Peter's Basilica.

The Blacks' conspicuous consumption began creating problems when evidence of his looting large sums of company money started to emerge. In 2001, as questions circulated about the couple's extravagant lifestyle, Toronto *Globe and Mail* columnist Margaret Wente wrote, 'Only a few hundred women in the world can afford to dress like Mrs. Black, and Mrs. Black may not be among them.'[18]

After his conviction for fraud, Black's thirty-seven months in a US prison temporarily constrained his lifestyle. But he downplayed the experience after his release: 'Let's not dramatize it. It was tedious and outrageous but it wasn't all that unpleasant.' He spent much of his jail time writing books – his hagiography subjects included US presidents Roosevelt, Nixon and Trump. Black described critics who claimed his reputation would never recover as the 'absolute bottom of the socio-educational spectrum of robotic credibility of a lumpen proletariat'.[19]

Silvio Berlusconi matched Maxwell and Black for slipperiness, but on a larger stage. Italians described their mogul prime minister as *furbo* – crafty – and not necessarily in a negative way. Only the wily get ahead, explained Maria Latella, magazine editor and anchorwoman on Italy's Sky 24 news network. 'Berlusconi succeeded because he was always a little more crafty than the others,' she said.[20]

If any single characteristic distinguished Berlusconi from other media dictators it was his recklessness. He was caught on tape in 2011 describing the German chancellor Angela Merkel as '*culona inchiavabile*' (an 'unfuckable lard-arse'). In the same phone call with an Italian journalist, recorded by police, he trashed Italy as a 'shitty country' that 'sickened' him.

Berlusconi's true priorities emerged at a critical summit in 2009 with European leaders Gordon Brown, Nicholas Sarkozy and Angela Merkel, held to address the global financial crisis. During a coffee break, according to Brown's account, Berlusconi chided the other heads of government in pigeon French: 'Amateurs, amateurs . . . don't they realize we've got a press conference in an hour and there's no makeup artist for any of us.'

———

Living lavishly is a sine qua non of mogul life. Joseph Pulitzer had homes in Manhattan; Bar Harbor, Maine; and on Jekyll Island, off the coast of Georgia. After he became blind at the age of forty-three, which made him an anxious, nervous wreck, his personal suite in a separate wing of each residence was known as a 'Tower of Silence'.

Hearst's 165-room hilltop castle in San Simeon, southern California, sat on a 60,000-acre estate, and encompassed an airstrip, roads, bridges, two Ancient Rome-styled swimming pools, and America's largest private zoo. Now called Hearst Castle, it is an incredibly popular state monument. George Bernard Shaw reportedly commented that it was 'what heaven would be like if God had your money'.[21]

Henry Luce was 'slightly uncomfortable' with the opulence of his lifestyle, according to biographer Alan Brinkley, but not so uncomfortable that he didn't tolerate the pleasures of a palatial apartment in Manhattan, a grand residence in Connecticut, and a 7,200-acre former plantation in South Carolina, 'all equipped with retinues of servants, important paintings on the walls, antiques and pottery'.[22]

Silvio Berlusconi's eighteenth-century Villa San Martino, near Milan, was the venue of his many so-called bunga bunga parties. Decorated with Old Masters, Renaissance antiques and Chinese porcelain, it was also dotted with huge Murano glass chandeliers and incorporated a family mausoleum in pink marble.

When Rupert Murdoch moved to Los Angeles in 1986 he acquired one of the great houses of Hollywood, a Spanish-style mansion, once owned by the impresario Jules Stein, perched on a hilltop overlooking the city. As of 2024, Murdoch's residential portfolio includes a $57 million, four-floor New York penthouse; a London townhouse; a $200 million, 340,000-acre working cattle farm in Montana; a 13-acre Californian winery incorporating a 7,500 square foot, Mediterranean-style residence; and a 20,000-hectare cattle stud in rural Australia.[23]

Lachlan Murdoch is even more Hearstian in his tastes. In 2019 he paid $150 million for the French chateau-style Bel Air mansion made famous by the 1960s TV series *The Beverly Hillbillies*. At the time it was reportedly the most expensive home ever sold in California. As well, he has a Sydney harbourside Georgian mansion with a $24 million boatshed nearby, and a 45-acre Aspen hideaway. To reach their residences, both father and son fly in private Gulfstream jets that can cruise from Sydney to Los Angeles in one hop.

Boats are another trophy item for the media magnate class. William Randolph Hearst's yacht *Vamoose* was the fastest steam craft in the world when it was built in 1890. Its power plant produced 'a thumping 875 brake horsepower and enough on-deck vibration to loosen a passenger's teeth', wrote Kenneth Whyte in *The Uncrowned King*.[24]

James Gordon Bennett Jr, owner of *The New York Herald*, effectively launched the era of the superyacht in 1900 when he spent the equivalent of $22 million to build the 285-foot *Lysistrata*. Bennett ran his newspaper from the boat, which had a Turkish bath, full-time masseur, and, according to journalist Lucius Beebe, 'a soft padded cell with special seagoing fittings for the ship's cow, an Alderney', that supplied Bennett's table butter and the ingredients for his 'brandy milk punches at breakfast'.[25]

Joseph Pulitzer lived for years on his 45-crew, 268-foot steam yacht *Liberty*. It travelled with enough coal to complete two return transatlantic crossings from the Riviera to New York without refuelling, and with a team of personal assistants who entertained and read to the increasingly blind Pulitzer. He died in bed on board.

The Murdochs also appreciate life afloat. Rupert has been sailing most of his adult life, starting with his yachting days on Sydney Harbour as a young publisher in the 1960s. He sold his 138-foot yacht *Rosehearty* in 2014 following his divorce from Wendi Deng, and according to unconfirmed rumours owns another superyacht, *Vertigo*. Lachlan splashed $150 million on a 60-metre sloop replete with a luxury open-air pool, multiple entertaining areas, and facilities for twelve guests and ten staff. While waiting several years for delivery of the craft in 2023 from shipyards in the Netherlands, he brought in a low-priced stopgap, a 42-meter Feadship superyacht, for around $20 million.[26]

———

Powerful men 'just take what they want', Dutch sociobiologist Johan van der Dennen told *Der Spiegel* in 2011. 'It is the position of power itself that makes men arrogant, narcissistic, egocentric, oversexed, paranoid, despotic, and craving even more power, though there are exceptions to this rule.'[27] These behavioural excesses are described as 'the banality of the abuses of power' by Dacher Keltner, a professor of psychology at the University of California, Berkeley, who says the experience of power is like having someone open up your skull and take out that part of your brain critical to empathy and socially appropriate behaviour.[28]

Taking what they wanted has been a trademark of the messy, complicated and often salacious private lives of moguls. Northcliffe's Irish mistress secretly bore him three children. Hearst had a wife in New York and a mistress in Los Angeles for much of his life. (She apparently bore him a child whose existence only became public decades after he died, when the *Los Angeles Times* obituary pages revealed the death of Patricia Van Cleve Lake, 'the only daughter of the famed movie star Marion Davies and the famed William Randolph Hearst'.)[29] Beaverbrook had two wives and numerous lovers; he was well known as a womaniser and was particularly fond of society ladies.

And in an escapade that reads like a script from *Succession*, Beaverbrook's 27-year-old granddaughter, Lady Jeanne Campbell, embarked on a torrid affair in the late 1950s with the married 58-year-old Henry Luce. Their intense relationship, which lasted several years, reached its apotheosis when she asked him to divorce his wife and marry her. Luce agreed, then reneged, and it was over. (Campbell later married the writer Norman Mailer.) Clare Boothe Luce once summarised her husband's approach to sex: 'He simply did it and then rolled over and thought about *Time*.'[30]

Rupert Murdoch has accumulated four wives (scheduled to increase to five at the time of writing). Berlusconi totted up hundreds of lovers. 'If I sleep for three hours, I still have enough energy to make love for another three,' he boasted when in his seventies.[31] The Australian media tycoon Kerry Packer, well known for his extramarital ventures, reportedly moved from his mistress's apartment to his family home to be with his wife shortly before he died. His father, Sir Frank Packer, who launched the family dynasty, had a predisposition for office trysts. He was a 'man of many mistresses', who had numerous affairs with women who worked on his *Daily Telegraph* and *Women's Weekly*, according to the Packer biographer Paul Barry. 'And no doubt there were benefits to be had from sleeping with the boss,' wrote Barry. 'But he could be both patronising and predatory.'[32]

The Norwegians invented a word for the excessive lives of power-obsessed authoritarians: *Stormannsgalskap* – the madness of great men. 'It is a particularly common condition among media barons,' according to *The Economist*'s Schumpeter columnist, 'not least because they frequently blur the line between reporting reality and shaping it.'

MALFEASANCE

The Moral
Compass

On a clear summer day in Aspen, Colorado in late June 1988, Rupert Murdoch and several dozen of his highest-ranking international editors and executives assembled in one of the fashionable ski town's conference centres. This was my first experience of a News Corp conclave, the infrequent cult-like gatherings where the senior disciples of the world's most powerful media pontiff soak up his company's special culture over several days and nights.

Murdoch presided over proceedings from a table at the front of the horseshoe-shaped lecture theatre. The agenda was packed with sessions covering world affairs, politics, media, and of course News Corp's unique form of journalism. Of all the notable guests who came to present us with confidential, state-of-the-world briefings, the most notable was Richard Nixon. The former US president arrived by helicopter in a whirr of noise, greeted Murdoch warmly, shook all our hands, then proceeded to deliver a lucid, almost magisterial foreign-policy *tour d'horizon*. In several other sessions, News Corp editors gave inside-baseball accounts of their strategies, challenges and secret sauce. My own presentation explained our attempt (which subsequently failed) to revive the once-great afternoon paper, the Melbourne *Herald*.

On this Sunday morning there was something different – an irreverent, vaudeville-style presentation from the veteran news editor of the London *Sun*, Tom Petrie. His subject (and manner) was

WIT (Whatever It Takes); the underhand tactics and chequebook journalism used by *The Sun* to land huge scoops and drive its tabloid competitors into the dust. 'We don't report the news, we make it,' boasted Petrie.

What happened next has entered the annals of Murdochian legend. Bruce Guthrie, my then deputy editor at the Melbourne *Herald*, raised his hand to ask Petrie a question. 'Tom,' he inquired, 'do you have any ethical framework at all at the London *Sun*?' They were thirteen words that had almost certainly never been uttered before inside any News Corp chamber. Guthrie's decision to wade into Petrie's 'morass of *Sun* exaggeration, invention and charac-ter assassination', as he described it, was one of the more serious misjudgements of his career. He outlined what happened next in his memoir *Man Bites Murdoch*:

> The place simply erupted. 'Ethics? At *The Sun*? You've got to be joking,' shouted one of the execs from the London broadsheets. All around were shouts of derision, raucous laughter and general hysteria. So much so that Petrie claimed to have not heard my question. He called for calm. 'Sorry, mate, but could you repeat the question? And would you shut up, you blokes?' pleaded the harried news editor. So I repeated the question. I don't remember looking at Rupert throughout any of this, which had lasted a good 90 seconds or so. But Beecher would later gleefully report that the proprietor had turned red when I first asked the question and blue when I repeated it. Soon Murdoch would have steam coming out of his ears as I was forced to ask it a third time. 'For God's sake,' said Petrie. 'Can you shut up? I'm sorry, mate, I missed it again.' By now, I was wishing Aspen would disappear in some summer blizzard. My future at News Limited was going to be, well, limited. I tried one last time, rushing the words to get the whole wretched thing over: 'DoyouhaveanyethicsatTheSun?' Petrie came to my rescue with a thoughtful reply. 'To tell you the truth, we don't really have any kind of ethical framework at all,' he admitted.[1]

Murdoch was shocked to discover a 'wanker' in his midst, as he later described Guthrie to one of his executives. To deflect attention from the unwelcome odour that was wafting through his inner sanctum, Murdoch diverted the discussion to the topic of *The Sun*'s great journalism. 'I would have thought it's news if the captain of the England cricket team is taking barmaids up to his room the night before a Test match,' he told his audience, a reference to a recent scoop that had fanned public outrage in Britain.

As for Guthrie, his career at News Corp continued for several years. He later became editor of one of its top-selling newspapers, before he was sacked and successfully sued the company in a widely publicised court case, winning AUD$580,000 in damages for breach of contract. But at that moment in Aspen, after dropping his hand grenade, he felt, he said, like 'the social equivalent of a leper'.[2]

The idea that ethics could be embarrassing subject matter inside a roomful of journalism professionals might seem paradoxical, but not when those professionals are hardened pragmatists whose primary role in life is to make money, and noise, for the proprietor who's sitting directly in front of them. Ethics in journalism, for many people in a profit-led media company, is viewed as a fringe topic that preoccupies wankers from pretentious newspapers or universities.

'Efficks? Efficks? In't that the place east o' London where they all wear white fuckin socks?' *The Sun*'s theatrical editor-from-central-casting, Kelvin MacKenzie, once allegedly roared at a reporter who used the word in a story. When asked by the Leveson Inquiry into the conduct of the British press in 2011 about the role of ethics in the print media, MacKenzie replied in his formal witness statement: 'The dictionary definition of ethics is; the philosophical study of the moral value of human conduct and the rules and principles that ought to govern it. They were not issues I bothered with.'[3]

Ignoring or joking about ethics in journalism at news organisations like News Corp and Fox News is a form of wilful blindness, constructed to ensure that moral principles don't interfere with the real priorities of igniting sensation, controversy, ratings, circulation, revenue, profit. It's the media manifestation of the famous injunction, usually misattributed to Edmund Burke, that 'the only thing necessary for the triumph of evil is for good men to do nothing'.

For years, Murdoch's native flagship *The Australian* has made an artform out of denigrating and humiliating its ideological enemies. One of those targets has been the admired Australian Indigenous journalist and author Stan Grant, whose storied career includes a long stint as a CNN presenter. In 2023 he accused the paper of acting like a 'racist hit squad that has been targeting me forever', as he described the impact on him and his family of the constant smearing of his gritty journalism, which offers an articulate First Nations perspective. 'Do they care that I am going to get death threats?' asked Grant. 'Do they care?'⁴

By incurring the paper's wrath, Grant joined a list of prominent figures targeted by *The Australian*. It attacked leading climate scientist Tim Flannery after he was selected by the federal government as Australian of the Year in 2007, denigrating him as a climate 'alarmist' and pursuing him in seventy-two articles over the following year, many negative or disparaging. 'They take any opportunity to belittle, besmirch, denigrate in any way they can,' said Flannery, who has made climate awareness one of the moral crusades of his life.⁵

Another victim was the Sudanese-Australian media presenter and writer Yassmin Abdel-Magied, who described herself as the 'most publicly-hated Muslim in Australia' following *The Australian*'s attacks on her comment on a national television program that Islam was a feminist religion. 'Whether or not one agrees with me isn't really the point,' wrote Abdel-Magied in *The Guardian*'s Australian edition. 'The reality is the visceral nature of the fury – almost every time I share a perspective or make a statement in any forum – is more about who I am than about what is said.'⁶

Stan Grant's anguished question – 'Do they care?' – exposes the moral culpability of a media organisation whose proprietor has absolute power to shut down his companies' personal and societal vitriol with a single phone call. That call, over the course of the seventy years of News Corp, has never been made, except under legal or criminal duress.

Instead, moguls like Hearst and Murdoch have defended and fortified their editorial behaviour by maintaining the false equivalence that their journalism is as important as anyone else's. This has empowered their editors and reporters to justify their work with well-worn phrases like *Freedom of the press means everyone should be subject to scrutiny* or *I support my owner because he is holding power to account.* What they don't say, but often think, is *I have kids and a mortgage and there are fewer and fewer jobs left in the media.* Of course, most of them don't have a choice. Or they share the sentiment of former US vice-president Hubert Humphrey, who, when asked by an aide why he tolerated constant mistreatment by President Lyndon Johnson, replied: 'I've eaten so much of Johnson's shit in this job that I've grown to like the taste of it.'[7]

Bruce Dover is an experienced foreign correspondent and editor who was News Corp's vice-president (China) for seven years in the 1990s. He conspicuously ended his own moral journey after Murdoch ordered his publishing company HarperCollins to kill Chris Patten's book. 'On a personal level, the Patten incident left me questioning for the first time the real cost of accepting the Murdoch dollar and working for News Corporation in China,' wrote Dover in *Rupert's Adventures in China.* 'Pragmatism was one thing but this bordered on the coldly amoral – doing whatever was needed to do to get the deal done.'[8]

Going public with his indignation was a risky career move for Dover. Another defector was a former *News of the World* reporter who decided to write her story anonymously on the British website *Byline Investigates*. Her career at the paper covered the gamut of tabloid populism – kiss 'n' tell exposés, serial killers, rapists, terrorists. She described the pressure to generate stories and stand them up – 'or, failing that, to pretty much make them up' – as the job consumed her life and challenged her values:

My conscience constantly bothered me. Was it right to doorstep the parents of a child who had just been murdered? To expose a celebrity cheating on his wife? To tell the world the whereabouts of child sex offenders who had served their time?

During my time at the paper I did all of these things with a heavy heart, and many apologies, yet I did them all the same, in desperation to get my name in the paper. I received letters telling me I was 'scum'. Publicly, I laughed it off. Privately, I agreed ... Eventually, I got to a point where – when faced with an ethical dilemma I found intolerable – I started to purposely sabotage stories I was working on, so that they wouldn't make the paper.[9]

Ethical dilemmas of this kind raise the question: Does journalism have a moral balance sheet? Can *any* amount of important or valuable reporting offset the worst excesses of unethical, malicious or illegal journalism within a single news organisation?

'The claim that because News Corp does some good journalism, its lying and lawbreaking can be forgiven relies on a flawed concept of character,' the ethicist Leslie Cannold told me. 'When a person of good character does something wrong, we see it is out of character, and even though that doesn't absolve them from having to make restitution for that wrong, it doesn't need to undermine our respect and belief that overall they are still a good person. But this has no relevance to News Corp, as they do not have a good reputation, for good reason, and therefore their wrongdoing is not a one-time slip that could be overlooked because of their consistent and reliable practice of doing good.'[10]

The perpetrators of unethical journalism often revert to a form of moral justification by portraying their work as socially acceptable because it purports to serve 'worthy or moral purposes', as the behavioral psychologist Albert Bandura explains it. This allows them to swat away their critics as they assuage their consciences.[11]

Rupert Murdoch has been a masterful performer in the theatrics of moral justification. When he retired as News Corp chairman in 2023, the 92-year-old grand-mogul highlighted his role, over seven decades, in defending what he described as 'the battle for the freedom of speech and, ultimately, the freedom of thought'. He lambasted 'self-serving bureaucracies' who seek to 'silence those who would question their provenance and purpose', and attacked elites who have 'open contempt for those who are not members of their rarefied class'. And he blasted most of the media for being 'in cahoots with those elites, peddling political narratives rather than pursuing the truth'.[12]

Murdoch talks a lot about his good works. 'We are not here just to sell newspapers, but if we look upon our role in the most idealistic light, that we are here to improve the world,' he told former British editor Bill Hagerty in a 1999 interview. 'I think my editors and the vast majority of the staff look upon our role as playing a very important part in society . . . they're aware of there being a certain influence and want to do good with it.'[13] News Corp's corporate website plays the same tune: 'There has always been a profound social purpose to what we do every day at News Corp, from providing news to inform the world, to sharing stories that change lives, to helping people find the homes of their dreams . . . We are committed to furthering our goals by enhancing the environment, maintaining strong governance practices, and building a diverse, equitable, inclusive and engaged workforce. We strive to be accountable and transparent about our goals and progress, and to make a meaningful contribution to the communities in which we work and live.'[14]

But not everyone in the Murdoch family has adopted the party line. James Murdoch, once seen as his father's likely successor, publicly and passionately criticised Fox News after it failed to condemn then president Trump for endorsing neo-Nazi rioters in Charlottesville, Virginia in 2017. He was joined by his wife Kathryn. 'If we're not going to say something about Nazis marching in Charlottesville, when are we going to say something?' she asked as the couple donated $1 million to the Anti-Defamation League to fight anti-Semitism.[15]

The younger Murdoch couple didn't stop there. Emboldened after banking his $2 billion personal share of the family's sale of film and broadcast assets to Disney, James harnessed his 'better angels and his better instincts', as one of his friends told *The New York Times*, to donate $100 million from the couple's non-profit foundation to progressive political causes during the 2020 presidential election cycle. After Fox News condoned Trump's denial of the election result and refused to condemn the mob attack on the US Capitol, James and Kathryn again went public, effectively declaring war on a hundred years of family media mythology. 'Spreading disinformation – whether about the election, public health, or climate change – has real world consequences,' they said. 'Many media property owners have as much responsibility for this as the elected officials who know the truth but choose instead to propagate lies.'[16]

This tension between journalism as a commercial product and journalism as a public trust has occupied the minds of principled media owners and editors for almost two centuries. Nowhere has that tension been more evident than at *The New York Times*. Since Adolph Ochs acquired the paper in 1896, the *Times* has operated more like a foundation or an educational institution than a commercial enterprise. The commitment by Ochs to journalism 'without fear or favor', write Susan Tifft and Alex Jones in their superb history of the paper, *The Trust*, is the 'enduring definition of journalistic integrity for newspapers everywhere'. When Arthur Sulzberger Jnr became the fifth *Times* publisher from the founding Ochs family in 1992, he recommitted another generation to the mission. 'Yes, we make money. But we make money to continue our search for truth,' he said.[17] The *Times* is 'a business wrapped around a church', according to a recent executive. Or as former *New Yorker* editor Robert Gottlieb explained it, 'The *Times* is in the same position as the Jews: it's expected to behave better than everybody else.'[18]

The first mainstream media owner to grapple with the conflict between journalistic profit and purpose was Joseph Pulitzer. On one hand he was largely responsible for inventing a style of newspaper sensationalism known as 'yellow journalism', which he later toned down. At the same time, he was passionately committed to the notion of the press as 'the only great organized force which is actively and as a body upholding the standard of civic righteousness'. The result – his New York *World* – was 'the most earnest, powerful and efficient social conscience yet seen in journalism', according to his biographer W.A. Swanberg.[19]

Pulitzer's serious intent was permanently cemented when he left a bequest in his will that created the Pulitzer Prizes, America's prestigious awards for journalism and other arts, and established Columbia University's school of journalism. 'Above knowledge, above news, above intelligence, the heart and soul of a paper lie in its moral sense, in its courage, its integrity, its humanity, its sympathy for the oppressed, its independence, its devotion to the public welfare, its anxiety to render public service' is how he encapsulated his view of the purpose of a newspaper. 'There is not a crime, there is not a dodge, there is not a trick, there is not a swindle, there is not a vice which does not live by secrecy,' he once told his secretary. 'Get these things out in the open, describe them, attack them, ridicule them in the press, and sooner or later public opinion will sweep them away.'[20]

One of Pulitzer's early competitors in St. Louis was another on-the-rise newspaper magnate with surprisingly egalitarian instincts for a capitalist. Edward Scripps, known to everyone as E.W., was the youngest of thirteen children and worked as a printer's apprentice before borrowing $10,000 from his family to launch his first news-paper, the *Cleveland Press*, in 1878. Over the next quarter-century he built America's first large-scale newspaper chain, with forty mast-heads. Where many newspapers in the late 1880s cost five cents, Scripps sold his for a penny, he said, to help working men and women 'protect themselves from the brutal force and chicanery of the ruling and employing class'.[21]

Scripps then embarked on what was an extraordinary pursuit for a wealthy media proprietor – he used his influence and his news-papers to agitate for rich Americans (like himself) to pay more tax.

In a telegram to President Woodrow Wilson on the eve of World War One, he argued that higher income and inheritance taxes were needed to fund the war. Anyone earning more than $100,000 ($2.2 million today) should pay the most, he said, while acknowledging that 'such legislation would cost me much more than half my present income'. He promoted the concept of 'a conscription of wealth' in a remarkably frank pitch to the House of Representatives Ways and Means Committee: 'Some of us have very large incomes. We employ servants who produce nothing for the common good and only minister to our vices. We purchase costly and showy clothing, houses, food, furniture, automobiles, jewelry, etc., etc., the production of which has taken the labor of many hundreds of thousands of men and women, who if they were not so employed would be producing other commodities in such quantity as to cheapen them and make them more accessible to the poor. An enormously high rate of Income Tax would have the effect of diverting all this labor, what is given to practically useless things, into other channels where production would be useful to the whole people.'[22]

The campaign led by Scripps was instrumental in recalibrating the US tax system. By the end of the war in 1918, the tax rate for the richest Americans had risen from 15 per cent to as high as 77 per cent. Although it soon dropped back down, Scripps himself began to grumble about the personal impact of his campaign. In 1921 he complained to President Warren Harding about 'absurd' and 'unreasonable' tax levels, but also admitted that by legally keeping profits inside his business he had successfully avoided his tax liability.[23]

Using journalism to make the world a better place was the ambition of *Time* magazine, Henry Luce's great twentieth-century editorial project. Luce was a media owner who was animated chiefly by ideas, not money. He tried to use his power to nudge the world towards his version of a better place. From the late 1930s, as fascism stalked Europe and Americans looked the other way, Luce positioned his magazines as a kind of alternative State Department, agitating for the US to enter the war to prevent a global catastrophe. *Time* and its stablemate

Life campaigned against the isolationists and 'appeasers' in America who, according to *Life*, were 'prepared to see Great Britain defeated and Hitler's power extended to the very sea gates of America'. Luce's belief in the idea of journalism-as-policy underpinned his landmark 1941 *Life* essay 'The American Century', in which he asserted that America's failure to act as a world power created 'disastrous consequences for themselves and for all mankind'.[24]

Two years later, as World War Two headed towards its conclusion, Luce attempted to map out an effective postwar terrain in 'The Reorganisation of the World', his ambitiously titled treatise that melded the immediacy of journalism with the gravitas of policy formulation. Operating like 'a state within a state', *Time* was unlike any other conventional media organisation. Stories filed by its national and international correspondents were pondered at the company's New York headquarters 'in the light of Lucean policy decisions', wrote Luce's biographer John Kobler. These deliberations were often accompanied by conferences and staff luncheons that resembled earnest meetings of the US National Security Council, and editors and executives would frequently take 'quick fact-finding trips like congressmen'.[25]

Unlike his mogul peers, Luce's sense of noblesse oblige extended well beyond journalism. Since its creation in 1936, the Luce Foundation has granted more than $1 billion to support Asian studies, theology, higher education, public affairs and public policy; it funds positions at American private colleges and universities, runs internships for potential leaders in Asia, and honours Luce's interest in 'ultimate questions'.

Luce wasn't the only media owner whose journalism was motivated by good intentions, not just money, throughout the twentieth century. After buying *The Washington Post* in 1933, Eugene Meyer not only pledged to pursue the truth, but to 'make sacrifices of its material fortunes, if such a course be necessary for public good'.[26] The *Post* spent eighty years under the custodianship of three generations of Meyers before it was sold to Amazon owner Jeff Bezos by Eugene's grandson Donald Graham, the family's last publisher.

It was a steely commitment to editorial integrity by Graham's mother, the much admired Katharine Graham, that provided the moral support for the Watergate investigation that ended Richard Nixon's presidency. Hers was the makeover story of an 'insecure, dowdy, poor little rich girl into The Most Powerful Woman in America, framed within the parallel tale of how a puny third-rate daily changed into a fearsome giant', wrote Gloria Cooper in the *Columbia Journalism Review*. Katharine Graham ran the *Post* for twenty-eight years in a commitment to her father's conviction that 'the American people could be relied upon to do the right thing when they know the facts'.[27] Several decades later, under the ownership of Bezos and the editorship of Marty Baron, the *Post* formalised that sentiment into a daily front-page slogan: 'Democracy Dies in Darkness'. It was Bezos who signed off on the new slogan and it has been Bezos who, under intense scrutiny from *Post* staff and the journalism world more broadly, has adhered to its ethos.

Roy (later Lord) Thomson was another magnate who refused to dumb down his journalism to make more money (although he still made plenty). The owner of more than 200 newspapers in Canada, the US and Britain, including *The Scotsman* and London's *Times* and *Sunday Times*, Thomson had a coy sense of duty that is reflected in the words on his memorial stone at St Paul's Cathedral in London: 'Lord Thomson of Fleet. He gave new direction to the British newspaper industry. A strange and adventurous man from nowhere, ennobled by the great virtues of courage, and integrity, and faithfulness.'[28] Thomson even handed out a printed card that explained his credo: 'I can state with the utmost emphasis that no person or group can buy or influence editorial support from any newspaper in the Thomson group ... I do not believe that a newspaper can be run properly unless its editorial columns are run freely and independently by a highly skilled and dedicated professional journalist. This is and will continue to be my policy.'[29]

The Fairfax family in Australia went further, creating a 'statement of principles' to distinguish *The Sydney Morning Herald* from its rough-and-tumble Murdoch tabloid competitors through the 1980s, beginning with four wholesome principles that now seem quaintly anachronistic:

Belief in the Christian faith, sympathy with those of other religions, and belief that those of no religion are still under the care of God;

Loyalty to the Sovereign and support of the British monarchy as an institution;

Belief that newspapers, existing as a service to the public, must inform the public accurately and impartially and must ensure fairness in advertising;

Belief that commentary should have no other aim but the welfare of the community, but with respect for the rights of people of other nations.

I joined an intimate lunch with two of those family custodians at a fashionable Indian restaurant in Washington in 2018. Don Graham and John B. Fairfax (a co-shareholder in my company, Private Media) were part of their family's last generation of ownership of two great newspapers, *The Washington Post* and *The Sydney Morning Herald*. Both in their seventies and sharp as tacks, they were far removed from the stereotypical image of omnivorous media moguls as the lunch table sparkled with discussion about the role and responsibility of journalism in the Trump era. There was no mention of deals or money, just the idea that owning an important newspaper was a business *and* a mission, especially in uncomfortable times.

Anyone looking for another working model of a modern news organisation built on editorial integrity should go to Paris, where *Le Monde* has become one of the great postwar journalism success stories. With more than 500 journalists reporting on international, national, economic and cultural news, this iconic French newspaper defends humanist and progressive values and supports democracy against all forms of authoritarianism. 'It is not linked to any political party,' declares the paper's ethics charter. 'Its editorials, which are not signed, are the opinion of the entire editorial staff. It strives to keep public debate alive, notably by publishing opinion pieces written by people outside the editorial staff. In reading *Le Monde*, the reader is empowered to freely form an opinion.'

This is a charter no autocratic media mogul would dream of supporting, but at *Le Monde* every shareholder is required to sign it. In 2019 that independence was threatened after a key shareholding change, provoking an intense public campaign that reaffirmed the paper's editorial integrity by forcing every shareholder to formally and publicly support the mission. An open letter demanding those guarantees from all shareholders was signed by 460 of the paper's journalists. 'Between those who read and those who write,' said the paper's director Jérôme Fenoglio, 'this show of force reflects a shared responsibility: the defense of a common good.'[30]

A few miles away, on the right bank of the Seine River, are the offices of another exceptional experiment in quality French journalism, *Mediapart*. Established in 2008 by *Le Monde*'s former editor-in-chief, Edwy Plenel, this subscription-only investigative website (which refuses to carry any advertising, to ensure its journalism can't be commercially influenced) is a success story of high-grade, independent journalism at scale. Owned by a non-profit endowment whose capital is mandated to be 'inviolable, non-transferable, and non-purchasable', *Mediapart* has some 150 staff, more than 200,000 paying subscribers, and generates around $24 million in annual revenues.[31]

Its decade-long investigation of former French president Nicolas Sarkozy over the illegal funding of his 2007 election campaign by Libyan dictator Muammar Gaddafi resulted in Sarkozy's conviction in 2021 for corruption and influence peddling. He was sentenced to three years in prison, two of them suspended and one year on home detention wearing an electronic bracelet, and was banned from public office or voting for three years.[32] *Mediapart* again made news, rather than just reporting it, when its offices were raided in 2019 by Paris prosecutors on a fishing expedition for sources behind an investigation into a disgraced former aide to French president Emmanuel Macron. The aide, Alexandre Benalla, had been fired after hitting a protester at a demonstration. *Mediapart*'s investigation revealed business dealings by Benalla and his associates at the Élysée Palace with a Russian oligarch close to Vladimir Putin. A French court later ruled that the state's attempted search of *Mediapart*'s office was 'neither necessary in a democratic society, nor proportionate to the objective sought'.[33]

Le Monde and *Mediapart* are the gold standard in safeguarding against proprietorial interference. They both started life with their editorial independence enshrined in a legal agreement, with no mogul in control, and supported by subscribers who passionately endorse those precepts. It's a construct that is almost unique to not-for-profit editorial entities, a small group that also includes *The Guardian*, the London-based multinational progressive-leaning news organisation owned by the 88-year-old philanthropic Scott Trust.

There aren't many independent newsrooms with the scale or risk appetite of *The Guardian* or *Mediapart*. Another global exemplar is *Rappler*, the Filipino website created in 2012 by the experienced news broadcaster Maria Ressa, together with a small group of like-minded journalists and financial backers. *Rappler* is explicit in its mission. 'Journalism and ethics go hand in hand because credibility is what makes journalists effective in what they do: truth-telling,' reads its website page covering editorial standards and guidelines. 'Journalism is about public service . . . It's not about self-indulgence, personal interest, or even privileges.'[34]

Four years after it was launched, following the election of Rodrigo Duterte as president of the Philippines, *Rappler* was presented with the challenge of reporting on a dictatorial leader whose so-called war on drugs killed more than 12,000 Filipinos, mostly urban poor, according to Human Rights Watch. 'For *Rappler*, the blowback was swift: first online, mostly on Facebook, with a deluge of insults and threats to its reporters and Ressa in particular,' reported *The New Yorker*. 'Then came a barrage of lawsuits, so many that if the potential jail sentences from them were added up, Ressa would be imprisoned for more than a hundred years.'[35]

Although Ressa still faces several criminal cases, her doggedness was acknowledged when she was awarded the 2021 Nobel Peace Prize, alongside the Russian editor Dmitry Muratov. In her typically feisty way, she used her increased profile to attack Facebook for failing to prevent the spread of disinformation and allowing its algorithms to 'prioritize the spread of lies laced with anger and hate over facts'.[36]

Authentic, robustly funded independent journalism stands in stark contrast to the business model of autocratic media proprietors, who instinctively view editorial autonomy by editors and staff as tantamount to allowing the lunatics to take over the asylum. The exception is the increasingly bizarre Elon Musk, the world's most recent mogul, who has created a case study in which the *owner* is the lunatic running the asylum.

Musk's purchase of Twitter in 2022 created a new paradigm for reckless abuse of media power. Within a year he had trashed almost everything about Twitter (which he renamed X). He reinstated previously banned accounts that had violated Twitter's rules. He cut back content moderation, unleashing a maelstrom of misinformation and disinformation by white nationalists, anti-Semites, election-deniers and trolls. Following the October 2023 terrorist attacks by Hamas against Israel, X published manipulated images of unrelated armed conflicts that originated, according to the European Union, from video games.[37] When X published a post claiming that 'Jewish communties [*sic*] have been pushing the exact kind of dialectical hatred against whites that they claim to want people to stop using against them', Musk himself responded personally with 'You have said the actual truth.'[38] According to the digital investigations firm Memetica, the hashtag #hitlerwasright appeared 46,000 times in the six weeks after the Hamas attacks, compared with fewer than 5,000 times per month previously.[39]

Musk's next gimmick was to visit Israel in the midst of the war, where he was escorted by prime minister Benjamin Netanyahu to inspect the site of a Hamas attack. 'Netanyahu is treating Musk like the leader of a country, not as a shambolic entrepreneur who seems to delight in offending people,' wrote Martin Peers in the technology website *The Information*.[40]

Musk has been off the leash since he bought Twitter. He has tweeted anti-Semitic remarks about billionaire investor George Soros, who supports progressive causes. He ordered the words 'state-sponsored media' be added to posts by the authoritative news sources BBC and NPR, treating them like State propaganda outlets Russia Today and Chinese government websites (a policy which was later rescinded after protests).

Musk has harnessed X as a tool against his perceived enemies by adding a five-second delay to sites that don't conform to his worldview, including *The New York Times* and Facebook. 'Targeting specific competitors and reputable media outlets shows he's not serious about free speech at all,' noted Jessica Lessin, owner of *The Information*. 'It shows he will wield his power to whatever ends he wants in the moment.'[41]

Musk is just the most recent example of plutocrats using their media properties as playthings for their views. Richard Mellon Scaife, the conservative conspiracy theorist and heir to the Mellon banking and oil fortune, lost more than $100 million from the 1960s until his death in 2014 by financing publications that evangelised his political philosophy. Scaife wasn't just a vocal opponent of liberalism in America, he believed its policies would lead to the annihilation of American civilisation. 'My prime motive as a publisher was and is ideological,' he acknowledged in his memoir. 'The profit element was not uppermost.'[42]

Scaife was the prime mover behind the so-called Arkansas Project, the anti-Democrat movement of the 1980s and 1990s that targeted the Clinton presidency with allegations of scandal and illegality, described by Hillary Clinton at the time as a 'vast right-wing conspiracy'. The project deployed Scaife-funded media – the right-wing *American Spectator* magazine and the daily *Pittsburgh Tribune-Review* in his home city – to attack the Clintons for their politics, calling for an investigation into the legality of their 1970s Whitewater real estate investment, along with accusations by Arkansas state worker Paula Jones of sexual harassment by Bill Clinton, and allegations that the Clintons were responsible for the suicide of Vincent Foster, Clinton's deputy White House counsel.[43]

Rupert Murdoch has been another backer of loss-making partisan media, despite already having a vast commercial empire to ply his ideological wares. In 1995 News Corp funded *The Weekly Standard*, a magazine created by conservative journalists Bill Kristol and Fred Barnes to spruik a neoconservative political playbook. Supporting a Reaganite foreign policy and cheerleading George W. Bush's invasion of Iraq, the magazine's Republican influence reached a point where it was touted as 'the in-flight magazine of Air Force One'.[44]

After incurring estimated losses of $30 million, and with Barack Obama ensconced in the White House, Murdoch sold the *Standard* in 2009 to Philip Anschutz, a Republican oil and railroad billionaire. When Donald Trump won the presidency, splitting the conservative movement, the magazine lost its raison d'être and alienated traditional Republicans by becoming a key voice in the Never Trump movement. In 2018, two years after Trump's election, Anschutz closed the publication, much to the president's glee. 'The pathetic and dishonest *Weekly Standard*, run by failed prognosticator Bill Kristol (who, like many others, never had a clue), is flat broke and out of business,' tweeted Trump. 'Too bad. May it rest in peace!'[45]

Brazenly partisan private media is nothing new in America; before the Civil War many newspapers were effectively arms of political parties, subsidised covertly or through government printing contracts. The spectacle of rich patrons acquiring media assets for their political influence has again become more common in recent decades as the prices of those assets, and the business models supporting them, have crumbled. The reclusive climate-denialist, Brexit-supporting, conservative hedge-fund billionaire Robert Mercer – the biggest single donor to Donald Trump's 2016 presidential campaign – plowed $10 million into the controversial right-wing news site *Breitbart News*. He later sold his stake to his daughter Rebekah, another fierce Republican culture warrior, who also took control of Parler, the extremist social media website that was booted offline after its alleged role in facilitating the plans of rioters at the US Capitol in 2021.

In 2017, the same year as Mercer invested in *Breitbart*, the philanthropist billionaire Laurene Powell Jobs, widow of Steve Jobs, acquired a majority stake in *The Atlantic*, the grand American cultural and political magazine that was founded in 1857. Worth an estimated $12 billion and with progressive instincts, Powell Jobs donated substantial amounts to Joe Biden's election campaigns in 2020 and 2023. But she hasn't interfered with the *The Atlantic*'s editorial direction, and in her desire to make it a sustainable model for quality journalism she's funded more than a hundred additional employees, half of them in the newsroom.

The English insurance magnate Sir Clive Cowdery is another wealthy benefactor with centre-left values who has bought himself an outlet for his views. His vehicle, *Prospect*, is a monthly magazine with a heavy emphasis on analysing and campaigning for serious British policy ideas. *Prospect* is owned by Cowdery's not-for-profit Resolution Foundation, and has been, in practice, consistently not for profit.

———

Making moral decisions in journalism – right/wrong, good/bad, honest/deceptive – is tricky and often highly subjective. Issues such as objectivity, privacy, legality, public interest and transparency sound like straightforward concepts until you're sitting behind a news desk making rapid-fire calls on what to publish or suppress while surrounded by conflicting advice, hovering lawyers, a wavering inner voice and an impending deadline.

Can subterfuge in journalism, for example, ever be justified? Is there a valid case for duplicity if it serves the public interest?

A classic example of one newspaper's approach to that ethical dilemma was the 25-part *Chicago Sun-Times* series in 1978 that uncovered corruption in the city's restaurants and bars. It began after reporter Pam Zekman, who had spent years gathering information about a system of bribes being paid to Chicago liquor and health inspectors and other public officials, couldn't convince her sources to confirm the illegality on the record. The only way to expose the corruption, Zekman told her editors, was to get *inside* the system. To do that, the *Sun-Times* came up with a radical, highly controversial idea – it bought a bar for $18,000, staffed it with reporters and concealed photographers, and called it The Mirage. Over four months of bartending and observing, they gathered evidence that resulted in the suspension or dismissal of more than a dozen officials, bribery convictions of eighteen city electrical inspectors, the establishing of an Office of Professional Review by Chicago's mayor, and the creation of an Illinois government taskforce, dubbed the 'Mirage Unit', to uncover tax fraud.[46]

The practice of undercover journalism – where reporters covertly infiltrate institutions to reveal important information that can't be accessed any other way – has a long and mainly proud history. In Ghana, investigative journalist Anas Aremeyaw Anas has spent decades posing as someone else to expose human rights violations and corruption. He started his career as an infiltrator working as a street hawker on a major highway in Accra, observing corrupt police officers taking bribes from unlicensed traders. Since then he has uncovered widespread child abuse; theft of food donations; bribery by the president of the country's top football body; pervasive judicial corruption that allowed accused murderers, drug traffickers and rapists to go free; trafficking of Chinese girls; bogus doctors providing illegal abortions; African businesses channelling government money into offshore accounts; abuse of patients in Ghana's biggest psychiatric hospital; teenagers forced into prostitution at a large brothel; maggot-infested flour used to produce biscuits at a large confectionery factory; the maltreatment and deaths of foreign prisoners in a Thai jail. All these exposures came about through deception.[47]

Many of investigative journalism's biggest exposés – political malpractice, conflict of interest, financial fraud, abuse of power, mismanagement of public money – have resulted from private information that someone wanted to conceal. 'Undercover investigative work has an honorable tradition and plays a vital role in exposing wrongdoing. It is part of an open society,' the British Press Complaints Committee stated after its investigation into News Corp's illegal phone hacking. 'But it risks being devalued if its use cannot be justified in the public interest.'[48]

New York University's database of undercover journalism, dating back to the 1800s, chronicles the scale of reporting that has used subversive techniques to unearth bad things. Journalists have revealed shocking conditions inside prisons, hospitals and clinics by working as guards or posing as patients or staff; they have joined cults and religious groups to show what happens inside them; they have become teachers or students to disclose the dark side of what goes on in certain schools; used hidden cameras to unmask perpetrators who solicit sex with minors online; taken jobs in sweatshops, factories and supermarkets to expose the poor working conditions; and have become debt collectors and slum dwellers. A white reporter from Pittsburgh went undercover in 1948 to live as a light-skinned black man in the deep south. In 1887 the famous New York journalist Nellie Bly immersed herself in the Women's Lunatic Asylum to document the appalling living conditions and maltreatment of patients.

The legality of undercover journalism remains fuzzy, even under US constitutional protections. In 1992 the *Primetime Live* program on ABC ran a story investigating employees in the meat department at Food Lion grocery stores in North and South Carolina, where old meat washed with bleach to kill the odour had been sold, along with cheese gnawed by rats. The program's producers secured jobs at the stores after submitting applications with false references, then used hidden cameras to secretly record employees. Three years later Food Lion sued ABC for fraud, breach of loyalty, trespass and unfair trade practices. A jury found ABC liable for fraud, awarding Food Lion $1,400 in compensatory damages, $5.5 million in punitive damages for fraud, and $2 in nominal damages for breach of loyalty and trespass. But two higher courts later struck out all but the $2 award, and in 2023 an appellate court lowered the bar for undercover reporting even further when it ruled in favour of constitutionally protected news-gathering in a case where PETA (People for the Ethical Treatment of Animals) challenged a North Carolina law against undercover investigations at agricultural facilities.

In their book *Undercover Reporting, Deception, and Betrayal in Journalism*, academics Andrea Carson and Denis Muller argue that deception is ethically justifiable 'under very specific conditions'. They provide a six-point checklist for journalists (and audiences) to test whether deception and betrayal are warranted:

- Is the information sufficiently vital to the public interest to justify deception?
- Were other methods considered and was deception the only way to get the story?
- Was the use of deception revealed to the audience and the reasons explained?
- Were there reasonable grounds for suspecting the target of the deception was engaged in activity contrary to the public interest?
- Was the operation carried out with a risk strategy so it would not imperil a formal investigation by competent authorities?
- Did the test of what is 'sufficiently vital' to the public interest include an objective assessment of harm or wrongdoing?[49]

In the end, of course, the judgements made by editors and owners about what is 'sufficiently vital' to the public interest are unmeasurable and unaccountable. This is the ambiguity that allows the purveyors of sensationalism, voyeurism and phone-hacking to justify almost *any* decision to publish *anything* with a straight face.

The same ethical challenges apply to so-called chequebook journalism, the practice – widespread in sensationalist popular media – of paying celebrities and other sources for their salacious stories. It's a technique that raises a fundamental question: Is it *ever* legitimate to pay for important public interest information that would otherwise never be revealed?

A classic case occurred in Britain in 2009 when *The Daily Telegraph* secured a computer disk containing four years' worth of confidential information about the misuse of expenses claims by members of parliament – a scoop later described by the then British prime minister Gordon Brown as 'the biggest parliamentary scandal for two centuries'. The leaked records revealed the details of extensive rorting by MPs who claimed expenses and mortgage interest payments on their second homes in London. The revelations led to numerous resignations, including the Speaker of the House of Commons, and the prosecution and imprisonment of members of parliament.[50]

When the *Telegraph* later revealed it had paid £110,000 to secure the files from a government official responsible for processing parliamentary expenses – described colourfully as a 'Whitehall mole' by other media – there was widespread support for the newspaper's decision to pay for critical information that would otherwise have remained secret.

But the biggest ethical minefield lurking in almost every newsroom in democratic societies is the issue of *objectivity*. 'Show me a man who claims he's completely objective, and I'll show you a man with self-delusions,' said Henry Luce. 'Impartiality is often an impediment to truth,' he told a gathering of his advertising salesmen in 1939. '*Time* will not allow the stuffed dummy of impartiality to stand in the way of telling the truth as it sees it.'[51]

In an age of fake news and social media misinformation, impartiality is sometimes disparaged by another name – 'both-sides-ism', which is the idea of giving equal weight to every opposing argument, regardless of its accuracy or validity. At the Australian Broadcasting Corporation, the national broadcaster, both-sides-ism was taken to a laughable level during the country's 2023 referendum on Indigenous recognition when all ABC television, radio and online producers were required to fill in a form after every referendum story listing the exact number of minutes allocated to the Yes case and the No case, so as to demonstrate an equal balance.

Maybe someone at the ABC should have asked a seasoned pro like Marty Baron, the *Washington Post*'s editor during the Trump years, about the practical meaning of objectivity. 'When we've done our work with requisite rigor and thoroughness (also known as solid, objective reporting) we should tell people what we've learned and what remains unknown – directly, straightforwardly, unflinchingly – just as people in lots of other professions do when they're doing their jobs correctly,' said Baron. 'That's what "objectivity" was intended to mean when the term was developed for journalism more than a century ago.'[52]

Not everyone agrees with Baron. Describing this traditional concept of objectivity as 'the view from nowhere', the respected New York University journalism professor Jay Rosen says journalists are effectively telling their audiences, 'I don't have a point of view, I don't have a starting point, I don't have a philosophy, I don't have an ideology. I'm just telling you the way it is. So believe it, because this is the way it is.'[53] Objective journalism, according to the famous twentieth-century gonzo reporter Hunter S. Thompson, is a 'pompous contradiction in terms' which can only be found in 'box scores, race results, and stock market tabulations'.[54] *New Yorker* writer Masha Gessen believes 'moral clarity' would be a better guiding ideal for journalism than objectivity, especially since the Trump presidency which 'served to normalize things that ought not be normalized'.[55]

The reason objectivity is a lie, says Mathias Döpfner, CEO of the giant German news publisher Axel Springer, is because journalism is made by human beings and humans all have preferences. 'If you run a story and if you position it prominently or big or small, that's already a judgment,' he told *The New Yorker*'s editor, David Remnick. 'I think it is not about objectivity or neutrality, it is about plurality.'[56]

Döpfner's company, which owns *Die Welt* and *Bild* in Germany, *Politico* globally, and many other media properties, has made its own attempt to apply ethical guardrails to its journalism by requiring its employees, in their contracts, to commit to a series of so-called 'Essentials', formulated by the company's founder Axel Springer in 1967 and since updated 'in order to adapt them to the social understanding of our company and our view of the world'. The company currently lists five Essentials:

- We stand up for freedom, the rule of law, democracy and a united Europe.
- We support the Jewish people and the right of existence of the State of Israel.
- We advocate the transatlantic alliance between the United States of America and Europe.
- We uphold the principles of a free market economy and its social responsibility.
- We reject political and religious extremism and all forms of racism and sexual discrimination.[57]

'I think it is a very important element of transparency and honesty of a media company,' Döpfner told Remnick. 'It is almost like a constitution of the company. Those are our fundamental social values, and that has nothing to do with party politics, with people politics, or with day-to-day politics.'

The obvious reason why no other serious mainstream media organisation has followed Springer's approach, regardless of the validity or otherwise of its Essentials, is that requiring editorial staff to follow specified policies is the antithesis of objective ethical journalism. It's precisely how media autocrats impose their views and preferences on their journalists – not by employment *contract* but by employment *tenure*.

There is no perfect template for the practice of ethical journalism, only examples of the least imperfect. The best of these, arguably, is the current model of *The New York Times* and *The Washington Post*, whereby a deeply supportive proprietor or board of owners, who are publicly committed to editorial excellence and fairness, appoint highly capable editors with whom they share a vision of journalism and society, and whose professional judgement they respect. In this model a culture of constant dialogue between owners and editors is maintained, with both dedicated to strong, long-term financial viability that secures the resources needed to underpin their mission.

But even the best models, in the end, are only as ethical as the people running them. A seemingly respectable news organisation may have an ethics charter, or a list of essentials, or rules of editorial independence. But if it's run by a scoundrel its journalism will be as tainted as the journalism of any news dictatorship.

The aspiration for objectivity in journalism is getting harder as the media polarises and its business model sags. 'With print media declining and Facebook and Google taking the lion's share of online ad revenue, news outlets must focus on getting paying customers,' says Matthew Pressman, assistant professor of journalism at Seton Hall University.[58] Another reason why old-fashioned impartial journalism is fading fast is that readers 'are bathed on the web in highly partisan content that whets their appetite for more opinionated news', says *The Economist*. 'The division between news and comment, clear on paper in American journalism, dissolves on the internet.' And unlike advertisers, 'readers love opinion'.[59]

In any case, as we've seen, the concept of editorial objectivity is superfluous in media organisations that are dominated by an owner's *personal* moral compass. While professions like medicine, science and the law have closely monitored processes of ethical oversight, the conduct of journalism is dependent entirely on the whims of its owners, ranging from rational (Luce and Ochs) to reckless (Musk and Murdoch).

Hearst was a dictator and an ideologue who supported Hitler's rise to power and constantly berated the so-called 'yellow races', especially the Japanese, who he claimed were conspiring to usurp the 'white races' internationally. 'He wielded vast and scary ideological power at the nexus of journalism, entertainment and politics for over fifty years, in an arc of greed and influence-mongering that bolted back and forth across the nation from the mining West to the intellectual and political control center of New York and back again to Hollywood,' wrote Frank Dana in *The Nation*. 'Money is simply power in cold storage,' Hearst once described his credo.[60]

Conrad Black's skewed morality first revealed itself when he was in grade nine: assisted by three other students at Toronto's elite, all-boys Upper Canada College, he was accused of stealing a cache of final exam papers from the school office and expelled for cheating. But the real scam, he later confessed, wasn't cheating, it was selling the stolen exam papers to other students, using copies of their academic records to identify those who would be prepared to pay the most for them. 'One supplicant actually knelt in front of me begging for an examination paper,' wrote Black in *A Life in Progress*, while admitting he was 'neither proud nor ashamed of what happened'.[61] He was still neither proud nor ashamed forty-eight years later, when his conviction for fraud landed him thirty-seven months in Cubicle 30, Unit B-1 at the Coleman Federal Correctional Complex in central Florida.

Robert Maxwell was another media owner with no detectable interest in ethics. He offered a window into his moral mindset when Conrad Black was visiting Headington Hall, Maxwell's family mansion in Oxford. Showing his visitor a large cabinet housing a formidable dinner service, Maxwell revealed he had unearthed it in the French zone while he was part of the British army occupation of Berlin in 1945. While he and his men were loading it onto their trucks, a representative of the French commandant arrived and told him to put it back. As he explained to Black, Maxwell had a better idea: 'You designate someone to assist my men to divide it exactly in two. I'll deliver one half to your attention anywhere you want in the three western allied zones, and I'll take care of the other half.' 'Very good idea, Captain,' came the reply.[62]

These were not individuals who concerned themselves with encumbrances like an ethical framework. Nor did most of them bother with the idea of giving back to society, despite being beneficiaries of a social licence that provided them with extraordinary power, money and influence. Rupert Murdoch, for example, has never expressed any visible interest in philanthropy or making a societal contribution, despite his $18 billion net worth. When his biographer William Shawcross asked him, in a *Vanity Fair* interview in 1999, 'Think of your predecessors as robber barons – people such as Rockefeller and Carnegie, fierce businessmen who also set up vast philanthropic institutions which have had a lasting impact for good ... Don't you want to do that?' Murdoch replied that he had already started putting aside a 'very large portion' of his family's assets for charitable giving. 'I feel very strongly that the cause private philanthropy can do a lot about is education,' he said. 'Seeing that every talented kid gets equal opportunity is the thing that interests me most.' Asked by Shawcross how big he hoped to grow his philanthropic giving, Murdoch responded, 'That depends, I guess, on how well News Corp does.'[63]

Fifteen years later, *Inside Philanthropy* reported that although Murdoch had a foundation in his name, it held no assets and hadn't made a grant since 2008. He did, however, donate $1 million to charities that supported the victims of crime, in memory of murdered British teenager Milly Dowler whose phone had been hacked by his newspaper. 'The behavior that the *News of the World* exhibited towards the Dowlers was abhorrent and I hope this donation underscores my regret for the company's role in this awful event,' he said as he announced a donation that constituted 0.011 per cent of News Corp's revenues at the time and had 'PR' stamped all over it.[64]

The reason Murdoch and his UK chief Rebekah Brooks were able to maintain plausible deniability for years after the phone hacking revelations, in the view of the Canadian management thinker Roger L. Martin, is because they never asked their editors and journalists one simple question: How did you get that scoop? 'Simply failing to ask the question would have sent an extremely powerful signal to the troops that it didn't matter how you got the scoop, just that you do indeed get it: Hack the cellphones of kidnapped children, bribe police, do whatever it takes,' Martin wrote in the *Daily Beast*, adding:

> I've no doubt that Brooks and Murdoch believe they were not responsible for the actions at the heart of this scandal, just as Col. Oran K. Henderson, the brigade commander who ordered the attack on My Lai in 1968, was certain he wasn't responsible for that outcome.
>
> Henderson had urged his officers to 'go in there aggressively, close with the enemy and wipe them out for good,' an order that immediately preceded his men executing between 350 and 500 Vietnamese women, children, and unarmed men. Accused of then taking part in an elaborate coverup, Henderson denied being told about the murder of civilians. Ultimately, the military court backed him up. But of course we all know that 'not guilty' is a legal outcome that should not be confused with 'innocent.'[65]

Murdoch's denial of responsibility for phone hacking sits uncomfortably even with his loyal corporate adviser Irwin Stelzer. 'Rupert is the only one who really knows in borderline cases just where the line between responsible and irresponsible, between acceptable and unacceptable, between what he characterizes as "the bawdy and the vulgar" can be drawn,' Stelzer wrote in his hagiography *The Murdoch Method: Notes on Running a Media Empire*.[66]

If Murdoch really knew the location of the line between 'responsible and irresponsible' during his seven decades at the helm of News Corp and Fox News, and if his subordinates were aware of that line, just like they've been acutely aware of everything else that's important to Murdoch, how is it possible to explain phone hacking, or police bribery by dozens of his senior staff? Or his TV network's support for a 'stolen' election, or its feverish attacks on climate science or Covid vaccines? Or the decades of personal denigration at *The Australian*, or the predatory culture of sexual harassment at Fox, which has resulted in more than $200 million in confidential settlements being paid to dozens of women? Or the payment of $900 million to competitors whose business secrets were stolen by a News Corp subsidiary that was led by an executive who, in his court testimony, stated, 'I work for a man who wants it all, and doesn't understand anybody telling him he can't have it all.'[67]

At its extreme, an ethically constrained media organisation led by a powerful autocrat has many of the characteristics of a cult. At News Corp's annual, black-tie journalism awards dinner in Australia, for example, the theme is corporate loyalty and the only prize winners are Murdoch employees. 'The journalism that we do at News Corp is so important,' the winner of the night's highest honour, the Sir Keith Murdoch Award, told her assembled colleagues in 2018. 'We should all be proud of it, and we should never allow ourselves to be defined by our critics.' Her fealty was reinforced by the company's global CEO Robert Thomson: 'Our journalistic vocation – our calling – is to question, to critique, to challenge,' he told the diners. 'We believe in the contest of ideas and not in the conquest of ideology.'[68]

It never occurred to me, when I resigned as a Murdoch editor, that I had been a member of a cult. But over the years, as I've watched News Corp and Fox News dissolve into propaganda operations that devalue facts, construct and attack lists of enemies, and treat ethics as an alien concept, the resemblance has become striking. Even though they operate under societal protections based on practising journalism in the interests of democracy, these companies have some of the key characteristics of a privately controlled messianic cult: they are led by an authoritarian leader, demand unwavering loyalty from adherents, follow a prescribed dogma, and exist in a culture of 'us versus them'.

When I told Rupert Murdoch I was leaving News Corp he offered me the deputy editorship of the London *Sunday Times* as an inducement to stay. It was a prestigious role; a clear signal that I could keep rising up his corporate ladder. But rather than motivating me to stay, his offer reinforced my principal reason for leaving. I needed to get out *before* I ascended any further up his corporate ladder, before ego became the quicksand that sucked me into a morally compromised place.

I was thirty-eight years old, earning one of the highest salaries in journalism, with access to anyone on Murdoch's Rolodex. Two years earlier, when I accepted his offer to run the Melbourne *Herald*, I'd tried to weigh the risks of working for a dominating proprietor. Before accepting, and after re-reading every Murdoch biography then published, I put my odds of surviving at News Corp at fifty-fifty. When I sent him a four-page outline of my vision for the paper, with a substantial list of resources, staff and budget needed to reinvent *The Herald*, he immediately faxed back with a scrawled 'Agreed'. And as he worked his persuasive charm on me, I became energised by the prospect of leading the revival of a once-great newspaper.

In my enthusiasm, I didn't envisage I was entering some kind of moral swamp. I'd come from a news organisation with a rock-solid ethical framework. But after a year at News Corp I found myself being tested, regularly, by ethical hurdles that became too precipitous for me to jump – pressure to sack a journalist because Murdoch didn't like his politics, pressure to downplay stories about airline crashes because News Corp at that time owned half an airline, pressure to support a favoured political party in a state election.

When I finally resigned, I left without a payout because I refused to sign a non-disclosure agreement that would have gagged me from ever talking or writing about my experiences at the company. We all need to decide for ourselves what we can live with; other people with their own financial, ideological or personal considerations often make a different choice.

But for me, the compromise was too great. I left without ever looking back because, naively or idealistically (or both), I believed, and still do, that professional journalism is a public trust.

Give 'em
What They Want

'Rupe doesn't dictate public tastes, you know. He has lots of bosses out there. Millions of them. The public tells him what they want to read and Rupe gives it to them.'[1]

Steve Dunleavy was a loud-mouthed defender of give-the-public-what-they-want journalism. Before his death in 2019, he worked for thirty-two years as a reporter at Murdoch's *New York Post* and its tabloid television stablemate *A Current Affair*. 'I lost count of the number of times I posed as a cop, a public servant or a funeral director,' he once boasted.[2]

Dunleavy was a practitioner of *journalism that interests the public* (not to be confused with *public interest journalism*), a formula embraced by William Randolph Hearst in San Francisco in 1887 and Rupert Murdoch in Adelaide in 1952, two privileged sons who created commercial media empires that pandered to populist tastes without bothering too much about civic responsibility. 'We're not here to pass ourselves off as intellectuals,' Murdoch told the *Los Angeles Times* in 1976. 'We're here to give the public what they want. You can have all the intellectual material you like, win Pulitzer prizes, and say you're great, but there's no way of testing whether the public likes it or not.'[3] A newspaper, said Lord Northcliffe, 'is to be made to pay. Let it deal with what interests the mass of people. Let it give the public what it wants.'[4]

Such journalism requires controversy, emotion or conflict. 'The modern editor of the popular journal does not care for facts,' said Hearst. 'The editor wants novelty. The editor has no objection to facts if they are also novelty. But he would prefer a novelty that is not a fact to a fact that is not a novelty.'[5] Papers with the highest news and literary quality, claimed Hearst, had the lowest circulations and made the least money. His top editor, Arthur McEwen, explained the three-step editorial methodology used by Hearst's newspapers to activate their readers: you wanted them to say, 'Gee whiz!' when they saw the front page, 'Holy Moses!' when they saw page two, and leap from their seats shouting, 'God a'mighty!' by page three.[6] Hearst's journalism, his star columnist Ambrose Bierce once observed, had 'all the reality of masturbation'.[7]

The rise of the Hearst empire was a crucial juncture in the evolution of commercial media. It was the story of how an amoral young man mastered the techniques of sensationalising journalism to 'seduce its public, and debauch its practitioners', as *Time*'s obituary later described the Hearstian formula that accumulated forty-three daily and Sunday newspapers, eight radio stations, thirteen national magazines, two film companies and three news services.[8] 'Truth and taste were tiresome encumbrances to Hearst's noisy, splashy brand of sensationalism,' wrote Richard Kluger in *The Paper*. 'His formula was a yet more lurid display of sex, crime, and scandal news, confected scoops and crusades, and an editorial page favoring such avowedly populist causes as the eight-hour workday, public ownership of utilities, and the cheap-money monetary policies of William Jennings Bryan.'[9]

As well as seducing and shocking its readers, Hearst's journalism enraged the American establishment by adopting 'every brand of faking, distortion, misquotation and dishonesty', according to Hamilton Basso in *The New Republic* in 1935. 'He has filled his papers with claptrap, triviality, sob-stuff and tripe. And, in doing so, he has debauched the minds, tastes and emotions of millions of his readers – glorifying all that is mean and tawdry, damning or ignoring all that is worthy and important.'[10]

But Hearst's success in twisting news into entertainment was grudgingly acknowledged by at least some of his critics. 'He shook journalism to its foundations, and exposed the incompetence of more than one highly smug newspaper proprietor,' wrote the famous columnist H.L. Mencken in *The American Mercury* in 1928. 'What the populace really wanted was simply a roaring show – and he brought to the business of giving it [*sic*] that show a resourcefulness that was unparalleled and a daring that was stupendous. It was quite impossible for the old-fashioned papers to stand up to him; they had to follow him or perish.'[11]

Nine years after Hearst introduced populist journalism to San Francisco, an equally radical newspaper was launched in England, pitched at the country's burgeoning lower middle-class. Alfred Harmsworth (later Lord Northcliffe) believed there was little interest in the earnest, bland reporting of the British newspapers of the day, but his intuition told him there would be a voracious market for journalism about entertainment and bad deeds. The result was the *Daily Mail*, an inspired vision by a 31-year-old publisher who had already proved his flair for tapping the popular mood with three successful magazines – *Answers* (answering questions from readers like 'How to Cure Freckles', 'Why Jews Don't Ride Bicycles' and 'Can Monkeys Smoke?'), *Comic Cuts* (tagline: 'Amusing without being Vulgar') and the women's journal *Forget-Me-Not*.

The *Mail* wasted no time mining the rich seam of British criminal life. 'Crime exclusives are noticed by the public more than any other sort of news,' explained Northcliffe. 'Watch the sales during a big murder mystery, especially if there is a woman in it. It is a revelation of how much the public is interested in realities, action and mystery. It is only human.' The headlines from a single edition of the *Daily Mail* in May 1896 reflected its owner's fascination with crime: 'A Spanish Lady's Death in Pimlico', 'Death From Excitement', 'Murder near Matlock: an Unaccountable Crime', 'Extraordinary Scare at Forest Hill', 'Corpse in a Burning House', 'Ghastly Scene in Camberwell'. Northcliffe described topics likely to excite readers as 'talking points'. When an editor informed him that long skirts had become fashionable in Paris, he replied, 'What a great talking point. Every woman in the country will be excited about it. We must start an illustrated discussion on "THE BATTLE OF THE SKIRTS: LONG V SHORT." Get different people's views. Cable to New York and Paris, get plenty of sketches by well-known artists ... plenty of legs.'[12]

To satisfy the values as well as the desires of middle England, the *Mail* cultivated a journalistic oeuvre, still active today, that shamelessly glorifies British white middle-class conservatism. The paper and its global website swoop on all forms of wokeness and political correctness – leniency in jailing criminals, snide exposés of sexual exploits of celebrities (especially 'gay' or 'kinky'), veiled racism that stirs up Britain's white ruling class, jingoistic support for 'our boys' in the military that demonises foreigners, and anything that arouses fear of the 'other'.

When Northcliffe's heirs confronted the existential challenge posed by digital technology at the beginning of the twenty-first century, they not only stuck with the formula that has never tired, they embellished it. The *Daily Mail* online is a trashy, raunchy, privacy-invading, give-em-wot-they-want global news website; a frenetic smorgasbord of gossip, paparazzi celebrity pictures and long titillating headlines. It is the most visited English-language newspaper site in the world outside China, attracting around 190 million unique visitors a month. But it became so factually dubious that in 2017 Wikipedia banned its content as a source or citation, pointing to its 'poor fact checking, sensationalism, and flat-out fabrication'.[13] Its conceit was summed up by the *Daily Mail*'s global chief brand officer, Sean Walsh: 'You tell us you're coming to read a story about Syria, but we know you'll end up looking at pictures of Kim Kardashian on the beach.'[14]

———

Popular journalism had risked becoming respectable, even boring, after William Randolph Hearst died in 1951. That vacuum was filled by a cherubic-looking 22-year-old Rupert Murdoch. His first acquisition after the Adelaide *News* was Perth's *Sunday Times* on Australia's remote west coast, where practically nothing he printed offended the locals. 'Thus was born in the mid-1950s what has since come to be known the world over as Murdochian journalism,' wrote Thomas Kiernan, an early Murdoch biographer – 'the exaggerated story filled with invented quotes; the rewriting of cryptic, laconic news-service wire copy into lavishly sensationalized yarns; the eye-shattering, usually ungrammatical, irrelevant, and gratuitously blood-curdling headline ... brisk, snappy, self-congratulatory editorials larded with boldface and underlinings, as though the reader had to be guided through the forest of verbiage; the insipid gossip column or two; the extensive space devoted to sports – all wrapped in cheap, smudgy tabloid form and promoted with the apocalyptic fervor and energy of Bible Belt evangelism.'[15]

Murdoch's next stop was Sydney, where he simulated Hearst's blazing entry into San Francisco eighty years earlier by plunging his newly acquired afternoon tabloid *Daily Mirror* into a bruising battle with its rival *The Sun*. It was the country's dirtiest newspaper war, fought every weekday on the streets of its biggest city. 'The *Mirror* had to out-lie the liars, out-distort the distorters, out-shock the shockers,' explained a veteran of Sydney's raffish newspaper world.[16]

Murdoch found his next juicy takeover target in London. The *News of the World*, known by local hacks as the 'Screws of the World', described itself as the 'Novelty of the Nation and the Wonder of the World' when it was launched in 1843. Read by millions of Britons every Sunday, the paper served up lashings of 'divorce, scandal, abduction, assault, murder and sport', as *Time* described it in 1941. 'Downstairs, rapt scullery maids devour its spicy morsels; so, upstairs, does many a lady of the house. Farmers, laborers and millworkers cherish its sinful revelations; so also do royalty, cabinet ministers, tycoons,' wrote *Time*. 'Without *News of the World*, Sunday morning in Britain would lack something as familiar as church bells.'[17]

Within months, Murdoch was mired in public controversy after the *News of the World* announced it had secured the memoirs of Christine Keeler, the callgirl whose scandalous affair with British war secretary John Profumo had forced him to resign six years earlier. Accused of cashing in on pornography and denigrating Profumo's attempts to rehabilitate himself as he assisted drug addicts and ex-convicts in London's East End, Murdoch replied candidly, 'People can sneer all they like, but I'll take the 150,000 extra copies we are going to sell.'

Now fully ensconced in Fleet Street's tabloid milieu, Murdoch's next acquisition reshaped popular journalism as emphatically as Hearst's purchase of the New York *Journal* had done almost eighty years earlier. The ailing London *Sun* was, according to its critics, a 'worthy, boring, leftish, popular broadsheet'. Not for long. Murdoch's reincarnated tabloid *Sun* stunned Fleet Street with its raciness, naked girls and punchy sports reporting. 'Not since Northcliffe's *Daily Mail* had a proprietor so instantly converted an editorial concept into a circulation success,' wrote media commentator Simon Jenkins. By 1978, selling more than 4 million copies a day, *The Sun* was like a splashy supermarket whose shelves were stocked with celebrity news, gossip, sport, comics, puzzles, while the central aisle displayed a product that was irresistible to most British working-class readers. Sex.

Murdoch's *Sun* started publishing pictures of semi-clothed young women from its first issue, positioning them alongside stories like 'The Geography of Love', 'Are You Getting your Share?', 'Do Men Still Want to Marry a Virgin?', 'The First Night of Love' and 'The Way into a Woman's Bed'.[18] A year later, the tops came off. The first 'genuine Page Three Girl' appeared on a Monday. Gradually, over subsequent days, there was an increase in breasts. First came a woman in a bikini, noted author George Munster; next came 'two views of Hylette', one of which displayed her left breast; the next day the bikini top was gone and both breasts were hidden under folded arms; finally, on Saturday, there was a 'deep cleavage harmonized with the late autumn'.[19]

Like much of Murdoch's *Sun*, the Page Three Girl production process was unlike anything else in conventional journalism. Pictures were retouched in the photographic department, with scribbled instructions to 'remove mole' or 'make jawline firmer'. On one memorable occasion a note came from the deputy editor Bernard Shrimsley: 'Make nipples less fantastic.' The models slowly evolved from 'girl-next-door types towards the visual cliches of the soft-porn industry', wrote Peter Chippindale and Chris Horrie in *Stick It Up Your Punter!*[20] Suspenders and black stockings were added as 'sex soon crept on to the menu of every part of the paper, with the sports pages enlivened by "artist's impressions" of female tennis stars in the nude, and crime reports which often led with the sex lives of either the villain or the victim.'[21]

But Murdoch was no Hugh Hefner. 'He had no interest in play-mates; he was personally prudish,' wrote Munster. 'The business of Rupert Murdoch was business.' His justification for introducing pornography into the British daily press was as brazen as the act itself – it was, he asserted, a 'daring experiment' and 'statement of youthfulness and freshness'.[22] But *The Sun* didn't invent the bosom, insisted Larry Lamb, the paper's first editor under Murdoch's owner-ship, any more than it invented the permissive society. 'Thousands of people, including many women, get great pleasure each day from looking at pictures of beautiful girls in a state of undress. Certainly I recall many occasions when the women in my family would discuss, at breakfast, the merits of that day's Page Three girl, without suggest-ing in any way that they felt women were thereby being exploited.'[23]

The Sun's startling success presented its commercial rivals with a choice: follow it downmarket or lose readers. It's the same dilemma that has confronted Murdoch competitors for seventy years: do you maintain your editorial standards because you believe journalism has a core place in civil society, or do you listen to the finance and marketing executives (and shareholders) who are telling you the only way to arrest falling revenues is to become more 'popular'?

'*The Sun* took the popular press into the gutter and they were successful at it,' bemoaned Robert Maxwell, owner of the rival *Daily Mirror*.[24] Murdoch defended *The Sun*'s prurience as a social inter-vention to improve British life. 'In every sense it's been a mouthpiece for a new young generation in this country, and this country changes very slowly and you still have a class system to a certain extent,' he told the media writer Raymond Snoddy in 1992. 'The elite here, the upper classes, see themselves threatened by papers like *The Sun*. We're saying to working-class people, "You are just as good as them." *The Sun* stands for opportunity for working people and for change in this society. It's a real catalyst for change. It's a very radical paper.'[25]

Murdoch's restlessness found its next landing spot in San Antonio, Texas. 'One day in 1973, the 42-year-old Australian breezed into Texas, met *San Antonio Express-News* owner Houston Harte at the airport's Continental ticket counter, signed an option for $18 million, and then, says Harte, "flew away to wherever he was going",' reported *Texas Monthly* under the headline 'Weirdo Paper Plagues S.A.' Murdoch imported a team of editors from Sydney to create 'a form of journalism heretofore unknown in these parts', featuring headlines like 'NUDE PRINCIPAL DEAD IN MOTEL', 'ARMIES OF INSECTS MARCHING ON S.A.', 'HANDLESS BODY FOUND', 'UNCLE TORTURES TOTS WITH HOT FORK'. Life in San Antonio, declared *Texas Monthly*, would never be the same again: 'The River still flows, the tourists still gawk, but nothing has been quite the same since Rupert Murdoch came to town.'[26]

Three years later, following the path of Pulitzer and Hearst almost a century earlier, Murdoch's tabloid caravan arrived in New York. His purchase of the dowdy liberal *New York Post* animated an establishment media that loves writing about itself. 'EXTRA!!! AUSSIE PRESS LORD TERRIFIES NEW YORK' screamed *Time*'s cover line over an image of King Kong with a Rupert Murdoch face trampling across the Manhattan skyline. *Newsweek* was similarly breathless: 'Aussie Tycoon's Amazing Story! – PRESS LORD TAKES CITY'.

But if Hearst and Murdoch were the most aggressive media owners to bastardise journalism in order to make more money, they weren't the only ones. 'We're a branch of showbiz, aren't we?' said Richard Desmond, one-time owner of the UK *Daily Express*.[27] Even the seemingly staid broadsheet *Daily Telegraph* is embellished with layers of titillation behind its respectable facade. It's a technique that was explained by Conrad Black after he bought the paper: 'The key to the *Daily Telegraph*'s immense success was a formula devised by Lord Camrose and faithfully continued by his son, Lord Hartwell, consisting of an excellent, fair, concise newspaper; good sports coverage; a page three in which the kinkiest, gamiest, most salacious and most scatological stories in Britain were set out in the most apparently sober manner, but with sadistically explicit quotations from court transcripts; and extreme veneration of the Royal Family ... [I]t was in some measure a brilliant confidence trick: a titillating chronicle, wrapped in a good but almost featureless news and sports paper.'[28]

Figuring out 'what people want' is an instinctual artform honed by seasoned tabloid editors and news directors. Obvious subjects include crime, greed and sex, but even more important than the topic is the requirement to stimulate the audience's *emotions*. Joseph Pulitzer plastered posters on his newsroom walls at *The World* in the early twentieth century to activate his editors: 'ACCURACY! TERSENESS! ACCURACY!' And he told them: 'Accuracy is to a newspaper what virtue is to a woman.'[29] Many decades later, the editor of Murdoch's London *Sun*, Kelvin MacKenzie, also posted signs across the walls of his news department: 'NEWS IS ANYTHING THAT MAKES THE READER SAY "GEE WHIZ!"'; 'IF YOU DO IT, DO IT BIG – OTHERWISE DON'T BOTHER, OLD BOY'; 'DO IT TO THEM BEFORE THEY DO IT TO US'; 'MAKE IT FAST, MAKE IT FIRST AND MAKE IT ACCURATE' (to which a wag on the staff added in felt-tip pen: 'IF ALL ELSE FAILS – MAKE IT UP').[30]

No-one at News Corp understood the prejudices and biases of readers better than MacKenzie. On one occasion, after being told that the new editor of the paper's Money Page was planning stories about ethical investments and Third World assistance, MacKenzie leaned over the new recruit's desk and, with slow emphasis on each word, said to him, 'Get this through your fucking head. Nobody gives a fuck about the Third World.'[31]

After decades of pushing the envelope, Murdoch can intuitively sense the base-level instincts of readers and viewers. In the early 1970s he arrived in remote Darwin for a visit to his northernmost Australian newspaper, the *Northern Territory News*, where he complained to the editor, Jim Bowditch, about the number of 'black faces' in the paper. 'Well, Rupert, Aborigines are one third of the population,' explained Bowditch. 'Yeah,' Murdoch replied, 'but they're not our readers.'[32]

Gays are another audience segment often sneeringly dismissed by editors and owners as peripheral to the interests of mass market readers. In the early days of *The Sun*, Murdoch told an editor who was planning a feature about what it's like to be a homosexual: 'Do you really think our readers are interested in poofters?'[33] In 1998 *The Sun* ran a front-page editorial under the headline 'Are we being run by a gay Mafia?', referring to four known homosexuals in Tony Blair's 21-member cabinet. 'The public has a right to know how many homosexuals occupy positions of high power,' proclaimed the paper. 'Their sexuality is not the problem ... [T]he worry is their membership of a closed world of men with a mutual self-interest ... there are widespread fears that Members of Parliament, even ministers, are beholden to others for reasons other than politics.' Accompanying the story was a shocking request to readers: 'Are you a gay MP who'd like to come out? *The Sun* has set up a hotline on 0171 782 4105 for ministers and MPs who are secretly homosexual. Don't worry about the cost, we'll ring you back.'[34]

Every boundary is stretched to breaking point in an editorial culture that's predicated on deceit, sensationalism and controversy. The *News of the World* employed a reporter for ten years known as the 'Fake Sheikh', who was armed with a wardrobe of full-length traditional Arab robes to impersonate Middle Eastern millionaires and entrap victims for his stories.[35] The same paper once concealed a camera behind a two-way mirror in a prostitute's bedroom, and used a tape recorder embedded inside a teddy bear to catch a junior government minister in bed with two women while smoking cannabis in 1973.[36] It was the motivation for publishing Hitler's fake diaries, and for concocting stories from rent boys, and for publishing photoshopped nude pictures of a female politician. It was why phone hacking continued for at least twelve years at News International.

Gossip, for Murdoch, is both commercial and personal. In *Vanity Fair* in 2008, his biographer Michael Wolff described a scene in the mogul's office that he witnessed together with his research assistant while they were there for an interview session. As they watched, Murdoch worked the phone in pursuit of a tip he had been given for a story. 'His side of the conversation was straight reporter stuff: Who could he call? How could he get in touch? Will they confirm? Barked, impatient, just the facts ... He was parsing each answer. Re-asking the question. Clarifying every point. His notepad going. He knew the trade. Of how many media-company C.E.O.'s could that be said? This wasn't a destroyer of journalism – this was a practitioner.' On the other hand, added Wolff, ' he was trying to smear somebody . . .'[37]

Murdoch once traced his tabloid instincts back to when his father staged Australia's first beauty contest, in the 1920s, to popularise *The Herald*. 'People were walking to the last block in Melbourne to buy the last edition with the result in it,' Rupert later recalled as he went on to critique the 'complacency and condescension that festers at the heart of some newsrooms' who find themselves competing for an audience they once took for granted.[38] 'It takes no special genius to point out that if you are contemptuous of your customers, you are going to have a hard time getting them to buy your product,' he said during his 2008 Boyer Lectures in Australia. 'Newspapers are no exception.'[39]

Avoiding contempt for your customers sounds like a textbook topic at any serious-minded business school. But would any MBA course recommend a strategy that involved illegally hacking into personal voicemails, bribing police officers, stirring up racism and homophobia, condoning election and climate denial, acquiring fake historical documents or impersonating sheikhs? Murdoch knew 'more viscerally than anyone, what postmodern societies wanted to satisfy their twisted appetites and he provided that material in all its gaudiness', wrote *New York Times* columnist Roger Cohen in the wake of the 2011 phone hacking scandal. 'I don't think he created those appetites. But he sure fed them.'[40]

In the aftermath of the 2020 US presidential election, Fox News broadcast lies and misinformation in order to assuage its customers' biases. Caught at the disjunction between journalism and revenue, Fox opted for the money. 'The business model revealed in startling detail in exchanges among Fox executives and stars depends on giving its viewers the red meat they want,' wrote Martin Wolf, the *Financial Times* columnist. 'If that includes falsehoods, so be it. Asked whether he could have told the top people at Fox to stop putting Rudy Giuliani (one of the most assiduous promoters of lies about the 2020 US election) on air, Rupert Murdoch replied "I could have. But I didn't." . . . A defender might argue that none of this was Fox's fault. It just did what it had to do, in order to give its customers what they wanted. This, one might note, is what a drug dealer would argue.'[41]

Meddling
with History

Reporters aren't used to getting instructions like the one received by James Creelman, the *New York Journal*'s London-based correspondent, on 28 May 1898:

> Dear Mr. Creelman,
>
> I wish you would at once make preparations, so that in case the Spanish fleet actually starts for Manila we will be prepared to buy or charter some English tramp steamer on the Eastern end of the Mediterranean and take her to some narrow and inaccessible portion of the Suez Canal and sink her where she will obstruct the passage of the Spanish fleet.[1]

That brazen proposition – that a newspaper would use its resources to subvert the course of military history – was the brainchild of the *New York Journal*'s proprietor, William Randolph Hearst, who devoted a career to interfering in national and international affairs. Hearst's role in pumping up the Spanish-American War in the final years of the nineteenth century, including his plan to physically obstruct Spain's naval fleet, was consistent with the credo he established as a boyish newspaper owner – 'Journalism That Acts'.

The US government had a strategic rationale for declaring war on Spain in Cuba, as well as listening to public support for the Cuban patriots waging guerrilla warfare against harsh Spanish rule. At the same time, the government was being dragged into an anciliary war alongside the military conflict: the fierce newspaper battle being fought on the streets of New York between Hearst's recently acquired *Journal* and its arch rival, Joseph Pulitzer's *World*.

Hearst was an unambiguously active participant in the Spanish–American War. When the artist he sent to provide sketches of the conflict couldn't find any fighting, and wanted to come home, Hearst supposedly cabled back: 'You furnish the pictures and I'll furnish the war.'[2] As part of its editorial high jinks, the *Journal* championed the cause of Evangelina Cisneros, a young Cuban sent to jail for attempting to kidnap a Spanish officer. Hearst dispatched a team of journalists to free Cisneros from her jail cell and accompany her to New York to appear at a public celebration. It was 'the greatest journalistic coup of this age', crowed the *Journal*.[3]

At times, Hearst acted like *he* was running the American government. When the battleship USS *Maine* exploded in Havana Harbor, killing 266 sailors, he appointed his own committee of US congressmen to go to Havana to validate his theory that the *Maine* was destroyed by an 'enemy's secret infernal machine', even though there was no evidence of Spanish involvement in the tragedy.[4] 'My father's angry headlines and stories on the sinking of [the] *Maine* virtually ignited the conflict,' William Randolph Hearst Jr acknowledged in his 1991 memoir.[5]

Hearst treated the war like a vanity publishing project. He offered US president William McKinley a volunteer cavalry regiment in which he proposed serving as an ordinary 'man in the ranks'.[6] That was rejected, but his next offer, to provide his fully manned 138-foot steam yacht *Buccaneer* at no cost, was accepted by the United States Navy, although his suggestion that he could serve 'either as commander or second in command' was declined.[7]

Hearst enthusiastically travelled to Cuba to cover the war himself, an assignment described by his correspondent James Creelman, who was wounded in fighting during the Battle of El Caney: 'Some one knelt in the grass beside me and put his hand on my fevered head. Opening my eyes, I saw Mr Hearst … The man who had provoked the war had come to see the result with his own eyes and, finding one of his own correspondents prostrate, was doing the work himself. Slowly he took down my story of the fight. Again and again the tinging of Mauser bullets interrupted. But he seemed unmoved. The battle had to be reported somehow. "I'm sorry you're hurt, but" – and his face was radiant with enthusiasm – "wasn't it a splendid fight? We must beat every paper in the world.'"[8]

The military conflict lasted only months, but Hearst maintained his circulation war for more than a year under a daily front-page slogan 'How Do You Like the Journal's War?' The war also inspired one of popular journalism's signature devices – the banner headline – as *Journal* readers watched the size of the paper's lurid page-one streamer headline grow from one inch, to three, and finally to five inches high.[9]

Hearst's next major geopolitical foray was a vitriolic campaign against American participation in World War One, motivated largely by his antipathy towards Britain. After he had to abandon this campaign when the US declared war on Germany, his next target for attack was America's allies in Europe. With American flags draped across his mastheads, Hearst campaigned against US aid to the Allies fighting Germany. 'Keep every dollar and every man and every weapon and all our supplies and stores AT HOME, for the defense of our own land, our own people, our own freedom, until that defense has been made ABSOLUTELY secure,' wrote Hearst across his fleet of newspapers in Trumpian style. 'After that we can think of other nations' troubles. But till then, America first!'[10]

Hearst's isolationist vitriol enraged politicians and readers. Advertisers boycotted his publications and his effigy was burned in cities across the country. 'While America has been engaged in the life and death struggle with civilization's enemy,' trumpeted his rival *New York Tribune*, 'the Hearst papers have printed: 74 attacks on our allies, 17 instances of defense or praise of Germany, 63 pieces of anti-war propaganda, 1 deletion of a Presidential proclamation – total 155 – or an average of nearly three a week.'[11]

After meddling in two major wars, Hearst was primed for another interventionist foray as Europe steamed towards World War Two. In the late summer of 1934 he arrived in Berlin just as Adolf Hitler was installed in the combined positions of German chancellor and president – effectively the country's absolute dictator. Accompanied by his mistress Marion Davies, her dachshund Gandhi, his three sons and other hangers-on, Hearst motored through southern and central Europe in a fleet of six black limousines. His grand tour included a meeting with the new Führer, who had been a columnist for Hearst's papers since 1930, earning $500 an article ($10,000 today) and reputedly often missing his deadline. Göring and Mussolini were also columnists in Hearst's op-ed stable during the 1930s.[12]

The publisher met his star writer at Berlin's sprawling *Reichspräsidentenpalais* (Reich President's Palace) on Wilhelmstrasse. Why am I so 'misunderstood' and despised in the US? Hitler asked Hearst. Because Americans are 'averse to dictatorship', replied the publisher. When conversation turned to the Nazis' treatment of Jews, Hitler responded by raising America's treatment of its native Indians, then dismissed the issue. 'All discrimination is disappearing and will soon entirely disappear, that is the policy of my government, and you will soon see ample evidence of that,' Hearst quoted Hitler in his memo summarising the meeting.[13]

Hearst also apparently ratified two extraordinary business deals with Hitler at the *Reichspräsidentenpalais*. One was a film-swapping arrangement, in which parts of his company's newsreels would be aired in Germany in return for newsreel footage featuring Nazi propaganda being shown to American audiences, claimed Kathryn Olmsted, author of *The Newspaper Axis*. In the other deal, Hitler agreed that his government would pay $400,000 a year (roughly $7.9 million today) for Hearst's nineteen daily newspapers to report happenings in Germany exclusively and in a 'friendly' manner, according to reports sent to Washington by William Dodd, the US ambassador in Berlin.[14]

'Everybody is for Hitler,' Hearst wrote to Julia Morgan, his architect, in a postcard from Germany: 'We think he is a tyrant in America but his own people don't think so. They regard him as a savior. Nine-tenths of the people are for him. Even the Communists – that is the working classes who were Communists – seem to be satisfied with him. His chief opposition is religious. The Catholics registered some objections in the recent elections and of course the Jews hate him. Everything is very quiet and orderly here. There are no evidences of disturbance.'[15]

Despite warnings from prominent American Jews about the looming Nazi maelstrom, Hearst continued to support Hitler. In early 1932 the president of Universal Pictures, Carl Laemmle, wrote to Hearst about 'the current political situation in Germany and the probable consequences to the Jewish population in that country in the event that Hitler is successful, as seems likely, in getting control of the Government'. Laemmle urged Hearst to use his influence: 'A protest from you would bring an echo from all corners of the civilized world, such as Mr. Hitler could not possibly fail to recognize.'[16]

Hearst ignored the pleas. For the next four years his newspapers became a mouthpiece for Nazi propaganda. They aggressively campaigned against US intervention in the war, using a front-page banner, 'AMERICA FIRST' (recycled from his World War One campaign), above the image of an eagle holding a ribbon with the words 'AN AMERICAN PAPER FOR THE AMERICAN PEOPLE'. In an NBC broadcast in October 1938, Hearst declared that 'it is no part of the duty of this English-speaking nation to support the British Empire in her ambitious schemes to dominate Europe, absorb Africa and control the Orient'. This came as President Roosevelt described most of the opposition to US government foreign policy as being from the Republicans, the Soviet press, the Nazi press 'and the Hearst press'.[17]

Hearst finally ended his infatuation with Hitler on Kristallnacht (Night of the Broken Glass), in November 1938, when Nazis rampaged across Germany, murdering nearly a hundred Jews, burning 200 synagogues, and destroying thousands of Jewish homes and businesses. Unable to ignore the reality, Hearst had no choice but to crank his media machine into reverse. 'The shocking outrages perpetuated against harmless and helpless Jews in Germany are not the result of any momentary animal impulse, nor the exhibition of any sporadic sentiment or action,' he wrote across his network of newspapers. 'The creed of violence and hatred is bearing its foul fruit, and the world is beginning to realize what a destructive and death-dealing fruit it is.'[18]

Hearst wasn't the only Anglophone press baron to be seduced by the Nazis. For a tumultuous decade, Harold Harmsworth, the first Viscount Rothermere, threw his mass circulation British flagship *Daily Mail* and his sixteen other daily and Sunday newspapers behind Hitler.

The Rothermere–Hitler dalliance began in 1930, as the Nazis morphed from beer hall thugs into a national presence after increasing their Reichstag seats from twelve to 107. This political upheaval attracted Rothermere to Munich for his first meeting with Hitler, followed by effusive praise. 'A new Germany is rising before our eyes,' he wrote in the *Daily Mail*. 'She is strong today; she will be much stronger a few years hence. She is determined now; she may before long be defiant.' The election, he predicted, would be seen as 'a landmark of this time ... the beginning of a new epoch in the relations between the German nation and the rest of the world.'[19] He was right, but not in the way he anticipated.

Rothermere viewed Hitler as a defence against Germany falling to the communists. As communism became entrenched in Russia during the 1920s, fears rose that it would spread across Europe. Rothermere continued his embrace of fascism through the 1930s, even as Hitler ramped up his attacks on German Jews and began invading surrounding countries. As his newspapers became propaganda sheets for Nazi anti-Semitism, the *Daily Mail* – led by Rothermere himself – was effectively the British mouthpiece in the Nazi spin machine.

'The Jews are everywhere,' he wrote in private correspondence, 'controlling everything.'[20]

When Hitler won the chancellorship in 1933, Rothermere was euphoric. 'This will prove to be one of the most historic days, if not the most historic day, in the latter day history of Europe,' he told his senior foreign correspondent George Ward Price, an active Nazi apologist. In March 1933, under the headline 'Hitler And The Jews', the paper's Berlin correspondent Rothay Reynolds interviewed Ernst 'Putzi' Hanfstaengl, then a Hitler confidante: 'Dr. Hanfstaengl, one of Herr Hitler's closest co-operators, told me today: "The Chancellor has authorized me to say that all the reports of the mishandling of Jews are barefaced lies." I asked him why many Jews are being discharged from public offices, and he replied: "Speaking for myself, I must say that the Jews have abused their power in Germany, politically, morally, and financially. They are being discharged from office because they are not national and because they have failed to protect the people from Marxist infection and from atheism."'[21]

A few months later, writing in the *Mail*, Rothermere claimed that Germany was 'rapidly falling under the control of its alien elements'. His invective was vicious. 'In the last days of the pre-Hitler regime there were twenty times as many Jewish government officials in Germany as had existed before the war,' he wrote. 'Israelites of international attachments were insinuating themselves into key positions in the German administrative machine. Three German ministers only had direct relations with the press, but in each case the official responsible for conveying news and interpreting policy to the public was a Jew.'[22]

Rothermere also championed fascism at home, throwing his support behind the British Union of Fascists – the so-called Blackshirts – led by the quixotic establishment figure Oswald Mosley. In January 1934 the paper published an infamous article written by Rothermere under the headline 'Hurrah for the Blackshirts' that lauded Mosley's movement for its 'sound common sense ... and Conservative doctrine', and urged Britain to follow a similar 'revival of national strength and spirit'. His papers offered free tickets to Mosley's rallies and printed the addresses of Blackshirt recruiting offices. Some of his staff started wearing black shirts to work.[23]

Five months later the *Mail* suddenly discontinued its support. According to Mosley this was the result of pressure 'at the point of an economic gun' from the paper's Jewish advertisers. Rothermere reportedly told Hitler that 'Jews cut off his complete revenue from advertising' and forced him to 'toe the line'.[24]

On 30 June 1934, the Night of the Long Knives, gangs of elite SS guards murdered hundreds of Hitler's perceived enemies in a frenzy of street violence across Germany designed to consolidate his power. 'Herr Adolf Hitler, the German Chancellor, has saved his country,' began the *Daily Mail*'s report on the brutality. Many in the British establishment were shocked by this stance – 'I was disgusted by the *Daily Mail*'s boosting of Hitler,' Winston Churchill wrote to his wife the same month – but elite British sentiment didn't constrain Rothermere and his son Esmond from attending a dinner party for foreigners hosted by Hitler at his official residence in Berlin a few months later, where they were guests of honour.[25]

When German troops marched into the Rhineland in 1936, the *Daily Mail* was undeterred. Hitler, it reported, had 'cleared the air'. And when the Nazis annexed Czechoslovakia two years later, Rothermere was again supportive. 'Czechoslovakia is not of the remotest concern to us,' he wrote, before sending this telegram to Hitler: 'PERSONAL MY DEAR FUHRER EVERYONE IN ENGLAND IS PROFOUNDLY MOVED BY THE BLOODLESS SOLUTION OF THE CZECHO-SLOVAKIAN PROBLEM STOP PEOPLE NOT SO MUCH CONCERNED WITH TERRITORIAL READJUSTMENT AS WITH DREAD OF ANOTHER WAR WITH ITS ACCOMPANYING BLOODBATH STOP FREDERICK THE GREAT WAS A GREAT POPULAR FIGURE IN ENGLAND MAY NOT ADOLFO THE GREAT BECOME AN EQUALLY POPULAR FIGURE STOP I SALUTE YOUR EXCELLENCYS STAR WHICH RISES HIGHER AND HIGHER.'[26]

Ward Price continued to churn out tame interviews with Hitler in the *Mail* and was filmed with the Führer's official party on the balcony of the Hofburg Palace in 1938 as the Nazis entered Vienna to annex Austria. The concentration camps, he reassured *Mail* readers, were a minor blip. 'To blacken the whole Nazi régime because a few subordinates may have abused their powers is as unfair as it would be to condemn the Government of the United States for the brutalities of some warder in charge of a chain-gang in the mountains of West Virginia.'[27]

Rothermere's personal relationship with Hitler lasted almost a decade. Following their first meeting in 1930, they met again in 1933 at Berchtesgaden, the Führer's Bavarian resort, and again in 1936, 1937 and 1938. Hitler was a 'simple and unaffected man' and a 'perfect gentleman', according to Rothermere, who also met several times during the 1930s with Joseph Goebbels, the Nazi propaganda chief. 'Rothermere pays me great compliments ... strongly anti-Jewish ... a strong supporter of the Führer,' Goebbels wrote in his diary.[28]

Rothermere and Hitler corresponded frequently in long, often gratuitous letters and cables, addressing each other as 'dear Lord Rothermere' and 'My dear Führer'. In April 1935, Rothermere wrote effusively: 'I esteem it a great honor and privilege to be in correspondence with Your Excellency. It is not often that anyone has an opportunity of learning the views of one who may occupy the first place in all European history.'[29]

Hitler often responded in kind. 'Your leading article published last week, which I have read with great interest, contains everything which coincides with my own ideas,' he wrote in May 1937.[30] Rothermere was 'the only Englishman who sees clearly the magnitude of this Bolshevist danger. His paper is doing an immense amount of good,' the Führer reportedly told Ward Price.[31]

Even as late as the summer of 1939 – months after Hitler's speech to the Reichstag threatening 'the annihilation of the Jewish race in Europe' if a war against Germany was started by 'Jewish financers' – Rothermere was still the sycophantic correspondent: 'My Dear Führer, I have watched with understanding and interest the progress of your great and superhuman work in regenerating your country ...

The British people, now like Germany strongly rearmed, regard the German people with admiration as valorous adversaries in the past, but I am sure that there is no problem between our two countries which cannot be settled by consultation and negotiation.'[32]

Of course, it ended in tears when World War Two started. After ten years as an unrelenting propagandist for a repugnant regime, Rothermere reversed direction only when he had no choice. 'We now fight,' the *Daily Mail* editorialised on 4 September 1939, 'against the blackest tyranny that has ever held men in bondage.'[33]

Not every Western media magnate fell under Hitler's spell. When Henry Luce visited Germany in the spring of 1938 he was shocked at the 'intensity' and 'brand of hatred' of the Nazis' anti-Semitism. 'It is my fault for not having insisted harder that we didn't blame Hitler enough for starting the war,' he told his *Time* editors after returning to New York.[34]

Luce, unlike Hearst, was a passionate advocate of US involvement in World War Two. In 1940, when Churchill appealed to President Roosevelt to provide naval destroyers to defend Britain against the Nazis 'as a matter of life or death', Luce joined the eminent non-partisan Century Group that met regularly at New York's Century Club to strategise support for the survival of the British Commonwealth as an 'important factor in the preservation of the American way of life'.[35]

Luce worked behind the scenes to broker the deal with Roosevelt that secured the destroyers for Britain and edged the US into the war. As the leader of a post-depression country that wasn't eager to join a costly war, Roosevelt was publicly isolationist before Japan's attack on Pearl Harbor, but he privately supported Churchill's efforts to stop Hitler, using workarounds like the destroyer deal to support Britain. And though the *Time* stable of magazines had actively opposed the president's policies and re-election, Luce and Roosevelt put aside their differences in the interests of supporting Britain in its moment of existential crisis. Luce and his author wife Clare Boothe Luce spent a night at the White House, where Roosevelt, after dinner and a movie, took Luce into his study to persuade him to actively throw the support of the *Time* empire behind the destroyers-for-bases deal. According to Clare, the president told her husband, 'Harry, I can't come out in favor of such a deal unless I can count on the support of the entire Time-Life organization for my foreign policy.'[36]

For Luce, a chief benefit of owning a vast publishing empire was the opportunity to contribute to public policy. It was almost as if he ran a government, rather than a media organisation whose role was to scrutinise governments. After Japan bombed Pearl Harbor, Luce established his own 'postwar planning department' to develop long-term policy positions on major domestic and foreign issues. Even though the US is 'the most powerful and the most vital nation in the world', Luce contended, Americans were failing to play their part as a world power – 'a failure which has had disastrous consequences for themselves and for all mankind'.[37]

In 1961 Luce committed Time Inc. to the 'dominant aim and purpose' of defeating communism throughout the world. Although he wasn't literally talking about waging a private war – 'of course, we of Time Inc. do not have the means to wage war as Francis Drake did … we have no ships, no guns, no bombs' – he did envisage a form of combat. 'Unlike the sixteenth century, ours *is* an age of journalism – and at least on that battleground, we can do some service,' explained Luce.[38]

———

The capacity of a media mogul to divert the rivers of history was on full display in 1936 when Lord Beaverbrook, owner of the *Daily Express*, conspired with King Edward VIII to conceal the crisis of the king's abdication from the British public. Edward had fallen in love with Wallis Simpson, a married American socialite, two years earlier. She wanted to marry the king after divorcing her husband, even though it was then constitutionally and morally unacceptable for a British king, who was the official head of the Church of England, to marry a divorcee.

For ten months in 1936, British newspapers concealed from their readers the fact that their country was embroiled in a constitutional crisis, even while the king's relationship with Mrs Simpson was reported with relish in the American and European media. Beaver-brook was the lead architect of this censorship conspiracy, later detailing his crucial meeting with the king at Buckingham Palace on 13 October 1936:

> The King asked me then to help in the suppression of the Simpson divorce case in the newspapers … [T]he reasons he gave for this were that the woman, Mrs Simpson, was unfortunate, that notoriety would attach to her because she had been a member of his party at Balmoral and in the Mediterranean … she was ill, unhappy and distressed by fear of publicity. And he for his part felt that he should protect her.
>
> These reasons appeared satisfactory to me. And so I took part in the suppression of the news before the divorce action took place and in the limitation of the publicity when it occurred.[39]

Assisted by Lord Rothermere, Beaverbrook persuaded the owners and editors of other major British newspapers to censor any mention of the king's affair with Mrs Simpson. By then, the king was in almost daily telephone contact with Beaverbrook, who would rise to his feet to take the calls and refer deferentially to the monarch as 'Sire'.

The news that Wallis Simpson's divorce had been finalised two weeks after that Buckingham Palace meeting was ignored by the British press. When the king informed the prime minister, Stanley Baldwin, that he intended to marry Mrs Simpson, Beaverbrook headed to the king's residence at Fort Belvedere, in Windsor Great Park, to act as intermediary between the monarch and the British government in the swirling constitutional crisis. The next day, Baldwin told the House of Commons that his cabinet had denied the king's request to create a law that would allow him to marry Mrs Simpson without her becoming queen and to exclude any children of the marriage from succession to the throne.

On December 3, the king informed Beaverbrook that he had decided to abdicate. 'Our cock won't fight,' Beaverbrook told his long-time political ally Winston Churchill, also a close supporter of the king.[40] It was only then that the country's newspapers broke their silence to report the constitutional conflagration they had kept under wraps for ten months.

At no point throughout 1936, as the crisis deepened, did Beaverbrook behave like a newspaper owner acting in the public interest. His *Daily Express* staff were instructed not to publish anything about the scandal, even though their proprietor knew more about it than anyone else in Britain apart from the king himself. When the *Express* published a photograph of the king standing on the deck of the royal yacht, where Mrs Simpson had been standing alongside him, it airbrushed her out of the picture.

Beaverbrook's manoeuvre to censor news of the king's love affair extended beyond England into most parts of the British empire, where loyal colonial governments and newspaper editors joined in opposing the marriage and abdication. On October 28, a short, single-column story appeared inconspicuously near the bottom of page 3 of the Melbourne *Herald*:

MRS SIMPSON GETS DIVORCE

Mrs Wallis Simpson, an American, and friend of King Edward, was granted a divorce in London yesterday from Ernest Aldrich Simpson. The suit was not defended. The parties were married in 1928. There are no children. Petitioner stated that she had lived happily with her husband until the autumn of 1934, when his manner toward her changed. He became indifferent and went off alone at week-ends.

The *Herald*'s managing director then was Sir Keith Murdoch, a staunch monarchist who, like Beaverbrook, was adept at using his papers to subvert or massage the news. First as a journalist and later as a media boss, he cultivated high-level relationships in London and Canberra, working the backrooms of political and media power.

Keith Murdoch's impact on twentieth-century history can be sheeted back to a fortuitous career move in the early months of World War One. He was then an up-and-coming newspaper reporter in his home city of Melbourne, thirty years old, about to depart for a new job in London as cable manager of the Australian newswire United Cable Service. As a political reporter, Murdoch had become friendly with the Australian prime minister Andrew Fisher. Before leaving for London, he suggested to Fisher and his defence minister that he travel via Turkey to report personally to them on the progress of Australian troops in the Gallipoli campaign, the massively costly Allied war initiative which included 70,000 soldiers from Australia and New Zealand. It was 'a peculiar mission for a newspaperman', wrote Murdoch's biographer Desmond Zwar. 'He was to conduct an investigation, not for his papers, but for his government.'[41]

Murdoch visited Anzac Cove, the site of the Gallipoli campaign, a month after an offensive was launched by the Allies against the defending Turks. He spent four days walking through trenches, talking to soldiers and officers. What he saw was a disaster. The campaign was failing, the summer heat created extreme conditions, dysentery had spread through the Allied troops, and bloated corpses lay unburied for weeks.

When Murdoch arrived in London, as an eyewitness to one of the most controversial campaigns of the war, he was in great demand. He lunched with the influential editor of *The Times*, Geoffrey Dawson, and briefed Sir Edward Carson, chairman of the British cabinet's Dardanelles committee.

He presented his findings in a 25-page, 8,000-word private letter to prime minister Fisher that became known as the 'Gallipoli letter'. In its opening pages, Murdoch describes the campaign as 'undoubtedly one of the most terrible chapters in our history', arguing that the risks of sending 'raw, young recruits on this perilous enterprise was to court disaster'. He revealed the troops' contempt for their commanding officers – 'sedition is talked round every tin of bully beef on the peninsula, and it is only loyalty that holds the forces together'. And he was scathing about General Sir Ian Hamilton, the British commander of the Gallipoli campaign – 'as a strategist he has completely failed ... [T]he essential and first step to restore the morale of the shaken forces is to recall him ... [T]he continuous and ghastly bungling over the Dardanelles enterprise was to be expected from such General Staff as the British Army possesses.'[42]

The contents of the letter soon became common knowledge inside Britain's corridors of power. After Murdoch met with senior members of the British government, prime minister Herbert Asquith had the letter printed as a State paper and distributed to the war cabinet. But just as quickly, doubts about the accuracy of Murdoch's obser-vations began to emerge. Asquith was soon repudiating the letter as 'largely composed of gossip and second-hand statements'. Winston Churchill, then a backbench member of parliament, sent Asquith a note from the editor of the *Daily Chronicle* saying he was 'not much impressed' when he met Murdoch. 'It is quite obvious that he had not seen the things which he described, nor has any personal knowledge of the men he condemned. His information was largely secondhand,' reported the editor.[43]

The Gallipoli letter ended Hamilton's military career. He was removed from his post by the war secretary, Lord Kitchener, and instructed to return to London. After reading Murdoch's letter, Hamilton was understandably upset. 'On every page inaccuracies of fact abound,' he wrote to his superiors. 'Here we have a man, a jour-nalist by profession, one who is quick to seize every point, and to coin epithets, which throws each fleeting impression into strongest relief.'[44]

The commander sent to replace Hamilton immediately ordered the evacuation of the Gallipoli Peninsula, resulting in a secretive withdrawal of 115,000 men in less than a week. It was a military volte-face that cemented Keith Murdoch's reputation as a multitasking player in the game. 'How Murdoch reconciled this double life – journalist one moment, emissary the next, observer today and player tomorrow – has never been explained,' wrote Les Carlyon in *The Great War*. 'Most journalists sought out government secrets and contrived ways to publish them; Murdoch kept government secrets and fed his readers platitudes.'[45] As the former war correspondent, editor and military historian Sir Max Hastings observed, 'Boy, Keith Murdoch understood how to promote Keith Murdoch.'[46]

Murdoch's role in exposing the Gallipoli military disaster, exaggerated as it appeared to be, catapulted him into the centre of political power in London while still in his early thirties. As World War One rolled on, he was viewed within Whitehall as a kind of de facto ambassador, working alongside the new Australian prime minister Billy Hughes as 'personal publicist, guide-to-the-British-mind, fixer, speech editor and errand boy', according to his biographer Desmond Zwar. Murdoch hosted a private dinner at his London apartment for Hughes in March 1916, attended by munitions minister Lloyd George, Lord Northcliffe, *Times* editor Geoffrey Dawson, chief of the imperial general staff William Robertson, and colonial secretary Andrew Bonar Law. By 1917, wrote Zwar, 'Hughes had Murdoch working hard for him, shuttling between Whitehall ministries, buttonholing officials and politicians. And as he met more and more of the great, Murdoch himself was becoming a little like the irascible little man who pulled the strings: *he* too started interfering. It was not enough to cable back his opinions to be printed in the various Australian newspapers ... Murdoch had started to urge Haig at British GHQ in France to listen to the Australian Government's desire for the formation of a single army corps under the command of Australian officers.'[47]

———

Like his father, Rupert Murdoch recognised a good war. When such a conflagration landed in his lap in April 1982, he was ready for action.

The improbable scene was the Falkland Islands, an archipelago of 778 tiny islands in the South Atlantic Ocean, off the bottom tip of South America. Britain's ownership of this overseas territory had long been disputed by near neighbour Argentina. As hostilities grew and diplomacy failed, the Argentinians invaded the Falklands. Britain responded with force. And so did Murdoch's *Sun*.

A remote South American location with a Spanish-speaking foreign enemy was a storyline straight out of central casting for a boisterous, jingoistic, circulation-hungry newspaper. Retitling itself 'The Paper That Supports Our Boys', *The Sun* supplied its own almost comedic form of tabloid braggadocio to the story of the war, featuring front-page headlines like 'THE SUN SAYS KNICKERS TO ARGENTINA' (above an article about how thousands of British women were 'sporting specially made underwear embroidered across the front with the proud name of the ship on which a husband or boyfriend is serving'), 'STICK IT UP YOUR JUNTA' (in response to an Argentinian peace proposal) and 'GOTCHA!' (after the British sank the Argentinian cruiser *General Belgrano*).

In its state of war, *The Sun*'s hostilities extended beyond Argentina to its arch rival the *Daily Mirror*, which alone among the UK tabloids adopted an anti-war stance. In an editorial titled 'The Traitors in Our Midst', *The Sun* turned its howitzers on the *Mirror*, which retaliated with an editorial titled 'The Harlot of Fleet Street' that described its rival as 'coarse and demented . . . The Sun today is to journalism what Dr Joseph Goebbels was to truth'.[48]

The real war raged for ten circulation-building weeks before Argentina surrendered. In that time *The Sun* increased its daily sales lead over the *Mirror* to more than a million copies. 'The cash, in both sales and advertising, for Murdoch simply crashed through the front door,' the paper's editor Kelvin MacKenzie later wrote. The scene inside *The Sun*'s office during its rollicking war was described by Roy Greenslade, then the paper's assistant editor: 'News editor Tom Petrie was wearing some sort of naval officer's cap and told me he now wished to be known as Commander Petrie. A map of the south Atlantic was pinned on the board behind him under a picture of Winston Churchill. Reporter Muriel Burden, who ran a pen pals service, was christened the "Darling of the Fleet".'[49]

The Sun's rambunctious Falklands war established its tabloid dominance in Britain. 'Sensing its power, and the support it was getting from Mrs Thatcher, it became louder and more aggressive than ever,' observed the distinguished BBC foreign correspondent John Simpson in *Unreliable Sources: How the Twentieth Century Was Reported*. Its coverage of the conflict challenged the stereotypical calmness and politeness of the British establishment – 'the Murdoch press had finally put paid to such outmoded conventions', wrote Simpson. 'They were the kind of things that Old Etonians clung to. Playing the game was finished.'[50]

Another opportunity for the Murdoch empire to position itself in service of the Anglosphere arrived as the US prepared to invade Iraq in 2003. Every one of News Corp's 175 newspapers across the globe supported the invasion – except one. After the Hobart *Mercury*, Murdoch's daily paper in Tasmania's small capital city, published an editorial arguing that 'it would be wrong for the US preemptively to attack Iraq', a sharp memo arrived from head office pointing out the company's position on Iraq. *The Mercury* swiftly U-turned, explaining that although 'no one wants a war', the alternative – 'to let a madman thumb his nose at the rule of international law' – is an 'obscenity'.[51]

As a citizen of the world who abandoned his native Australia to take up US citizenship in 1985, and who has lived in Britain and America since the 1970s, Murdoch portrays himself as a passionate nationalist in each country where he exerts political power.

As an American patriot, he implored his fellow citizens to support the US invasion of Iraq: '*We* have an inferiority complex, it seems. I think what's important is that the world respects *us*, much more important than they love *us*.'[52] He later praised the virtues of his adopted country's exceptionalism in a *Wall Street Journal* op-ed: 'I chose to come to America and become a citizen because America was – and remains – the most free and entrepreneurial nation in the world. *Our* history is defined by people whose character and culture have been shaped by ambition, imagination and hard work, bound together by a dream of a better life.' When rival US newspapers described him as an Australian, he complained, 'I'm an American citizen and have been for many years and consider myself an American.'[53]

As a British patriot, he urged his fellow British companies to compete globally. '*We* need to attract the brightest talent, regardless of background and ethnicity,' he proclaimed in London in 2010 when presenting the inaugural Margaret Thatcher Lecture.[54]

As a patriot down under, Murdoch paraded his Australianness before the country's Broadcasting Tribunal in 1979 when he sought regulatory approval to buy the Channel 10 television network. He was residing overseas at that time and told the inquiry, 'I am now accused of not being an Australian. Who in this room can say I am not a good Australian, or a patriotic one? . . . I carry an Australian passport. My children are Australian. I pay my taxes in Australia, I have a home in Australia . . . I certainly intend to come back to this country and certainly when my children are old enough to leave home I trust I will in fact put them through Australian universities.'[55] The Tribunal approved the takeover; none of Murdoch's promises about himself or his children eventuated. Then in 2008, when addressing his native country's challenges in the prestigious Boyer Lectures, he argued that '*we* alone must define our future. An independent Australia will have no excuses for failure because the mistakes will be all *our* own. But I have few doubts that *we* will prosper because I have much confidence in this country and its people.'

One of the issues which has most controversially enmeshed this global citizen in the slipstream of modern history is global warming. Although Murdoch was an early advocate of climate action – in 2007 he told his shareholders that 'climate change poses clear, catastrophic threats' – he soon changed his mind, despite the vast majority of scientists agreeing that climate change has been caused by human activity. As a result of his volte-face, Murdoch has presided over an international media empire that leads the world in climate science denialism.

Top-rating commentators at Fox News regularly assail viewers with conspiracy theories alleging that climate change is a left-wing plot designed to destroy the economy and control lives. 'The entire theory is absurd,' said Tucker Carlson, who was sacked by the network in early 2023, of the scientific validity of human-caused climate change.[56] Another leading conservative Fox commentator, Laura Ingraham, described climate change as a scientific fraud and a lie. Young people, she claimed, are being 'indoctrinated into critical climate theory just like critical race theory'.[57] In the first half of 2019, according to the nonprofit consumer advocacy organisation Public Citizen, 212 of the 247 segments that Fox News devoted to climate issues were dismissive or doubtful about the climate crisis. Fox has been the 'greatest promoter of climate change disinformation over the past two decades', claimed Pennsylvania State University climate scientist Michael Mann in 2021.[58]

Murdoch's Australian news channel Sky News is 'ground zero' for climate science antagonists around the world, according to analysis conducted in mid-2022 by the Institute for Strategic Dialogue, a British think tank. And a 2020 investigation by the advocacy group GetUp into climate coverage at News Corp's four biggest Australian daily newspapers found that over a year, 45 per cent of 8,612 news and commentary items either rejected or cast doubt on consensus scientific findings.

A raging summer of wildfires in Australia in 2019–2020 – known as the country's Black Summer – generated a fresh surge of hostility towards the Murdoch empire's climate denialism. It was led by James Murdoch, who left the company later in 2020, and his activist wife Kathryn. Many of News Corp's Australian newspapers and Sky News commentators claimed that arsonists – not climate change – were largely responsible for the fires, which were the worst in decades and claimed twenty-seven lives, destroyed thousands of properties, and killed an estimated one billion animals. 'Hysterical efforts to blame the fires on climate change continue, even though we have always faced this threat and always will,' columnist Chris Kenny wrote in *The Australian*, the company's flagship.[59] At Fox News, Laura Ingraham talked of a 'climate change flameout' and claimed that 'celebrities in the media have been pressing the narrative that the wildfires in Australia are caused by climate change'.[60]

James and Kathryn Murdoch, both passionate environmentalists, were appalled by their family company's rejection of climate science reality. 'Kathryn and James' views on climate are well established and their frustration with some of the News Corp and Fox coverage of the topic is also well known,' their spokesperson told *The Daily Beast* website in what was an unprecedented mutiny, carried out in the public glare, from within the Murdoch family. 'They are particularly disappointed with the ongoing denial among the news outlets in Australia given obvious evidence to the contrary.'[61]

James Murdoch's freedom to openly criticise his family companies was undoubtedly made less onorous by the billions of dollars in his pocket that resulted from the earlier sale of assets to Disney. But it's much harder for employees with a conscience *and* a mortgage to say what they really think. One exception was Emily Townsend, a News Corp commercial finance manager in Sydney, who was so incensed by her company's climate coverage that she sent an email to News Corp's Australian chairman, Michael Miller, and copied it to all Australian staff members:

I have been severely impacted by the coverage of News Corp publications in relation to the fires, in particular the misinformation campaign that has tried to divert attention away from the real issue which is climate change to rather focus on arson (including misrepresenting facts).

I find it unconscionable to continue working for this company, knowing I am contributing to the spread of climate-change denial and lies. The reporting I have witnessed in *The Australian*, *The Daily Telegraph*, and *Herald Sun* is not only irresponsible, but dangerous and damaging to our communities and beautiful planet that needs us more than ever to acknowledge the destruction we have caused and start doing something about it.[62]

After pressing 'send' on an email that was swiftly deleted from staff inboxes, Townsend departed the company.

'We Go Out and Destroy Other People's Lives'

Fossicking through the personal lives of public figures has always been foundational to the commercial success of tabloid media. 'As far as journalists are concerned, celebrities forfeit their rights once they become famous,' says the British journalism professor and former newspaper editor Roy Greenslade. 'They have wealth and fame and should be happy to pay the price for it which means accepting that they are fair game for media misbehaviour.'[1]

No-one has understood this for as long, or as profitably, as Rupert Murdoch. His privacy-invasion business model (including the billion-dollar-plus costs of paying off victims to keep them quiet) has been a central feature of his newspapers since the mid-twentieth century. In that time, News Corp has spied on thousands of people across three continents, illegally hacked the voicemails of public figures, bribed public officials to extract private information, and concocted or embellished stories about the private lives of public figures under the guise of 'public interest'.

Industrial-scale intrusion into personal privacy started at News Corp at least two decades before it was exposed by the phone hacking scandal. In 1987 *The Sun* published a front-page story under the headline 'ELTON IN VICE BOYS SCANDAL' which alleged that the singer Elton John and his manager had paid a 'minimum of 100 pounds plus all the cocaine they could stand' to ten rent boys in exchange for sex, and that 'the singer had snorted cocaine while begging tattooed skinheads to indulge in bondage'. Elton John issued seventeen libel writs against *The Sun* before it finally conceded the story was false, paid him a £1 million settlement and published a front-page apology under the headline 'SORRY ELTON'. Six months later, the rent boy who made the allegations told the rival *Daily Mirror* he only did it for the money: '*The Sun* was easy to con. I've never met Elton John . . . it's all a pack of lies, I made it all up.'[2]

Three years later, News Corp's Sydney *Sunday Telegraph* splashed two 'secret photos' of the well-known right-wing Australian politician Pauline Hanson, topless and scantily decked in black lingerie, across its front page. The pictures claimed to show Hanson as a nineteen-year-old posing naked in the 1970s for a photographer who was then her boyfriend. A week later, under the headline 'Pauline: we're sorry, they weren't you', the paper's editor acknowledged the pictures had been photoshopped – 'part of an elaborate con' – but justified publishing them because 'firstly, we believed it was Pauline Hanson in the pictures and, secondly, she was a public figure, running for election in Queensland in a return to front-line politics, who had written a detailed book about her life in which she laid her private life bare. The paper believed – and still believes – there is massive public interest in Ms Hanson's life.'[3]

When asked in a later interview what public interest the story served, deputy editor Helen McCabe didn't even attempt to dissemble. 'That will be determined by the number of people that buy the paper,' she said, a response that sat uncomfortably alongside News Corporation Australia's code of professional conduct: 'Journalists have no general right to report the private behavior of public figures unless public interest issues arise.'[4]

Stories of 'massive public interest' that embarrass politicians, celebrities and sports stars are the most valuable items on display in the shop window of privacy-invasion journalism. In its pre-phone-hacking days, the *News of the World* was so brazen about its requirements that it ran ads asking its readers to invade other people's privacy: 'We pay big money for sizzling shots of showbiz love-cheats doing what they shouldn't ought to. A-listers looking the worse for wear or Premiership idols on the lash the night before a crucial game.'[5]

Members of royal families are prime targets. Princess Diana's death in 1997, in a crash that allegedly resulted from photographers following her chauffeur-driven car through Paris, created international outrage. In 2018 the French magazine *Closer* was fined for breach of privacy after it published photographs of the Duchess of Cambridge sunbathing topless on holiday at a private chateau in southeast France. The magazine, its editor and publisher were fined €45,000 and ordered to pay €100,000 in damages to the duchess and her husband Prince William.

The actor Sienna Miller, the first person to sue the *News of the World* for hacking her phone, became a kind of unofficial spokesperson for the victims of privacy intrusion by the media. In 2005 *The Sun* revealed she was pregnant after one of its journalists extracted her private medical information from a 'medical records tracer', who then invoiced the paper for 'Sienns [*sic*] Miller Pregnant research'.[6] In 2011 she was awarded £100,000 in compensation from the *News of the World* after it accepted unconditional liability for hacking her voicemail to produce stories about her troubled relationship with actor Jude Law.

Initially, she was nervous about taking on one of the world's most powerful media machines. 'Everyone was scared of Rupert Murdoch, even governments,' she said. 'People are terrified for their own reputations. They want the press on their side.' She eventually decided to pursue legal action because 'the tabloid media culture in this country had got to a point where it was completely immoral. There was no consideration for you as a human being. You were successful, you were making money, therefore you deserved it and it was a very medieval way of behaving.'[7]

In his own victim statement when he settled a phone-hacking case, Jude Law described an organisation that was 'prepared to do anything to sell their newspapers and to make money, irrespective of the impact it had on people's lives ... No aspect of my private life was safe from intrusion by News Group newspapers, including the lives of my children and the people who work for me. It was not just that my phone messages were listened to. News Group also paid people to watch me and my house for days at a time and to follow me and those close to me both in this country and abroad.'[8] Another celebrity, singer Charlotte Church, who was paid £600,000 by News International to settle her phone-hacking lawsuit, expressed the views of many of the victims: 'They are not truly sorry; they are just sorry they got caught.'[9]

In 2017 the actor Geoffrey Rush woke up to find himself plastered over the front page of News Corp's Sydney *Daily Telegraph* under the headline 'KING LEER'. The story, which had no source and was based entirely on rumour, alleged that Rush had engaged in 'inappropriate behavior' while appearing in a Sydney Theatre Company production of *King Lear*. Rush sued the *Telegraph* for libel, claiming the stories portrayed him as a 'pervert' and a 'sexual predator'. During the trial his wife, Jane Menelaus, told the court how her husband 'wept' on seeing the front page. 'I saw a man so altered and changed. His eyes sunk into his head. He retreated very much from the world,' said Menelaus. 'It will take us a very long time to get over this. Our approach to the people and the world has changed.' Her husband had spent the previous eleven months, she said, asking, 'Why must they hate me so much so [*sic*] say these things about me?'[10]

Rush won the court case comprehensively. He was awarded AUD$2.9 million in damages, a record for an Australian libel action. The judge condemned the *Telegraph* for its 'recklessly irresponsible pieces of sensationalist journalism of the very worst kind'.[11] When the paper appealed the judgement, it lost. Yet the defamation case initiated by Rush to protect his reputation – he was an acclaimed Hollywood and stage actor with Oscar, Emmy and Tony awards – created public humiliation on a scale that has severely damaged his career.

Every journalist who participates in voyeuristic privacy invasion understands why they do it: to generate clicks, increase ratings or circulation, advance their career, make more money for their owner – all under the pretext of public interest. 'What I want to know,' *The Sun*'s features editor in the late 1980s, Wendy Henry, told her editorial staff, 'is who's fucking who?'[12] Henry later went on to edit *The People* newspaper where, following a burst of proprietorial conscience by its owner Robert Maxwell, she was sacked after six months for publishing a photograph of seven-year-old Prince William urinating in a park, and another of singer Sammy Davis Jr showing scars from his throat cancer treatment – both in the same edition.[13]

Even *The Sun*'s long-time editor Kelvin MacKenzie, arguably the godfather of twentieth-century British beat-up journalism, has acknowledged the central role of invading privacy in the tabloid business model. Following the death of the paper's veteran chief reporter John Kay, who lost his job after News International turned over evidence of payments to one of his sources at the Ministry of Defence, as part of the police investigation into phone hacking, MacKenzie told the UK *Press Gazette*, 'John was among twenty-two staff that Murdoch threw under the bus to save his own skin when threatened with a corporate charge which would have forced him out of his own company. In my years of running *The Sun* Murdoch never asked where John's fantastic tales came from; he was only interested that we had them so we could sell more papers, make more money and stuff the opposition.'[14]

———

Intruding into the private lives of celebrities and public figures has spawned a sub-industry – the paparazzi – staffed by freelance photographers who stalk celebrities, athletes and politicians to snap private pictures they can sell to gossip websites, newspapers and magazines. Ron Galella, the one-time king of the paparazzi photographers, was injuncted in 1973 by an American federal appeals court that constrained his pursuit of former US first lady Jacqueline Onassis and her children. The judge described the paparazzi as 'literally a kind of annoying insect, perhaps roughly equivalent to the English "gadfly"'.[15]

That case was unusual in the US, where there is limited protection for the targets of paparazzi. The federal Protection from Personal Intrusion Act and the Privacy Protection Act include criminal penalties for photographers if their conduct causes physical harm. In California, paparazzi are legally prohibited from pursuing targets in cars, trespassing, and using telephoto lenses to film on private property. Despite those laws, these issues are rarely tested in a country where press freedom is protected by the constitution's first amendment.

Even more toothless are the official-sounding 'codes of editorial practice' that have become a fig leaf for media companies to feign responsible behaviour. In the UK, for example, it's instructive to compare the Editors' Code of Practice with the actual practices of the worst-offending journalists. This is Clause 2 of the code, on privacy:

i) Everyone is entitled to respect for their private and family life, home, physical and mental health, and correspondence, including digital communications.

ii) Editors will be expected to justify intrusions into any individual's private life without consent. In considering an individual's reasonable expectation of privacy, account will be taken of the complainant's own public disclosures of information and the extent to which the material complained about is already in the public domain or will become so.

iii) It is unacceptable to photograph individuals, without their consent, in public or private places where there is a reasonable expectation of privacy.[16]

Over recent decades, the internet has ratcheted up privacy invasion to a whole new level. The online version of the Northcliffes' *Daily Mail* is a relentless showcase of paparazzi activity, delivering daily, sometimes hourly exposés. Often the most vulnerable victims are ordinary people, who don't have agents, advisers and publicists, who don't use the media for self-promotion, and who have almost never interacted with journalists. This distorted system was exposed in granular detail by Julia Dahl, a young journalist, writing in the *Columbia Journalism Review* in 2017. Dahl had been sent as a freelancer for the *New York Post* to talk to a student at the College of Staten Island who had done jail time for child pornography charges and had recently been released on parole. The *Post*'s editor had told her to ask this man 'if he thinks the students should feel unsafe around him', and to be sure to get a picture of him.

Dahl and a photographer went to the man's house, where he was working with his father in the garage. After a brief altercation the photographer got his picture. '"Why can't you leave him alone," wailed the father, trying to pull his son back into the garage. "He's just trying to make a better life. Please,"' recounted Dahl. 'The next day, the paper ran an article announcing that the "pervy pupil" had been barred from enrollment.'

For its subjects and victims, Dahl wrote, such journalism 'reduces the greatest tragedy of their life to alliterative shorthand, will have consequences for them, their family, and maybe their attitude toward the news for the rest of their lives. Knocking on doors for the *Post* forced me to acknowledge that power each day.'[17]

Not many reporters, editors or proprietors acknowledge that power, because it would force them to confront the duplicity used by journalists who invade private lives. In July 2005, after London was rocked by suicide bomb blasts, there was intense media competition for interviews with survivors. One of those survivors, university professor John Tulloch, sustained cut eyes and shrapnel embedded in his head from a bomb on his train carriage. He was lying in a hospital bed on strong painkillers, without his glasses and suffering from hearing problems, when a sad-looking young woman carrying flowers entered his room.

Sharri Markson was a News Corp reporter from Australia, then on vacation in Europe. 'I just saw this massive pack of media out the front and I thought there's no way I'm going to get an interview if I just join that pack, so I bought a bunch of flowers and I walked straight into the hospital and no one would ever think I was media,' she later told her newspaper, *The Australian*. 'I was 21, looking even younger, in casual clothes because that's all I had, holding a bunch of flowers. So I just went in and said, "Oh I'm here to visit [John Tulloch]", and I didn't lie, I was very careful, I just said I was here to visit John Tulloch and I went up there and when I got in with him I gave him my card immediately ... The hospital was furious because a journalist got in but at no time did I lie and he agreed to be photographed so I got the exclusive interview with him.' According to the hospital's press officer, Markson duped a nurse to enter Tulloch's room: 'In the 13 years I've worked in PR, I have never once come across such outrageous reporting practices.'[18]

The power imbalance that exists between the subjects and the controllers of the news gnaws at the moral heart of journalism. 'As anyone in the business will tell you, the standards and culture of a journalistic institution are set from the top down, by its owner, publisher, and top editors,' the Watergate reporter Carl Bernstein wrote in the aftermath of the phone hacking scandal. 'Reporters and editors do not routinely break the law, bribe policemen, wiretap, and generally conduct themselves like thugs unless it is a matter of recognized and understood policy. Private detectives and phone hackers do not become the primary sources of a newspaper's information without the tacit knowledge and approval of the people at the top, all the more so in the case of newspapers owned by Rupert Murdoch, according to those who know him best.'[19]

One of Murdoch's many editors of the London *Sun*, David Yelland, explained his power by imagining the presence of a permanent 'big red button' sitting on his desk. By pressing it, a giant explosion is created somewhere the next morning – bang goes a career, bang goes a family, bang goes a life.[20] *News of the World* reporter Greg Miskiw, who spent a career unmasking the private lives of celebrities, was once caught on tape explaining the purpose of tabloid journalism to a young reporter: 'That is what we do – we go out and destroy other people's lives.'[21]

In scale, moral contempt and criminality, nothing in the history of journalism compares to the systemic phone hacking and bribery perpetrated by Rupert Murdoch's British newspapers throughout the first decade of the twenty-first century. The voicemails of more than 5,000 unsuspecting celebrities, sports stars, politicians, parents, spouses, Buckingham Palace staff and ordinary people were secretly monitored by private detectives and reporters employed by the *News of the World* and *The Sun*. The juiciest information was used to write exclusive stories or as blackmail. Public officials and police were bribed to supply personal information to the newspapers.

This institutionalised criminal behaviour effectively started in 1999 when reporters at *The Sun* intercepted voicemails in order to uncover dirt about the divorce of Mick Jagger and – deep irony – Murdoch's subsequent wife Jerry Hall. By 2002, *News of the World* journalists had begun buying phone and credit records from a private detective agency, according to evidence produced by *The Guardian*.

In 2003, staff from the UK information commissioner's office discovered a large cache of handwritten requests from newspapers, including the *News of the World*, asking the private investigator Steve Whittamore to uncover personal information about public figures. In 2005, at Blackfriars Crown Court in London, four men pleaded guilty to procuring confidential police data to sell to newspapers, including the *News of the World*. During the same year, three *News of the World* journalists commissioned another private investigator, Glenn Mulcaire, to start hacking the voicemails of public figures and celebrities.

A year later, Scotland Yard detectives arrived at the *News of the World* office with a search warrant. This followed a six-month police investigation into the voicemail hacking of princes William and Harry and the royal family household by two of the paper's journalists, its royal editor Clive Goodman, and Mulcaire. Some 11,000 pages of handwritten notes, containing the names of nearly 4,000 celebrities, politicians, sports stars, police officials and victims of crime, were seized by the detectives. The voicemail of one royal aide had been called 433 times, those records revealed, and evidence later emerged in court that Goodman had hacked Kate Middleton's phone 155 times.

Mulcaire and Goodman were immediately arrested and charged with conspiracy to intercept communications without lawful authority. Five months later, after pleading guilty, they were sentenced to several months in jail and lost their jobs at News International. Goodman's world was one where 'ethical lines are not always so clearly defined or at least observed', his lawyer told the court.[22] After that case, Mulcaire admitted to hacking the voicemails of the chief executive of the Professional Footballers' Association, a member of parliament, the model Elle Macpherson, an influential public-relations agent, and a powerful soccer agent.

Even after the resignation of the *News of the World*'s editor, Andy Coulson, the alarm bells were muffled by the noise of News Corp's righteous denials. Bugging the voicemails of the royal family was merely 'an exceptional and unhappy event in the 163 year history of the *News of the World*, involving one journalist', said Colin Myler, the paper's new editor. Clive Goodman was 'the only person' at the paper who knew about the hacking, insisted Les Hinton, executive chairman of News International.[23]

A formal inquiry by Britain's Press Complaints Commission supported News Corp's facade of blamelessness. The PCC lamely promised to write to Myler for 'detailed information on what had gone wrong and to find out what steps would be taken to ensure that the situation did not recur', and pledged to conduct a 'broad inquiry across the whole of the press to find out the extent of internal controls aimed at preventing similar abuses'. Two years later the commission reported reassuringly that its earlier work on phone hacking had 'raised standards'.[24] Nothing to see here.

But the issue just wouldn't go away. In mid-2008, News International was told privately by a senior specialist in media law, Michael Silverleaf QC, that 'there is or was a culture of illegal information access used at News Group Newspapers to produce stories for publication'.[25] It was another two years before Sienna Miller took civil action in the High Court against the paper for hacking her voicemail. By now, the scandal was attracting attention in the US, where News Corp was headquartered and subject to tough corporate and anti-bribery laws. *The New York Times* cited several *News of the World* former staff who alleged that phone-hacking at the paper was widespread. Under the weight of this increasing evidence, the PCC finally found its teeth. 'Evidence we have seen makes it inconceivable that no-one else at the *News of the World*, bar Clive Goodman, knew about the phone-hacking,' it concluded.[26]

News Corp's nothing-to-see-here obfuscation strategy might have survived if not for two dogged investigative reporters from *The Guardian*, Nick Davies and Amelia Hill. On 4 July 2011 they detonated the story, across their paper's front page, that blew the lid on years of denials and deceit:

Missing Milly Dowler's voicemail was hacked by News of the World

- Deleted voicemails gave family false hope
- Hacking interfered with police hunt
- Family lawyer: actions 'heinous and despicable'

The News of the World illegally targeted the missing schoolgirl Milly Dowler and her family in March 2002, interfering with police inquiries into her disappearance, an investigation by the *Guardian* has established.[27]

All hell broke loose. Not only had News Corp employees hacked the voicemail of a kidnapped and murdered thirteen-year-old schoolgirl, it was revealed that the phones of relatives of deceased British soldiers and victims of the 7 July 2005 London bombings had also been intercepted. No longer could the company conduct its 'important public interest journalism' in secret. Describing the *News of the*

World's behaviour as 'heinous' and 'despicable', the Dowler family's lawyer announced that a damages claim would be pursued against the paper. (Five months later, *The Guardian* reported that although the *News of the World* did hack Milly Dowler's phone, new police evidence showed that 'the newspaper is unlikely to have been responsible for the deletion of a set of voicemails from the phone that caused her parents to have false hopes that she was alive'.)

Three days after *The Guardian*'s revelation, another bombshell dropped. James Murdoch, who ran his father's UK operation, announced the closure of the *News of the World*. This was followed by a grovelling full-page ad placed in British newspapers:

We are sorry.

The *News of the World* was in the business of holding others to account.

It failed when it came to itself.

We are sorry for the serious wrongdoing that occurred.

We are deeply sorry for the hurt suffered by the individuals affected.

We regret not acting faster to sort things out.

I realize that simply apologizing is not enough.

Our business was founded on the idea that a free and open press should be a positive force in society. We need to live up to this.

In the coming days, as we take further concrete steps to resolve these issues and make amends for the damage they have caused, you will hear more from us.

Sincerely,

Rupert Murdoch

Rupert and James were summoned to appear before the Culture, Media and Sport Committee of the House of Commons. Neither Murdoch was prepared to admit personal responsibility for their company's criminal behaviour, although they did express contrition. 'First, I would like to say ... how sorry I am, and how sorry we are, to particularly the victims of illegal voice-mail interceptions and to their families,' James began. 'It is a matter of great regret to me, my father, and everyone at News Corporation.' Then Rupert put his hand on his son's arm and uttered the most quoted words of the entire phone hacking scandal: 'I would just like to say one sentence. This is the most humble day of my life.'[28]

It was a singular public humiliation for a mogul who had spent a career humiliating others without sanction. 'He mumbled. He looked confused. He couldn't remember anything very specific,' wrote Sarah Ellison in *Vanity Fair*. 'The idea that he might have any influence on what his newspapers published seemed to strike him as absurd. Murdoch told the committee that he talked to the editors of the *News of the World* and *The Sun* "very seldom".' His son, meanwhile, appeared naive and helpless. When committee member Tom Watson said to him, 'You must be the first mafia boss in history who didn't realize he was running a criminal enterprise,' James Murdoch replied contritely: 'Mr Watson, please, I think that is inappropriate.'[29]

The next day, a government that had always deferred to Murdoch was forced by public disgust to launch a judicial inquiry into the culture, practices and ethics of the British press. After a nine-month investigation involving 337 witnesses and almost 300 statements, Lord Justice Leveson's 2,000-page final report recommended establishing a new independent media standards body with sanction powers, including fines and the ability to force media companies to publish prominent apologies and corrections. Prime minister David Cameron said he welcomed many of Leveson's findings, but rejected legislating to implement Leveson's proposal for a new journalism regulator. All major national newspapers, except *The Guardian*, agreed with Cameron's position.

In his final report, Justice Leveson grappled with the underlying conundrum of press freedom, noting that on one hand, journalism is 'one of the true safeguards of our democracy', and on the other that phone hacking 'damaged the public interest, caused real hardship and on occasion, wreaked havoc on the lives of innocent people'. His conclusion was a sharp statement of the obvious: 'I know of no organized profession, industry or trade in which the serious failings of the few are overlooked or ignored because of the good done by the many.' As he noted, self-evidently, the press itself would be 'the very first to expose such practices' in any other case.[30]

———

Listening to voicemail messages was so pervasive in the *News of the World* newsroom that, as one long-time reporter told *The New York Times*, 'everyone knew ... the office cat knew'. One of the paper's showbusiness reporters explained how Coulson never instructed him to hack voicemails, but veiled his request in 'metaphorical language' by asking him to use his 'dark arts' to procure stories. A former *News of the World* senior editor talked of being at 'dozens if not hundreds of meetings with Andy' where Coulson was told about stories procured by 'pulling the phone records' or 'listening to the phone messages'. According to Clive Goodman, the reporter who left the paper after pleading guilty to bugging the phones of the royal family, 'the practice was widely discussed in the daily editorial conference, until explicit reference to it was banned by the editor'.[31] It took years, but willful blindness eventually trumped newsroom chatter.

The mechanics of phone hacking were not complicated. Reporters in the *News of the World* newsroom were like amateur telephone technicians, illegally infiltrating a target's voicemail using either electronic or human intervention. 'Often, all it took was a standard four-digit security code, like 1111 or 4444, which many users did not bother to change after buying their mobile phones,' explained *The New York Times*. 'Reporters called one method of hacking "double screwing" because it required two simultaneous calls to the same number. The first would engage the phone line, forcing the second call into voice mail. A reporter then punched in the code to hear messages, often deleting them to prevent access by rival papers.'[32]

Phone numbers were procured through a practice known as blagging, which is defined in dictionaries as wheedling or cadging. Reporters, or their private-investigator collaborators, blagged personal medical data from hospitals by pretending to be a doctor or by befriending hospital employees. They gleaned financial information from banks by posing as customers (on six occasions a blagger acting for *The Sunday Times*, another Murdoch masthead, posed as Gordon Brown, then Britain's chancellor of the exchequer and later prime minister, to gain details from his account). They gathered social security information from probation services and benefit agencies by purporting to be beneficiaries.

John Ford, who blagged for fifteen years for *The Sunday Times*, explained in an interview with *The Guardian* in 2018 how he extracted personal financial details of hundreds of cabinet ministers, publishers, businessmen and celebrities. 'He tricked call centre staff and company employees, typically using a fake identity, to obtain bank statements, mortgage records, utility bills and ex-directory numbers. He blagged unpublished autobiographies from publishers, emptied the bins of the powerful in pursuit of secrets . . . he targeted the most powerful people of the era: Tony Blair, Gordon Brown, William Hague, John Prescott, the former head of MI6 and celebrities such as Paul McCartney at the time of his marriage to Heather Mills.'

When *The Sunday Times* agreed to Ford's suggestion to steal rubbish in the hope of finding secrets, he raided the bins of a dozen prominent figures in the Labour government in the spring and summer of 2000. Ford was assisted by a friend he called George in a practice they described as 'bin-spinning'.

His rates, he told *The Guardian*, were £80–120 for obtaining an ex-directory number, and £120–250 to get into a UK bank account, rising to £350 for international accounts. 'In those days, you could get anything,' Ford told *The Guardian*. 'There is one basic law of the blag. And that is to give something to someone.' He would find the account numbers of his targets by calling the bank and telling them he owed them money: '[L]ooking at my direct debits, the money should have gone to you and it has not gone through,' to which they would say that it had come through. 'What do you mean? From my sort code 20 23 31?' No, he was told, sort code 64. He would say, 'From account 5721.' And they would reply, 'No, account number . . .' And he would sign off: 'Thanks very much.'[33]

The private investigator whose arrest led to the closure of the *News of the World*, Glenn Mulcaire, would call his target's mobile carrier posing as a credit control employee to get the voicemail PIN changed back to default. Paul McMullan, a former *News of the World* reporter, described for *The Guardian* another typical sting: '[A celebrity] checked into a hotel room in Paris with a new girlfriend who wasn't his wife. So what we did is we rang up the hotel pretending to be his accountant and said, we need the entire bill, please with all the phone calls so we can itemize it. And the hotel rather stupidly just faxed over his bill and we just rang all of the numbers until we found the home number of his girlfriend, then sent some paparazzis to get a picture.'[34]

If deception didn't work, there was always the most old-fashioned of procurement techniques: bribery. According to Sue Akers, Scotland Yard's deputy assistant commissioner, *The Sun* established a network of corrupted officials in the police, health service, military and prison service, who received multiple payments over several years. This scheme had been in operation for years before the phone hacking scandal broke. Appearing before the House of Commons' Culture, Media and Sport Committee in 2003, then *Sun* editor Rebekah Brooks acknowledged 'we have paid the police for information in the past'.[35] And when Kelvin MacKenzie was asked by the Leveson Inquiry nine years later whether he was aware of payments made to police officers for information while he was editor of *The Sun*, he replied, 'I wasn't but it wouldn't surprise me if they were made.'[36] Police eventually charged or arrested thirty-four journalists with illegally paying for stories, but only one *Sun* reporter, several public officials, and, in total, only nine of the company's employees were convicted for hacking crimes between 2005 and 2014.

Andy Coulson's behaviour embodied News International's response to the phone hacking revelations. First, deception (it was the work of a single 'rogue reporter'). Then denial ('my instructions to the staff were clear – we did not use subterfuge of any kind unless there was a clear public interest in doing so').[37] When he was finally imprisoned, having been found guilty in June 2014 of conspiracy to intercept voicemails, he served less than five months of his eighteen-month prison sentence. Coulson has since drawn on his hacking and tabloid experiences to create a post-penal career running a PR agency that specialises in crisis management for high-profile victims. He also presents 'Crisis What Crisis?', a serious, non-tabloid-style podcast that 'delivers invaluable lessons for when life unravels'.

More than a decade after it was first exposed, phone hacking remains the time bomb that never stops ticking at News Corp. By 2024, Murdoch's companies had paid $1.3 *billion* in damages to more than a thousand victims to legally prevent them from telling their stories. This included $66 million in 2022 alone, a sum reported obscurely in the News Corp accounts as 'UK newspaper matters'.[38]

And the legal assault on the company by high-profile victims continues to roll on. Actor Hugh Grant, who had already received substantial damages from *News of the World*, lobbed a further damages claim in 2022, this time against *The Sun*. Among others who lodged claims around the same time were the government minister Zac Goldsmith, former cabinet minister Chris Huhne, Spice Girl Mel B, and actors Gillian Anderson and Kate Winslet. And in 2023, fourteen years after *The Guardian* first broke the story, Prince Harry became the highest profile litigant so far.

Meanwhile, the man whose company committed crimes against thousands of victims continues to disclaim any personal responsibility, either for the practices or the culture that nurtured them. Instead, Rupert Murdoch blames his executives and their underlings: 'With the wisdom of hindsight, I have learned that even experienced and long serving members of staff can fail to meet their responsibilities.'[39] News Corp, he insisted, handled the crisis 'extremely well in every way possible', making just 'minor mistakes'.[40]

At the height of his company's embarrassment in 2013, Murdoch met privately with a group of *Sun* journalists who had been arrested or charged by police. At the meeting – which was taped and later exposed by the British investigative website *Exaro News* – the paper's former managing editor Graham Dudman introduced Murdoch to the group: 'Until their arrests, everybody that you're looking at in this room today was a loyal, hard-working employee devoted to you personally, to *The Sun*, to News International and everything that this company and you stand for, and have been proud to work here. One thing that everybody in this room shares . . . is that we were arrested, thrown into police cells, treated as common criminals in front of our children, our families, and our neighbours, and our friends and our colleagues, for doing nothing more than the company expected of us – nothing.'[41]

In response, Murdoch told the gathered journalists, 'I don't know of anybody, or anything, that did anything that wasn't being done across Fleet Street and wasn't the culture . . . we're talking about payments for news tips from cops: that's been going on a hundred years, absolutely.'[42] It was an excuse that sits uncomfortably alongside the email written by a junior editor working at the *News of the World* at the height of phone hacking to a colleague: 'Sometimes I think we're just dazzled by traces and checks and shady stuff, and [so] we don't try obvious journalistic techniques.'[43]

One of the biggest victims of the 'shady stuff' was Prince Harry, the Duke of Sussex, who in early 2023 made an appearance in the British High Court in a £200,000 damages case, claiming *The Sun* had hacked into his voicemails and employed private investigators to ferret out personal information about his relationships.

Reflecting on the role of senior News Group executives, who both knew about and condoned phone hacking, and actively sought to cover it up, the prince told the court that his 'immediate thoughts are that this makes them criminals, not journalists, and the fourth estate is too important and rightly powerful to have criminals masquerading as journalists running the show'.[44]

Fox News

Nothing in the history of abuse of media power since the 1880s comes close to the squalid role played by Fox News in monetising bigotry and resentment. Conceived by Rupert Murdoch, the network was constructed as an American propaganda machine, in tone and substance, by its founding chairman and chief executive, Roger Ailes.

Ailes subscribed to the propangandist's maxim (attributed to Joseph Goebbels), 'Make the lie big, make it simple, keep saying it, and eventually they will believe it.' His mindset was crudely exposed in 2010 when he publicly attacked his liberal public broad-casting competitor National Public Radio. 'They are, of course, Nazis. They have a kind of Nazi attitude. They are the left wing of Nazism. These guys don't want any other point of view. They don't even feel guilty using tax dollars to spout their propaganda,' he told *The Daily Beast*.[1]

In the same interview, Ailes defended a three-part series by Fox News commentator Glenn Beck that parodied liberal billionaire philanthropist George Soros as a 'Jewish boy helping send the Jews to the death camps' during World War Two. Ailes described critics who decried the program as 'left-wing rabbis who basically don't think that anybody can ever use the word "Holocaust" on the air'.[2]

Fox News practises Hannah Arendt's description of the essen-tial tactic of the totalitarian movement – 'a mixture of gullibility and cynicism'. Her analysis, made in 1951, is even more relevant today:

'In an ever-changing, incomprehensible world the masses had reached the point where they would, at the same time, believe everything and nothing, think that everything was possible and nothing was true.'[3]

The true power of Fox News lies in its role as a *player* in the political tumult. It may look like a regular TV news network covering the game, but it is actually an on-field participant, a cheerleader and often the referee as well. Fox became so enmeshed in supporting Donald Trump that its titular boss, Lachlan Murdoch, was merely stating the obvious when he described his network as 'the loyal opposition' in a post-Trump world after the 2020 presidential election. 'That's what our job is now with the Biden administration.'[4] No ambiguity about the mission. *Our job. The loyal opposition.*

None of us in the modern Western media have ever witnessed a distortion of journalism on this scale. In my two years as a Murdoch editor in the late 1980s I saw things that offended my ethical sensibilities, but the worst offences in those days were sensationalism and privacy invasion pursued for profit – not journalism that endangered civic, political or democratic norms.

Fox News was launched in 1996 as a spiritual partnership with the Republican Party, and has never veered off course. Ailes was the perfectly credentialled helmsman, having spent years working as a political consultant for Republican presidents Nixon, Reagan and George H.W. Bush. He believed he had an instinctive understanding of the heartbeat of his largely working-class conservative target audience. 'I built this channel from my life experience,' he once told *The New York Times*. 'My first qualification is I didn't go to Columbia Journalism School. There are no parties in this town that I want to go to.'[5] With the full-throated support of his financier and co-conspirator Rupert Murdoch, Ailes created a partisan 'news' network that used slogans like 'Fair and Balanced' and 'We report. You decide' to obfuscate its real purpose.

For its political partner, however, the rapid growth of Fox News soon became a double-edged sword. 'Republicans originally thought that Fox worked for us and now we're discovering we work for Fox,' said former George W. Bush speechwriter David Frum in 2010.[6] Such was its control over the party that by 2015 Fox had become the kingmaker in Republican presidential primaries, and it has remained a kingmaker, albeit impersonating as an observer, ever since.

It was the election of Donald Trump in 2016 that wholly disconfigured Fox News, just as it disconfigured America. Trump rose to power using Fox as his personal mouthpiece and trusted adviser on policy. This created symbiosis on a scale never attempted by a media owner or a national leader. To those watching closely, Trump's White House and Murdoch's Fox News were interchangeable cogs in the same spin machine. Personnel, policy ideas, talking points and political tactics shifted seamlessly between two peak organisations in the topography of American power.

The enmeshment started at the top. Rupert Murdoch talked to Trump and his son-in-law Jared Kushner regularly, often weekly, according to *The New York Times*. 'Mr. Murdoch has felt comfortable enough to offer counsel that others may shy away from, such as urging the president to stop tweeting and advising him to improve his relationship with Secretary of State Rex W. Tillerson,' noted the *Times* in late 2017.[7] This easy alliance flowed naturally through to policy formulation. Fox News hosts Pete Hegseth and Lou Dobbs were patched into Oval Office meetings by speakerphone to offer strategic advice, while Sean Hannity – dubbed the Shadow Chief of Staff by White House advisers – spoke to the president virtually every night, reported *The New Yorker*.[8]

Trump spent up to four hours a day watching Fox News during his presidency, creating not just blurred boundaries, but, often, no boundaries. When a study by the liberal website *Media Matters for America* tracked the correlation between Fox shows and Trump's Twitter feed in 2019, it found more than 200 examples of Trump disseminating specific Fox News items to his 58 million followers, often within minutes of the broadcast.[9]

Then there was the revolving door of personnel between Fox HQ at 1211 Avenue of the Americas in New York, and the United

States government HQ at 1600 Pennsylvania Avenue in Washington, DC. When the former co-president of Fox News, Bill Shine, was appointed as Trump's director of communications and deputy chief of staff in 2018, he continued to receive his $14 million bonus payments from Fox while working in the White House.[10] Shine's connections to Fox were deep: he led the programming division for more than a decade; he was so close to the Fox commentator Sean Hannity that their children called them 'Uncle Bill' and 'Uncle Sean'; and he was allegedly complicit in a culture of cover-ups, payoffs and victim intimidation in several lawsuits, which led to the dismissal of Fox supremo Roger Ailes and star host Bill O'Reilly.[11]

Other notable Trump political appointments included Fox commentators Ben Carson and John Bolton, who were given cabinet positions by Trump; another commentator, K.T. McFarland, became deputy national security adviser (she resigned after four months); ex-Fox News anchor Heather Nauert was appointed US ambassador to the United Nations (she later withdrew because her nanny apparently lacked a migrant work permit); and former Fox co-host Kimberly Guilfoyle left the network to become a Trump adviser, working on his re-election campaign and later announcing her engagement to Donald Trump Jr.

Fox is the closest America has to State TV, says Nicole Hemmer, author of *Messengers of the Right*, a history of the conservative media in US politics. It acts as a force multiplier for Trump, not just taking the temperature of his base, but raising the temperature. 'It's a radicalization model,' says Hemmer.[12] In 2021, when asked what Fox News is for, an unnamed former News Corp executive told *The Economist*: 'Fomenting insurrection.'[13]

To understand the Fox News phenomenon, wrote David French in his *New York Times* column in 2023, you have to realise its role in conservative America. 'It's no mere source of news. It's the place where Red America goes to feel seen and heard. If there's an important good news story in Red America, the first call is to Fox. If conservative Christians face a threat to their civil liberties, the first call is to Fox. If you're a conservative celebrity and you need to sell a book, the first call is to Fox. And Fox takes those calls.'[14]

The effectiveness of Fox News as an activist broadcaster has been recognised by no less an expert than the Russian government. 'We understood long ago that there is no such thing as an independent Western media,' Sergey Lavrov, Russia's foreign minister, told his country's State television station RT in 2022. 'Only Fox News is trying to present some alternative point of view.'[15] Mentions of Fox in Russian-language media increased significantly after Putin invaded Ukraine. This was hardly surprising given Fox's pro-Russian stance, exemplified by a diatribe from the network's then prevailing star commentator, Tucker Carlson, in late 2022, after the Ukrainian president Volodymyr Zelensky addressed US lawmakers in Washington. 'No one's ever addressed the United States Congress in a sweatshirt before,' declared Carlson, describing Zelensky as a 'strip club' manager whose speech to Congress was 'humiliating' to 'the greatest country on Earth'.[16]

———

The proof that Fox News debased and distorted its content to please its viewers would never have emerged were it not for Dominion Voting Systems, a small technology outfit whose electronic voting machines processed ballots in twenty-eight states in the 2020 presidential election. The company, then worth around $60 million, came to the attention of Fox News commentators following the risible claims made by Donald Trump and his lawyers that Dominion's machines had flipped millions of votes from Trump to Biden to rig the election.

Fox News recklessly embraced Trump's stolen-election conspiracy theories. Without any fact checking, the network aired false accusations that Dominion had been launched in Venezuela to steal elections on behalf of dictator Hugo Chávez, and had bribed US officials to use its machines.[17] Fox hosts and Trump apologists used tracts of airtime to vent their spurious claims. 'The 2020 election is a cyber

Pearl Harbor,' declared commentator Lou Dobbs. 'We have techni-
cal presentations that prove there is an embedded controller in every
Dominion machine, that allows an election supervisor to move votes
from one candidate to another.'[18] Trump lawyer Rudy Giuliani told
Fox viewers that the Dominion machine was 'as filled with holes as
Swiss cheese and was developed to steal elections'.[19] Another Trump
lawyer, Sidney Powell, claimed 'the system was set up to shave and
flip different votes in different states', as part of 'the most massive
and historical egregious fraud the world has ever seen'.[20]

Four months after the election, Dominion sued Fox for defamation, seeking $1.6 billion in damages. This set off two years of legal
contretemps that ended, literally, on the steps of the courtroom when
the Murdochs threw in the towel and agreed to pay their tiny adver-
sary the largest publicly known defamation settlement involving a
media company in US history – $787.5 million.[21]

The already tarnished Fox News brand was trashed even more
during those lengthy pretrial skirmishes. At one stage the trial
judge, Eric Davis of the Delaware Superior Court, ruled that it was
'CRYSTAL clear that none of the Statements relating to Dominion
about the 2020 election are true' (his capital letters).[22] Then Davis
unsealed more than 6,500 pages of internal Fox News texts, emails,
and transcripts of deposition testimony that revealed, in excruciating detail, how the network's executives, personalities and both
Murdochs *knew* the claims about Dominion were untrue, but
continued to broadcast them.[23]

No media company has ever been forced to watch its own
mendacity aired so publicly. This is where we see the private Rupert
Murdoch at work. Emailing his Fox CEO, Suzanne Scott: 'We don't
want to antagonize Trump further, but Giuliani [should be] taken
with a large grain of salt. Everything's at stake here.'[24] Handing
Trump's son-in-law Jared Kushner a confidential preview of Biden's
ads before they were aired on Fox during the 2020 election campaign.
Asking Scott to ensure that Sean Hannity says 'something supportive' about Republican senator Lindsey Graham ahead of the election

because 'we cannot lose the Senate if at all possible'. (*We!*) Telling Scott, after Trump had asked for assistance to defeat a candidate in West Virginia, 'anything during day helpful but Sean [Hannity] and Laura [Ingraham] dumping on him hard might save the day'. Sending an internal text message acknowledging that Trump's voter fraud claims were 'really crazy stuff', yet admitting, 'I would have liked us to be stronger in denouncing it in hindsight.'[25] And conceding that Fox executives who knowingly pushed lies 'should be reprimanded' or 'maybe got rid of'. (*Maybe!*)[26]

Here is Lachlan Murdoch, messaging Scott to complain about comments made by Fox anchors covering Trump's support rally: 'News guys have to be careful how they cover this rally. So far some of the side comments are slightly anti, and they shouldn't be. The narrative should be this is a huge celebration of the president. Etc.'[27]

And here is Tucker Carlson, Fox's star host, privately describing the Trump election conspiracy theories as 'insane' to colleagues, while simultaneously defending his audience's belief in those theories: 'Our viewers are good people and they believe it.'[28] And Sean Hannity, after Trump lawyer Sidney Powell appeared on his show to allege that Dominion machines had been rigged, admitting privately, 'I did not believe it for one second.'[29]

The Dominion discovery documents and deposition testimony exposed Fox's primary mission – making money – out of the mouths of the people who ran and fronted the network. The tension between truth and profits was never more palpable than after the Fox election desk predicted that Biden had won Arizona during the 2020 election-night live TV coverage. It was a call that stunned the Trump camp because it set in train their path to defeat. 'What the f— is Fox doing?' Trump reportedly screamed. 'What the f— are these guys doing? How could they call this this early? Call Rupert! Call James and Lachlan!' he instructed Jared Kushner. But it was too late. Rupert Murdoch's response to Trump was 'a signature grunt' and a pithy message – 'Fuck him' – according to Michael Wolff's book on the Trump presidency, *Landslide*.[30]

The Arizona call roiled the network's heavyweights. 'Do the executives understand how much credibility and trust we've lost with our audience?' Tucker Carlson texted his producer in reference to the call, which proved accurate.[31] This has caused 'incalculable' damage that could allow a competitor to usurp Fox, texted Sean Hannity – 'Serious $$ with serious distribution could be a real problem.'[32] Meanwhile Suzanne Scott texted Lachlan Murdoch reassuringly: 'We will highlight our stars and plant flags letting the viewers know we hear them and respect them.'[33]

The Dominion revelations released the cat from the bag. Fox was *only* about the money. Credible news journalism was a facade – its Potemkin village. The demarcation line within the Murdoch business had been unmasked. 'On one side, journalism, constitutionally protected, even in its nastiest, most slanted and ideological form as part of the brutal scrum of democracy,' wrote Jim Rutenberg, who has been covering Fox for most of his career at *The New York Times*. 'On the other side, knowing lies, reckless disregard for the truth – the "actual malice" that is at the heart of the Dominion case.'[34]

The temperature continued to rise at Fox, and among its audience, as rioters marched on the US Capitol on 6 January 2021. While Trump remained silent, three prominent Fox News anchors – Sean Hannity, Laura Ingraham and Brian Kilmeade – pleaded privately with Trump's chief of staff Mark Meadows to urge the president to try to stop the violence. 'Mark, the president needs to tell people in the Capitol to go home. This is hurting all of us. He is destroying his legacy,' Ingraham texted – in stark contrast to her comments on air a few hours later claiming the Capitol was 'under siege by people who can only be described as antithetical to the MAGA movement … they were likely not all Trump supporters, and there are some reports that antifa sympathizers may have been sprinkled throughout the crowd'.[35]

Never in the messy history of journalism has cynicism and greed been conflated on such a scale. Anyone who participates in the news business understands the inherent tensions that can arise when a story, or storyline, butts up against the sensitivities of the audience. But to run an entire organisation on lies and quackery in order to mollify the audience? That's the work of a cult, not the work of a broadcaster or publisher. 'At issue here were not errors of fact, framing, or even ideological blind spots,' observed Adam Serwer in *The Atlantic*. 'The lawsuit shows these were conscious decisions to mislead, made for self-interested and partisan reasons.'[36]

———

Unlike the skills required for regular news programming – accuracy, judgement and balance – the key elements of propaganda TV are language, emotion and messaging. Images are nuanced with symbolism. Subtlety lurks. There's always a sense of urgency and movement.

Fox uses two crucial pronouns: *you* and *they*. (*You* are under attack; *they* are the attackers.) And one tone: indignation. 'Its grammar is grievance. Its effect is totalizing,' wrote Megan Garber in *The Atlantic* in 2020, citing touchstone Fox words and phrases like *mob, PC police, deep state, socialist agenda, libs, hordes, hoax, dirty, violent, invasion, open borders, anarchy, liberty, Donald Trump.*[37]

Incendiary language has two complementary functions in the propaganda TV toolkit: entertainment and resentment. Tucker Carlson was the master of the Fox one-liner: Joe Biden and Kamala Harris were 'a senile man and an imbecile'; the chairman of the Joint Chiefs of Staff General Mark Milley was 'not just a pig, he's stupid'; in America's schools 'your children are being taught by some of the most ignorant people in the country'.[38] In 2023, as talk host Laura Ingraham used the brutal Hamas assault on Israel to foment fear in the US, the on-air graphic was typically Fox: 'AMERICA NEXT?'[39]

Roger Ailes was the network's first professor of propaganda. He created a vast stage set designed to resemble an actual news network, hardwired into the homes of millions of conservative Americans. Republican candidates use Fox as their platform to communicate with their base, 'bypassing the professional journalists Ailes once denounced as "matadors" who want to "tear down the social order" with their "elitist, horse-dung, socialist thinking",' observed Tim Dickinson in *Rolling Stone*.⁴⁰

No news story fitted Fox's hysteria matrix more perfectly than the 9/11 terror attacks. In a back-channel memo from Fox to the US government, Ailes urged President Bush to ramp up the War on Terror: 'The American public would tolerate waiting and would be patient, but only as long as they were convinced that Bush was using the harshest measures possible,' he advised the White House, as reported by Bob Woodward.⁴¹ Not unlike the London *Sun's* glorious Falklands campaign, Fox quickly shifted to a war footing, plastering an American flag in the corner of the screen, dressing a host in camouflage clothing, and having another host make rhetorical on-air threats to pursue Osama bin Laden with a pistol.

The visual impact of a news network – especially a faux news network – relies heavily on chyrons, the crafty, ever-present, ever-moving digital captions that appear in the lower third of the screen. Normally a device used to report breaking news, chyrons at Fox News are often tools used to generate urgency and emotion. When Donald Trump was arraigned in June 2023 on criminal charges over the handling of classified documents, Fox ran a banana-republic-style chyron under images of Biden and Trump: WANNABE DICTATOR SPEAKS AT THE WHITE HOUSE AFTER HAVING HIS POLITICAL RIVAL ARRESTED.

The presence of chyrons across the bottom of the screen normalises Fox as a regular 'news network', even if the messages are often inflammatory, like this one during the 2016 presidential election campaign: A TALE OF TWO CANDIDATES ... HILLARY IN HIDING WHILE TRUMP'S OUT ON THE TRAIL.

The range of Fox News chyrons in the days immediately after the January 6 assault on the US Capitol in 2021, presented under a 'BATTLE FOR AMERICA' banner, paints a gritty picture of a network devoted to entrenching Trump's election denial narrative:

- LEFTIST MEDIA WAKES UP TO MOB VIOLENCE
- D.C. CHAOS EXPOSES MEDIA'S DOUBLE STANDARDS ON VIOLENCE

- LIBERAL DEMAGOGUERY EXPOSED
- CANCEL CULTURE RAGE MOBS WILL USE CAPITOL HILL RIOTS AS AN EXCUSE TO SILENCE ALL CONSERVATIVES
- D.C. ELITE WANTS TO MALIGN EVERY TRUMP SUPPORTER
- CRACKDOWN ON CIVIL LIBERTIES DIDN'T TAKE LONG
- MEDIA HYPOCRISY. PRESS DOWNPLAYED SUMMER VIOLENCE, RIPS CAPITOL RIOT

The bombardment of chyrons on the screen 'reduces our ability to be critically analytical', says cognitive expert Maryanne Wolf, who directs the Center for Reading and Language Research at Tufts University. This intensifies confusion, which can make viewers more susceptible to false or inaccurate information, she told *The Washington Post* in 2018. 'You're getting information, but you really don't have the time to process it.'[42]

Propaganda techniques work even more effectively when they're hooked into topics that evoke fear, anger or grievance (ideally all three). At Fox News in recent years, the code words that pushed those buttons most viscerally were 'birther', 'replacement theory' and 'vaccines'.

The 'birther' narrative was a concoction about 'Barack Hussein Obama' – as the president was constantly referred to on Fox – promoted by Donald Trump and fuelled by Fox commentators who claimed Obama was a Marxist Muslim black nationalist who was born in Kenya and therefore ineligible to be US president. It engrossed an audience that was 1.38 per cent African-American, with a median age of sixty-five at the time. When Trump used a weekly segment on *Fox & Friends* to push his spurious theory in 2011, well into the first Obama term, Fox host Sean Hannity defended those who promoted the theory as being unfairly 'crucified and beaten up and smeared and besmirched'.[43] By implying that the black president wasn't a true American, Fox News was able to make the two terms of Obama's presidency franchise-building years that produced record ratings.

For presenters and viewers living in a world of racist conspiracies, it was an almost seamless pathway from 'birther' to The Great Replacement theory. This Fox-fuelled conspiracy is based on the notion that liberals, Democrats and Jewish people are creating the conditions for political dominance, whereby falling birth rates in Western countries will lead to the replacement of white people by non-whites. It is a phrase that echoes the chants of white supremacists in the streets of Charlottesville, Virginia in 2017 – 'You will not replace us, Jews will not replace us' – and it later became the title of the document released by the murderer of fifty people in New Zealand mosques in 2019.[44] It's a trope that feeds probably the most effective audience activation strategy in the entire Fox News repertoire – the idea of *us* being supplanted by *them*, the conviction of many ordinary Americans that they have become increasingly powerless, socially and economically, in their own country.

Replacement theory was the topic that kept on giving for *Tucker Carlson Tonight* (the highest-rating cable news show in history at its peak), from its launch in 2016 until Carlson was peremptorily sacked by Fox in 2023. He was relentless in railing against immigration ('it makes our own country poorer, and dirtier, and more divided'), and accused President Biden of meddling with America's racial mix 'to reduce the political power of people whose ancestors lived here, and dramatically increase the proportion of Americans newly arrived from the Third World'.[45]

By the time he was booted from Fox, Carlson had referenced replacement theory well over 400 times on his show. And across Fox News the term 'critical race theory' was mentioned up to 700 times a month in 2021, six times more than on CNN or MSNBC, according to the media monitoring service Critical Mention. 'Night after night, hour by hour, Mr. Carlson warns his viewers that they inhabit a civilization under siege – by violent Black Lives Matter protesters in American cities, by diseased migrants from south of the border, by refugees importing alien cultures, and by tech companies and cultural elites who will silence them, or label them racist, if they complain,' wrote Nicholas Confessore in *The New York Times* in mid-2022.[46]

But the Murdochs were unmoved by criticism that their network was a torchbearer for race theory. If anything, it seemed to galvanise them, just as they were energised when 'liberals' questioned their methods of journalism. In 2022 the Democrat majority leader Senator Chuck Schumer wrote to Rupert Murdoch, his executives and Carlson, urging them to 'immediately cease the reckless amplification of the so-called "Great Replacement" theory on your network's broadcasts'. His plea followed an anti-black rampage in a Buffalo, New York supermarket where a white supremacist gunman killed ten people. 'This pernicious theory, which has no basis in fact, has been injected into the mainstream thanks in large part to a dangerous level of amplification by your network and its anchors,' wrote Schumer.[47]

Lachlan Murdoch had staunchly defended Carlson a year earlier after the Anti-Defamation League's CEO, Jonathan Greenblatt, described his on-air statements as 'racist and toxic'. Murdoch junior informed Greenblatt that he 'respectfully disagreed', claiming Carlson had 'decried and rejected' replacement theory, and asserting that Fox 'shares your values and abhors anti-Semitism, white supremacy and racism of any kind'. In fact, added Murdoch, 'I remember fondly the ADL honoring my father with your International Leadership Award, and we continue to support your mission.' Greenblatt acknowledged that the ADL had indeed honoured his father over a decade ago, 'but let me be clear that we would not do so today, and it does not absolve you, him, the network, or its board from the moral failure of not taking action against Mr. Carlson'.[48]

In 2020 an even juicier opportunity for stirring up indignation and resentment landed on the Fox doorstep. *A global pandemic.* This was ratings gold for a propaganda network, offering the chance to peddle conspiracy theories, undermine government health advice, threaten an economic collapse, all laced with threats to personal freedom amid growing State power. It was the perfect menu of red meat to serve up a culture war.

As early signs of the pandemic emerged in March 2020, Fox's resident medical analyst, Marc Siegel, informed viewers that 'at worst, at worst-worst-case scenario, it could be the flu'.[49] This set the tone for two years of cynicism and denialism as Fox hosts constantly undermined the US government's vaccination campaigns. Tucker Carlson compared vaccine mandates to Nazi and Japanese wartime medical experiments. 'I mean, after watching what the imperial Japanese army and the Nazis did in their medical experiments, I thought that American physicians agreed that compulsory medical care was unethical, it was immoral and it could never be imposed on anyone,' claimed Carlson, while applauding the 'brave souls', particularly health care workers, who refused to 'go along' with the 'lunacy' of mandatory vaccination. And he accused the highly respected director of the National Institute of Allergy and Infectious Diseases, Dr Anthony Fauci, of helping to create COVID-19 in a lab.[50]

Laura Ingraham pilloried health experts as liars who 'think that parents should trust them and inject their kids with an experimental drug to prevent a disease almost none of those kids will ever get sick from'.[51] To reinforce its anti-vaccine rhetoric, Fox aired months of interviews with dozens of nurses, teachers, police and military officers who claimed to have been fired or had resigned from their jobs because they defied vaccine mandates.

A former News Corp vice-president, Joseph Azam, accused Fox of being 'almost single-handedly responsible for the politicization of public health in the US and the creation of vaccine hesitancy in a significant portion of the population'.[52] The network's vaccine narrative was 'simple and sinister', wrote Alex Shephard in *The New Republic* in July 2021. 'The vaccines are unproven and may be worse than the disease itself. The government is covering up the risks involved for reasons that are never quite specified but always amount to the Orwellian: It wants to control everything about your life, down to what you choose to put in your body.'[53]

Once again, Lachlan Murdoch sprang to the defence of his network and its ratings darlings. He claimed Carlson's vaccine comments were 'brave' because he was using data from the Centers for Disease Control and Prevention – 'so there's nothing the CDC itself isn't saying'.[54]

Fox News's coverage of the pandemic raised the most basic questions for news journalists. Do you have a duty of care towards your audience? Should journalists trust government health experts? Who holds moral responsibility for editorial coverage: the owners, producers, presenters, everyone? As former Australian prime minister Malcolm Turnbull pointed out, anyone who promotes conspiracy theories about vaccines or discourages people from getting vaccinated is 'contributing to death and disease'. Rupert Murdoch was one of the first people in the world to receive a Covid vaccination. '[S]urely,' noted Turnbull, 'you would think you would have enough affection for your viewers not to encourage them to follow a course of action that is likely to result in their illness and death.'[55]

Another culture-wars topic that never fails to activate Fox News, as it does at Murdoch's Australian newspapers, is climate change (or, more accurately, climate *denial*). Analysis by the Public Citizen advocacy group in 2019 revealed that 212 of the network's 247 segments on the subject over a six-month period were dismissive of the climate crisis, cast doubts on the reality of global warming, or employed fearmongering when discussing climate solutions. Fox News hosts and guests constantly roll out denialist tropes to denounce the reality of climate change – 'the big climate con' (Laura Ingraham), 'a political movement, not a scientific movement' (contributor Sean Duffy), 'not even climate experts understand the climate' (Tucker Carlson), 'as this climate gets warmer, people's lives improve' (Greg Gutfeld).[56]

———

The Fox News business model is a breathtaking case study in cash generation. Its parent company, Fox Corporation, rakes in around $1.5 billion in annual *profit* a year, the majority of which comes from Fox News.[57] This is profitability on an unprecedented scale in the history of news journalism, in any medium. Even at their peak last century, the world's most commercially successful newspapers – often described as a licence to print money – generated profits of a few hundred million dollars a year (and one of those papers, *The Washington Post*, was on track to *lose* around $100 million in 2023).[58]

At the heart of this goldmine is the $2-a-month licensing fee, also known as a carriage fee, paid to Fox News and its sister channel, Fox Business, by America's 70 million cable and satellite subscribers (down from 100 million over the past decade). This is more than twice the carriage fee received by CNN, and five times that of MSNBC. Even though Fox News is watched by a relatively small number of viewers – around 1.5 million a night in a country of over 300 million people – its appeal to an older TV-watching demographic means cable carriers need to include it on their bundle of available channels.[59] And like many of Murdoch's newspapers, whose circulations are tiny compared to their glory days last century, Fox News is a megaphone: its content ricochets into social media and other media channels, where it reaches a mass audience, including (and especially) politicians.

But there are two reasons why those gobsmacking numbers may not keep rolling on. First, as media consumption habits ebb and flow, US cable subscriber numbers are falling at a rate of around 10 million every two or three years. And second, the network's ratings are tied to the political fortunes of Donald Trump, as Fox discovered when it tried to disentangle itself from supporting Trump after his election defeat in 2020.

The Fox business model requires the network to *follow*, not lead, its audience of sixty-plus-year-old traditional white Americans, predominantly Republican voters, committed Christians, supporters of the NRA, who are opposed to gay rights. As *Rolling Stone* explained in 2011, this delivers advertisers with a cohort of rusted-on viewers who are attracted to ads catering to the elderly, the immobile, the infirm and the incontinent, with appeals to join class-action lawsuits on hip replacements, spots for products like Colon Flow, and testimonials for the services of Liberator Medical ('Liberator gave me back the freedom I haven't had since I started using catheters').[60]

Another plank of the business model – one which *loses* a lot of cash – is the payment of large settlements to former employees to keep them silent about the culture inside Fox News. For the past decade, settlements paid to victims of sexual and racial harassment and other bad behaviour by the network's male presenters and executives (including Roger Ailes, its founding CEO) have been staggering in their size, duration and frequency. They include:

- $20 million to former star presenter Gretchen Carlson after she was fired from her program for refusing Ailes' sexual advances.[61]
- $3.15 million to news booker Laurie Luhn after she spent two decades sexually 'servicing' Ailes, who had kept her quiet for years by blackmailing her with compromising videotapes. (Fox then sacked Ailes and paid *him* a $40 million severance package.)[62]
- $32 million reportedly paid to former Fox News legal analyst Lis Wiehl after Bill O'Reilly allegedly initiated a 'non-consensual sexual relationship' with her.[63]
- $4 million (or more) to a female employee who accused the former co-host of *The Five*, Kimberly Guilfoyle, of workplace impropriety and displaying lewd pictures of male genitalia.[64]
- $9 million (estimated) to Andrea Mackris, a former producer of *The O'Reilly Factor*, after she sued O'Reilly for sexual harassment and engaging in a crude phone conversation.[65]
- $2.5 million to Fox News contributor Tamara Holder, who reported that a network executive tried to force her to perform oral sex on him in his office.[66]
- $1.6 million to former Fox host Juliet Huddy after she alleged O'Reilly pursued a romantic relationship with her and made lewd remarks.[67]
- $2.4 million to three other female employees who accused O'Reilly of sexual harassment or inappropriate behaviour.[68]
- $1 million in fines handed down by New York City's Commission on Human Rights over #MeToo allegations from female employees, the highest civil penalty ordered in the commission's history.[69]

- $12 million to former producer Abby Grossberg after she accused the network of fostering a 'toxic atmosphere victimizing women' and claimed its legal team 'coerced, intimidated, and misinformed' her.[70]
- $15 million to former host Melissa Francis for gender-based pay disparities from 2012 to 2020.[71]

Fox shareholders have also been compensated for the financial and reputational harm caused by the company culture, by way of $90 million in settlement of 'derivative' shareholder claims against network personnel, including Rupert Murdoch.[72]

All of which raises the question of why anyone would work at a disinformation factory that practices this kind of culture. Inevitably, the answer is the money. Fox News pays its top talent excessively well because it's the most profitable news machine in history. But for some Fox commentators even the money wasn't enough to assuage their consciences. When the military affairs analyst Ralph Peters, a retired army lieutenant colonel, departed Fox News in 2018, his farewell email included a withering attack on the network: 'When prime-time hosts – who have never served our country in any capacity – dismiss facts and empirical reality to launch profoundly dishonest attacks on the FBI, the Justice Department, the courts, the intelligence community (in which I served) and, not least, a model public servant and genuine war hero such as Robert Mueller – all the while scaremongering with lurid warnings of "deep-state" machinations – I cannot be part of the same organization, even at a remove. To me, Fox News is now wittingly harming our system of government for profit.'[73]

When the conservative commentator Jonah Goldberg left Fox News in 2021 he said it was because he was surrounded by too many lies. 'I never deliberately lied on Fox,' he wrote in *The Dispatch*, 'but over time I felt like I was becoming complicit in a series of lies of omission.'[74]

The Ends Justify
the Means

'Bury your mistakes,' advised Rupert Murdoch in a *New York Times* interview in 1990.[1] Since then, News Corp and Fox News have built a $3 billion graveyard filled with the bodies of individuals and companies they have paid to go away and keep their mouths shut: $1.3 billion (so far) to the victims and for the legal costs of British phone hacking, $787 million to Dominion Voting Systems for insinuating they had rigged a presidential election, more than $200 million to at least eleven women involved in sexual harassment and abuse cases at Fox News, and tens of millions to departing editors and executives who signed non-disclosure agreements to stay *shtum*.

There's more. Between 2009 and 2017 a News Corp subsidiary paid over $900 million to three competitors to settle charges of corporate espionage and anticompetitive behaviour in the side-alley business of supermarket advertising. In one of these cases, News America Marketing – a Murdoch company that sold advertising on supermarket floors, shopping carts and shelves, and in direct-mail discount coupons – admitted hacking into the computer system of a smaller competitor, Floorgraphics, to disseminate 'false, misleading and malicious information about the plaintiff'. In another case, $500 million was paid to Valassis Communications by News America after coercing its customers to sign long-term contracts or incur large price increases for their in-store advertising. And a further $125 million settlement was made with Insignia Systems for violating antitrust laws. News America Marketing during much of this activity was led by an executive who motivated his sales staff by screening the scene from *The Untouchables* where Al Capone beats a man to death with a baseball bat.[2]

And more. Another $139 million in 2013 to two large News Corp shareholders, the Amalgamated Bank of New York and the Central Laborers Pension Fund, who sued Murdoch and his board for failing in their fiduciary duty to prevent the phone-hacking scandal and for treating News Corp 'like a wholly owned family candy store' when it purchased daughter Elisabeth Murdoch's TV production company Shine for $675 million. In that case the money didn't come directly from the graveyard of buried mistakes, it was paid to the shareholders from insurance policies held by board members, including Rupert, James and Lachlan Murdoch.[3]

As well, there was the Fox broadcasting bribery scandal that shook the sporting world in 2015 when Swiss authorities raided a five-star hotel and arrested nine officials from FIFA, soccer's governing body. The case dragged on for eight years before Alejandro Burzaco, a banker-turned-sports marketing executive, admitted to a New York federal court that he and two former Fox executives had paid tens of millions of dollars to bribe soccer officials to help win the TV rights to the 2022 World Cup, plus another big tournament, over rival network ESPN. The former head of Fox International Channels, Hernan Lopez, was later convicted for his role in the bribery scheme. Burzaco forfeited the $21.7 million he received from the scam, telling the court that Rupert Murdoch was so grateful for his work at the time that he sent a complimentary note to one of the FIFA bosses.

Murdoch's seventy-year career has been pockmarked by legal confrontations with competitors, ex-employees, celebrities, shareholders, defamation litigants, sexual harassment victims, tax agencies and antitrust regulators. He doesn't always win, but if there's an opportunity to legally circumvent laws and regulations, he takes it.

Early one Washington, DC morning in May 2003, Murdoch found himself sitting in a hearing room in the Russell Senate Office

Building, taking questions from US senators about proposed new media ownership laws designed to place limits on radio and TV licences. This led to a fascinating exchange with Barbara Boxer, a Democrat senator from California, about media power. 'Do you believe there should be any limits – at all – on how much media one individual or one company can control?' she asked Murdoch. The result was a David Mamet-style dialogue, reported by James Fallows in *The Atlantic*:

MURDOCH: I don't know what the right limits are, but I'm certainly in favor of relaxing the existing limits, Senator.

BOXER: You're in favor of relaxing the limits! . . . Well, what if you owned everything?

MURDOCH: If I owned everything?

BOXER: Do you think there ought to be limits on you?

MURDOCH: No, of course not. And we don't —

BOXER: You think there should be limits?

MURDOCH: I think there should be competition everywhere. My life has been built, and my business, [by] starting competition and starting up against —

BOXER: So we've gotten this far.

MURDOCH: — other people and providing diversity.

BOXER: So we've gotten this far. So you agree there should be limits. And the —

MURDOCH: I think there should always be diversity.

BOXER: Good. Limits and diversity. We agree. So then the question is how much? And that's – you're saying you can't put a number on it.

MURDOCH: There should be no limit to diversity.[4]

(Laughter)

Antitrust and ownership laws are constant irritants for media moguls with large appetites. In 1987, in the biggest deal of his career to date, Murdoch acquired his father's old company the Herald and

Weekly Times, Australia's dominant newspaper group. Soon after that he started sniffing around *The Canberra Times*, the influential newspaper in the national capital. That's when Australia's competition regulator, the Trade Practices Commission, informed News, in writing, that it would not be permitted to buy the paper because it had reached its ownership limit in Australia. At the same time, Murdoch was ordered to divest two of his existing newspapers, the Brisbane *Sun* and Adelaide *News*, to prevent monopolies in those cities as a result of his Herald and Weekly Times acquisition.

News Corp's solution to these impediments was to 'warehouse' the three newspapers it couldn't own but didn't want to fall into the hands of competitors or new entrants. Warehousing is a technique used by companies to control or influence another company without directly owning its shares or assets, usually through loans and often with some kind of option to acquire the business down the track.

Murdoch found the perfect 'buyers' for his Brisbane and Adelaide mastheads. Frank Moore and Roger Holden were both long-serving senior News Corp editors who unexpectedly became newspaper proprietors in their home cities – funded, it later emerged, by Citibank loans guaranteed by News. The company also provided printing presses, distribution, offices and editorial services to the new mini-moguls (for a fee). I once spotted Holden entering the News Corp head office in Sydney to visit his previous chief executive, just as he had done when he wasn't the owner of their direct competitor.

As expected, the two papers struggled financially up against their revitalised News Corp competitors. The charade ended four years later when they were both peremptorily closed, creating the newspaper monopolies in Brisbane and Adelaide that the corporate regulator had specifically tried to avoid.

The Canberra Times was also 'acquired' by a new owner – Kerry Stokes, then an up-and-coming media entrepreneur who later became a billionaire media magnate with a friendly relationship with Murdoch. What wasn't revealed at the time, but later surfaced at a federal government inquiry, was that Stokes was loaned the money to buy the paper by News Corp in a friendly deal that included a future option to buy it (although Murdoch never did).

The opaqueness of Murdoch's influence over his competitors in Adelaide and Brisbane in the 1980s was as murky as Lord Beaverbrook's furtive ownership of the *Daily Express* in Britain earlier in the twentieth century, but for entirely different reasons. Beaverbrook took financial control of the *Express* in 1916, but hid his ownership for another two years so he could pull strings, without complications, at the highest level of British politics, including a pivotal role in the destruction of the Asquith government. As well as his secret control of the *Express*, Beaverbrook's power stemmed from his close association with Bonar Law, who later became prime minister. The editor of *The Observer*, J.L. Garvin, once compared Beaverbrook to a 'hermit crab' who always put himself into the other man's ear, 'swaying in his sinister, insistent way as he likes that strange unfixed feeble mass of timidity and ambition'.[5]

———

Evading tax is another pragmatic priority for big media operators. For Rupert Murdoch, tax minimisation has been a lifetime preoccupation, and News Corp has been a prime target of tax authorities for at least four decades as it has aggressively exploited loopholes, tax havens and international boundaries.

Since the 1980s, News Corp has built a tax minimisation regimen that optimises profits in subsidiary companies registered in global tax havens. A 1988 Australian government report found that *all* of News Corp's profits in the previous year – AUD$387 million – were earned through tax havens. 'By a strange alchemy, each year hundreds of millions of dollars of News Corporation earnings bounced around some of the most exotic parts of the world, touring the archipelagos of offshore tax havens,' wrote Neil Chenoweth, a finance reporter who has followed the company assiduously for decades, in his book *Virtual Murdoch*. 'Huge money streams flowed through more than 75 News Corporation companies in the British Virgin Islands, the

Cayman Islands, the Netherlands, the Netherland Antilles, Hong Kong and Bermuda.' The result, reported Chenoweth, was that most of News Corp's tax bill 'disappeared'.[6]

Throughout the 1990s, Murdoch's corporate taxes were one-fifth the size of his main American competitors, according to *The Washington Post*. 'The international tax and accounting strategies employed by News Corp may, in fact, make Murdoch a model for the 21st-century entrepreneur – a captain of industry who operates under so many flags at once that it's hard to know where his allegiances lie or how his businesses function,' wrote Paul Farhi in the *Post*.[7]

A secret taskforce of US, Australian, British and Canadian tax officials met in Sydney in late 1997 to discuss international tax structures in general, and the Murdoch company's tax arrangements in particular. By then, News Limited (as it was then called) had been under scrutiny by the Australian Tax Office for more than a year. 'The risk assessment in respect of News Limited shows substantial funds movements from unlisted CFCs [Controlled Foreign Companies] to listed CFCs and the audit team is presently identifying the transactions and structures responsible for these movements,' tax authorities explained in bureaucratic jargon in a memo uncovered by Chenoweth.[8]

By 2015 News Corp was the only company in the highest risk category of tax avoidance in Australia. 'Historically, this particular taxpayer has made it quite clear that they have not had an interest in being open with us and discussing any of their affairs with us prior to their doing transactions,' the tax commissioner Chris Jordan told a parliamentary committee, referring to 'the history of their aggressive behaviour in tax over a period of time'.[9] Over five years from 2014 to 2019, the company generated revenue of $9 billion and profits of $476 million – yet paid tax of just $5.7 million.[10]

News Corp's aggressiveness in challenging tax rulings has paid off. In 2010 the company won an appeal against a decision by the Australian Tax Office to disallow almost $1 billion in capital losses. Three years later, 21st Century Fox received an Australian tax rebate of US$589 million over paper losses on currency transactions dating back to 1989. The rebate was so large, *The Australian Financial Review* calculated, that it became the 'single biggest factor' that contributed to the entire country's budget deterioration over four months.[11]

All the while, in editorials and columns in *The Wall Street Journal*, the London *Times*, *The Australian*, and in other News Corp publications, governments and politicians are counselled on how to manage tax and fiscal policies in their respective countries. Conveniently, none of that journalism carries a declaration of the newspaper owner's conflict of interest in publishing commentary about an issue – national and global tax policy – in which he and his family are deeply invested.

Murdoch himself has assisted at least one other media magnate to stretch the boundaries of tax avoidance. In 1989 he appeared as a witness in a blockbuster tax case involving the Newhouse publishing family. Like Murdoch, Sam Newhouse had created complex structures to avoid tax before he died. According to a 1976 *Business Week* investigation, the Newhouse 'corporate labyrinth' had a convoluted ownership structure whereby newspapers in his group owned other newspapers in order to shuffle their tax liabilities. This meant that the Staten Island paper owned the Long Island paper, which owned Syracuse, which in turn owned Portland, which owned Newark, which owned Springfield, which owned Harrisburg, which owned Cleveland, and so on.[12]

When Sam Newhouse died in 1979, his estate was valued at $182 million, a figure that the US Internal Revenue Service argued was an undervaluation of more than $1 billion. This higher value would have meant his sons were liable for a further $914 million in estate taxes and penalties. The dispute ended up in a protracted landmark trial in Washington, which was won comprehensively by Newhouse's two sons, Si and Donald. A surprise witness at the trial, Murdoch turned up to argue the Newhouse case against the IRS 'out of a kind of professional courtesy – one media mogul helping another – and self-interest, because he could easily imagine his heirs facing the same problem', according to Carol Felsenthal in *Citizen Newhouse*.[13]

———

Extracting large wads of cash from your company is another obvious necessity for a media baron. During the 1930s, William Randolph Hearst and his top executives allocated 10 per cent of the total annual payroll of all their companies to themselves in salaries. Of that chunk, Hearst himself took 10 per cent. In 1936 that made him the highest salaried employee in the US, according to the Treasury Department, earning $500,000 a year (roughly $11 million today).[14]

Conrad Black was another magnate with an appetite for meaty remuneration. After he and his three closest associates paid themselves nearly $391 million in management fees and salaries over seven years from 1997, the issue boiled over at Hollinger Inc.'s shareholder meeting at the New York Metropolitan Club in May 2002. 'I've been listening to what my distinguished – and I do mean distinguished – colleagues have been saying to you,' Edward Shufro, an investor who had recently sold most of his Hollinger stock, told Black in front of the assembled stockholders. 'They're trying to be polite about it, but what they're telling you is that they consider you a thief.'[15] Black was outraged, but a year later he stepped down as CEO of Hollinger International, triggering a series of criminal charges and court cases that resulted in a three-and-a-half-year prison sentence.

The Murdochs have been more transparent than Black in extracting executive compensation from Fox and News Corp – and much better remunerated. Between 1998 and 2023 Rupert, Lachlan and James took home combined salaries and bonuses of almost $1.2 billion from the public companies they control. As well, Rupert received $141 million in pension benefits after he retired as Fox Corp chairman in November 2023.

Another mechanism used by control-obsessed media owners to keep ordinary schmuck shareholders at bay is the dual-class share structure. Under this ethically questionable but perfectly legal

arrangement, founders or their successors control their companies by owning a majority of *voting* shares, which empowers them
to make all key decisions even if they own a minority of *financial*
shares. At *The New York Times*, the Ochs Sulzberger family owns 20
per cent of the business while controlling 70 per cent of the board.
The Murdochs, who own around 15 per cent of News Corp, control
almost 40 per cent of its voting shares. At Facebook, Mark Zuckerberg and a small group of insiders control almost 70 per cent of the
voting shares. Google's founders, Larry Page and Sergey Brin, hold
around 51 per cent of the company's voting power through 'super-
voting shares' that carry ten times as many votes as those of the
economic shareholders.[16]

In 2005, when the News Corp board needed non-Murdoch shareholder votes to support its proposal to relocate the company from
Australia to the US, it reluctantly agreed to dismantle the Murdoch
family's voting-share control, then reneged on its pledge soon after
winning shareholder approval. 'The company's behaviour simply
confirms that the thing that matters at News Corp is Murdoch family
control,' observed Australian business journalist Alan Kohler (who
later sold his business news website, in which I was a co-shareholder,
to News). 'Shareholders are a distant fourth – not even among the
places. News Corp is nothing but a badly performing business mostly
run by untrustworthy people.'[17]

———

Negotiating is the heartbeat of moguldom. It's where hubris, courage
and ruthlessness converge to build – and sometimes destroy – media
empires. Rupert Murdoch's first big international negotiation took
place in 1968 over breakfast at the London home of Sir William Carr,
owner of the huge-selling *News of the World*. After Murdoch laid out
his demands, including full operational control of the business, Carr
and his associates balked. 'Gentlemen, either you concede to my wishes
or I catch the next plane home,' Murdoch reportedly told them. 'I've
come here at my own expense. It has cost you nothing. I'll cut my

losses and go home if we can't agree right now.' Murdoch had positioned himself as the preferred Anglosphere buyer over his main rival for the paper, the Jewish Czech-born Robert Maxwell. And his tactic worked. 'Rupert is a gentleman,' Carr was reported as saying after the deal was completed. Six months later he was sacked by Murdoch.[18]

Murdoch's negotiating style became increasingly self-assured as he accumulated more media properties. His deal to buy American football rights in 1993 was typically brazen. Fox Sports at the time was a minor player in the lucrative business of television sports broadcasting and Murdoch believed he had been used as a stalking horse to push up bidding by CBS and NBC in his two previous attempts to acquire National Football League rights. Now he wanted to use football coverage to transform Fox into a top-tier network, but to do that, he was told by his network chief Chase Carey, he needed 'a number that – I don't have a better word for it – made them choke'.[19]

Murdoch figured out the choking point was $1.6 billion over four years. 'In 1993, it was an astonishing figure,' reported *The Ringer*. 'It was half a billion dollars more than CBS had paid under their old deal, and 60 per cent more than CBS was offering on the current one.' After his victory, Murdoch took his key executives back to his apartment to celebrate. 'OK, now somebody tell me how they play this game,' he said to them as he rubbed his hands in glee. It was all about the money, not the sport.[20]

Like Murdoch, Conrad Black's carpet ride into media's top tier was fuelled by deals. He became the third-largest newspaper publisher in the world (before he lost it all) by buying hundreds of mainly small, provincial Canadian newspapers over thirty years. His operating style was brutal. 'When he buys papers, Black usually fires a significant chunk of the staff,' wrote David Plotz in *Slate*. 'He calls this, delightedly, "drowning the kittens".'[21]

Black's predatory style should have surprised no-one. In his early days as a corporate raider in Canada he was charged with (and cleared of) wrongdoing in the failed takeover of a mining company, then attracted negative publicity when a supermarket chain he controlled pulled $60 million from a pension plan while the company was closing down stores and laying off thousands of workers. 'He repeatedly bought into companies promising to be a passive investor or an ally against hostile takeovers, only to turn around and make a play for the company himself or make common cause with other raiders,' wrote Steven Pearlstein in *The Washington Post* in 1998.[22]

When Black took control in 1991 of Australia's premier newspaper group, Fairfax, it was a deal that played out like a *Succession* pastiche. Max Hastings, the London *Daily Telegraph* editor, was inside the room to watch his boss negotiate with the Australian media tycoon Kerry Packer in a delicate political arrangement that needed to skirt competition and foreign investment laws for both men. The meeting took place over lunch in Packer's permanent suite at the Savoy Hotel in London. 'From the outset, the occasion defied parody,' wrote Hastings in his memoir *Editor*. The prelude to the meeting was a *Fawlty Towers* performance by the Savoy's waiters, whom Packer finally instructed in exasperation, 'Put the ****ing food down there, put the ****ing bottles here, and get your useless ****ing asses out of here.'[23]

Packer outlined a deal that, from his point of view, was heavily focused on how he could use the Fairfax papers to crucify his many political and business enemies. 'Right, Conrad. We're all agreed, then,' said Packer. 'I shall take a back seat on this one. You'll lead the band. I'll fix Canberra. I'll deal with the state government. I'll square the banks. All I want out of this one is to see certain people's heads so deep in the shit that the tops of their heads will only be visible through a powerful microscope!'[24]

My own peripheral involvement in the deal, as an unofficial sounding board to another investor in the Black-Packer consortium, gave me a brief, first-hand view of Black's trademark arrogance and verbosity, traits he seemed to exaggerate in the presence of inferior Australians. It was the same kind of cockiness displayed by William Randolph Hearst when he attempted to buy *The New York Herald*, the ailing competitor to his *New York Journal*. Not wanting to waste time on a lengthy negotiation, Hearst cabled the *Herald*'s owner, James Gordon Bennett, to ask whether his paper was for sale, and if so at what price. 'PRICE OF HERALD THREE CENTS. FIVE CENTS SUNDAY. BENNETT' came the response.[25]

———

Delivering and receiving insults are a daily part of a mogul's life. Pulitzer was berated by his competitor Charles Dana, owner of *The New York Sun*, in a vernacular that was considered acceptable in the late-nineteenth-century corridors of power. 'The insuperable obstacle in the way of his social progress is not the fact that he is a Jew, but in certain offensive personal qualities,' said Dana as the two rivals faced off in a bitter newspaper war. 'His face is repulsive, not because the physiognomy is Hebraic, but because it is Pulitzeresque ... Cunning, malice, falsehood, treachery, dishonesty, greed and venal self-abasement have stamped their unmistakable traits ... No art can eradicate them.'[26]

A few years later Hearst described his competitor Adolph Ochs, the Jewish owner of *The New York Times*, as an 'uneducated ... oily little commercial gentleman' with 'obsequiously curved shoulders'.[27]

When asked in 2003 what he'd learned about being powerful in America, Rupert Murdoch summed it up in six words: 'You make a lot of enemies.' He should know: few people in history have been as vilified for as long as Murdoch. In 1994 the dying British playwright Dennis Potter named his cancer Rupert because 'no man is more responsible for polluting the press and, in turn, polluting political life'.[28] Ted Turner, the creator of CNN, claimed that talking to Murdoch was 'like confronting the late Führer'. (The comparison 'referred only to the way Hitler managed the news in Germany', Turner later amplified.)[29]

When Oxford University established a Rupert Murdoch Chair in Communications in 1991, the English actor-playwright Alan Bennett wrote in *The Spectator*: 'If the University thinks it's appropriate to take Rupert Murdoch's money perhaps they ought to approach Saddam Hussein to found a chair in Peace Studies.'[30] During a takeover battle for Britain's storied *Observer* newspaper, the writer and poet Clive James compared the prospect of Murdoch owning *The Observer* to 'giving your lovely 18-year-old daughter to a gorilla'. When Murdoch acquired the *Chicago Sun-Times*, its star columnist Mike Royko immediately quit. 'No self-respecting fish would care to be wrapped in a Murdoch-owned paper,' he said. Around the same time, the *Columbia Journalism Review* described the *New York Post* as 'a social problem – a force for evil'. In 1985, after Murdoch took US citizenship, the New York *Daily News* columnist Jimmy Breslin characterised Murdoch's papers as 'headlines about killer bees and newspapers filled with pictures of blacks in handcuffs'. Murdoch 'gave you thuggery and called it a newspaper', said Breslin.[31]

But there have been few more acerbic judgements made about Murdoch than the one delivered by Prince Harry, Duke of Sussex, in his 2022 memoir *Spare*:

> Once you've been chased by someone's henchmen through the streets of a busy modern city you lose all doubt about where they stand on the Great Moral Continuum. All my life I'd heard jokes about the links between royal misbehaviour and centuries of inbreeding, but it was then that I realized: Lack of genetic diversity was nothing compared to press gaslighting. Marrying your cousin is far less dicey than becoming a profit centre for Murdoch Inc.
>
> Indeed, I couldn't think of a single human being in the 300,000-year history of the species who'd done more collective damage to our sense of reality. But what really sickened and frightened me in 2012 was Murdoch's ever-expanding circle of flunkies: young, broken desperate men willing to do whatever was necessary to earn one of his Grinchy smiles.[32]

But unlike regular people, media magnates possess a unique weapon they can use to foil their denigrators. *Retribution.*

If you get on the wrong side of Murdoch, explained the first editor of *The Australian*, Maxwell Newton, 'all he has to do is put a cross next to your name and you cease to exist'. (Newton lasted less than a year before falling out with Murdoch).[33] Individuals or organisations who 'cease to exist' are often placed on an unofficial Enemies List (also known as a Shit List). I was once chastised by a general manager at News Corp for hiring a former high-profile, moderately progressive Australian government minister as a new columnist. 'He's not one of us,' I was informed, because he had opposed changes to laws that affected News Corp's stranglehold on Australian media ownership. I ignored the advice and hired him anyway. Neither of us lasted very long.

Of all News Corp's publications, the *New York Post* has been the most weaponised to manhandle Murdoch's enemies. 'The *Post* did not give you a sixty-forty break if you were on its shit list,' according to Steve Cuozzo, the paper's former executive editor. Actor Paul Newman, who supported a range of progressive causes, including opposition to the Vietnam War, was the paper's Public Enemy #1 during Cuozzo's period. Stories about him were banned unless they contained bad news and his name was even barred from the TV listings guide. 'He topped our permanent, eradicable hate list,' said Cuozzo.[34] (Newman was also on President Richard Nixon's list of enemies, unearthed in 1971, but neither listing seemed to diminish respect for Newman or his beliefs.)

Life as an enemy of the Murdoch state was chronicled in detail by the British Labour Party parliamentarian Tom Watson after he resigned as the country's defence minister in 2006. Watson had quit after calling for the resignation of his prime minister, Tony Blair, a Murdoch favourite at the time. From then on, Watson later told the PBS *Frontline* program, every story written about him as an MP was negative, particularly his role as a member of the parliamentary Culture, Media and Sport Committee, which scrutinised the *News of the World* phone hacking scandal. Watson was placed under News Corp surveillance at least twice – by a private investigator employed by News International and again when it emerged that *News of the World* reporters had spied on the entire committee. 'The objective was to find as much embarrassing sleaze on as many members as possible in order to blackmail them into backing off from its highly probing inquiry,' former senior *News of the World* journalist Neville Thurlbeck told the *New Statesman*. 'It wasn't journalism, it was corporate espionage.'[35] And despite the committee's conclusion that Murdoch was 'not a fit person to exercise the stewardship of a major international company', he continued stewarding a major international company for another thirteen years.

———

'Dog doesn't eat dog' is the unwritten code that cushions media owners against public attacks from fellow members of the moguls' club. This self-protective mechanism operates in many countries; in Spain, for example, it's called *perro no come perro*.

'There is a shameless, self-serving compact between companies, that the personal embarrassments of newspaper owners are not reported by competitors,' says Max Hastings, editor of the London *Daily Telegraph* under Conrad Black's ownership. 'Anyone who attempts to write about Rupert Murdoch or his family's domestic arrangements for another publication is likely to receive a call . . . drawing attention to the proprietors' pact, and warning without much subtlety about the inevitability of retaliation if the convention is breached.' Black's policy position was equally pragmatic: 'My eleventh commandment as a London newspaper chairman is never to speak ill of another such chairman and my relations have been almost uninterruptedly cordial with all of them.'[36]

When the proprietor of the San Francisco *Chronicle* became embroiled in a financial scandal in 1924, the owner of the rival *Examiner*, a young William Randolph Hearst, issued an instruction to his editors: 'Nothing unpleasant about Mr de Young is to be printed whether it is news or not.' He added for good measure: 'I think it would be a good policy to adopt not to print any unpleasant things about any newspaperman.'[37]

In the late 1980s, after Murdoch's *Sunday Times* acquired serial-isation rights to a highly critical biography of rival publisher Robert Maxwell, the paper's editor Andrew Neil started getting calls from his proprietor reminding him of the 'unwritten agreement that propri-etor does not attack proprietor'. Even though Murdoch disliked Maxwell – the latter had described him as a 'moth-eaten, empty-pouched kangaroo' twenty years earlier when they battled for control of the *News of the World* – self-interest outweighed emotion.[38]

The tycoon protection racket continued when Black came to Murdoch's aid in late 1990, during News Corp's existential finan-cial crisis. In a speech to the Media Society at London's Café Royal, he expressed confidence that 'Murdoch would come through his problems and that most of his critics were motivated by spite and envy'. According to Black, Murdoch wrote to thank him for his support.[39]

Thirteen years later Murdoch chose not to reciprocate when Black was imprisoned for fraud and his empire imploded. 'Rupert Murdoch had terminated twenty-five years of our cordial coexistence when my legal problems broke in 2003 and ordered the most malicious possible demolition of me throughout his media group,' wrote Black in his memoir, describing his one-time competitor as a 'sleazy and vicious Anglophone' who was 'neurotically sensitive' to any public criticism. 'He used to phone me from all over the world to complain about puckish asides even in *The Spectator*,' added Black.[40]

Some stories about rival owners were harder to suppress. When Robert Maxwell drowned in suspicious circumstances in 1991, after swindling millions of pounds from his company's pension fund, Black told editor Hastings: 'Don't be too hard on Bob, Max . . . I know he was a crook, but he was a not uninteresting character as well. He had his moments.' Hastings wrote a *Telegraph* obituary that included a string of stories about Maxwell's ghastly behaviour, but concluded that 'those of us who had never experienced anything to match his journey from the basest childhood poverty in Czechoslovakia would not, perhaps, condemn him absolutely'. Black complimented him warmly on the piece, but when the scope of Maxwell's crimes later became apparent, Hastings acknowledged that he 'felt cross with myself for having succumbed to an impulse of generosity'.[41]

But *perro no come perro* doesn't work without the cooperation of all dogs. In 2000, when *The Wall Street Journal* started working on a profile of Murdoch's new wife, Wendi Deng, News Corp executives were 'almost apoplectic' to quash the story, according to author Sarah Ellison. 'Murdoch himself called the paper's managing editor Paul Steiger to ask him to protect his wife's privacy, but the *Journal* published anyway.' Murdoch's embarrassment was understandable; the story traced Deng's rise 'as the daughter of a Guangzhou factory manager who came to America as a 19-year-old student, married her 53-year-old American host father, left him for another man she called her "husband" while she was still married, then met Murdoch'.[42]

But there are limits to even the power of media moguls, as Hearst discovered when he attempted to block the release of *Citizen Kane*, Orson Welles' brilliant 1941 movie about an unlikeable, lonely, Hearstian newspaper-owning tyrant named Charles Foster Kane. Unable to prevent the RKO studio from making the film, Hearst instructed his editors not to publish any stories about the 'crooks' at RKO and refused to run advertising for any of the studio's films in his newspapers. Part of this retaliatory campaign was led by Louella Parsons, Hearst newspapers' chief gossip columnist, who convinced most of the big movie theatre chains to blackball the movie. Some Hearst operatives allegedly went even further: during a lecture tour ahead of the film's release, Welles was reportedly warned by a police investigator not to go back to his hotel because 'they've got a 14-year-old girl in the closet and two photographers waiting for you to come in'.[43]

Apart from conveniently ignoring the misdeeds of their competitors, most media organisations also ban any mention of embarrassing moments in the lives of their owners. That wasn't the case in 2019 when the *National Enquirer* exposed the extramarital affair, replete with racy personal text messages, of *Washington Post* owner Jeff Bezos. Initially, the *Post* avoided covering the topic, but within weeks it was reporting the story without constraint (with Bezos's approval). That certainly wasn't the case after Rupert Murdoch left his wife Anna in 1998 and, a year later, began living with Wendi Deng in New York's fashionable Mercer Hotel. 'Not a single word' about their liaison was published in Murdoch's British newspapers, wrote Stephen Glover in *The Spectator*, who used the affair to highlight the hypocrisy of the 'two worlds' of the media universe; 'in one world Rupert Murdoch sets up with a woman half his age while he is still married, and largely escapes being written about, let alone censored. And, in the other world, this man's newspapers rant and rave against "love rats" who betray their spouses and live with younger women who are not their wives.' Murdoch, concluded Glover, 'constructs a moral universe for the rest of us to live in, and then withdraws into the delights of the Mercer Hotel'.[44]

———

Unauthorised books and biographies are another source of sensitivity for most media moguls. The permanent record they create, with few exceptions, never satisfy the subject's ego.

No media owner has attacked more biographers more aggressively than Conrad Black. After publication of *The Establishment Man* in 1982, Black castigated its author, Peter C. Newman, for the 'largely fictitious image that you created for me, of a chillingly ruthless and rather conceited person, obsessed with materialism, pontificating endlessly, and viewing the world through the prism of a "reactionary proprietor"'.[45] Black continued his assault after Newman's autobiography contained an unfriendly reference to Barbara Amiel, Black's wife, calling it 'the lowest, nastiest, most revolting piece of journalistic sewage I have read'. In his memoir, Black accused Newman of using his 'lurid and neurotic imagination' to claim that 'Barbara hooked me with her sexual wiles'.[46]

Black was just as vituperative towards the British investigative journalist Tom Bower when he requested an interview for his planned biography of the mogul in 2006:

Dear Tom,

Many people have contacted Barbara and me asking if they should talk with you. Our usual response is that you have made it clear that you consider this whole matter a heart-warming story of two sleazy, spivvy, contemptible people, who enjoyed a fraudulent and unjust elevation; were exposed, and ground to powder in a just system, have been ostracized; and largely impoverished, and that I am on my way to the prison cell where I belong. It is the false rise and well-deserved downfall of crooked charlatans; a variant on your treatments of Maxwell, Fayed and Rowland. You have expressed essentially this view many times that have been reported to me.

The rough facts are that I am an honest businessman; the chances of my committing an illegality are less than zero, this will be clear when my accusers have to prove beyond a reasonable doubt the guilt of innocent people and not just manipulate the agencies of the US and Canadian governments to act on the pre-emptive presumption of guilt and conduct a prolonged assassination of careers and reputations.[47]

Beaverbrook faced a similar dilemma in 1954 after he gave a free hand to the journalist-politician Tom Driberg to write what became *Beaverbrook: A Study in Power and Frustration*. 'This fellow with cunning persuaded me to help him with his project in the belief that he was doing something that would be critical but fair,' Beaverbrook complained. 'Instead I find that I am subjected to accusations of a very disagreeable character.' After lawyers squabbled over the book for months, Beaverbrook agreed to its publication and allowed an extract to appear in the *Daily Express* under the heading 'Lord Beaverbrook: a hostile biography'. Driberg, meanwhile, continued to describe the book as 'unauthorized and independent'.[48]

Rupert Murdoch is such juicy fodder for authors that he has spawned a multimillion-dollar micro-publishing industry that continues to churn out books about his private life, his deals and his corporate dexterity. Most have been unauthorised, and even those involving the subject's cooperation have usually ended badly.

Murdoch claims not to read books about himself, but he has a retinue of loyal henchmen available to launch counterattacks against his critics. His praetorian guard was led for decades by Les Hinton, who started as a copy boy at the Adelaide *News* in 1959. In a 2015 essay in the *British Journalism Review*, Hinton described the procession of Murdoch biographies as 'far-fetched tales of scabrous, plundering, capitalist, debasing cultures across the globe', usually written by 'the militant wing of AntiMurdochMania ... The Murdoch they hate doesn't exist. This view of him is so risible, so nuts, it must be a hallucination,' he wrote. 'It's a crowd-sourced apparition, a vessel where these people pour their rage and grief about big business, great power, global inequity and everything else they see wrong with the world. This virtual Murdoch is their devil.'[49]

Whatever it takes.

'I Didn't Know that Hitler Kept a Diary'

For the purveyors of populist news, nothing triggers a bigger eruption than a world scoop, even if it later turns out to be completely wrong. A bombshell on such a scale landed in the laps of Rupert Murdoch's *Sunday Times*, Germany's *Stern* and America's *Newsweek* in early 1983.

The first hint of this journalistic coup was relayed by Murdoch to one of his senior editors, Ed Kosner of *New York* magazine, who recalled the moment in his memoir: "'I'm calling from Switzerland," said Rupert in a conspiratorial whisper, "and do you know what's in the next room?" I confessed that I didn't. "Hitler's diaries," murmured Murdoch. "I didn't know that Hitler kept a diary, chief," I piped up. "That's just the point," said Rupert. "Nobody did. How big a story do you think this is?"'[1]

The saga had begun two years earlier when Gerd Heidemann, a German reporter who revelled in Nazi-era stories, was tipped off that sixty-two volumes of a secret, handwritten diary kept by Adolf Hitler were on the market. The diaries, allegedly compiled by the Führer from 1932 until his death in 1945, were among personal items of his that had been aboard an aircraft that crashed near Dresden just after the war, Heidemann was told. They had reportedly been found by local farmers.

Heidemann took his world scoop, supported by samples of the diaries, to his editors at *Stern*, the mass-circulation liberal weekly German news magazine, who quickly assigned a team of researchers to validate their authenticity. Once that was done, *Stern*'s owner, the giant German publisher Gruner + Jahr, handed over 9.3 million deutschemarks ($3.7 million) to acquire them from Heidemann. To recoup part of this outlay, local republication rights were sold to a string of international publishers, including News Corp, which paid $800,000 for US rights and $400,000 for the British and Australian rights.[2]

Several historians sent by the syndicating publishers to scrutinise the diaries, which were locked in a Zurich bank vault, also vouched for their authenticity. These experts included Hugh Trevor-Roper (who later became Lord Dacre of Glanton), the highly respected British historian whose 1947 book *The Last Days of Hitler* was regarded as one of the definitive accounts of the Nazi era. Comfortingly for Murdoch, Lord Dacre was also independent director of Times Newspapers, owner of *The Sunday Times*. He was glowing in his endorsement of the diaries in *The Times*: 'When I entered the back room in the Swiss bank, and turned the pages of those volumes, my doubts gradually dissolved. I am now satisfied that the documents are authentic; that the history of their wanderings since 1945 is true; and that the standard accounts of Hitler's writing habits, of his personality, and even, perhaps, some public events may, in consequence, have to be revised.'[3]

Armed with that confirmation, *Stern* launched a massive pre-publication publicity blitz that included a press conference, advertising campaign, TV documentary, and testimonials from Dacre proclaiming the diaries as 'the most important historical discovery of the decade and a scoop of Watergate proportions'. And on 24 April 1983 *The Sunday Times* splashed its scoop over five broadsheet pages under the headline 'WORLD EXCLUSIVE ... The secrets of Hitler's War'.[4]

The evening before, as the printing presses began to roll in the basement several levels below their newsroom, senior staff gathered for their traditional Saturday drinks in the office of the editor, Frank Giles. 'There was a mood of self-congratulation' in the room, wrote Robert Harris in *Selling Hitler*, his masterful account of the saga. As the various editors discussed their coup, the conversation turned to the following week's paper. 'Giles suggested they should invite

Trevor-Roper to write an article demolishing "all these carping crit-
icisms" about the diaries' authenticity. This was considered a good
idea. Giles picked up the telephone.' Harris describes the excruciating discussion that followed:

> 'Hugh? . . . Frank Giles . . . Very well, thank you . . .'
>
> There had been a murmur of conversation in the room, but
> this gradually died away as more of the *Sunday Times* men began
> listening to one side of the telephone conversation.
>
> 'I think we'd like just a quiet, scholarly, detailed piece,
> rebutting . . .'
>
> There was a pause. 'Frank didn't go white exactly,' recalled
> [senior writer Phillip] Knightley, 'but his tone suddenly changed.'
>
> 'Well, naturally, Hugh, one has doubts. There are no certain-
> ties in this life. But these doubts aren't strong enough to do a
> complete 180-degree turn on that? . . . Oh, I see. You *are* doing
> a 180-degree turn . . .'

At that point, wrote Harris, 'the editorial conference froze into a
tableau of despair . . . nobody spoke . . . After Giles had hung up there
was, according to one participant, "a tense fifteen-minute conversation". Should the presses be stopped? That would require Murdoch's
agreement.'

The paper's managing editor, Brian MacArthur, tracked Murdoch
down in the United States. MacArthur outlined the problem caused
by Lord Dacre's change of heart. Should they stop the print run and
remake the paper?

Murdoch's reply was brusque. 'Fuck Dacre. Publish.'[5]

Two days later *Stern* followed suit with a spectacular special
edition carrying more than forty pages of extracts, background
and analysis, titled 'Hitler's Diary Discovered'. With a print run of
2.3 million copies, it was the biggest issue in the magazine's history.

In the New York offices of *Newsweek*, however, there was a
distinctly more cautious mood. In a sign of the brewing uncertainty

about the validity of the diaries, the magazine had withdrawn from negotiations to buy the diaries from *Stern*, citing price. Instead, *Newsweek* decided to mine the content it had seen during the negotiations to pump up its circulation, supported by an advertising and PR blitz. The magazine's ambivalence permeated its front cover: 'HITLER'S SECRET DIARIES: Are they Genuine? How They Could Rewrite History; Hitler and the Jews'.

Within days, the mood at *Stern* headquarters began turning bleak. A press conference scheduled to boast about its world scoop degenerated into a debacle as Dacre expressed doubts over whether the purported diaries were actually found in the crashed aircraft. 'I regret that the, er, normal method of historical verification, er, has, perhaps necessarily, been to some extent sacrificed to the requirements of a journalistic scoop,' he admitted as he navigated the final stages of his U-turn.[6]

As the journalistic coup of the decade began to unravel, the German government stepped in to clarify the legitimacy of documents that, if genuine, would have reshaped the world's perspectives on the worst period in the country's history. After examining the diaries for barely a day, scientists at Germany's federal archives, the Bundesarchiv, confirmed they were clumsy forgeries:

- The paper used in the diaries contained a chemical whitener that didn't exist before 1955.
- The ink didn't match inks used during the war.
- Chemical analysis showed the books were produced over the past two years.
- They were littered with factual mistakes.
- Much of the content was lifted from a two-volume edition of *Hitler: Speeches and Proclamations*.[7]

It was a volte-face moment. Almost 250,000 copies of *Stern*'s second Hitler Diaries edition, carrying thirty-four pages drawn from the now-debunked documents, were pulped. And in Manhattan, the cover of *Newsweek*'s next issue carried just one word: 'FORGERY'.

Back in London, meanwhile, Murdoch's *Sunday Times* was in no mood for apologies. Its front-page headline – 'The Hitler Diaries: the hunt for the forger' – was a 'reverse ferret' of the kind often executed by its tabloid stablemate *The Sun* to whitewash its embarrassing editorial missteps. 'We did not act irresponsibly,' declared the paper in a public statement. 'Serious journalism is a high-risk enterprise ... our mistake was to rely on other people's evidence.' Rupert Murdoch brushed off the experience as 'nothing ventured, nothing gained ... after all, we are in the entertainment business'. News International was refunded the $200,000 it had paid *Stern*, and the *Sunday Times* added 60,000 copies to its circulation.[8]

For *Stern*, the affair had a traumatic effect. 'Politicians treated them as a laughing stock; prominent West Germans pulled out of interviews; young East German pacifists refused to cooperate with a planned *Stern* feature article on the ground that the magazine was "a Hitler sheet",' wrote Harris.[9] *Stern*'s two chief editors, Peter Koch and Felix Schmidt, resigned immediately after the German Ministry of the Interior confirmed the diaries were forgeries. Circulation slumped and never revived. The disaster cost the magazine more than $5 million.

———

The architect of the fraud was a confidence trickster from the German branch of central casting. A Stuttgart antiques dealer, Konrad Kujau was also a painter, petty thief, and collector of Nazi memorabilia. His parents had been members of the Nazi Party. By the time he began forging the diaries in Hitler's handwriting in the late 1970s he had already been faking banknotes and fabricating Hitler paintings for years. Using notebooks he acquired in East Germany, Kujau aged the forged documents by bashing them on a desk and sprinkling them with spilt tea. Hitler's embossed gold initials on each edition came from a set of plastic letters made in Hong Kong (although they accidentally read 'FH' rather than 'AH', a mistake none of the experts seemed to notice in their early examination). After two years spent practising Hitler's handwriting, Kujau gleaned the content of his diaries from an official 1935 Nazi party yearbook, lists of Nazi party promotions and official engagements, and from books, newspapers and magazines covering Hitler's life.

Ironically, it was the sheer tedium of the diary's content that made it more credible. Something this boring, many people figured, *had* to be real. 'I couldn't believe that anyone would have gone to the trouble of forging something so banal,' said Henri Nannen, the founder of *Stern*.[10]

At the end of each month's entries, Kujau included a 'personal' section where he invented speculative material that alluded to a more humanised Führer than history had recorded. He had Hitler worrying about his health and expressing his affection for Eva Braun. By adding hitherto unknown personality traits to titillate the publishers viewing the material, Kujau portrayed the Nazi dictator as a far kinder, gentler person than the monster who perpetrated humanity's worst atrocities:

- The measures against the Jews were too strong for me.
- My health is poorly – the result of too little sleep.
- Must get tickets for the Olympic Games for Eva.
- On Eva's wishes, I am thoroughly examined by my doctors. Because of the new pills I have violent flatulence, and – says Eva – bad breath.
- The English are driving me crazy – should I let them escape [from Dunkirk], or not? How is this Churchill reacting?
- This man Bormann has become indispensable to me. If I had had five Bormanns, I would not be sitting here now [in the Berlin bunker].[11]

Police arrested Heidemann and Kujau fifteen months after the fake diaries were published. After a ten-month trial they were each sentenced to four and a half years in jail for defrauding *Stern*. Heidemann allegedly kept at least $600,000 of the $3.1 million he was paid by *Stern* for the fake diaries, while Kujau reportedly got $500,000 of the money.

Apart from the two conmen, a string of high-profile reputations were shredded by the fiasco. Frank Giles was sacked by Murdoch as *Sunday Times* editor two months after the diaries were published, even though he had followed his boss's specific instruction ('Fuck Dacre. Publish'). Giles was handed the title of editor emeritus for the two years remaining on his contract. When he asked what editor emeritus meant, Murdoch reportedly replied, 'It's Latin, Frank ... the "e" means you're out, and the "meritus" means you deserve it.'[12] (Ironically, Murdoch appointed himself chairman emeritus of News Corp and Fox Corp when he stepped down as an executive in 2023.)

Giles initially steered most of the blame for the disaster onto *Stern* rather than Murdoch, but a few years later he took a big swing at his former proprietor in his memoir, *Sundry Times*. 'Murdoch, the supposedly shrewd publisher with a reputation for seeing off most of his rivals and opponents, was the dupe, comparable to a man who buys a horse upon the recommendation of its vendor's vet,' wrote Giles.[13]

Lord Dacre's reputation as a historian was both skewered and parodied following his authentication of the diaries that were quickly debunked. A limerick circulated around Cambridge University following his humiliation:

> There once was a fellow named Dacre,
> Who was God in his own little acre,
> But in the matter of diaries,
> He was quite *ultra vires*,
> And unable to spot an old faker.[14]

Another shock to emerge from the debris was the revelation that this was the *second* time *The Sunday Times* had been fooled into buying the fake diaries of a World War Two dictator. In 1968, during its Thomson-ownership era, the paper outlaid £100,000 as a down payment to a Polish arms dealer for the alleged diaries of Benito Mussolini, as well as £3,500 in a brown paper bag to the Italian dictator's son Vittorio, who had confirmed they were written by his father. The forgeries turned out to be the work of an Italian woman and her 84-year-old mother. Although *The Sunday Times* never published those diaries, after finally realising they were fakes, the paper was highly embarrassed by the ruse. One of the *Sunday Times'* most senior reporters, Phillip Knightley, who was involved in the Mussolini ruse, had argued with his editors fifteen years later against publishing the Hitler diaries. 'We should insist on doing our own checks and not accept the checks of any other publication,' Knightley concluded in a detailed memo to Giles and Murdoch before publication. They never bothered to reply to him.[15]

William Randolph Hearst had his own Hitler Diaries moment in 1951 when a correspondent sent him a batch of clippings from the French newspaper *Le Figaro*, claiming that US president Roosevelt had designated the president of the National Council of Young Israel, Jacob Zabronsky, as his secret emissary to Stalin. Roosevelt allegedly instructed Zabronsky to hand over Finland, the Baltic states and a Mediterranean port to Stalin, according to a letter cited by the paper.

Like Murdoch and *Stern* thirty-two years later, Hearst excitedly ordered all his newspapers to run big with the story without doing any checking, in the belief he had a scoop of international proportions. 'F.D.R.'S SECRET OFFER TO SHARE WORLD POWER WITH THE KREMLIN', screamed the front page of the *New York Journal-American*. The story lasted just one day before the State Department officially confirmed the letter was 'fashioned from fact, half-truth, rumor and inaccuracy'.[16]

Ouch.

THE FUTURE

The New Moguls

After more than a century dominated by newspaper tycoons and family dynasties, the levers of media power have been shifting into the hands of ultra-rich industrialists and state oligarchs. Seduced by the prospect of owning the journalism that influences society, and attracted by collapsing media asset prices, billionaires who made their money in mining, luxury brands, defence equipment, electric cars, logistics, rockets, software and retail have been acquiring large slabs of powerful news media. Four of the five wealthiest people in the world in early 2023 – Bernard Arnault, Elon Musk, Gautam Adani and Jeff Bezos – held controlling stakes in big media companies in the US, India and France. 'They buy up media not to increase media pluralism but to extend the scope of their own influence or the influence of their friends,' says Christophe Deloire, secretary-general of Reporters Without Borders.[1]

The other breed of emerging 21st-century media chieftains are the national dictators who use journalism as a crude instrument of state power. They run countries where the resident media autocrat is not a Murdoch or a Hearst, it's a president, general or strongman. Like private media autocrats, their mission is to report the truth selectively as they fortify the power of their regimes and their cronies.

Owning an influential newspaper or television network is the perfect vehicle for rich business people who want to cosy up to governments and politicians. And nowhere is the nexus between media ownership and political power more conspicuous than in France, where most of the country's serious journalism is owned or heavily influenced by industrialists and billionaires. A new generation of media puppeteers has largely replaced the lively, independent French press that emerged when several dozen new daily papers were launched after World War Two. By 2015 most of the influential French news outlets had been sold to conglomerates with business ties to government.

The fusion of French commercial and media power is daunting. At the top of the tree is Bernard Arnault, the world's richest individual, who controls luxury goods company LVMH (whose brands include Moët Hennessy, Tiffany, Dior, Fendi, Louis Vuitton, Dom Perignon) and owns and editorially interferes in the daily *Le Parisien* and the leading financial paper *Les Echos*. The Dassault family, manufacturers of military aircraft and business jets (a business in which the French government is a co-shareholder), own *Le Figaro*, the country's oldest national newspaper. Telecom and cable TV entrepreneur Patrick Drahi, France's third-wealthiest individual and owner of Sotheby's auction house, controls two broadcasters and the weekly news magazine *L'Express*. The Bouygues family, construction and telecoms operators in more than a hundred countries, own France's most popular domestic TV network, TF1, and the news channel LCI. François Pinault, founder of the luxury fashion group Artémis, owns and controls the conservative magazine *Le Point*. Xavier Niel, founder of the telecommunications company Free, is the largest shareholder in the influential newspaper *Le Monde*, but can't exercise any clout because under the paper's charter his shares sit in an autonomous fund created to defend press freedom.

The industrialist with the highest media mogul status in France is the logistics and transport billionaire Vincent Bolloré, whose family conglomerate controls extensive television, movie, advertising, PR, publishing and digital-content distribution assets. Bolloré's media power derives mainly from his high-rating, conservative, 24-hour news channel, CNews, dubbed 'France's Fox News' for its often hysterical attacks on intellectuals, 'wokistes' and 'islamo-leftists'. His network heaves with anti-immigration rhetoric, warnings about the breakdown of French law and order, and the glorification of Napoleon. In 2021 CNews was fined €200,000 by France's broadcast regulator for inciting racial hatred after it aired the extreme far-right Éric Zemmour describing child migrants as 'thieves, murderers and rapists'. During the 2022 French presidential election campaign, Bolloré devoted several hours a week on CNews to pushing the aspirations of Zemmour, a former political journalist.[2] 'It's clear in his media that his aim is a culture war, an ideological battle,' media historian Alexis Lévrier told *The Guardian*. 'It's more a cultural, religious and political crusade to defend a Catholic France which would close its borders and turn in on itself.'[3]

Another billionaire who uses his wealth for political influence is Gautam Adani, who became the majority shareholder in India's first private 24-hour news network, NDTV (New Delhi Television), in late 2022. A first-generation entrepreneur, Adani began with a coal business before expanding into infrastructure, defence equipment, data centres, urban water management and green energy. Adani's wealth has grown from $7 billion to an estimated $51 billion since Narendra Modi became Indian prime minister in 2014. 'Their influence has continued to grow in tandem,' wrote Anchal Vohra in *Foreign Policy*. 'He [Adani] is widely seen as the government's preferred business partner.'[4]

Adani's control of NDTV has raised more questions about political influence in India's already murky media landscape. Ravish Kumar, one of the country's most influential broadcasters, resigned from NDTV the day after Adani bought in, following a 26-year career. 'How can a channel, bought by a corporat[ion] whose success is seen to be linked to contracts granted by the government, now criticize the government?' asked Kumar, who has aggressively critiqued both the Modi government and its connections with Adani. 'It was clear to me I had to quit.'[5]

Adani's motive in influencing the news agenda appears to be largely commercial. But whatever inspires a billionaire to become a media tycoon, it rarely involves humility. In 2009 Russian-born Evgeny Lebedev bought a controlling stake in the storied London *Evening Standard*, together with his father, Alexander, a former banker and oligarch and ex-KGB agent. They later acquired *The Independent*, another financially stretched but prestigious newspaper. After five years its print edition was shut down, making it the first major British daily to go fully online. By buying into print newspapers at the very end of their profitable life, the Lebedevs have reportedly lost more than £100 million, according to the *Financial Times*.

But there have also been non-commercial benefits. Following in the path of twentieth-century newspaper-owning toffs like North-cliffe and Beaverbrook, Evgeny Lebedev was handed a life peerage by a British prime minister – in this case, his friend Boris Johnson. Afterwards, he basked openly in his own glory: 'Is it not remarkable that the son of a KGB agent, and a first-generation immigrant to this country, has become such an assimilated and contributing member of British society?' he reflected. 'What a success for our system. Don't you think?'[6]

Described by Marina Hyde in *The Guardian* as 'London's biggest starfucker', Lord Lebedev has been a regular fixture on London's nightclub scene.[7] But he has also used the *Standard* to advocate for a resolution of the Russia–Ukraine war, publishing an open letter on the paper's front page in early 2022 pleading with Vladimir Putin to stop the invasion. 'As a Russian citizen I plead with you to stop Russians killing their Ukrainian brothers and sisters,' wrote Lebedev. 'As a British citizen I ask you to save Europe from war. As a Russian patriot I plead that you prevent any more young Russian soldiers from dying needlessly. As a citizen of the world I ask you to save the world from annihilation.'[8] A few months later he returned to the topic with a very personal column criticising anti-Russian sentiment in Britain: 'It's not enough that I called for the war to end in the first week of the invasion, on the front page of the free London paper I rescued from financial ruin. I need a new surname, a new passport, and a new speech therapist to train the Ruski accent out of me. Businesses that were once so far up my backside you couldn't see their legs are so deluded they feel they can now pass judgment on me based purely on hearsay.'[9]

———

Over recent years, *The Washington Post, Los Angeles Times, The Boston Globe* and *The Atlantic* have all been acquired by incredibly rich people with no previous media experience. While those four billionaires were undoubtedly conscious of their newfound proximity to power and influence, they also talked about the importance of journalism in a democracy as a motivation for becoming media barons.

Jeff Bezos, the controlling shareholder of Amazon, acquired *The Washington Post* from the Graham family in 2013 for $250 million. It was a sad moment for the family, especially its doyen Donald Graham, who was 'like a desperate but loving mother placing a newborn in a basket and sticking it on the doorstep of somebody she hoped would clasp it to heart', according to *Vanity Fair*. Bezos told the newsroom staff that 'one of the things I can give you is runway', recalled the *Post*'s senior political reporter, Dan Balz. 'The paper's duty will remain to its readers and not to the private interests of its owners,' Bezos pledged. And the new proprietor quickly slipped into media mogul mode by acquiring a $23 million Washington mansion where guests are served food on dishes displaying the *Post* logo, and can view a memorabilia collection that includes a lock broken by the Watergate burglars.[10]

Bezos invested heavily in overhauling the *Post*'s technology and marketing, increased its newsroom staff from 700 to more than 1000, and so far hasn't interfered editorially. But the potential for conflict of interest is ever-present when one of the world's most respected newspapers becomes a collector's piece for such a ferocious entrepreneur. 'Pretty much every public-policy issue the *Post* covers affects Bezos's sprawling personal and business interests in material ways,' noted Dan Froomkin in the *Columbia Journalism Review*. When the Biden administration floated plans in 2022 to increase taxes on the wealthy, Bezos posted tweets accusing the president of 'straight ahead misdirection or a deep misunderstanding of basic market dynamics'. Being owned by someone with economic interests on that scale, argued media ethicist Edward Wasserman, 'is not compatible with the kind of independence we normally associate with independent news organizations'.[11]

Although Bezos says he bought the *Post* as a benevolent gesture, taking the baton when the public-spirited Graham family felt they didn't have pockets deep enough to support its mission in a tumultuous digital era, he still views the paper as a business that needs to be self-sustaining, not as philanthropy. 'If he treated us like a charity and later tired of us, we'd be in deep trouble, left with operations as unsustainable as the day he bought *The Post*,' the paper's former editor Marty Baron wrote in his memoir *Collision of Power*.[12]

For a wealthy acquirer of an iconic masthead, the real test of commitment will come if, or when, the business falters to the point that it requires permanent cash support to stay afloat. At that stage, the question won't be: Can I afford to fund my editorial toy? It will be: Am I prepared to wear the embarrassment of being seen in public as the piggybank of a bottomless pit of losses, staff resentment and diminishing influence?

Bezos seems to understand that one of the key roles of a newspaper proprietor is to resist pressure from the citadels of power. In 2017 he attended a dinner in the White House, along with his paper's editor and publisher, where then president Trump strongly criticised the *Post*. A year later, Trump launched a tirade against Bezos, claiming Amazon had failed to pay its share of taxes and Bezos had used his newspaper to advance his own interests. 'Amazon is just not on an even playing field,' Trump told reporters. 'You know, they have a tremendous lobbying effort, in addition to having *The Washington Post*, which is, as far as I'm concerned, another lobbyist.'[13] Trump again attacked Bezos the following year, calling him 'Jeff Bozo' after the *National Enquirer* published an exposé of the billionaire's extramarital relationship with a former news anchor.

Bezos resisted Trump's taunting. 'He stood by us, despite enormous pressure from the president of the United States, undoubtedly the most powerful person in the world, who wanted to sabotage Amazon, his primary business interest and the principal source of his enormous wealth,' Baron told *Vanity Fair*. 'There are a lot of business people who would've caved under that pressure, and he didn't.'[14]

Among the other grand American media icons to fall into billionaire-benefactor hands in recent years, the *Los Angeles Times* and *The San Diego Union-Tribune* were picked up by biotech businessman Patrick Soon-Shiong; *The Boston Globe* was acquired by John Henry, owner of the Boston Red Sox baseball club, and the Liverpool football team in England; *Time* magazine was bought for $190 million by Marc Benioff, chairman of software giant Salesforce; and Laurene Powell Jobs, the wealthy widow of Apple founder Steve Jobs, took a majority stake in *The Atlantic*.

All those transitions were calm, almost boring, compared with Elon Musk's $44 billion purchase of Twitter in 2022. The world's second-richest man, a self-styled 'free speech absolutist' who made his money in electric cars and dabbles in space exploration, has converted Twitter from a pervasive global marketplace of ideas into a plaything. 'Twitter obviously cannot become a free-for-all hell-scape, where anything can be said with no consequences!' he tweeted soon after the acquisition, before turning it into exactly that.[15]

Musk is an entirely different animal to the other rich media acquirers. He's rash, impetuous, often uncommercial, and at least a bit mad. In less than a year, he transformed a platform with tens of millions of users into a personal playground for his own increasingly anti-woke, right-wing ideology and conspiracy theories. 'Disinformation and misinformation proliferated on the platform prior to Musk's takeover,' wrote Claire Berlinski in *Politico* in the aftermath of the Hamas attack on Israel in late 2023. 'But the difference in degree is so significant now as to amount to a difference in kind. Almost every significant change Musk has made has reduced its value as a source of reliable information from and for people affected by a disaster, and every change, similarly, has increased its utility to malicious propagandists and scammers.'[16]

In Musk's first year as owner, staff numbers fell from 7500 to about 1500, and revenue declined by more than 60 per cent as advertisers fled the toxic platform. As a result, Twitter/X's valuation was marked down by investors from $44 billion to $19 billion. Musk remained unrepentant amid the financial bloodbath. 'I'll say what I want,' he told CNBC, 'and if the consequence of that is losing money, so be it.'[17] A widespread view about Musk's impact on Twitter was summarised in early 2023 by *New York Times* political reporter Jonathan Swan: 'I'm not sure I've ever seen a company owner destroy a product's basic functionality as quickly as Musk has done with Twitter. I find it borderline useless as a fast news service these days and my feed is full of tweets from people I don't follow.'

———

The idea of journalism that is independent of government is a peculiarly Western democratic concept. In Putin's Russia, every television channel, newspaper, news website and radio station is effectively controlled by the Kremlin. Editors and producers are regularly issued with *metodichki* (guidance manuals) by the government to ensure they comply with official talking points and topics.

The noose of Russian censorship has tightened further during the war in Ukraine, as the government's media control agency Roskomnadzor (the Federal Service for Supervision of Communications, Information Technology and Mass Media) systemically stomped out independent sources of information. In early 2022 the *Financial Times* Moscow bureau chief Max Seddon tweeted: 'Russia's media censor will block any website that calls Moscow's war with Ukraine "an, invasion, or declaration of war." It's a "special military operation" in Donbas – or you get banned. Say Russia fired on cities and killed civilians – get banned.'[18]

A few months later the government introduced a law that criminalised independent reporting of the war, including calling it a war.

This followed Putin's so-called fake news law in 2019, which introduced grounds for criminal prosecution of media outlets that publish 'unreliable information' or show 'disrespect for society, government, state symbols, the constitution and government institutions'.[19]

Putin's decade-long assault on Russia's media can be encapsulated in the story of one newspaper, *Novaya Gazeta*. Established by several dozen journalists in 1993 as an experiment in independent journalism, this staff-owned collective also had two early external financial supporters: Mikhail Gorbachev, the last leader of the Soviet Union, and Alexander Lebedev, the billionaire former KGB agent who is now an aspiring mini-media-mogul in London. But as Putin's government tightened the screws on unbiased domestic news coverage of the war in Ukraine, *Novaya Gazeta*'s position became increasingly untenable. After its website was blocked and its media licence revoked, the paper was forced to suspend publication in March 2022.

Novaya Gazeta's credentials as a journalism crusader are impressive. In 2021 the paper's founding editor-in-chief, Dmitry Muratov, and the courageous Filipino editor Maria Ressa were jointly awarded the Nobel Peace Prize for their combined attempts to safeguard freedom of expression. Another marker of the paper's fearlessness are its seven journalists who have been murdered since 2000. Their pictures hung in the *Novaya Gazeta* conference room, a sombre reminder of the high price of investigative reporting in Russia. 'Every time a new portrait goes up, we try to hang it so that there is no more room on the wall,' lamented *Novaya* journalist Elena Kostyuchenko in her 2023 memoir *I Love Russia*, just before the paper's suspension.[20]

The best-known of those seven murdered *Novaya Gazeta* journalists was Anna Politkovskaya, the Putin critic who was shot dead in the elevator of her Moscow apartment block in 2006, in what was widely regarded as a government contract killing in retaliation for her reporting of the Chechnyan war. In her posthumously published book *Is Journalism Worth Dying For?* Politkovskaya described the topography of the Russian media at the time:

Koverny [was] a Russian clown whose job in the olden days was to keep the audience laughing while the circus arena was changed between acts. If he failed to make them laugh, the ladies and gentlemen booed him and the management sacked him.

Almost the entire present generation of Russian journalists, and those sections of the mass media which have survived to date, are clowns of this kind, a Big Top of *kovernys* whose job is to keep the public entertained and, if they do have to write about anything serious, then merely to tell everyone how wonderful the Pyramid of Power is in all its manifestations. The P of Power is something President Putin has been busy constructing for the past five years, in which every official – from top to bottom, the entire bureaucratic hierarchy – is appointed either by him person-ally or by his appointees ... Journalists and television presenters have taken enthusiastically to their new role in the Big Top. The battle for the right to convey impartial information, rather than act as servants of the Presidential Administration, is already a thing of the past. An atmosphere of intellectual and moral stag-nation prevails in the profession to which I belong, and it has to be said that most of my fellow journalists are not greatly troubled by this reversion from journalism to propagandizing on behalf of the powers that be.

What happens to journalists who don't want to perform in the Big Top? They become pariahs.[21]

It's a similar storyline across all the other faux democracies of Europe, Asia and the Middle East, where effective control of the media resides in the hands of governments and their cronies. Regimes in these countries employ an uncannily similar playbook to suppress independent journalism: they force the ownership of TV, radio, websites and newspapers into friendly hands; they close down or suspend unfriendly outlets; they fine, prosecute or jail owners and journalists who breach state editorial 'regulations'; they control news coverage via edicts from government agencies; they withhold state advertising from independent media; they reward and enrich loyal owners and editors.

In Turkey, the media is owned largely by a handful of pro-government business groups who are active in strategic sectors like telecommunications, banking and public works. 'Editorial content is strictly controlled by media bosses who have other business interests and are submissive to the government,' says Yavuz Baydar, a well-known journalist and campaigner for Turkish media freedom. President Erdogan's 1500-employee Directorate of Communications regularly issues directions to newsrooms on what to publish. And regulators routinely fine independent or opposition news providers for breaching Turkey's media code – for example, criticising the president or alleging official corruption is an offence – and suspend their state advertising contracts.[22] In 2016 the Erdogan government closed down more than a hundred media outlets following an unsuccessful coup. More than forty journalists languished in Turkish jails at the end of 2022, according to the Committee to Protect Journalists. Reporters Without Borders describes Turkey as the world's 'biggest prison for journalists'.[23]

Egypt is just as bad. As of 2019, almost all media organisations toed the government line 'either because they are directly controlled by the state or the intelligence agencies, or they are owned by a small number of wealthy businessmen allied with the government', according to Reporters Without Borders. In his decade of authoritarian rule, Egyptian president Abdel Fattah el-Sisi has presided over a systemic crackdown on press freedom. At least 170 journalists have been jailed, more than 500 news websites have been blocked, and six journalists have been killed. 'Persecution and the law operate side by side,' an Egyptian lawyer told Reporters Without Borders. 'The laws are so terrible for press freedom that, even if they comply with them, journalists risk being arrested or censored.'[24]

In Hungary, independent journalism has been steadily suffocating since Viktor Orbán returned as prime minister in 2010. One method cooked up in Budapest to control the country editorially was the creation of a pro-government media conglomerate called KESMA (Közép-Európai Sajtó és Média Alapítvány, the Central European Press and Media Foundation). KESMA owns more than 500 pro-government media outlets previously controlled by oligarchs allied with Orbán's Fidesz party. And in a country where the government accounts for around a third of all advertising expenditure – with the Prime Minister's Office being the single largest advertiser – critical journalism is starved of financial support.

In Mexico, as in Hungary, government advertising is the country's single biggest source of media revenue. The country is technically democratic but highly corrupt, plagued by drug cartels. There's little incentive to practise fearless journalism from either government or the big media owners, who must ingratiate themselves with politicians to get their slice of government advertising. Most Mexican media owners are powerful billionaires and magnates. 'The result is a media landscape across Mexico in which federal and state officials routinely dictate the news, telling outlets what they should – and should not – report,' explained *The New York Times* in 2017. 'Two-thirds of Mexican journalists admit to censoring themselves.' The relationship between the media and politicians is 'carrot and stick', says Javier Corral, the former governor of Mexico's largest state, Chihuahua. 'Behave well, and I'll give you lots of money and advertising. Act bad and I'll get rid of it.'[25]

Practising respectable journalism in Mexico became even more problematic after the election of Andrés Manuel López Obrador as president in 2018. Openly hostile towards the media, López Obrador vents against individual journalists during his daily 7am press briefings, known as the *mañaneras* ('morning show'). In a segment called 'Who's Who' he separates journalists and publications into the 'good', who report positively on his administration, and the 'bad' neoliberals and government critics. A day after he was criticised by the president, Ciro Gómez Leyva, a prominent television anchor, was gunned down by two men on a motorcycle and survived only because his car had bulletproof windows.[26]

Mexico is one of the deadliest countries for journalists – 163 were murdered between 2000 and 2022, most of them in states where prominent drug cartels operate. Journalism in Mexico is so dangerous that federal and state governments – despite the president's antipathy towards the media – run protection programs, providing camera systems, panic buttons, police protection, and relocation assistance for journalists under threat. Nine have been killed while receiving protection; 521 were under protection by mid-2022, while others who requested protection were killed before they received it, reported Human Rights Watch. Journalists in Mexico are killed just for doing their job, says Open Democracy.

In India, the world's biggest democracy, a tight government–crony axis has been expanding since 2014 under the prime-ministership of Narendra Modi. 'There is a coup underway in India,' says writer and journalist Manu Joseph.[27] 'Some people who are inconvenienced by democracy have taken over nearly all the country's television news channels.' Another Indian journalist, Ravish Kumar, has coined the Hindi term '*godi* media' – 'lapdog media' in English – to describe the vast bulk of his country's compliant news operators, who are entrenched in industries that depend on government contracts. 'In India, there are hundreds of news channels, but their content has become communal and criminal,' says Kumar.[28] 'Journalists are sent legal notices by government departments under any pretext now,' a former NDTV employee told *Foreign Policy* magazine. 'If nothing else you will be charged with sedition.'[29]

In Hong Kong, the era of independent journalism is over. The famously robust media ecosystem that was a hallmark of the former British colony collapsed following China's takeover in 1997. Beijing's imposition of widespread national security laws has triggered the closure or emasculation of almost all legitimate editorial platforms. In their place, much of Hong Kong's media has fallen into the hands of mainland Chinese owners or publishers backed by the Beijing government. There's no editorial independence left at the once-respected public broadcaster Radio Television

Hong Kong (RTHK), which is now run by a bureaucrat who has no media experience.

The *South China Morning Post*, the city's famous English-language paper, established in 1903, has been a litmus test for Beijing's tolerance of journalism that isn't propaganda. Now owned by mainland tech giant Alibaba, the *Post* is increasingly seen as the polite face of Chinese authoritarianism. In covering the 2019 pro-democracy protests, the largest demonstrations in Hong Kong's history, 'reporters found themselves butting up against senior editors who often appeared to be overly deferential to authorities and largely unquestioning of police narratives, even as evidence of misconduct mounted', reported *The Atlantic*.[30] Two years later, two reporters quit after the paper's editors axed their three-month investigation into human rights abuses in China's Xinjiang region, according to the *Hong Kong Free Press*.

The disintegration of Hong Kong's spirit of open journalism is also the story of the rise and fall of a remarkably brave media mogul. At the age of twelve, Jimmy Lai stowed away on a fishing boat from mainland China to Hong Kong. He worked his way up to a fortune by building a clothing brand, Giordano, which he was forced to sell by the Chinese government after he publicly described China's then premier Li Peng as 'the son of a turtle's egg with zero IQ'. It was a comment that embodied the free-speech ethos of his most spectacular creation, *Apple Daily*, launched in 1995.[31]

Within months of its launch, *Apple Daily* became the second-biggest-selling paper in Hong Kong. 'From the start, the newspaper engaged in a complicated interplay of politics, capitalism, and populism,' the Chinese-American journalist Jiayang Fan wrote in *The New Yorker*. 'Although always pro-democracy in its outlook, it first acquired a reputation for its eye-catching headlines and sensationalist exposés, in the style of the *Sun*, in Britain, or the *New York Post*. But, over time, alongside the celebrity gossip, it began publishing unsparing stories about political and economic malfeasance.'

Those stories led to its undoing. The Chinese leader, Xi Jinping, had made his government's position clear in 2016 when he declared,

'All news media run by the Party must work to speak for the Party's will and its propositions, and protect the Party's authority and unity.' In 2020, after the introduction of upgraded security laws, the paper was raided twice and Lai was arrested, and charged with colluding with foreign forces, fraud, sedition, and organising an unlawful assembly to protest the laws. He was sentenced to fourteen months in jail and now sits in solitary confinement in a maximum-security prison, awaiting a further trial on other charges. 'Jimmy Lai is essentially being charged with conspiracy to commit journalism,' his lawyer told CNN in early 2024.[32]

Elsewhere across Asia there's an entrenched, hand-in-glove relationship between autocratic governments and compliant media owners. In Singapore, the government regulates newspaper ownership through the Newspaper and Printing Presses Act, and imposes criminal penalties on media companies for 'speech deemed to be seditious, defamatory, or injurious to religious sensitivities'. It is almost never criticised, because most local media are controlled by Temasek Holdings, the state's investment arm.

Next door, Malaysia issues annual permits to all print media, prosecutes publishers of news stories deemed critical or derogatory of the government, and harasses the country's independent digital media. In 2016 the Malaysian *Insider* news website shut down after it was constantly blocked by the government's internet regulatory body on the grounds of national security. And in 2021 the country's dominant independent news website, *Malaysiakini*, was fined $123,000 by the federal court over comments posted by readers.

In Vietnam, privately owned media are banned or shut down if they publish 'non compliant' content; all newspapers and television channels are state-run; bloggers are routinely arrested, and all mass media are supervised by the Ministry of Culture and Information. In 2019, according to Reporters Without Borders, at least thirty journalists and bloggers were being held in Vietnam's jails.[33]

Cambodia practises an even more draconian form of media strangulation. Hun Sen, the country's dictator for thirty-eight years, systematically demolished independent journalism, before handing over the prime-ministership to his son in 2023. Over recent years, Hun Sen shut down or reallocated ownership of almost every non-compliant media outlet. Ahead of the 2023 election (where his Cambodian People's Party won 120 of the 125 seats), he further cleared the decks by ordering the closure of *Voice of Democracy*, one of the country's last independent news outlets, and blocking the websites and social media accounts of *The Cambodia Daily*. He also removed the US-government-funded broadcaster Radio Free Asia. This followed the closure in 2017 of the print edition of the vigorously independent *Cambodia Daily*. 'Descent Into Outright Dictatorship', was the paper's final headline. Ten months later, its rival *Phnom Penh Post* was sold to a Malaysian businessman who immediately sacked the editor-in-chief for refusing to remove an article about the new owner's apparent links to Hun Sen.

Cambodia's media 'is in a perilous state'.[34] That was an assessment by the United Nations High Commission on Human Rights, but it could have been talking about the state of journalism in nearly every dictatorship, banana republic or quasi-democracy in the world.

The Media
is Broken

In a 2012 *New Yorker* cartoon, two fifteenth-century scholars are standing in front of a hand-operated printing press looking at the newfangled invention known as a book. 'Nice,' says one to the other, 'but as long as there are readers there will be scrolls.'

Six centuries later, almost no-one believes that as long as there are readers or viewers there will always be newspapers, magazines, conventional TV or radio. The media as we've known it for generations has shattered. Advertising has fled elsewhere and can no longer fund journalism at scale. News is increasingly shaped by personal preference, not by facts. Trust in news producers is collapsing. Social media is unconstrained and ubiquitous. Artificial intelligence is meddling with human-created content. 'We're collectively living through [the year] 1500, when it's easier to see what's broken than what will replace it,' says media analyst Clay Shirky.[1]

The business models of traditional media have been unravelling at high speed ever since the internet transfigured communications more than two decades ago. It's a process that has created financial disaster for many owners and investors, and that's *their* problem. But because those businesses can no longer bankroll the resources needed for quality journalism, creating a dilemma for democracies, that's *our* problem.

Raw statistics tell the story of the demise of newspapers, the primary funding source of journalism for more than a century.

Since 2000, global newspaper revenue has fallen from $107 billion to around $30 billion, and it's still falling. Over the same period, global internet advertising revenue has grown from around $8 billion to more than $600 billion, and it's still growing. In 1930, newspapers scooped up almost 80 per cent of all US advertising revenue; by 2020 that figure was closer to 5 per cent. Since 1990, employment at American newspapers has declined from 455,000 to below 90,000.

Yet even as those trends accelerated in the early 2000s, many traditional publishers couldn't envision a world without mass-produced journalism funded by mass-market advertising. 'A lot of people say the internet is the future for newspapers,' the editor of the *Daily Mail*, Paul Dacre, told his staff at their annual summer party in 1999. 'Well, I say to that: bullshit.com.'[2]

What Dacre (and most of us) didn't realise in 1999 was how vulnerable the existing advertising model was to the emergence of a better – digital – mousetrap. It should have been obvious because most pre-internet advertising was little more than a game of chance. 'Half the money I spend on advertising is wasted,' the American department store owner John Wanamaker famously observed in the late 1800s, 'the trouble is I don't know which half.'[3]

Today, digital advertising is a *science*, not a gamble. Advertisers no longer waste half their money on newspapers, magazines, TV or radio. Instead of a single ad addressed at millions of people that goes largely unread or unviewed, digital technology and artificial intelligence can deliver the *right* ads to the *right* customers at the *right* time – personally, geographically, psychographically, professionally, demographically – on interactive devices that sit in the pockets of their owners. Digital advertising harvests users' data via tiny pieces of code known as cookies, that are embedded in web browsers and reach their targets using rapid-fire algorithms. It's a science that makes analogue advertising look like horses-and-buggies in an age of rockets.

Meanwhile, the vast pipelines of advertising continue to flow: worldwide ad spending in 2023 was estimated at $889 billion (more than the individual GDP of all but the top twenty countries in the world). Much of that revenue lines the pockets of giant new social media start-ups like Facebook, Twitter/X, Instagram, TikTok, YouTube and LinkedIn; and the pockets of Google, Amazon, digital TV, so-called retail media, out-of-home advertising, and a plethora of platforms created primarily to entertain, not to inform, and definitely not to subsidise quality journalism. 'Almost nothing short of a biological virus can spread as quickly, efficiently or aggressively as these technology platforms,' wrote Eric Schmidt and Jared Cohen in *The New Digital Age*.[4]

We are now watching the world's third great transfer of media power, following the invention of the printing press in the fifteenth century and the evolution of commercial media in the nineteenth and early- to mid-twentieth centuries. And the biggest winner in this power shift has been Google. Launched from a friend's garage in 1998 by two Stanford University computer science graduate students, Sergey Brin and Larry Page, Google has succeeded brilliantly in its mission to 'organize the world's information and make it universally accessible and useful'. It now controls more than 70 per cent of worldwide online search requests, sending 9,000 clicks *per second* to the websites of news publishers, generating some $224 billion of annual revenue (more than a quarter of all global advertising), profits of nearly $80 billion, and a market capitalisation of around $1.8 trillion – all hoovered up from ads that used to appear in print in local newspapers, Yellow Pages directories, direct mail, retail catalogues, specialist publications and magazines, and on TV and radio.

'For more than two decades, publishers big and small have packaged their content to rank highly in Google's search results,' explained a *New York Times* analysis. Known as search engine optimisation (SEO to industry insiders), this practice involves creating headlines that mimic Google user queries, and lacing editorial content with links to other sites, all with the objective of driving clicks from Google to their websites. Acting as an alluring shop window,

Google generates nearly 40 per cent of publishers' traffic, according to *The Wall Street Journal*.[5]

All that power means that when Google blinks, news journalism can shudder. And that's what happened in late 2023 when referral traffic to news publishers plummeted after Google adjusted its algorithms to more effectively 'show helpful and reliable results'. Following that shockwave, publishers are bracing for an even worse nightmare from the likely impact of Google's recently introduced generative-AI-powered search. Under that scenario, users will get a complete answer to their Google search, integrated by AI, without needing to click on a news website.

Google's lopsided relationship with the news industry was laid out in indelicate detail in 2014 by Mathias Döpfner, CEO of the German publisher Axel Springer, in an open letter to then Google CEO Eric Schmidt. Published in *Frankfurter Allgemeine* under the heading 'Why we fear Google', Döpfner's passionate letter started with a frank acknowledgement – 'Google doesn't need us. But we need Google' – and continued in the same vein:

> We are afraid of Google. I must state this very clearly and frankly, because few of my colleagues dare do so publicly ... Google knows more about every digitally active citizen than George Orwell dared to imagine in his wildest dreams in 1984 ... Behind this statement there is a state of mind and an image of humanity that is typically cultivated in totalitarian regimes – not in liberal societies ... Only dictatorships want transparent citizens instead of a free press ... Does this mean that Google is planning to operate in a legal vacuum, without troublesome antitrust authorities and data protection? A kind of superstate that can navigate its floating kingdom undisturbed by any and all nation-states and their laws? ... On the Internet, in the beautiful colorful Google world, so much seems to be free of charge: from search services up to journalistic offerings. In truth we are paying with our behavior – with the predictability and commercial exploitation of our behavior. Anyone who has a

car accident today, and mentions it in an e-mail, can receive an offer for a new car from a manufacturer on his mobile phone tomorrow ... Google is the world's most powerful bank – but dealing only in behavioral currency ... Nobody capitalizes on their knowledge about us as effectively as Google.[6]

As bad as that sounds, at least Google has a *complementary* relationship with news, unlike other social media platforms that have appropriated large chunks of the advertising revenue and audiences that once supported news journalism. Google's underlying business model is to provide instant information on demand – mainly consumer information, with news and commentary as a side dish – accompanied by relevant advertising content designed to assist users (and advertisers, of course).

For the dominant social media platforms – Facebook, TikTok, Instagram, Twitter/X and YouTube – news and journalism are all but irrelevant. Their remit is to drive massive social engagement that converts into advertising dollars (currently around $180 billion combined, more than five times the global advertising revenue of newspapers). They are in the addiction business.

Social media is like making magic, says Tristan Harris, a former Google design ethicist. 'Magicians start by looking for blind spots, edges, vulnerabilities and limits of people's perception, so they can influence what people do without them even realizing it,' he says. Once you know how to push people's buttons 'you can play them like a piano', by constructing the menu so people think they win, no matter what they choose. It's a manifestation of Clarke's Third Law, the axiom created by the futurist Arthur C. Clarke in 1973: 'Any sufficiently advanced technology is indistinguishable from magic.'[7]

This illusion was described by Harvard law professor Lawrence Lessig in *The Verge* in late 2023: 'People have a naïve view: they open up their X feed or their Facebook feed, and [they think] they're just getting stuff that's given to them in some kind of neutral way, not recognizing that behind what's given to them is the most extraordinary intelligence that we have ever created in AI that is extremely good at figuring out how to tweak the attitudes or emotions of the people they're engaging with to drive them down rabbit holes of engagement. The only thing they care about is engagement.'[8]

At the heart of the social media business model are the algorithms that lure people down those rabbit holes, where they're welcomed by advertisers who have paid to connect with them, based on automated personal data about their individual online activities. That sounds harmless enough – and is often useful – if the algorithms are used to sell prams to expectant mothers or hotel rooms to travellers.

But it's not just about prams and hotel rooms. In 2017 ProPublica revealed that Facebook advertisers were targeting the newsfeeds of people who expressed interest in the topics of 'Jew hater', 'How to burn jews', or 'History of "why jews ruin the world"'. Facebook's response to this revelation was to remove those targeting fields and explain that a *human* wasn't responsible for creating them. 'That was true. It was the AI that generated that category,' noted Lessig. 'The point is that we've got to break the tyranny of analogical reasoning here.'[9]

Data, according to X's owner Elon Musk, is 'probably more valuable than gold'.[10] Driving that calculus is a psychological seduction process that was teased out by the historian Yuval Noah Harari in his book *21 Lessons for the 21st Century*: 'Suppose a shady billionaire offered you the following shady deal: "I will pay you $30 a month and, in exchange, you will allow me to brainwash you for an hour every day, installing in your mind whichever political and commercial biases I want." Would you take the deal? Few sane people would. So the shady billionaire offers a slightly different deal: "You will allow me to brainwash you for one hour every day, and in exchange, I will not charge you anything for this service." Now the deal suddenly sounds tempting to hundreds of millions of people.'[11]

There have been ongoing attempts by regulators and courts to curb the excesses of online data collection. Meta, Facebook's parent company, was fined more than $400 million by the Irish Data Protection Commission in early 2023 for breaching European rules over its targeted advertising. And later that year, Google settled a Californian lawsuit that claimed more than $5 billion in damages for millions of users who were secretly tracked, even though they had set their browsers to 'incognito' or 'private' mode. This allowed Google to access information about their friends, hobbies, consumer habits and 'potentially embarrassing things' they sought online. But these fines are drops in an ocean of advertising revenue for the behemoths who control the multi-billion-dollar digital advertising bonanza.

If social media and search engines were the only predators plundering the revenue that once flowed to news publishers, that would be bad enough. But they are part of a pincer movement of non-traditional advertising that's carving large slices from the pie that used to feed journalism. The biggest of these is so-called retail media, a booming $130 billion-a-year business that places ads on retailers' ecommerce websites and targets consumers before the point of purchase in stores, all based on their online behaviour. Amazon is the biggest player in this space, scooping up around $45 billion of ad revenue in 2023, more than the whole global newspaper industry combined. To that you can add a further $38 billion of 'out-of-home' advertising – billboards, outdoor posters, and ads in lifts, airports, sports arenas and railway stations – which is becoming increasingly digital, sophisticated and targeted, a constant array of giant TV screens dotted through freeways, city streets, public spaces, sports stadiums and almost everywhere that people gather.

And the digital uprising hasn't just decapitated newspapers and magazines, it threatens the viability of network television, the last dominant 'traditional' medium that's still in survival mode. 'The old-fashioned TV business is slowly but surely sliding into the ocean,' wrote Martin Peers in *The Information* in mid-2023.[12] Streaming channels like Netflix and Disney+, where the majority of subscribers pay to skip the ads, have overtaken cable and broadcast networks as the most-watched television in the US. The business model for television is refracting as younger viewers bypass conventional TV and advertisers follow the eyeballs.

———

Technological brilliance creates turbulence that creates opportunities. It happened in the late nineteenth century when Pulitzer, Hearst and Northcliffe exploited the new potency of printing presses to kick-start the mass-market newspaper business. And it happened again at the beginning of this century when a blazing burst of journal-ism start-ups exploited the internet to (briefly) transform the media landscape, offering outsider voices to audiences who were 'sick of the stuffy mainstream media', as described by one of those entrepreneurs, Ben Smith.[13]

First came *Gawker*, the snarky gossip website launched in 2002 from the New York living room of its founder, Nick Denton, an expat British former *Financial Times* reporter described in *Salon* as 'a serious journalist, a cynic, an idealist, a free-speech crusader, and someone (at times) with a very loose sense of ethics'.[14] *Gawker* shook the media establishment to its bootstraps by presenting rumour and innuendo (usually unsourced, often scurrilous) as journalism.

That vicarious recipe worked until, inevitably, it went too far. In 2012 *Gawker* published a private sex tape showing the American professional wrestler Hulk Hogan intertwined with the estranged wife of a radio personality known as Bubba the Love Sponge. Hogan successfully sued *Gawker* for invasion of privacy, eventually winning $140 million in damages. It later emerged that Hogan's legal case had been secretly funded by the billionaire PayPal co-founder and Facebook investor, Peter Thiel, who had been outed as gay by *Gawker*'s Valleywag blog a few years earlier under the headline 'Peter Thiel is totally gay, people'.

That single item motivated Thiel to launch a covert legal pursuit of *Gawker* and Denton. 'It's less about revenge and more about specific deterrence,' he told *The New York Times*. 'I saw *Gawker* pioneer a unique and incredibly damaging way of getting attention by bullying people even when there was no connection with the public interest.' Thiel's vendetta worked: after he spent $10 million to bankroll Hogan's case, *Gawker* was forced to file for Chapter 11 bankruptcy and ceased publishing soon after.[15]

Next came *Vice*. Created as a printed lifestyle magazine in Canada in the 1990s, it expanded into digital video in 2007, rolling out separate news, music, technology and sports sites and channels. Soon *Vice* was riding high. Rupert Murdoch's 21st Century Fox invested $70 million in the business-everyone-was-talking-about, after Murdoch reportedly drank tequila with Shane Smith, *Vice*'s bearded, tattooed founder, at his cool Brooklyn office.

By 2017 the company had launched *Vice* the HBO news program and *Vice News Tonight*, and had banked a $450 million investment from a private-equity firm that valued the parent company, Vice Media, at a stratospheric $5.7 billion. 'News Corp, Time Warner, Bertelsmann, Condé Nast ... everyone is after us,' Smith had told the *Financial Times* in 2012. Four years later he predicted *Vice* could soon be worth $50 billion. The media business, he said, was on the verge of a 'bloodbath' and 'we will be sitting there laughing our heads off'.[16]

The laughter never happened. As the company's vision floundered, it began laying off staff, and many of its online TV channels were consolidated into website feature sections. The dream effectively ended in mid-2023 when *Vice* formally filed for Chapter 11 bankruptcy and was sold to its former lenders for $350 million, wiping out everyone else's equity.

Gawker and *Vice* were the splashy stars of the new media firmament. But the two other notable start-ups, *The Huffington Post* and *BuzzFeed News*, had a weightier ambition: to reconstruct news journalism in an original, entertaining digital fashion. 'We celebrated and immersed ourselves in an optimistic web culture that imagined a reader who cared about which Disney princess she was, and also the worst of how the American justice system treated abused women, who wanted to argue about the color of the dress and also understand the science behind it,' explained the founding editor-in-chief of *BuzzFeed News* Ben Smith, writing later in his next news website iteration, *Semafor*.

Arianna Huffington, a whip-smart, well-connected 55-year-old Republican-turned-Democrat, Greek-turned-American, launched *The Huffington Post* in 2005 as a hybrid news/celebrity website that published the opinions of thousands of unpaid bloggers and had a voracious appetite for clicks. 'Old-media types tend to cringe if a headline oversells a story or a story is trumped up solely to grab eyeballs,' wrote media critic Jack Shafer in *Slate*. 'Huffington suffers no such shame. There is no celebrity slide show beneath her tastes and no SEO [search engine optimisation] trick she won't employ if it will get her traffic.'[17]

As the Obama presidency began its eight-year course in 2009, *The Huffington Post* became an established Washington liberal fixture. 'Arianna, I want you to know that I don't agree with everything you say,' the president reportedly told the new mini-media mogul at his first White House holiday party, 'but I read *The Huffington Post* every day.' He was part of the Zeitgeist: within a few years her site was reaching 26 million unique visitors a month. 'An astonishing number,' as William Cohan explained in *Vanity Fair*, 'but in the Internet business, sites either grow or shrink.'[18]

Huffington wasn't for shrinking. In 2011 she sold *The Huffington Post* for $315 million to the online service provider and web portal AOL (formerly America Online). AOL's deep pockets fuelled a global expansion. When the site unveiled its sixth international edition in Italy in 2012, Huffington went to Rome to immodestly spruik her egalitarian model of journalism. 'I'm sure there will always be a *New York Times* and *La Repubblica*,' she told an Italian reporter. 'But we must also recognize that in certain circumstances any citizen can become a correspondent or a journalist.'[19] Two years later she was back in her country of birth to launch *The Huffington Post*'s fourteenth international edition at the Acropolis Museum in Athens. 'For me personally, it's the ultimate homecoming,' she told her audience.[20]

As with the other start-ups, the euphoria at *The Huffington Post* lasted only as long as the advertising revenue matched the aggressive valuations that had been sold to investors. When it didn't, AOL pressured Huffington to reduce costs and began easing her out of daily management, using an approach one former executive described to *Vanity Fair* as the 'Popemobile strategy': she was encouraged to go on trips and, on her way out the door, wave 'like the Pope to all the people in the newsroom'. A further blow landed in 2015 when AOL was acquired by the telecom giant Verizon, with the tiny *Huffington Post* trailing in its wake. As Verizon focused on creating video content, not website news reporting, the site was redesigned, repositioned and renamed *HuffPost*. 'A decade into its life – a veritable century in the Digital Age – *The Huffington Post* was being treated not as a high-quality news source but as another Web site for click-bait infotainment,' observed *Vanity Fair*'s William Cohan.[21]

We now come to Jonah Peretti, one of the co-founders of *The Huffington Post*, a curly-haired 31-year-old computer science nerd with a passion for delving into what was in 2006 an obscure artform: how to spread ideas virally. While helping Huffington build her business, Peretti also began toying with an experimental project he called *BuzzFeed* – 'a lab where I could continue to play and do research and experiment', as he described it.[22] Gradually his attention shifted towards his buzzy side hustle and by 2011, when AOL acquired *The Huffington Post*, he created what *Business Insider* predicted would be 'a great media company for the social age'.

By 2013 *BuzzFeed*, along with its sister site *Buzzfeed News* under the direction of Ben Smith as editor-in-chief, had become a media darling. Its oeuvre was described vividly by Andrew Rice in *New York* magazine as 'a hyperactive amalgam' of 'really serious news by first-rate journalists' and 'an enormous amount of stuff like "The 40 Greatest Dog GIFs of All Time."' Rice explained the modus operandi:

BuzzFeed's articles only nominally live on the website, spending most of their time out of the house as links on social networks like Facebook and Twitter.

Peretti's assembly line produces hundreds of posts a day, applying his theories of virality to both original articles and – more important to *BuzzFeed*'s mission – on behalf of paid advertisers. *BuzzFeed*'s ads are meant to be just as clickable as the site's most popular and uplifting posts. Prominent clients include GE, Pepsi, VW – and Nike.

BuzzFeed's model, known in the industry as 'native advertising,' has caused some trepidation among traditional ad agencies, which see its potential to cut out their intermediary role. It's also the sort of intermingling of editorial content and business – 'church and state' – that used to be considered heretical at any respectable journalism institution.[23]

By 2014, after reportedly passing $100 million in revenue, *BuzzFeed* raised $50 million from the savvy venture capital firm Andreessen Horowitz. The next year saw a $200 million investment by NBCUniversal, valuing *BuzzFeed* at a spectacular $1.7 billion. 'The money was enough for us to keep paying the growing bills – for a staff of about 1,700, a dozen offices, and a culture that tried to keep up with the perks of the tech industry, from a frozen yogurt machine to lavish holiday parties,' wrote Smith in *Traffic: Genius, Rivalry, and Delusion in the Billion-Dollar Race to Go Viral*, his granular account of the early-21st-century digital journalism revolution. 'In reality, it arrived just in time to prevent the floor from falling out.'[24]

By 2017, as the floor began to wobble, the company announced it would accept banner ads and no longer rely on native advertising – 'an obvious admission that *BuzzFeed*'s model, its belief in its own ability to make anything spread virally across an open internet, was no longer working', wrote Smith. Then came staff layoffs, Smith's own departure, and the closure of the Australian and British operations.[25]

Nothing typified *BuzzFeed*'s in-your-face editorial ethos better (or worse) than its decision in 2017 to publish the so-called Steele Dossier – thirty-five pages of raw intelligence it described as 'specific, unverified, and potentially unverifiable allegations of contact between Trump aides and Russian operatives'. Compiled by Christopher Steele, a former British counterintelligence operative, on behalf of Hillary Clinton's 2016 presidential campaign, the explosive dossier claimed that the Russian government possessed a video of Donald Trump in compromising positions with prostitutes at Moscow's Ritz-Carlton hotel, and referred to secret meetings by one of Trump's aides with Russian officials in Prague years before Trump was elected.[26]

Publication of the dossier was widely criticised as reckless and unsubstantiated by rival journalists and editors. Trump's response was to pillory *BuzzFeed* as a 'failing pile of garbage'.[27] Ben Smith attempted to justify publication of the dossier, which had been circulating at the highest levels of American government, on the grounds that it had 'enormous explanatory power' and revealed 'the strange and intriguing document that elites had tried to keep from them, and we stated plainly what we knew and what we didn't'.[28]

The unravelling of *The Huffington Post* and *Buzzfeed News* converged in late 2020 when the companies announced that *BuzzFeed* was buying *HuffPost* from Verizon, who in turn invested in *BuzzFeed* – a sad, obtuse ending to a two-decade rollercoaster ride that had promised so much. By the end of 2023, the headlines on the *BuzzFeed* home page told the grim story of its withdrawal from news: 'Eat Nothing But Fried Foods And I'll Accurately Guess Your Height'; 'My Mother Was A Cult Leader. At Her Funeral, One Of Her Followers Put A Curse On Me'; 'I Know I Shouldn't Laugh But These 85 Extremely Dumb Things People Posted On The Internet Last Month Are Killing Me'.

Gawker, Vice, The Huffington Post and *BuzzFeed*, Ben Smith concluded, 'didn't turn out to be the future'.[29] A chapter in the grand experiment to reinvent news for the digital era was effectively over. 'They had it all – the coolness of the tech world, the chops of the best newspapers, the know-how of the internet,' wrote *Slate*'s editor-in-chief Hillary Frey. 'They did great work that mattered and won awards. They raised up a generation of journalists that have made our industry better and smarter.'[30] Maybe, but as James Hennessy wrote in *The Guardian*, they are more likely to be remembered 'not as the revolutionary disrupters of the industry they were once thought to be, but as a decade-long intermission to the whim of the famously mercurial tech titans who briefly offered them patronage'.[31]

Their failure, after such a promising start, raises questions about what, if anything, can replace the civic function of newspaper journalism in the digital age. Even podcasting, the great editorial invention of my lifetime, has hit a commercial roadblock. The depth and intelligence of the best podcasts is stunning; it's a compellingly intimate and conversational medium that isn't constrained by the time or space limitations imposed on most other journalism; podcasts are accessible to anyone with a phone and nearly always free.

But where once the format was seen as a ray of sunlight in an otherwise troubled media landscape, it's now clear that there are severe limits to the scale of revenue available to fund and nourish quality podcasting. In 2023 it was estimated that US podcasting advertising was worth $3.4 billion, just *one per cent* of all media advertising revenue – a paltry level of income to finance the costs of talent and satisfy the expectations of an influx of investors who have piled into the medium in recent years. The result has been a dramatic consolidation of the fledgling industry, large-scale layoffs, and growing pessimism about the economics – but not the programming quality – of podcasting as a business. 'From 2018 to 2020, highly-produced podcasting went from a fairly easy way to make a decent profit to a near-guaranteed way to lose a fortune,' observed the writer and analyst Adam Davidson, co-creator of the highly successful podcast 'Planet Money'.[32]

Podcasting as a medium is unlikely to fade away like *BuzzFeed*, *Huffington Post* or *Vice* as it attempts to pivot towards video, where YouTube is a ready-made hosting platform. But as it cuts costs and tries to attract paying subscribers – a hard ask when there's so much quality podcasting content available for nothing – it's looking more like a niche and less like a panacea for the problems facing journalism.

———

If there is one individual who most epitomises the economic, political, technological and editorial turbulence that has emerged in the unfolding media revolution, it is Facebook founder Mark Zuckerberg. His societal power, measured by outcome, is almost certainly greater than that of Hearst, Beaverbrook and Murdoch combined. In some countries, Facebook *is* the internet, the place where elections are fought, national issues are debated and influence resides.

'Nobody believes Mark Zuckerberg woke up one morning and decided to destroy the media industry,' wrote Matthew Ingram in the *Columbia Journalism Review*. 'His company's behavior is a lot more like an elephant accidentally stepping on an ant – something that has happened while Facebook has gone about its business.'[33]

It was a business that started serendipitously by mining personal information, as this 2004 exchange of messages between Zuckerberg and a friend, unearthed by *Business Insider* in 2010, revealed:

> Zuck: Yeah so if you ever need info about anyone at Harvard
> Zuck: Just ask.
> Zuck: I have over 4,000 emails, pictures, addresses, SNS
> [Redacted Friend's Name]: What? How'd you manage that one?
> Zuck: People just submitted it.
> Zuck: I don't know why.
> Zuck: They "trust me"
> Zuck: Dumb fucks.[34]

A picture of Zuckerberg the corporate titan going about his business was sketched by the company's co-founder Chris Hughes in *The New York Times* in 2019: 'Facebook's board works more like an advisory committee than an overseer, because Mark controls around

60 per cent of voting shares. Mark alone can decide how to configure Facebook's algorithms to determine what people see in their News Feeds, what privacy settings they can use and even which messages get delivered. He sets the rules for how to distinguish violent and incendiary speech from the merely offensive, and he can choose to shut down a competitor by acquiring, blocking or copying it.'[35]

Analysing Zuckerberg's motives and impulses has become an obsession among the global tech and media elite. 'The company's ambition, its ruthlessness, and its lack of a moral compass scare me,' wrote John Lanchester in the *London Review of Books* in 2017. Growth has been so fundamental to the company's raison d'être that it has become, in many respects, 'more like a virus than it is like a business'. And Facebook's motivation? 'It does things because it can.'[36]

The story of Facebook and Zuckerberg is a disturbing study in how a disruptive *economic* force can be configured into a disruptive *political* and *social* force. Facebook possesses the personal data of more than a quarter of the world's people, 2.8 billion out of 8 billion, and governs the flow of information among them, wrote Jill Lepore in *The New Yorker*, making the company 'in important respects, larger than any country'.[37] Adrienne LaFrance extended the analogy further in *The Atlantic* in 2021 under the headline 'The Largest Autocracy on Earth': 'GDP makes for a telling comparison, not just because it gestures at Facebook's extraordinary power, but because it helps us see Facebook for what it really is. Facebook is not merely a website, or a platform, or a publisher, or a social network, or an online directory, or a corporation, or a utility. It is all of these things. But Facebook is also, effectively, a hostile foreign power.' LaFrance went on to cite the company's 'single-minded focus on its own expansion; its immunity to any sense of civic obligation; its record of facilitating the undermining of elections; its antipathy toward the free press; its rulers' callousness and hubris; and its indifference to the endurance of American democracy.'[38]

Hillary Clinton told LaFrance that she had always caught a whiff of authoritarianism from Zuckerberg. 'I feel like you're nego-tiating with a foreign power sometimes,' she said. 'He's immensely powerful.'³⁹ On the eve of Germany's federal election in 2017, as Zuckerberg took steps to increase the transparency of political advertising on Facebook, he announced that 'we have been working to ensure the integrity of the German elections this weekend'. It was a comforting statement that showed Zuckerberg and Facebook were eager to restore trust in their system, wrote Max Read in *New York* magazine, but 'it's not the kind of language we expect from media organizations, even the largest ones. It's the language of governments, or political parties, or NGOs. A private company, working unilaterally to ensure election integrity in a country it's not even based in?'⁴⁰

One of Zuckerberg's catchphrases early in Facebook's life was 'company over country', a mantra that sat uneasily during the Trump era when the US needed its media to prioritise coverage of country over company. By 2020, according to *The Wall Street Journal*, Zuckerberg was 'an active political operator', dining with President Trump, in regular contact with White House senior adviser and Trump son-in-law Jared Kushner, and 'playing a hands-on role in setting Facebook's policies for the upcoming presidential election'.⁴¹

Then came the 2021 assault on the Capitol. 'Facebook groups swelled with at least 650,000 posts attacking the legitimacy of Joe Biden's victory between Election Day and the Jan. 6 siege of the US Capitol, with many calling for executions or other political violence,' reported a joint investigation by ProPublica and *The Washington Post*. 'Many posts portrayed Biden's election as the result of widespread fraud that required extraordinary action – including the use of force – to prevent the nation from falling into the hands of traitors.' One post showed an image of a Civil War-era gallows featuring nooses and hooded figures waiting to be hanged. 'LOOKS LIKE CIVIL WAR IS BECOMING INEVITABLE!!!' read a Facebook post a month ahead of the Capitol attack. 'WE CANNOT ALLOW FRAUDULENT ELECTIONS TO STAND ! SILENT NO MORE MAJORITY MUST RISE UP NOW AND DEMAND BATTLEGROUND STATES NOT TO CERTIFY FRAUDULENT ELECTIONS NOW!'⁴²

Facebook and Google – and the other start-ups who have undermined the advertising-funded system of journalism by sequestering most of that advertising – are not malign actors. They're innovators who created a new algorithmic order that has transformed (and muddied) the world of information. They didn't set out to disrupt democracy or kill news. They followed their financial incentives. They aren't innocent, or blameless, and should be doing a lot more to moderate and control their most egregious content. But unlike the media barons who created their own journalism, then manipulated it for money and power, the tech entrepreneurs did no more than create conduits for other people's content. They weren't allocated the responsibility of protecting news journalism.

The truth is, journalism has always operated as a kind of mirage. The people who consume it have never paid what it costs to produce. And the people who funded most of those costs, the advertisers, never had a say in what was produced because they were paying for a different product – access to the audience. To me, this misalignment of incentives always felt uneasy. And, finally, it has proved to be untenable.

I gleaned my first insight into the perversity of that business model as a young reporter during the golden era of newspapers in the late 1970s. My first big story was about to be published across the front page of the Melbourne *Age*. Chuffed with pride, I waited at the office until midnight, when the first of the 400,000 or so copies of the huge weekend edition (more than 200 broadsheet pages incorporating a news section and bulky employment, property and automotive classified-advertising sections) started rolling off the massive lines of printing presses that filled the vast basement and shook the building for hours every night.

In those days, hundreds of people would queue up outside the *Age* offices at midnight every Friday to buy the first copies of the paper. There were traffic jams and illegal parking. Rubbish bins were placed by *Age* staff along an entire city block to handle the debris. Standing on the dark street that night, I watched the readers pick up their papers, each plucking out the advertising section they came for and dumping the rest of the paper – including my journalism – into garbage bins.

Reimagining
Journalism

When I typed the query 'Can AI replace journalism?' into ChatGPT and Google Bard, two of the world's biggest AI platforms, they offered responses that felt rational, yet darkly unconvincing:

'While AI can assist in various journalistic tasks like fact-checking, data analysis, and even generating certain types of news articles,' responded ChatGPT, 'it's unlikely to entirely replace journalism.' *Entirely?*

'Journalism involves complex tasks that go beyond just reporting facts. It requires critical thinking, investigative skills, contextual understanding, empathy, and the ability to ask insightful questions,' continued ChatGPT. 'These qualities are deeply human and aren't easily replicated by AI.' *Easily?*

'While AI is a powerful tool that enhances journalistic capabilities, it's unlikely to fully replace the role of journalists in interpreting, investigating, and providing the depth of analysis and understanding that audiences expect,' added ChatGPT. *Unlikely? Fully replace?*

Google Bard agreed that AI wasn't likely to 'completely replace journalism in the foreseeable future'. *Completely?*

Bard then cited AI's strengths (efficiency, speed and personalisation) and its limitations ('lack of creativity and critical thinking ... ethical concerns ... job displacement'), concluding that instead of replacing journalists, AI is more likely to become 'a powerful tool' that will augment human journalists and create new roles. *Augment humans? Create new roles?*

The future of journalism, concluded Bard, 'lies in harnessing the power of AI while upholding the core values of the profession: accuracy, objectivity, and accountability. It's still an evolving field with complex considerations, and ongoing discussions will be vital as we navigate the future of journalism in the age of AI.' *Complex considerations? Ongoing discussions?*

We used to believe the challenges confronting the news media could only be resolved by humans armed with good intentions and smart business models. Now an entirely different set of non-human dangers threatens the integrity and viability of news journalism. The image of old-style moguls lounging on yachts and summoning politicians may have faded, but media manipulation is arguably more pernicious in an age of artificial intelligence, automated news, sham content, misinformation, stalking algorithms and surveillance technology. The once-feared human 'dark arts' – phone hacking, invasion of privacy, compiling lists of enemies, and blackmailing prime ministers – seem almost quaint compared to their modern, invisible, technological equivalents.

'AI will rain a hellfire of fake and doctored content on the world,' says Jim VandeHei, founder of the successful US news-analysis website *Axios*.[1] 'AI and large language models have the potential to destroy journalism and media brands as we know them,' proclaims Axel Springer boss Mathias Döpfner.[2] The arrival of generative AI could spell 'the end for our business model', according to Louis Dreyfus, chief executive of *Le Monde*.[3]

Barely a year since the first generative AI platforms were launched, the media world is roiling with alarm and uncertainty. This is a different and more foreboding mood than the one that prevailed during the early years of the internet, when media companies were still gushing money and hardly anyone could foresee the looming dangers ahead. Now, the memory of what *did* eventuate during that painful internet revolution is scaring the pants off media owners and decision-makers.

This early stage of AI is eerily reminiscent of the 1950s when slow, bulky computers were being used for a narrow range of tasks. ChatGPT is currently in its 'giant room-size machine phase', says David Baggett, founder of cybersecurity firm Inky.[4] 'I think part of the reason news organizations are now looking so carefully at OpenAI,' explained the publisher of *The Atlanta Journal-Constitution*, Andrew Morse, 'is because they have 20 years of history indicating that if we're not careful, we'll give away the keys to the kingdom.'[5]

The current dangers posed by artificial intelligence to the existing models of journalism are alarming, and numerous:

- AI CAN REPLICATE REAL JOURNALISM. By packaging text, images, video and graphics that adopt the patterns and structure of the best professional content, AI can create a sham alternative publishing ecosystem that looks real. NewsGuard, a company established by several American journalism professionals to monitor online misinformation, identified 623 so-called UAINS – Unreliable AI-Generated News and Information Websites – in late 2023. Using generic names like *iBusiness Day*, *Ireland Top News* and *Daily Time Update*, these simulated sites operate with little or no human oversight and collectively publish thousands of generic articles about subjects that include politics, technology, entertainment and travel, and which are written largely or entirely by bots. By attracting mass traffic, these sites can generate automated programmatic advertising revenue, often unintentionally supported by well-known brands.

- AI-CONCEIVED SUMMARIES CAN REPLACE GOOGLE LINKS TO CREDIBLE NEWS. In what could become a disastrous scenario for news publishers, Google has introduced highly efficient AI-generated summary paragraphs at the top of search queries, reducing or eliminating the need for users to click onto links to reputable news sites. After only a few months of this innovation, clicks from Google to news websites have fallen dramatically. 'If somebody can type a question, or write stories, using our content or mixing it with some low-quality content, it's a risk for the political debate, political society,' warns *Le Monde*'s Dreyfus.[6]

- AI CAN CREATE AND NORMALISE DISINFORMATION. 'Well-dressed AI-generated news anchors are spewing pro-Chinese propaganda, amplified by bot networks sympathetic to Beijing,' reported *The Washington Post* in late 2023. 'In Slovakia, politicians up for election found their voices had been cloned to say controversial things they never uttered, days before voters went to the polls.' This is now happening: AI can empower almost anyone to create professional-looking disinformation that most consumers can't distinguish from real news.[7]

- AI COMPANIES CAN DECIDE WHO GETS REMUNERATED FOR CONTENT. When the German publisher Axel Springer signed a content-licensing deal in late 2023 with OpenAI, owner of ChatGPT, it became the first major news publisher to give an AI company legal access to its content. The deal, worth tens of millions of euros a year to Springer, allows ChatGPT to summarise and link to articles from *Politico*, *Bild*, *Business Insider* and its other media brands. In contrast, other big publishing companies have blocked AI web crawlers from scraping their content. *The New York Times* has gone even further, suing OpenAI and Microsoft for billions of dollars for 'unlawful copying and use of *The Times*'s uniquely valuable works'.[8] Licensing editorial content gives AI companies the power to 'play middleman' in the news business. That's a risky bet because it means people won't need to visit publisher sites to get information; they can just go to OpenAI, according to Jacob Donnelly, who runs the 'Media Operator' newsletter. 'And when News Corp, *The New York Times*, IAC, and various other large content library owners do these deals, OpenAI only gets stronger,' says Donnelly.[9]

- AI CAN REPLACE THOUSANDS OF JOURNALISTS' JOBS. For several years this threat sounded more like a science fiction trope, but when Europe's largest newspaper *Bild* (owned by Axel Springer) retrenched around 200 staff in mid-2023 it became a gritty reality. In an internal email later leaked to *Frankfurter Allgemeine*, *Bild* informed its employees it was 'starting a clear AI offensive . . . for our move to digital-only . . . AI will soon be able to completely take over the layout of the printed newspaper . . . the functions of editor-in-chief, editors, proofreaders, secretaries, and photo editors will no longer exist as they do today'. As a result, *Bild* told its staff, it is 'parting ways with colleagues who have tasks that are replaced by AI and/ or automated processes in the digital world, or who do not find themselves in this new team with their current skills'.[10] Another German newspaper, *Express*, has created a virtual journalist called Klara Indernach that now writes more than 5 per cent of all its stories, overseen by human editors. And Rádio Expres in Slovakia covers its nightshift using the cloned voice of a popular presenter to broadcast commentary about news and music from the company's news website.

Inside the world's biggest newsrooms, AI is now viewed as a kind of frenemy. *The New York Times* has appointed its first 'editorial director of Artificial Intelligence Initiatives' to establish the principles and tools for the paper's use of artificial intelligence. It's an acknowledgement that to remain competitive as a business, AI 'will need to be delicately infused one way or another into the organization's DNA', said Oliver Darcy on CNN's *Reliable Sources*.[11] Across the Atlantic, the *Financial Times* is developing a team that can 'experiment responsibly with AI tools to assist journalists in tasks such as mining data, analyzing text and images and translation', *FT* editor Roula Khalaf wrote in mid-2023. In the same letter to readers, Khalaf made a pledge that would have sounded bizarre at any time in the previous two centuries: 'FT journalism in the new AI age will continue to be reported and written by humans.' It says a lot about the current anxiety sweeping the world of media, and democracy, that the editor of one of the world's prestige newspapers needs to publicly reassure her staff and readers that its journalism will continue to be carried out by 'humans'.[12]

———

The Hearsts, Beaverbrooks and Murdochs have now banked or spent the fortunes they made from milking journalism for profit and power for more than a century. The Mogul Era has almost ended. While democracy still needs a free press to hold power to account, the funding model that paid for that function (and for the moguls' mansions and boats) has become redundant.

Accountability journalism is now stranded. There's no commercial incentive to own it and no obvious business model to fund it. Yet it's no less important to democracy, and no less expensive to run. This raises a most uncomfortable question for anyone who believes in the role of independent media in a civilised society: Is it possible for journalism to fulfill its civic role without being permanently propped up by massive financial subsidies? The short answer, sadly, is no.

One way of understanding that answer is to see it through the lens of the most successful news platform, commercially and editorially, in the internet-AI era, *The New York Times*. It has 1700 journalists, publishes around 200 fresh stories every day, and generates $2.3 billion in annual revenue and some $200 million in operating profit. As a business it's a modest success; as a *journalism* business it is the gold standard. Its 10 million paying subscribers (mainly digital) add up to more than *all* the subscribers combined of *The Washington Post*, *The Guardian*, the *Los Angeles Times*, *The Boston Globe*, the London *Times*, *Daily Telegraph*, *Le Monde*, *Bild*, *The Sydney Morning Herald*, *The Economist* and *The New Yorker*.

As advertising revenue evaporates and printed newspaper sales disappear, finding enough digital subscribers has become key to the survival of news publishers. Like almost every other regular retail product, journalism now relies on its customers to pay for it. But in a world of ubiquitous news, information and entertainment, the biggest competitor isn't just other media, it's *time*. 'We actually compete with sleep,' Netflix boss Reed Hastings, one of journalism's big competitors, explained, 'and we're winning.'[13]

As a result of these convulsions, mass media has become an anachronism. Apart from *The New York Times*, the only viable spaces left for commercial journalism are narrow, specialised and niche. There are definitely winners, just not many of them. One of the biggest is financial and business publishing, where *The Wall Street Journal*, the *Financial Times* and comparable mastheads in other countries produce compulsory, high-level news reporting and analysis for audiences who effectively (and financially) can't live without it; who happily pay premium subscription rates for information that is essential to their working lives, whose preferred medium is digital because that's where they spend much of their professional time, and who represent a compelling, well-heeled audience for advertisers in a trusted editorial environment. The *FT* and the *Journal* are the Michelin-starred restaurants of the media biosphere.

Smaller scale quality content is also served up successfully at places like *The New Yorker*, *The Economist*, *The Atlantic*, *Politico*, *Axios*, *Vox*, *Semafor*, and their equivalents in other countries. Although they don't have the muscle or breadth to save journalism, they may end up being the last mastheads standing. 'Many publishers will need to confront the need to get smaller and more focused,' says respected US industry analyst Brian Morrissey in *The Rebooting*.[14] 'Publishers need to prepare for a world of infinite content, and the inevitable effect that has on marketplace dynamics.' Ben Thompson, on his tech site *Stratechery*, observes that instead of focusing on journalism and getting the business model for free, 'publishers need to start with a sustainable business model and focus on journalism that works hand-in-hand with the business model they have chosen'.[15]

One of those business models, if that's an apt description, is the phenomenon of well-intentioned billionaires buying media properties. But deep-pocketed benefactors are not the panacea for funding journalism at scale; in any case, they almost always come without guarantees and with no strings attached. 'Plutocrats the world over delight in owning media properties,' wrote the media critic Jack Shafer in 2013. 'Money can buy a lot, but unless you own a publication you're just one of the world's 1,426 billionaires – human cargo on a private jet, a delegator, an employer of lobbyists, another yakker in the opinion chorus.'[16]

Because wealthy benefactors don't invest in journalism without self-interest, the more relevant question is: What's the nature of their self-interest? In France, a large chunk of journalism is owned or controlled by billionaire industrialists who extract commercial or political influence from a system in which back-scratching is institutionalised. But if Jeff Bezos bought *The Washington Post* for its political or commercial influence, it hasn't worked. In every utterance from Bezos since he bought the *Post* in 2013, he has supported its function as an independent news publication holding power to account. Similarly, when the billionaire sports entrepreneur John Henry bought *The Boston Globe* he made his motive clear in a published mission statement: 'The truth matters. At the end of the day it may be the only thing that matters. Finding it is our job, and our pledge to anyone who takes the time to read or watch or listen to what we've found out.'[17]

Jack Shafer sketched this cynical yet plausible scenario of a hypothetical 'vanity press mogul' who uses some of his excess millions to dabble in the media: 'In the opening phases, the mogul opens the money throttle wide, hiring the best journalists and designers, and even voices the view that he'll make money where his predecessors made none to little. Then comes the morning after and with it sobriety. Too much red ink is flowing, too many projects over-budget and late, too many gifted wunderkinds spending wildly. Not even billionaires enjoy losing money forever. Then comes the reality adjustment, the downsizing, the prospecting for partners or "synergies," and often an exit from the media business, which attracts a fresh vanity mogul and restarts the cycle.'[18]

Of course, there aren't enough benevolent billionaires to fund quality journalism. So where else could the money come from? Ideas to reinvent the current model are regularly disgorged from universities, journalism schools, philanthropic foundations, NGOs and think tanks – schemes with names like Engagement Journalism, Solutions Journalism, Collaborative Journalism, Constructive Journalism, Reparative Journalism, Dialog Journalism, and Deliberative Journalism, as recently cataloged by media critic Jeff Jarvis. These movements are largely based on worthy but ultimately theoretical concepts to improve journalism and make it more credible, not schemes that will generate the big licks of money needed for its survival.

If there is to be a solution to civic journalism's funding crisis, it's likely to come from an amalgam of sources; paid subscriptions (which, for most news organisations won't be enough to pay for their aspirations, but might be enough to support some of them) and other strands of commercial revenue, including sponsored or subsidised editorial content, live events, high-priced special reports, 'clipping the ticket' on selling products, and branching into adjacent specialist content categories, like sports and cooking. But the three biggest sources of financing journalism that have emerged in recent years are government funding, philanthropic funding, and grants from large digital platforms.

The arguments in favour of governments helping to bankroll civic journalism are obvious: informing citizens, supporting democracy and free speech, covering elected political power, spreading ideas. But it's a deeply controversial proposition because it involves collaboration between adversaries: the scrutinised (politicians) and the scrutineers (journalists). It can only work if the funding is systemically apolitical and administered at arm's length.

Denmark, Norway and Sweden have subsidies, including reduced or exempted VAT, which are designed to encourage digital innovation and foster diversity of media ownership by supporting newspapers that are not in market-leading positions. In France, government grants have been rolling out since the end of the Second World War, on a scale that has created an unhealthy dependency at news organisations, even though many of them are controlled by wealthy industrialists who happily accept the government's largesse. Public funding of the French press in 2021 was €367 million, including payments of €13 million to *Le Parisien*, owned by France's richest man Bernard Arnault, and €7.7 million to *Le Figaro*, owned by the arms manufacturer Dassault. By doling out cash to media-owning billionaires, the government makes the press–politics relationship even cosier. 'French media companies claim that their independence isn't threatened at all by their dependence on handouts,' commented Jonathan Miller in *The Spectator*. 'The evidence is that awash in unearned income, none will bite the hand that feeds them.'[19]

The idea of governments funding news journalism is opposed in principle by many journalists and editors, and the current parlous state of the media industry makes the concept even riskier. With their survival at stake, media owners and editors are vulnerable to becoming supplicants who depend on handouts from a source that's also the main target of their editorial scrutiny. Even at public broadcasters like Britain's BBC, Canada's CBC and Australia's ABC, there is growing pressure on news creators from their government 'owners' to practise 'balanced' journalism that doesn't offend political sensitivities. 'He who pays the piper calls the tune' is, after all, a theme song that has played loudly throughout the sweep of journalism history.

Although philanthropy is becoming a material source of funding nonprofit news, this is mainly at a community media level, covering courts, city councils, schools, crime and civic affairs. But philanthropy, like government, can only assist, never solve, a problem on this scale. And philanthropic funding, by its nature, is rarely permanent. According to the Boston Consulting Group, US nonprofit news outlets currently receive around $150 million a year, a tiny slice of the estimated $1.75 billion a year needed by a news industry that has seen the closure of 2,200 local newspapers since 2005.

The biggest influx of cash to news publishers in recent years has come from an improbable source: Google and Facebook. Those payments have been delivered through several channels, dressed up under different names, but should really be described as *guilt money*.

After commandeering much of the advertising revenue that once paid for civic journalism, the world's two biggest digital platforms have been generously tossing a few coins from their vast war chests in the direction of struggling publishers who believe they wuz robbed.

In truth, they weren't robbed. They were out-innovated. Google and Facebook invented incredible pieces of machinery that give advertisers vastly better results than the half-my-ads-are-wasted jalopies operated by the old-style media barons. In response, the moguls – one in particular, first name Rupert – have used their power over politicians to pressure the digital platforms to recompense them because, claim the publishers, Google and Facebook have 'stolen' their content as well as hijacking their ad revenue. Under that logic, as Mike Masnick pointed out in *Techdirt*, 'any business that successfully competes with a legacy business should be forced to share its revenue with the business they out competed'.[20] Both companies were already providing modest financial support (tens, not hundreds, of millions) to news journalism before Murdoch and his executives, around 2018, began pushing the conservative Australian government to legislate a substantive solution. The result was the News Media Bargaining Code, introduced in 2021 to 'address a bargaining power imbalance that exists between digital platforms and Australian news businesses'. The law forces large technology platforms to pay news publishers, ostensibly for content summarised or linked on their platforms, but with no formula for how payments are calculated, or for how publishers must use their windfalls, just a stipulation that the platforms bargain in good faith. Since then, Google and Facebook have handed AUD$200–300 million a year to around two dozen Australian news publishers (including my company, Private Media, which has received a small portion of that kitty).

Canada followed in 2023 with a similar piece of legislation, the Online News Act. After months of tense negotiations, Google, having threatened to pull all news content from its Canadian platform, finally agreed to pay Canadian news media companies $75 million annually. But Facebook's parent company Meta refused to play ball. Not only did it block Canadian news from its two social media platforms, Facebook and Instagram, it also killed off its news tab in Australia, France, Germany and the UK, and began ending funding for local news projects across the world. The Facebook gravy train, it seems, has been decommissioned.

In the world's biggest media market, the US Congress has been considering an Australian-style law, the Journalism Competition and Preservation Act, to force digital platforms to compensate only local news outlets, not large national newspapers and broadcast networks. The industry hopes to collect billions of dollars a year if these measures are enacted. Meanwhile Google continues to dole out significant financial support to US journalism, separate from any obligations under legislation, including a $100 million, three-year deal with *The New York Times* to showcase its stories in Google news products.

———

The news media today is like a once-prosperous man about town who now tramps the same streets, shabbily dressed, looking for handouts. It has lost its advertising rivers of gold. It has become increasingly dependent for funding on governments and competitors. It pleads for philanthropic assistance. It must constantly downsize, retrench, remodel.

But there's another – arguably greater – indignity. *The media has never been less trusted or respected.* Thirty-eight per cent of Americans say they have no confidence 'at all' in the media.[21] Globally, 42 per cent believe the media is a source of false or misleading information.[22] Only 13 per cent of Britons and 18 per cent of Australians say they have a 'great deal' or 'quite a lot' of confidence in the press.[23]

'Journalists like to think of themselves as the people's surrogate, covering society's waterfront in the public interest. Increasingly, however, the public doesn't believe them,' write Bill Kovach and Tom Rosenstiel in *The Elements of Journalism*. 'People see sensationalism, exploitation, and they sense journalists are in it for a buck, or

29. Felsenthal, Carol, *Citizen Newhouse: Portrait of a Media Merchant*, Seven Stories Press, New York 1998, p. 119.

30. Ibid., p. 153.

31. Kandell, Jonathan, 'S.I. Newhouse Jr., who turned Condé Nast into a magazine powerhouse, Dies at 89', *New York Times*, 1 October 2017, <https://www.nytimes.com/2017/10/01/obituaries/si-newhouse-dead.html>.

32. Bower, Tom, *Outrageous Fortune: The Rise and Ruin of Conrad and Lady Black*, Harper Collins, 2006, pp. 30, 106.

33. Baistow, Tom, 'Lord Hartwell: Last of the press barons, whose miscalculation cost his family the Daily and Sunday Telegraphs', *The Guardian*, 4 April 2001, <https://www.theguardian.com/news/2001/apr/04/guardianobituaries2>.

34. Bower, Tom, *Outrageous Fortune*, pp. 113–14.

35. Black, Conrad, *A Life in Progress*, Random House, Australia, 1993, p. 354.

36. Martinson, Jane, *You May Never See Us Again: The Barclay Dynasty: A Story of Survival, Secrecy and Succession*, Penguin Business, 2023, p. 149.

37. Auletta, Ken, 'Citizens Jain', *New Yorker*, 1 October 2012, <https://www.newyorker.com/magazine/2012/10/08/citizens-jain>.

38. Jagannathan, R, 'Media moguls: inside the minds of Samir and Vineet Jain', *First Post India*, 5 October 2012, <https://www.firstpost.com/india/media-moguls-inside-the-minds-of-samir-and-vineet-jain-479062.html>.

Succession

1. Auletta, Ken, 'The Heiress', *New Yorker*, 2 December 2012, <https://www.newyorker.com/magazine/2012/12/10/the-heiress-2>.

2. Sloan, Allan, 'Shareholder money funds Murdoch family deals', *Washington Post*, 24 February 2011, <https://www.washingtonpost.com/wp-dyn/content/article/2011/02/24/AR2011022407828.html>.

3. Felsenthal, Carol, *Citizen Newhouse*, p. 79.

4. Stelzer, Irwin, *The Murdoch Method: Notes on Running a Media Empire*, Atlantic, 2019, Kindle edition, p. 212.

5. Martin, Ralph G., *Henry and Clare*, p. 192.

6. Jane Martinson, 'Frederick Barclay received £800,000 to settle the espionage case , court told', *The Guardian*, 22 July 2022, <https://www.theguardian.com/uk-news/2022/jul/26/frederick-barclay-paid-800000-to-settle-ritz-espionage-case-court-told>.

7. Martinson, Jane, *You May Never See Us Again*, p. 241.

8. Ellison, Sarah, 'Rupert Murdoch hands control of Fox media empire to son Lachlan Murdoch', *Washington Post*, 21 September 2023, <https://

personal fame, or, perhaps worse, a kind of perverse joy in unhappiness. To reconnect people with news, and through the news to the larger world, journalism must reestablish the allegiance to citizens that the news industry has mistakenly helped to subvert.'[24]

At the heart of journalism's credibility problem is the question of 'why we're deserving of the public trust and the special protections afforded the free press', says Arthur ('A.G.') Sulzberger, publisher of *The New York Times*. 'It will take years, if not decades, to win over people who have been told again and again by those they admire and trust – including a former president of the United States – that the media hates them and hates this country,' he argues. 'But news organizations can't act as if they are powerless to reverse the growing distrust in journalism more broadly. They need to do a far better job fighting for their reputations and explaining how they make journalistic decisions.'[25]

Sulzberger is the custodian of a newspaper whose owners have spent more than 125 years promoting and defending independent journalism. 'My great-great-grandfather, the founder of the modern *New York Times*, helped establish the model of independent journalism – "without fear or favor," in his now famous motto ... "entirely fearless, free of ulterior influence and unselfishly devoted to the public welfare",' he wrote in the *Columbia Journalism Review*.[26]

Sulzberger isn't alone in fighting the uphill battle to defend the integrity of civic journalism. There are many other news publications practising serious-minded journalism in different parts of the free world, applying the same principles and passion. They include *Le Monde*, France's centre-left quality paper of record, which is protected against shareholder interference by a charter and by an ever-vigilant staff and readership. Its values and independence are conspicuous in a French media landscape dominated by transactional industrialist and billionaire owners.

Founded in 1944 at the behest of General Charles de Gaulle, five months before the end of World War Two, *Le Monde*'s charter of ethics and professional conduct is a model of its kind and includes rules and guidance like this: 'Journalists have the necessary means to rigorously exercise their profession, collect and verify information, independently of any external pressure. They refrain from any manipulation and plagiarism, do not relay rumors, and avoid sensationalism, approximations and bias. They must avoid any links of interest with actors in the sectors on which they write, and undertake to declare any conflict of interest.'

Across the channel, *The Guardian* flexes similar editorial muscles. Founded in 1821 as *The Manchester Guardian* to 'promote the liberal interest', and owned by the not-for-profit Scott Trust whose core purpose is 'to secure the financial and editorial independence of the Guardian in perpetuity', it has a cool £1.2 billion in the bank to support that obligation. *The Guardian* has a novel loyalty payment scheme that successfully taps its international readers for voluntary annual 'donations' (not 'subscriptions'), which contribute more than a third of its £264 million annual revenues.

Haaretz is another quality journalism act. Described by *The New Yorker* as 'arguably the most important liberal institution in Israel', it is the country's longest-running newspaper currently in print. Owned since 1935 by the Schocken family, who invest heavily in its quality and objectivity, its coverage of the 2023 Gaza war was so fearlessly independent that Israel's right-wing government proposed imposing financial sanctions on the paper for 'sabotaging Israel in wartime'. *Haaretz* publisher Amos Schocken's response to that threat was succinct: 'If the government wants to close *Haaretz*, that's the time to read *Haaretz*.'[27]

The Washington Post, now in its post-Graham family ownership phase, after being sold to Amazon billionaire Jeff Bezos in 2013, no longer basks in its glory days of Watergate and the Pentagon Papers. Today it confronts financial challenges (it reportedly lost $100 million in 2023) and fewer subscribers (down 500,000 in three years). Bezos's money 'changed everything,' after he bought the paper, reported the *Columbia Journalism Review*, 'bulking up the newsroom, revolutionizing its technology, and firmly reestablishing it as a dominant voice in the national media'. But now, even as its journalism still shines, everything is tougher for the *Post*.[28]

The Economist, a 180-year-old weekly magazine and website that still describes itself as a newspaper, in that stuffy British way, is a global exemplar of effective *modern* journalism. Sharp, elegant, insightful and authoritative, still committed to liberal capitalism with a beating heart, *The Economist* remains passionately committed to the mandate laid out in 1843 by its founding editor James Wilson: 'A severe contest between intelligence, which presses forward, and an unworthy, timid ignorance obstructing our progress.'[29] With a pragmatic commercial mindset supporting its editorial prowess, and almost 1.2 million subscribers worldwide, and rigid protections on shareholder interference, *The Economist* is a media icon.

Yet precisely because of their principles and quality, these news publishers essentially preach to the converted. They can't save journalism on their own, just a slither of it. Their readers are part of a minority of socially and politically aware collaborators in upholding democracy; they're people who don't need to be told about the importance of trustworthy journalism, because that's what they buy.

But even as technology is changing everything, as the presses have almost stopped and the advertisers have run for the hills, much of the mistrust that plagues journalism is still controlled by moguls wielding power. And no individuals or platforms have contributed more viscerally to that mistrust than Rupert Murdoch at Fox News and Elon Musk at X. But while Murdoch's participation in destabilising American democracy at Fox News is almost entirely profit-motivated, Musk is a different animal. Under his ownership, X has been erratic and unpredictable because he *isn't* commercially motivated. And that makes him dangerous in a different way.

After X fired 1213 people from its global trust and safety team following Musk's acquisition of the company in 2022, the European Commission reported in late 2023 that the platform had Europe's 'highest discoverability' of disinformation. When asked at a *New York Times* business summit to comment on his own trustworthiness,

Musk replied mockingly, 'You could not trust me.' Questioned about how he felt when large firms pulled their ads over concerns about unsavoury content on the platform, he blustered: 'If somebody's going to try to blackmail me, go fuck yourself.'[30] No media mogul has said *that* before.

The modern reality, however, is that misinformation can now be found across the full sweep of social *and* conventional media. This was never more evident than during the Gaza conflagration that erupted in October 2023. 'The era of social news – when we could trust social media platforms to help us understand what is going on in the world – is over,' wrote *Crikey's* technology reporter Cam Wilson a few weeks into the war. 'Platforms such as X, TikTok, Reddit, Telegram and YouTube are overflowing with untold amounts of footage purporting to show different perspectives of what's really happening in the conflict . . . [O]ld footage, mislead-ing framing, AI-generated content and even video-game clips have gone viral from users presenting them as updates from the ground.' Social media doesn't provide a window into the real world anymore, says Wilson. 'It's been replaced with a funhouse mirror that warps, populated with visions of people trying to convince you that it's real.'[31]

Another factor adding to the mistrust of media is the modern cultural realignment that has fractured concepts like 'objectivity' and 'balance' and forced many news organisations into taking politi-cally correct defensive postures – often reluctantly – to appease their audiences and staff. Although this fissure has appeared across the ideological spectrum, its main critics are conservatives who attack what they perceive as an elite media dominated by liberals.

'We are at a stage where people can no longer talk to each other because they don't even recognize each other's moral language,' soci-ology professor James Davison Hunter told *Le Figaro*. It was his prophetic 1991 book *Culture Wars* that created the term, adapted from the German word *Kulturkampf*, that now frames these uncomfort-able currents.[32]

In many major news organisations, this failure to recognise different dialects of 'moral language' has created a kind of panic. 'On all sides of the political spectrum, we are presented with opinions by activists who do not want any kind of dialogue,' writes columnist Suzanne Moore, of the conservative London *Daily Telegraph*. 'The result is the chaos of millions of people screaming into the void.' She cites her own previous experience at *The Guardian*, where she claims she was told that issues involving the conflict between trans rights and women's rights could only be 'reported', not presented as 'comment'. The idea of neutrality is impossible, says Moore. 'We all start from a conscious or unconscious perspective, we are all complicated, but a central liberal tenet is surely that we can tolerate differences. Increasingly, this is not so and the staff of liberal institutions have mislaid their moral compasses at a time when we urgently need them.'[33]

Nowhere has this discomfort surfaced more conspicuously than at *The New York Times*, where entrenched institutional liberalism has collided with previous norms of objectivity, balance and curiosity. This predicament was unpicked by former *Times* opinion editor James Bennet, whose 18,000-word essay in *The Economist* (now his employer) attempted to confront the issue that led to his dismissal in 2020. Bennet had approved publication in the *Times* of a controversial op-ed by the Republican senator Tom Cotton, advocating the use of the military to suppress violent democratic protests during the Trump era. Its publication created an uproar among his colleagues and senior editorial leaders, who Bennet believes caved in to a culture of 'illiberalism' that silences debate in the ideological interests of the paper's left-leaning staffers (and subscribers). 'What is lacking here is genuine journalistic curiosity, alongside a self-righteous worldview that can brook no opposition,' wrote Bennet. 'This refusal to confront readers with anything uncomfortable is a journalistic failure of nerve.'

As he explained, Bennet traces much of the paper's problem with cultural identity to the successful transformation of its business model from a traditional, advertising-funded print newspaper into a quality digital powerhouse funded by a spectacular growth in online subscriptions:

> As the number of subscribers ballooned, the marketing department tracked their expectations, and came to a nuanced conclusion. More than 95% of *Times* subscribers described themselves as Democrats or independents, and a vast majority of them believed the *Times* was also liberal. A similar majority applauded that bias; it had become 'a selling point', reported one internal marketing memo. Yet at the same time, the marketers concluded, subscribers wanted to believe that the *Times* was independent.
>
> Perception is one thing, and actual independence another. Readers could cancel their subscriptions if the *Times* challenged their worldview by reporting the truth without regard to politics. As a result, the *Times*'s long-term civic value was coming into conflict with the paper's short-term shareholder value.[34]

Working in journalism now, argues Bennet, requires a particular kind of courage – 'not just the devil-may-care courage to choose a profession on the brink of the abyss; not just the bulldog courage to endlessly pick yourself up and embrace the ever-evolving technology; but also, in an era when polarization and social media viciously enforce rigid orthodoxies, the moral and intellectual courage to take the other side seriously and to report truths and ideas that your own side demonizes for fear they will harm its cause.'[35]

There's nothing new about mistrust in the media, of course. When John Norvell, a newspaper editor and later US senator, wrote to then president Thomas Jefferson in 1807 asking to 'have your opinion of the manner in which a newspaper, to be most extensively beneficial, should be conducted', Jefferson's response was excoriating. 'Nothing can now be believed which is seen in a newspaper. Truth itself becomes suspicious by being put into that polluted vehicle,' replied the president. 'I will add, that the man who never looks into a newspaper is better informed than he who reads them; inasmuch as he who knows nothing is nearer to truth than he whose mind is filled with falsehoods & errors.'[36]

More than two hundred years later, the media gatekeepers have been usurped by tech platforms and, prospectively, by generative artificial intelligence. Nothing and everything has changed. Trust in journalism still languishes in an era where social media allows almost anyone to become an op-ed pundit. Instead of news being convened professionally (and sometimes recklessly) by traditional gatekeepers, it is now no longer *the* news, or *their* news; it's *my* news.

The media dictators who failed to act accountably or transparently, and sowed those seeds of mistrust, got away with it because they owned the gates, the drawbridges and the moats that prevented almost anyone else from becoming a custodian of the news. Now that the castle has been overrun and the contents ransacked, nothing matters more for the remaining custodians of professional civic journalism than finding ways to think like Joseph Pulitzer, who, unlike many of his mogul successors, understood that *trust* is the lifeblood of journalism. 'Influence cannot exist without public confidence,' he wrote in *The North American Review* in 1904. 'And that confidence must have a human basis. It must rest in the end on the character of the journalist ... he must be known as one who would resign rather than sacrifice his principles to any business interest.'[37]

Sentiments like those used to be widely accepted, even respected. But we no longer live in those times. The internet, despite all its benefits, has unleashed a series of missiles that have attacked the durability of the free press. Landing one after another, those missiles have demolished the business model, accelerated mistrust in journalism, and impugned its motives and authority.

The responsibility for this wave of mistrust lies in several hands. Media owners who spent a century trashing journalism for profits. Social media that breeds venom and misinformation. And self-interested politicians who fail to defend the importance of independent media and, instead, spread relentless anti-press propaganda to blame journalists for doing their jobs.

Of all those culprits, Donald Trump has done more damage to institutional journalism than any other public figure. He has described the press as 'the enemy of the people', labelled news organisations as 'fake news', and called reporters 'slime', 'scum' and 'sick people' – vitriol that spurs his loyal followers to take up media-bashing as a contact sport. 'The Democrats don't matter. The real opposition is the media,' Trump's former adviser Steve Bannon once gloated. 'And the way to deal with them is to flood the zone with shit.'[38]

Trump has exploited the media's tectonic moment by turning millions of Americans against its raison d'être. 'He knows well that the American press is hardly popular and, in many ways, is on the defensive,' writes *The New Yorker*'s David Remnick. 'He knows that many news outlets are, in his pitiless term, "failing," or at least struggling for survival in the wake of vast changes in technology and in the advertising market ... and he has figured out how to exploit that change. He has seized on the capacities of right-wing radio, cable television, and social media to form an alternative, fact-free, Trumpian universe.'[39]

Can journalism rebuild trust in itself amid all this mess? On a broad scale, almost certainly not. The roots of media mistrust are too deep, sown in the Jefferson era, thoroughly watered and nurtured during the Hearst-Murdoch mogul century, and fertilised over recent decades by social media. Younger people who haven't grown up with formalised professional journalism – 'a generation of social natives that are not bound by traditional definitions of news', as Nic Newman at the Reuters Institute for the Study of Journalism describes them – are unlikely to suddenly demand or embrace trustworthy professional reporting.[40] For sceptics and partisans, meanwhile, media mistrust has become a central plank of their worldview.

If the people who do democracy's heavy lifting can't convince a wider public why their journalism is essential to a socially functional society, they will continue to lose audiences, credibility and viability. News publishers need to both explain and assert their importance, to boldly demonstrate their commitment to ethical journalism and professional conduct in a manner that is non-partisan, non-ideological, non-arrogant and *believable*.

Without a rescue mission, news will become more of a specialist niche, like vintage cars, vinyl records or antiquarian books. Journalism will survive, but it will be smaller, narrower and vastly less impactful. The stakes are high, the downside is precipitous. If nothing changes, the era of media power – the *right* kind of media power – will fade even further, allowing more people like the former head of the CBS television network, Les Moonves, to compromise the role and practice of journalism, as he did in 2015 when asked about Trump's decision to seek the presidency. 'It may not be good for America,' said Moonves, 'but it's damn good for CBS.'[41]

Afterword

When I first began to think about writing this book, a decade ago, its central premise was uncomplicated. The owners and practitioners of news journalism either exercised their social licence responsibly or they abused it, but they *used* it.

Ten years on, as media power has shifted rapidly into the hands of the owners of social-media algorithms and partisan propaganda platforms, technology is replacing the humans. Scale is no longer a limitation. The century-old idea that greedy, malign media moguls are the greatest danger to moral journalism has become almost quaint.

Just before this book went to press in mid-2024, Jack Brewster, an editor at NewsGuard, a company that monitors online mis-information, spent a few hours and $105 to launch a fully automated, AI-generated news website that could publish thousands of politic-ally partisan news articles a day, nearly all of them rewritten from legitimate sources without acknowledgement. His experimental website joined thousands of other so-called 'pink slime' propaganda news sites, created by humans working with artificial intelligence, which masquerade as local news outlets and almost outnumber local newspapers.[1]

The ability to create off-the-shelf, algorithmic, AI-fuelled, partisan news-making sausage machines has partly reshaped the thesis behind this book. No longer is it just *men* who have killed the news. Now it's also *machines* that are killing the news.

The proliferation of more editorial slime and partisanship will, in theory at least, even further diminish the stature of professional news journalism. But it could also have the opposite effect. To anyone who knows the difference between authentic journalism and trash journalism, the real thing is even more valued when it can be seen floating conspicuously in a sea of muck. As trust in democratic institutions erodes, have we reached a point where Steve Bannon's desolate recipe for managing the media – 'flood the zone with shit' – will end up driving more people towards the trustworthy journalism that operates outside the sewer?

If Bannon and his cohorts continue to infest the zone, there will inevitably be increasing pressure on governments to regulate journalism's ethical behaviour, in the way that they regulate the ethics of other professions and industries. Many people are shocked when they discover that the news media has no mandated ethical guidelines and is entirely self-regulated – often camouflaged by authentic-sounding 'codes of ethics' that sit like shop-window dummies on the websites of media organisations. ('We do not let revenue sources dictate our news and opinion content,' declares the Fox News Statement of Business Ethics. 'Our opinions do not drive our news reporting.')[2] Media operators like Fox News have run their businesses for almost two centuries under the pretence that no-one else in society is qualified to meddle with the sanctity of the free press.

Government regulation is an idea opposed vehemently by nearly everyone in the media because we know it would inevitably undermine the credibility and functionality of a free press. But it's now clear that journalism desperately *needs* stronger regulation – not by governments, but by its *owners*. If enough news organisations recognised this juncture as an opportunity to work collaboratively to implement an enforceable code of ethical conduct, it might be possible to rebuild trust. And if those organisations included News Corp and Fox News – which is unlikely unless or until James Murdoch's siblings put him in charge after his father's eventual departure – the ethics of global journalism could be recast.

Media power wielded by humans matters more, not less, in the age of algorithms. In a world where the revenue has collapsed and mass media is disintegrating, that power is narrower and vastly less profitable, and it will need to become smarter and more innovative in order to survive. This new reality – the end of the era of large editorial sources of trusted information – is described as the 'shards of glass phenomenon' by the founders of news website *Axios*, Jim VandeHei and Mike Allen. 'Where you get your news, the voices you trust, and even the topics and cultural figures you follow could be wholly different from the person sitting next to you,' they explain.[3]

In *The Press*, his 1961 critique of journalism, media pundit A.J. Liebling wrote: 'The function of the press in society is to inform, but its role is to make money.'[4] Now, increasingly, it does neither. But for any country that views itself as a civilised democracy, that is an untenable outcome.

To successfully chaperone journalism into the algorithm era, and keep it viable, will require the emergence of modern-day versions of Ochs, Luce, Thomson, the Fairfaxes and the Grahams. It will need their resolve to fight for the standards and principles that differentiate authentic journalism from slime – the kind of resolve exhibited by Ochs' great-grandson A.G. Sulzberger, the current *New York Times* publisher. As a young *Times* news reporter, Sulzberger was covering wild storms in South Dakota in 2008 when he introduced himself to a local farmer, who told him, 'My friends on talk radio have told me not to trust you,' to which Sulzberger replied, 'When was the last time your friends on talk radio showed up at your farm in an effort to understand what you're going through?'[5]

I knew, when I embarked on this project, that the story of media power would be less than pretty because it involved, at least in part, humans behaving badly. But I never imagined that the intervention of machines, controlled by another group of humans behaving badly, could usurp the moguls and make things worse.

No-one knows how this story will play out because the traps are so freshly laid. It will take a new and different kind of media power to counter the forces that are lining up to kill the news: the power to demonstrate, through performance, that respectable, professional civic journalism, despite its imperfections, is a prerequisite for a decent society.

Notes

Why this Book?

1. Thomas Jefferson to James Currie, 28 January 1786, Thomas Jefferson Papers in the Library of Congress, Washington DC.

Introduction

1. Chuda, Nancy, 'Raising More Than Kane: Steve Hearst Great Grandson of William Randolph Hearst Will Screen for Citizens at The Hearst Castle', *The Huffington Post*, 9 March 2012, <https://www.huffpost.com/entry/raising-more-than-kane-st_b_1335099>.

An Encounter with Lachlan Murdoch

1. Keane, Bernard, 'Trump is a confirmed unhinged traitor. And Murdoch is his unindicted co-conspirator', *Crikey*, 29 June 2022, <https://www.crikey.com.au/2022/06/29/january-six-hearing-donald-trump-comfirmed-unhinged-traitor/>.

2. Moore, Thomas, 'Fox Corp. CEO Lachlan Murdoch calls Fox News Biden's loyal opposition', *The Hill*, 4 March 2021, <https://thehill.com/homenews/media/541750-fox-corp-ceo-lachlan-murdoch-calls-fox-news-bidens-loyal-opposition/>.

3. Beecher, Eric and Fray, Peter, 'The power of one: how Lachlan Murdoch turned nuclear over a legitimate piece of journalism', *Crikey*, 22 August 2022, <https://www.crikey.com.au/2022/08/22/lachlan-murdoch-letters-crikey-journalism-nuclear/>.

4. Masnick, Mike, 'Lachlan Murdoch is big mad that Crikey called him out on his bullshit; so now he's suing to shut them up', *Techdirt*, 25 August 2022, <https://www.techdirt.com/2022/08/25/lachlan-murdoch-is-big-mad-that-crikey-called-him-out-on-his-bullshit-so-now-hes-suing-to-shut-them-up/>.

5. Editorial, 'Hang on, doesn't Murdoch support free speech?', *The Age*, 25 August 2022, <https://www.theage.com.au/business/companies/hang-on-doesn-t-murdoch-support-free-speech-20220825-p5bcmu.html>.

6. Le Grand, Chip, 'Crikey and Murdoch stoush a bonfire of inanities', *The Age*, 24 August 2022, <https://www.theage.com.au/national/crikey-and-murdoch-stoush-a-bonfire-of-inanities-20220824-p5bc8q.html>.

7. White, Sam, 'The excruciating irony of Lachlan Murdoch's Crikey lawsuit', *Sydney Morning Herald*, 24 October 2022, <https://www.smh.com.au/business/companies/the-excruciating-irony-of-lachlan-murdoch-s-crikey-lawsuit-20221023-p5bs5g.html>.

8. Pompeo, Joe, '"I Think Lachlan's Trying to Peter Thiel Crikey": Inside a scrappy Australian news site's war with the Murdochs', *Vanity Fair*, 3 October 2022, <https://www.vanityfair.com/news/2022/10/lachlan-murdoch-crikey-lawsuit>.

9. Cartwright, Lachlan, 'Lachlan Murdoch goes to war with website blaming him for Jan.6', *The Daily Beast*, 15 August 2022, <https://www.thedailybeast.com/lachlan-murdoch-goes-to-war-with-website-blaming-him-for-jan-6>.

10. An article in *The Guardian* on 24 September 2018 noted: 'At the 2002 Andrew Olle lecture Lachlan took on Eric Beecher, publisher of Crikey, who had given the lecture two years earlier. Beecher had sought to distinguish between the "commercial media" driven by the need to make money, and "the serious media", which he defined as those whose journalism is subsidised like the ABC via taxpayers, and the broadsheets, through classifieds.'

11. Down, Rhiannon, 'Crikey "virtually begged to be sued"', *The Australian*, 31 January 2023.

12. Meade, Amanda, 'The mouse that roared: how a little Australian website stared down Murdoch's millions', *The Guardian*, 22 April 2023, <https://www.theguardian.com/media/2023/apr/22/crikey-how-a-little-australian-website-stared-down-murdoch-mighty-news-corp>.

13. 'Hi everyone! It's me, Lachlan Murdoch!', *The Chaser*, Issue 225, 21 April 2023, <https://mailchi.mp/chaser.com.au/a-special-message-from-lachlan-murdoch>.

Gutenberg to Zuckerberg

1. Jessup, John K., *The Ideas of Henry Luce*, Atheneum, New York, 1969, p. 27.

2. Nasaw, David, *The Chief: The Life of William Randolph Hearst*, Houghton Mifflin, 2000, p. 514.

3. Chisolm, Anne and Davie, Michael, *Beaverbrook: A Life*, Hutchinson, 1992, p. 524.

4. Stelter, Brian, 'Biden called Murdoch the "most dangerous man in the world," new book alleges', *CNN*, 3 April 2022, <https://edition.cnn.com/2022/04/03/media/reliable-sources-biden-murdoch-fox-news/index.html>.

5. Blair, Tony, 'Full Transcript of Blair Speech', Reuters, 2007, <https://www.reuters.com/article/idUSZWE245852/>.

6. Kobler, John, *Luce: His Time, Life and Fortune*, Doubleday, 1968, p. 106.

7. New York Times Co. v. United States 'The Pentagon Papers Case', *National Constitution Centre*, 1971.

8. 'Extract from Thomas Jefferson to Edward Carrington', *The Jefferson Monticello*, 16 January 1787, <https://tjrs.monticello.org/letter/1289>.

9. Thomas Jefferson to James Currie, 28 January 1786, <https://tjrs.monticello.org/letter/2141>.

10. O'Rourke, K.C., *John Stuart Mill and Freedom of Expression: The Genesis of a Theory*, Routledge, 2001, p.38.

11. Kovach, Bill and Rosensteil, Tom, *The Elements of Journalism: What Newspeople Should Know and the Public Should Expect*, Three Rivers Press, 2001, p. 180.

12. David and Wallace, Irving, 'History of International Newspapers: The Times in England Part 1', Trivia-Library, 1975–81, <https://www.trivia-library.com/a/history-of-international-newspapers-the-times-in-england-part-1.htm>.

13. Swanberg, W.A., *Pulitzer*, Charles Scribner's Sons, New York, 1967, p. 70.

14. Denis, Brian, *Pulitzer: A Life*, Wiley Publishers, 2002, p. 41.

15. Jenkins, Simon, *Newspapers, the Money and the Power*, Faber & Faber, 1979, p. 17.

16. Nasaw, David, *The Chief*, p. 77.

17. Swanberg, W.A., *Pulitzer*, pp. 205–07.

18. 'The Press: Hearst's Legacy', *Time*, 22 September 1961, <https://content.time.com/time/subscriber/article/0,33009,873422,00.html>.

19. Dudding, Will, 'Impartial Coverage: As Good for Business as It Is for Journalism', *The New York Times*, 16 January 2009, <https://www.nytimes.com/2019/01/16/reader-center/impartial-news-coverage-history.html>.

20. Ibid.

21. Leff, Laurel, *Buried by the Times: The Holocaust and America's Most Important Newspaper*, illustrated edition, Cambridge University Press, 2005, pp. 2–3.

22. White, Michael, 'Why the Daily Mail hates Britain', *Prospect Magazine*, 12 April 2017, <https://www.prospectmagazine.co.uk/culture/44189/why-the-daily-mail-hates-britain#:~:text=Lord%20Salisbury%2C%20who%20dismissed%20the,to%20pass%20one%20million%20sales.>.

23. Potter, Simon, 'Rupert Murdoch and the rise and fall of the press barons: how much power do newspapers still have?', *The Conversation*, 22 September 2023, <https://theconversation.com/rupert-murdoch-and-the-rise-and-fall-of-the-press-barons-how-much-power-do-newspapers-still-have-213283>.

24. Goldfarb, Michael, 'British tabloid's hit piece on Miliband dredges up anti-Semitic past', *The World*, 4 October 2013.

25. Young, Kenneth, *Churchill and Beaverbrook*, Eyre & Spottiswoode, London, 1966, p. 52.

26. Snoddy, Raymond, *Good, the Bad and the Unacceptable: Hard News About the British Press*, Faber & Faber, 1992, p. 78.

27. Hetherington, John, *Nine Profiles*, F.W. Cheshire, 1960, p. 93.

28. Younger, R.M., *Keith Murdoch: Founder of a Media Empire*, Harper Collins, Australia, 2003, p. 186.

29. Young, Sally, *Paper Emperors, The Rise of Australia's Newspaper Empires*, NewSouth Publishing, Sydney, 2019.

30. Roberts, Andrew, *The Chief: The Life of Lord Northcliffe Britain's Greatest Press Baron*, Simon & Schuster, London, 2023, p. 416.

31. Jenkins, Simon, *The Market for Glory: Fleet Street Ownership in the Twentieth Century*, Faber & Faber, 1986, p. 116.

32. Stelzer, Irwin, *The Murdoch Method: Notes on Running a Media Empire*, Atlantic Books, 2018, p. 39.

33. Ibid., p. 194.

Building the Empires

1. Brenner, Joel Glenn and Weil, Martin, 'Publisher Malcolm Forbes dies at 70', *The Washington Post*, 25 February 1990, <https://www.washingtonpost.com/archive/politics/1990/02/25/publisher-malcolm-forbes-dies-at-70/5fb9f9ff-3f60-4753-bc90-f070b4a2d3c3/>.

2. Jones, Bryony, 'Rupert Murdoch: The last press baron', *CNN*, 16 August 2011, <http://edition.cnn.com/2011/WORLD/europe/07/18/rupert.murdoch.profile/index.html>.

3. Whyte, Kenneth, *The Uncrowned King*, Counterpoint, Berkeley, 2009, p. 27.

4. Ibid.

5. Ibid.

6. Ibid., p. 29.

7. Roberts, Andrew, *The Chief*, p. 69.

8. Denis, Brian, *Pulitzer: A Life*, John Wiley and Sons, New York, 2002, p. 70.

9. Gibbs, Wolcott, 'Time … Fortune … Life … Luce', *New Yorker*, 20 November 1936, <https://www.newyorker.com/magazine/1936/11/28/time-fortune-life-luce>.

10. Wilner, Isaiah, 'The Man *Time* Forgot', *Vanity Fair*, 23 May 2014, <https://www.vanityfair.com/news/2006/10/henry-luce-briton-hadden-rivalry>.

11. 'Life (magazine)', Wikipedia, <https://en.wikipedia.org/wiki/Life_(magazine)>, accessed September 2023.

12. Martin, Ralph G., *Henry and Clare: An Intimate Portrait of the Luces*, Putnam, New Jersey, 1991, p. 168.

13. Marsh, Walter, *Young Murdoch*, Scribe, Melbourne, 2023, p. 14.

14. Morris, Madeleine and Hegarty, Stephanie, 'How a young Murdoch fought his early battles, and won', *BBC News*, 23 July 2011, <https://www.bbc.com/news/world-14220332>.

15. Jenkins, Simon, 'News of the World was not such a steal for Murdoch', *The Guardian*, July 8, 2011, <https://www.theguardian.com/commentisfree/2011/jul/08/news-of-the-world-rupert-murdoch>.

16. Preston, John, 'The man was obviously a crook: the decline and fall of Robert Maxwell', *The Guardian*, 22 February 2021, <https://www.theguardian.com/books/2021/feb/22/the-man-was-obviously-a-crook-the-decline-and-fall-of-robert-maxwell>.

17. Wolff, Michael, *The Man Who Owns the News: Inside the Secret World of Rupert Murdoch*, Broadway Books, 2008, p. 19.

18. Tuccille, Jerome, *Rupert Murdoch*, Donald I. Fine Inc, 1989, p. 52.

19. Shawcross, William, *Murdoch*, Chatto & Windus, Sydney, 1992, pp. 316, 365, 372, 377, 381.

20. Rosenstiel, Thomas B., 'Murdoch may be no. 1 media mogul with triangle deal', *Los Angeles Times*, 9 August 1988, <https://www.latimes.com/archives/la-xpm-1988-08-09-fi-271-story.html>.

21. Neil, Andrew, 'Murdoch and me', *Vanity Fair*, 3 January 2012, <https://www.vanityfair.com/news/1996/12/rupert-murdoch-199612>.

22. Shawcross, William, *Murdoch*, p.403.

23. Ellison, Sarah, 'War at the Wall Street Journal', Houghton Mifflin Harcourt, Boston, 2010, p.107.

24. Associated Press, 'News Corp.'s Murdoch: newspapers must embrace internet, *Fox News*, 13 April 2005, <https://www.foxnews.com/story/news-corp-s-murdoch-newspapers-must-embrace-internet>.

25. Bylund, Anders, 'Doing the math on News Corp.'s disastrous MySpace years', *Ars Technica*, 6 June 2011, <https://arstechnica.com/tech-policy/2011/06/doing-the-math-on-news-corps-disastrous-myspace-years/>.

26. Jones, Tim, 'Robert R. McCormick', *Chicago Tribune*, 19 December 2007, <https://www.chicagotribune.com/nation-world/chi-chicagodays-robertmccormick-story-story.html>.

27. Perrone, Pierre, 'Obituary: Robert Hersant', *Independent*, 25 April 1996, <https://www.independent.co.uk/news/people/obituary-robert-hersant-1306862.html>.

28. Ball, James, 'The man who would be media king', *The New European*, 20 October 2022, <https://www.theneweuropean.co.uk/mathias-dopfner-the-man-who-would-be-media-king/>.

www.washingtonpost.com/style/media/2023/09/21/rupert-murdoch-steps-down-fox-news-corp/>.

9. Neil, Andrew, 'How the bitter feud between the two Murdoch brothers makes William and Harry's fallout look like a tea party', *Daily Mail*, 30 September 2023, <https://www.dailymail.co.uk/debate/article-12576871/ANDREW-NEIL-feud-Murdoch-brothers-William-Harrys-fallout.html>.

10. Ibid.

11. Kruger, Colin, 'Rupert Murdoch has a plan if Lachlan and James are dud hires, it involves $US44m', *Sydney Morning Herald*, 20 July 2015 <https://www.smh.com.au/business/rupert-murdoch-has-a-plan-if-lachlan-and-james-are-dud-hires-it-involves-us44m-20150720-gifyiy.html>.

12. Ibid.

13. Chenoweth, N., 'The Story Behind News' Super Shares', *Australian Financial Review*, 3 November 1993, <https://neilchenoweth.com/2013/12/11/ruperts-sweetest-deal-of-all-was-at-his-familys-expense/>.

14. Chenoweth, N., *Virtual Murdoch*, Secker and Warburg, London, 2001, p. 116.

15. Clark, Andrew, 'Murdoch the munificent: media tycoon gives his six children $100m each', *The Guardian*, 3 February 2007.

16. Chozick, Amy, 'Fox-Disney deal gives Rupert Murdoch his King Lear moment', *New York Times*, 14 December 2017, <https://www.nytimes.com/2017/12/14/business/media/rupert-murdoch-21st-century-fox.html#:~:text=%E2%80%9CHe%20tried%20to%20buy%2C%20and,the%20best%2>.

17. Ibid.

18. Fishman, Steve, 'The boy who wouldn't be king', *New York Magazine*, 9 September 2005, <https://nymag.com/nymetro/news/media/features/14302/>.

19. Ellison, Sarah, 'Inside the final days of Roger Ailes's reign at Fox News', 22 September 2016, <https://www.vanityfair.com/news/2016/09/roger-ailes-fox-news-final-days>.

20. Seal, Mark, 'Seduced and abandoned', *Vanity Fair*, March 2014 <https://www.vanityfair.com/style/2014/03/wendi-deng-note-tony-blair>.

21. Ibid.

22. Sherman, Gabriel, 'Inside Rupert Murdoch's succession drama', *Vanity Fair*, 12 April 2023, <https://www.vanityfair.com/news/2023/04/rupert-murdoch-cover-story>.

23. Hearst, William Randolph Jr., *The Hearsts: Father and Son*, Roberts Rinehart, 1991, p. 175.

24. Ibid., pp. 254–56.
25. Ibid.

Decline and Fall
1. Chaney, Lindsay and Cieply, Michael, *The Hearsts: Family and Empire The Later Years*, Simon & Schuster, New York, 1981, p. 24.
2. Ibid., p. 89.
3. Shawcross, William, *Murdoch*, 1992, pp. 8–17.
4. Preston, John, *Fall: The Mystery of Robert Maxwell*, Viking, 2020, pp. 276–77.
5. Davies, Caroline, 'The murky life and death of Robert Maxwell – and how it shaped his daughter Ghislaine', *The Guardian*, 22 August 2019, <https://www.theguardian.com/us-news/2019/aug/22/the-murky-life-and-death-of-robert-maxwell-and-how-it-shaped-his-daughter-ghislaine#>.
6. Oxford Dictionary of National Biography, <https://www.oxforddnb.com/browse;jsessionid=DE4D20EF8AD65349375E93A31AC744C7?pageSize=10&sort=titlesort&t=OccupationsAndRealmsOfRenown%3A489&to=OccupationsAndRealmsOfRenown%3A1815>.
7. Kirsch, Noah, 'Long before Ghislaine Maxwell disappeared, her mogul father died mysteriously', *Forbes*, 28 February 2020, <https://www.forbes.com/sites/noahkirsch/2020/02/28/long-before-ghislaine-maxwell-disappeared-came-her-mogul-fathers-mysterious-death/?sh=6e2d0fb15869>.
8. Preston, John, *Fall*, p. 67.
9. Fabrikant, Geraldine, 'Hollinger files stinging report on ex-officials', *New York Times*, 1 September 2004, <https://www.nytimes.com/2004/09/01/business/media/hollinger-files-stinging-report-on-exofficials.html>.
10. Nish Jacquie and Stewart Sinclair, *Wrong Way: The Fall of Conrad Black*, Overlook Press, New York, 2004, p. 92.
11. Ibid.
12. Breedon, Richard C., 'Report of the special committee of the company', U.S. Securities and Exchange Commission, 30 August 2004, p. 2, <https://www.sec.gov/Archives/edgar/data/868512/000095012304010413/y01437exv99w2.htm>.
13. Laville, Sandra, 'The Guardian profile: Barbara Amiel', *The Guardian*, 3 September 2004, <https://www.theguardian.com/media/2004/sep/03/pressandpublishing.citynews>.
14. Burrough, Bryan, 'The convictions of Conrad Black', *Vanity Fair*, October 2011, <https://archive.vanityfair.com/article/2011/10/the-convictions-of-conrad-black>.
15. Black, Conrad, *A Matter of Principle*, McClelland & Stewart, Canada, 2011, p. 2.

16. McDonald, Duff, 'The man who wanted more', *Vanity Fair*, 2 April 2007, <https://www.vanityfair.com/news/2004/04/black200404>.
17. Haughney, Christine, 'New York Times Company sells Boston Globe', *New York Times*, 3 August 2013, <https://www.nytimes.com/2013/08/04/business/media/new-york-times-company-sells-boston-globe.html>.
18. Lee, Edmund, 'New York Times hits 7 million subscribers as digital revenue rises', *New York Times*, 5 November 2023, <https://www.nytimes.com/2020/11/05/business/media/new-york-times-q3-2020-earnings-nyt.html>.
19. Morrissey, Brian, 'The state of subscriptions', *The Rebooting*, 9 November 2023, <https://www.therebooting.com/the-state-of-subscriptions/>.
20. Shirky, Clay, 'Is The New York Times a tech company?', WNYC Studios, 22 July 2023, <https://www.wnycstudios.org/podcasts/otm/segments/is-the-new-york-times-tech-company-on-the-media>.
21. Reed, Roy, 'London's Beaverbrook papers sold', *New York Times*, 1 July 1977, <https://www.nytimes.com/1977/07/01/archives/londons-beaverbrook-papers-sold.html>.
22. Pappu, Sridhar and Stowe, Jay, 'The last days of Time Inc.', *New York Times*, 21 May 2018, <https://www.nytimes.com/interactive/2018/05/19/business/media/time-inc-oral-history.html>.
23. <https://halloffame.melbournepressclub.com/article/john-fairfax>.
24. Bagwell, Sheryle, 'Warwick goes quietly', *Australian Financial Review*, 11 December 1990, <https://www.afr.com/politics/warwick-goes-quietly-19901211-k47l5>.

Editorial Dictators

1. Snoddy, Raymond, *The Good, the Bad and the Unacceptable*, Faber & Faber, 1992, p. 131.
2. Black, Conrad, *A Matter of Principle*, p. 15.
3. Hastings, Max, *Editor*, Macmillan, London, 2002, p. 22.
4. Ibid., pp. 250–51.
5. Halberstam, David, *The Powers That Be*, Alfred A. Knopf, New York, 1979, p. 48.
6. Brendon, Piers, *The Life and Death of the Press Barons*, Atheneum, New York, 1983, p. 156.
7. Gourlay, Logan, ed,. *The Beaverbrook I Knew*, Quartet Books, 1984, p. 182.
8. Chisolm, Anne and Davie, Michael, *Beaverbrook*, p. 335.
9. Christensen, Arthur, *Headlines All My Life*, Heinemann, 1961, p. 219.
10. Gourlay, Logan, ed., *The Beaverbrook I Knew*, p. 10.
11. Winkler, John, K., *William Randolph Hearst: A New Appraisal*, Kessinger Publishing, 2007, p. 262.

12. Nasaw, David, *The Chief.*
13. Winkler, John, K., *William Randolph Hearst*, p. 262.
14. Cannon, Michael, 'Shaping the Herald: Sir Keith Murdoch seen through his confidential memoranda', *Inside Story*, 29 June 2013, <https://insidestory.org.au/shaping-the-herald-sir-keith-murdoch-seen-through-his-confidential-memoranda/>.
15. Shawcross, William, *Murdoch*, p. 144.
16. Kiernan, Thomas, *Citizen Murdoch: The Unexpurgated Story of Rupert Murdoch—The World's Most Powerful and Controversial Media Lord*, Dodd Mead, 1986, p. 78.
17. UK Parliament Select Committee on Communications, 'House of Lords–Communications–First Report', Q1650, <https://publications.parliament.uk/pa/ld200708/ldselect/ldcomuni/122/12206.htm>.
18. Kelly, Paul, 'Conspiracy debunked: The truth about Murdoch editors', *The Australian*, 9 July 2014.
19. Shawcross, William, *Murdoch*, 1992, pp. 8–17.
20. Ellison, Sarah, 'Murdoch and the vicious circle', *Vanity Fair*, 6 February 2013, <https://www.vanityfair.com/news/2011/10/murdoch-201110>.
21. Mackenzie, Kelvin, 'Dominic Raab is no bully – and I should know', *The Spectator*, 8 February 2023, <https://www.spectator.co.uk/article/dominic-raab-is-no-bully-and-i-should-know/>.
22. Ellison, Sarah, *War at the Wall Street Journal: Inside the Struggle to Control an American Business Empire*, Houghton Mifflin Harcourt, 2010, pp. 102–03
23. Peers, Martin and Patrick, Aaron O., 'Murdoch's editors know his voice', *Wall Street Journal*, 3 May 2007, <https://www.wsj.com/articles/SB117815037579090204>.
24. Tobitt, Charlotte, 'Andrew Neil: Line between Murdoch press and state became blurred during Blair era', *Press Gazette*, 16 July 2020, <https://pressgazette.co.uk/news/rupert-murdoch-documentary-rise-of-dynasty-bbc-tony-blair/>.
25. Gourlay, Logan, ed., *The Beaverbrook I Knew*, p. 31.
26. Warzel, Charlie, Twitter is a far-right social network, *The Atlantic*, 23 May 2023, <https://www.theatlantic.com/technology/archive/2023/05/elon-musk-ron-desantis-2024-twitter/674149/>.
27. Milmo, Dan, 'Eight things we learned from the Elon Musk biography', *The Guardian*, 12 September 2023, <https://www.theguardian.com/technology/2023/sep/12/elon-musk-biography-eight-things-learned>.
28. Breiner, James, 'What freedom of the press means for those who own one', *Mediashift*, 10 December 2014, <https://mediashift.org/2014/12/what-freedom-of-the-press-means-for-those-who-own-one/>.

The Exercise of Power

1. Halberstam, David, *The Powers That Be*, p. 355.

2. Knightley, Phillip, *A Hack's Progress*, Roli Books, 2005, p. 28.

3. Williams, Francis, *Dangerous Estate: The Anatomy of Newspapers*, Longmans, Green, 1957, p. 215.

4. Gibson, Matthew, 'May's praise on 100th birthday of Sunday Express', *Sunday Express*, 30 December 2018, <https://www.express.co.uk/news/uk/1065148/theresa-may-tribute-sunday-express-100th-birthday>.

5. Brendon, Piers, *The Life and Death of the Press Barons*, p. 42.

6. Evans, Harold, 'Rupert Murdoch is the stiletto, a man of method, a cold-eyed manipulator', *The Guardian*, 19 September 2011, <https://www.theguardian.com/media/2011/sep/18/harold-evans-rupert-murdoch-leadership>.

7. Belfield, Richard, Hird, Christopher, & Kelly, Sharon, *Murdoch: The Decline of an Empire*, Macdonald, London, p. 80.

8. Hoskins, Paul, 'Rebekah Brooks to revisit her parliamentary past', *Reuters*, 15 July 2011, <https://www.reuters.com/article/idUSTRE76E1I1/>.

9. Hurst, Daniel, 'Kevin Rudd says Australian politicians "frightened" of "Murdoch media beast" in Senate inquiry', *The Guardian*, 19 February 2021, <https://www.theguardian.com/australia-news/2021/feb/19/kevin-rudd-says-australian-politicians-frightened-of-murdoch-media-beast-in-senate-inquiry>.

10. Robert Duffield quoted in Chubb, Philip, 'Politics, power and the pen', *The Age*, 1 October 1980.

11. Massie, Alex, 'Revenge of the MPs', *Foreign Policy*, 13 July 2011, <https://foreignpolicy.com/2011/07/13/revenge-of-the-mps/>.

12. Price, Lance, *Where Power Lies: Prime Ministers V the Media*, Simon & Schuster, 2010, p. 43.

13. Jenkins, Simon, *The Market for Glory: Fleet Street Ownership in the Twentieth Century*, Faber & Faber, 1986, p. 22.

14. Chisolm, Anne and Davie, Michael, *Beaverbrook*, p. 298.

15. Gourlay, Logan, ed., *The Beaverbrook I Knew*, p. 10.

16. 'Lord Beaverbrook dead at 85; founder of newspaper empire; member of Churchill's war cabinet guided Britain's aircraft production', *New York Times*, 10 June 1964, <https://www.nytimes.com/1964/06/10/archives/lord-beaverbrook-dead-at-85-founder-of-newspaper-empire-member-of.html>.

17. 'Benjamin Netanyahu: What are the corruption charges?' BBC, 22 May 2020, <https://www.bbc.com/news/world-middle-east-47409739>.

18. Addley, Esther, 'Alastair Campbell back at the Leveson inquiry – and with great clunking balls', *The Guardian*, 15 May 2012, <https://www.theguardian.com/media/2012/may/14/alastair-campbell-leveson-inquiry>.

19. Shawcross, William, *Rupert Murdoch: Ringmaster of the Information Circus*, Chatto & Windus, 1992, p. 47.

20. Manning, Paddy, *The Successor*, Black Inc., Victoria, 2022, p. 242.

21. Young, Sally, *Paper Emperors: The Rise of Australia's Newspaper Empires*, NewSouth Publising, 2019, pp. 437–38.

22. Clarke, Peter and Kingston, Margo, 'Transcript of interview with former Prime Minister Malcolm Turnbull', *No Fibs*, recorded 11 August 2012, <https://nofibs.com.au/transcript-of-interview-by-peter-clarke-and-margo-kingston-with-former-prime-minister-malcolm-turnbull-recorded-august-11-2012-lightly-edited-for-clarity-and-succinctness/>.

23. Wolff, Michael, *Fire and Fury: Inside the Trump White House*, Henry Holt, 2018, p. 36.

24. Chozick, Amy, 'Rupert Murdoch and President Trump: a friendship of convenience', *New York Times*, 23 December 2017, <https://www.nytimes.com/2017/12/23/business/media/murdoch-trump-relationship.html>.

25. Henderson, Alex, 'Jared Kushner's new memoir reveals 2020 election night call with Fox News' Rupert Murdoch', *Salon*, 28 July 2022, <https://www.salon.com/2022/07/28/jared-kushners-new-memoir-reveals-2020-night-call-with-fox-news-rupert-murdoch_partner/>.

26. 'Donald Trump, Democrats are obsessed with 2020 – GOP should look to the future', *New York Post*, 10 June 2022, <https://nypost.com/2022/06/10/trump-and-dems-remain-obsessed-with-2020-republicans-should-look-to-the-future-instead/>.

27. Rahman, Khaleda, 'Steve Bannon says Fox News has "turned on Trump," favors DeSantis', *Newsweek*, 23 June 2022, <https://www.newsweek.com/steve-bannon-fox-news-turned-trump-1718395>.

28. Sweeney, Mark, 'Murdoch tells Trump he will not back fresh White House bid – report', *The Guardian*, 16 November 2022, <https://www.theguardian.com/us-news/2022/nov/15/murdoch-press-turns-on-donald-trump-in-favour-of-defuture-ron-desantis>.

29. Shafer, Jack, 'Why Rupert Murdoch is finally done with Donald Trump', *Politico*, 25 July 2022, <https://www.politico.com/news/magazine/2022/07/25/rupert-murdoch-donald-trump-splitsville-00047748>.

30. Munster, George, *Rupert Murdoch: A Paper Prince*, Penguin, 1987, p. 95.

31. Oakes, Laurie and Solomon, David, *The Making of an Australian Prime Minister*, Cheshire, 1987, p. 278.

32. Griffen-Foley, Bridget, *Party Games*, Text Publishing, 2003, p. 201.

33. Menadue, John, 'Gough, Rupert and the London job', *Pearls and Irritations*, 27 August 2022, <https://johnmenadue.com/murdoch-whitlam-and-the-job-in-london/>.

34. Kiernan, Thomas, *Citizen Murdoch: The Unexpurgated Story of Rupert Murdoch – The World's Most Powerful and Controversial Media Lord*, Dodd Mead, 1986, p. 141.

35. Dorling, Philip, 'Murdoch editors told to "kill Whitlam" in 1975', *Sydney Morning Herald*, 28 June 2014, <https://www.smh.com.au/national/murdoch-editors-told-to-kill-whitlam-in-1975-20140627-zson7.html>.

36. Cryle, Denis, *Murdoch's Flagship: Twenty-Five Years of the Australian Newspaper*, Melbourne University Publishing, 2008, p. 135.

37. Leapman, Michael, *Arrogant Aussie: The Rupert Murdoch Story*, Lyle Stuart, 1985, p. 75

38. Cryle, Denis, *Murdoch's Flagship*, p. 148.

39. Shafer, Jack, 'Why Rupert Murdoch is finally done with Donald Trump'.

40. Menadue, John, 'Gough, Rupert and the London job'.

41. Halberstam, David, *The Powers That Be*, p. 90.

42. Brinkley, Alan, *The Publisher: Henry Luce and His American Century*, Knopf, New York, 2011, p. 384.

43. Felsenthal, Carol, *Citizen Newhouse*, p. 140.

44. Price, Lance, *Where Power Lies: Prime Ministers V the Media*, Simon & Schuster, 2010, p. 252.

45. Barry, Paul, *Breaking News: Sex, Lies & the Murdoch Succession*, Allen & Unwin, 2013, p. 54.

46. Kiernan, Thomas, *Citizen Murdoch*, p. 311.

47. Simpson, John, *Unreliable Sources: How the Twentieth Century Was Reported*, Macmillan, 2010, ch. 18.

48. Neil, Andrew, *Full Disclosure*, Macmillan, 1996, p. 248.

49. Simpson, John, *Unreliable Sources*.

50. Lusher, Adam, 'John Major told ministers to avoid attending "jamboree" for Rupert Murdoch, newly released files reveal', *Independent*, 28 December 2018, <https://www.independent.co.uk/news/uk/home-news/john-major-cabinet-papers-rupert-murdoch-michael-howard-eu-bastards-maastricht-conservative-party-1990s-a8691211.html>.

51. Plunkett John and O'Carroll, Lisa, 'John Major tells Leveson inquiry Murdoch demanded policy changes', *The Guardian*, 13 June 2012, <https://www.theguardian.com/media/2012/jun/12/john-major-leveson-inquiry-rupert-murdoch>.

52. Campbell, Alistair, *The Blair Years: Extracts from the Alastair Campbell Diaries*, Arrow, 2008, pp. 75–76.

53. Ibid., p.160.

54. Hickman, Martin, 'The world according to Rupert Murdoch', *Independent*, 26 April 2021, <https://www.independent.co.uk/news/uk/crime/the-world-according-to-rupert-murdoch-7679254.html>.

55. Tobitt, Charlotte, 'Andrew Neil: line between Murdoch press and state became blurred during Blair era', *PressGazette*, 16 July 2020, <https://

pressgazette.co.uk/news/rupert-murdoch-documentary-rise-of-dynasty-bbc-tony-blair/>.

56. Price, Lance, *Where the Power Lies*.

57. Tuccille, Jerome, *Rupert Murdoch*, Donald I. Fine Inc., 1989, p. 131.

58. Shawcross, William, *Rupert Murdoch*, p. 190.

59. Dickinson, Tim, 'Rupert Murdoch's American Scandals', *Rolling Stone*, 3 August 2011, <https://www.rollingstone.com/politics/politics-news/rupert-murdochs-american-scandals-243127/>.

60. Dover, Bruce, *Rupert's Adventures in China: How Murdoch Lost a Fortune and Found a Wife*, Mainstream Publishing, 2009, pp. 152–55.

61. Chisolm, Anne and Davie, Michael, *Beaverbrook*, pp. 352–53.

62. Roberts, Andrew, *The Chief: The Life of Lord Northcliffe Britain's Greatest Press Baron*, Simon & Schuster, London, 2023, pp. 114, 122.

63. Martinson, Jane, *You May Never See Us Again: The Barclay Dynasty: A Story of Survival, Secrecy and Succession*, Kindle ed., Penguin, 2023, p. 181.

64. Taylor, Matthew, 'Margaret Thatcher's estate still a family secret', *The Guardian*, 10 April 2013, <https://www.theguardian.com/politics/2013/apr/09/margaret-thatcher-estate-family-secret>.

65. Karni, Annie, 'President Trump grants pardon to Conrad Black', *The New York Times*, 15 May 2019, <https://www.nytimes.com/2019/05/15/us/politics/conrad-black-pardon.html>.

66. Oborne, Peter, 'The great Murdoch conspiracy', *The Telgraph*, 14 July 2011, <https://www.telegraph.co.uk/news/uknews/phone-hacking/8638614/The-great-Murdoch-conspiracy.html>.

67. Ibid.

68. Ellison, Sarah, 'The Dark Arts', *Vanity Fair*, 5 May 2011, <https://www.vanityfair.com/news/2011/06/rupert-murdoch-news-of-the-world-201106>.

69. Moore, Martin, *Who Was Hacked*, Media Standards Trust, March 2015, p. 44, <https://www.mediareform.org.uk/wp-content/uploads/2015/11/Who_was_hacked-An_investigation_into_phone_hacking_and_its_victims-Part_1-News_of_the_World.pdf>.

70. Davies, Nick, *Hack Attack: How the Truth Caught up with Rupert Murdoch*, Vintage, 2015.

71. Ellison, Sarah, 'Murdoch and the Vicious Circle'.

72. Bauder, David and Horwitz, Jeff, 'Relationship between Trump, Enquirer goes beyond headlines', AP News, 23 August 2018, <https://apnews.com/united-states-government-general-news-arts-and-entertainment-74c03eb6b2a04f828af36a4227951309>.

73. Farrow, Ronan, 'Donald Trump, a Playboy model, and a system for concealing infidelity', *New Yorker*, 18 February 2018, <https://www.

newyorker.com/news/news-desk/donald-trump-a-playboy-model-and-a-system-for-concealing-infidelity-national-enquirer-karen-mcdougal>.

74. Twohey, Megan; Kantor, Jodi: Dominus, Susan: Rutenberg, Jim and Eder, Steve, 'Weinstein's Complicity Machine', *New York Times*, 5 December 2017, <https://www.nytimes.com/interactive/2017/12/05/us/harvey-weinstein-complicity.html#>.

75. Davies, Nick, *Hack Attack*, pp. 174–75.

76. Rusbridger, Alan, 'News of the World was "probably beyond reform" says Rusbridger ten years after closure', *PressGazette*, 9 July 2021, <https://pressgazette.co.uk/news/news-of-the-world-was-probably-beyond-reform-says-rusbridger-ten-years-after-closure/>.

77. Waterson, Jim, 'News of the World: 10 years since phone-hacking scandal brought down tabloid', *The Guardian*, 10 July 2021, <https://www.theguardian.com/media/2021/jul/10/news-of-the-world-10-years-since-phone-hacking-scandal-brought-down-tabloid>.

Sycophants and Sackings

1. Evans, Harold, 'Murdoch in good times and bad, Reuters, 20 September 2011, <https://jp.reuters.com/article/idUS1576992271/>.

2. Neil, Andrew, *Full Disclosure*, p. 160.

3. Goldman Rohm, Wendy, *The Murdoch Vision: The Digital Transformation of a Media Empire*, John Wiley & Sons, 2001, p. 61.

4. <https://newscorp.com/2014/10/10/remarks-of-robert-thomson-at-the-victorian-media-hall-of-fame/>, accessed June 2023.

5. Meade, Amanda, 'Rupert Murdoch eases into retirement as Lachlan takes up baton of "philosophical integrity"', *The Guardian*, 10 November 2023, <https://www.theguardian.com/media/commentisfree/2023/nov/10/rupert-murdoch-eases-into-retirement-as-lachlan-takes-up-baton-of-philosophical-integrity>.

6. Hinton, Les 'Life with Murdoch, *British Journal Review*, Vol. 26, No. 3, 8 September 2015, pp. 18–23.

7. Swanberg, W.A., *Citizen Hearst: A Biography of William Randolph Hearst*, Bantam Books, 1967, p.520.

8. Cudlipp, Hugh, 'The Deathbed Repentance', *British Journalism Review*, Vol.1, No.2, January 1990, p.3.

9. Hastings, Max, *Editor: An Inside Story of Newspapers*, Macmillan, London, 2002, p. 256.

10. Schlesinger, Arthur, M., *A Thousand Days: John F. Kennedy in the White House*, HarperCollins, New York, 2002, p. 63.

11. Lundberg, Ferdinand and Beard, Charles, A., *Imperial Hearst: A Social Biography*, The Modern Library, New York, 1936.

12. Rogers, Simon, 'James and Rupert Murdoch at the Culture, Media and Sport Select Committee – full transcript', *The Guardian*, 20 July 2011, <https://www.theguardian.com/news/datablog/2011/jul/20/james-rupert-murdoch-full-transcript>.

13. Stephens, Bret, 'The Tragedy of Fox News', *New York Times*, 24 April 2023, <https://www.nytimes.com/2023/04/24/opinion/tucker-carlson-fox-news-murdoch.html>.

14. Kiernan, Thomas, *Citizen Murdoch*.

15. Somerfield, Stafford, *Banner Headlines*, Scan Publishing, 1979, p. 192.

16. Hills, Ben, *Breaking News: The Golden Age of Graham Perkin*, Scribe, 2013, pp. 371, 372.

17. Evans, Harold, *My Paper Chase: True Stories of Vanished Times: An Autobiography*, Little Brown, 2009, p. 498.

18. D'Arcy, John, *Media Mayhem: Playing with the BIG BOYS in Media*, Brolga Publishing, 2005, p. 171.

19. Ellison, Sarah, *War at The Wall Street Journal*, Houghton Mifflin Harcourt, 2010, pp. 203–04.

20. Tiffen, Rodney, 'Ruffling the hair apparent', *Inside Story*, 2 November 2022, <https://insidestory.org.au/ruffling-the-hair-apparent/>.

21. Ibid.

22. Brooks, Geraldine, 'Murdoch', *New York Times Magazine*, 19 July 1998 <https://www.nytimes.com/1998/07/19/magazine/murdoch.html#:~:text=But%20unlike%20his%20father%2C%20Lachlan,only%20general%2Dinterest%20national%20daily.>.

23. Maier, Thomas, *Newhouse: All That Glitter, Power and Glory of America's Richest Media Empire and the Secretive Man Behind It*, St Martins Press, 1994, p.3.

24. Felsenthal, Carol, *Citizen Newhouse*, pp. 387–88.

25. Taylor, A.J.P., *Beaverbrook*, Hamish Hamilton, London, 1972, p.623.

26. Bourne, Richard, *Lords of Fleet Street: The Harmsworth Dynasty*, Unwin Hyman, London, 1990, p.37.

The Mogul Politicians

1. Pinkerton, Stewart, *The Fall of the House of Forbes: The Inside Story of the Collapse of a Media Empire*, St Martin's Press, 2011, p.29.

2. Swanberg, W.A., *Citizen Hearst*, p. 342.

3. Rutland, Robert Allen, *The Newsmongers; Journalism in the Life of the Nation, 1690-1972*, Dial Press, 1973, p. 274

4. Nasaw, David, *The Chief: The Life of William Randolph Hearst*, Houghton Mifflin Harcourt, 2000, p. 175.

5. Ibid., p. 200.

6. Zimmerman, Jonathan, 'William Randolph Hearst for President', *Lapham's Quarterly*, 22 January 2018, <https://www.laphamsquarterly.org/roundtable/hearst-president>.

7. Taylor, A.J.P, *Beaverbrook: A Biography*, Hamish Hamilton, 1972, p. 415.

8. Bachrach, Judy, 'Arrivederci, Berlusconi?', *Vanity Fair*, January 1995, <https://archive.vanityfair.com/article/share/ee84c7fb-93dd-4534-a180-d73a665eaceb>.

9. Peretz, Evgenia, 'La Dolce Viagra', *Vanity Fair*, 31 May 2011, <https://www.vanityfair.com/news/2011/07/silvio-berlusconi-201107>.

10. Peretz, Evgenia, 'La Dolce Viagra'.

11. Stille, Alexander, 'The World's Greatest Salesman', *New York Times Magazine*, 17 March 1996, <https://www.nytimes.com/1996/03/17/magazine/the-world-s-greatest-salesman.html>.

12. <https://www.economist.com/leaders/2011/06/09/the-man-who-screwed-an-entire-country>.

13. Stille, Alexander, *The Sack of Rome: Media + Money + Celebrity = Power = Silvio Berlusconi*, Penguin, 2007, p. 174.

14. Davies, Lizzy, 'Paulo: as offensive as his brother Silvio?', *The Guardian*, 7 February 2013, <https://www.theguardian.com/world/shortcuts/2013/feb/06/paolo-berlusconi-offensive-brother-silvio>.

15. 'In quotes: Italy's Silvio Berlusconi in his own words', BBC, 2 August 2013, <https://www.bbc.com/news/world-europe-15642201>.

16. Peretz, Evgenia, 'La Dolce Viagra'.

17. Day, Michael, 'Silvio Berlusconi caught out trying to stifle media', *Independent*, 18 March 2010, <https://www.independent.co.uk/news/world/europe/silvio-berlusconi-caught-out-trying-to-stifle-media-1923147.html>.

18. Stille, Alexander, *The Sack of Rome: Media + Money + Celebrity = Power = Silvio Berlusconi*, Penguin Books, 2007, p. 72.

19. Lloyd, John & Giugliano, Ferdinando, 'Intimate fusion: media and political power in Silvio Berlusconi's Italy', *Open Democracy*, 8 April 2013, <https://www.opendemocracy.net/en/intimate-fusion-media-and-political-power-in-silvio-berlusconis-ital/>.

20. Davies, Lizzie, 'Silvio Berlusconi supporters stage "we are all whores" protest over conviction', *The Guardian*, 26 June 2013, <https://www.theguardian.com/world/2013/jun/25/silvio-berlusconi-supporters-protest-conviction>.

The Madness of Great Men

1. Becher, Jonathan, 'The Poison of Power', *Forbes*, 5 January 2011, <https://www.forbes.com/sites/sap/2011/01/05/the-poison-of-power/?sh=2a458ead5of3>.

2. Chaney, Lindsay and Cieply, Michael, *The Hearsts: Family and Empire: The Later Years*, Simon and Schuster, New York, 1981, p. 39.

3. Morris, James McGrath, *Pulitzer: A Life in Politics, Print, and Power*, Harper Perennial, 2011, p. 411. Roberts, Andrew, *The Chief, The Life of Lord Northcliffe, The Life of Lord Northcliffe Britain's Greatest Press Baron*, Simon & Schuster, London, 2022, p. 41.

4. Neil, Andrew, 'Murdoch and Me', *Vanity Fair*, 3 January 2012, <https://www.vanityfair.com/news/1996/12/rupert-murdoch-199612>.

5. Ellison, Sarah, 'Two Men and a Newsstand', *Vanity Fair*, 6 September 2010, <https://www.vanityfair.com/news/2010/10/times-versus-wall-street-journal-201010>.

6. Taylor, S.J., *The Great Outsiders: Northcliffe, Rothermere and the Daily Mail*, Weidenfeld & Nicholson, 1996, p. 79.

7. Gourlay, Logan, ed., *The Beaverbrook I Knew*, p.2.

8. Ibid., p. 89

9. Nasaw, David, *The Chief: The Life of William Randolph Hearst*, Houghton Mifflin Company, Boston, 2000, p. xii.

10. . Lanchester, John, 'Bravo l'artiste', *London Review of Books*, Vol. 26, No. 3, 5 February 2004, <https://www.lrb.co.uk/the-paper/v26/no3/john-lanchester/bravo-l-artiste>.

11. Hutcheon, Stephen, 'Murdoch shackled by a new cult of self', *Sydney Morning Herald*, 2 November, 2013, <https://www.smh.com.au/technology/murdoch-shackled-by-a-new-cult-of-self-20131101-2ws4s.html>.

12. Sherman, Gabriel, 'Inside Rupert Murdoch's Succession Drama', *Vanity Fair*, 12 April 2023, <https://www.vanityfair.com/news/2023/04/rupert-murdoch-cover-story#:~:text=While%20examining%20the%20X%2Dray,spent%20weeks%20on%20the%20couch.>.

13. Pattinson, Terry, 'Monster of the Mirror', *UK Press Gazette*, 6 April 2001, p.13.

14. Maxwell, Betty, *A Mind of My Own: My Life with Robert Maxwell*, Pan Books, 1995, p. 613.

15. Black, Conrad, *A Matter of Principle*, p. 3.

16. McDonald, Duff, 'The man who wanted more', *Vanity Fair*, 2 April 2007, <https://www.vanityfair.com/news/2004/04/black200404>.

17. Burrough, Bryan, 'The convictions of Conrad Black', *Vanity Fair*, October 2011, <https://archive.vanityfair.com/article/2011/10/the-convictions-of-conrad-black>.

18. McDonald, Duff, 'The Man Who Wanted More'.

19. Hopper, Tristin, 'Conrad Black says his comeback is already under way', *National Post*, 21 May 2012, <https://nationalpost.com/news/canada/conrad-black-says-his-comeback-is-already-underway>.

20. Nadeau, Barbie Latza, 'Berlusconi embodies Italy's greatest weaknesses, worst instincts', *Newsweek*, 13 November 2011, <https://www.newsweek.com/berlusconi-embodies-italys-greatest-weaknesses-worst-instincts-66387>.

21. Hearst, William Randolph Jr, *The Hearsts: Father and Son*, Roberts Rinehart, 1991, p. 5.

22. Brinkley, Alan, *The Publisher: Henry Luce and His American Century*, Alfred A. Knopf, 2010, p. 207.

23. Dufraigne, Annabelle, 'The Murdoch family's staggering real estate portfolio', *Architectural Digest*, 17 November 2023, <https://www.architecturaldigest.com/story/the-murdoch-familys-staggering-real-estate-portfolio>.

24. Whyte, Kenneth, *The Uncrowned King: The Sensational Rise of William Randolph Hearst*, Counterpoint, Berkeley, 2009, p. 5.

25. Lysistrata (1900); Recreation vessel; Passenger vessel; Yacht', *Royal Museums Greenwich*, <https://www.rmg.co.uk/collections/objects/rmgc-object-67262>.

26. 'Explore SY Vertigo: A Luxurious Sailing Yacht with Impressive Design and Unmatched Comfort', *Superyacht Fan*, <https://www.superyachtfan.com/yacht/vertigo/#google_vignette>, accessed February 2024. Vincent, Peter, 'Lachlan Murdoch expands his superyacht fleet with an award-winning $30million vessel - as he awaits the completion of his brand-new $175million boat', *Daily Mail*, 2 April 2022, <https://www.dailymail.co.uk/news/article-10677913/Lachlan-Murdoch-expands-superyacht-fleet-30million-boat-new-150million-yacht-built.html>.

27. van der Dennen, Johan, 'Powerful men have an overactive libido', *Spiegel International*, 27 May 2011, <https://www.spiegel.de/international/world/sex-and-power-powerful-men-have-an-overactive-libido-a-765316.html>.

28. Keltner, Dacher, 'The Power Paradox', *Greater Good Magazine*, 1 December 2007, <https://greatergood.berkeley.edu/article/item/power_paradox>.

29. Rasmussen, Cecilia, 'It was one of the first architectural ...', *Los Angeles Times*, 23 May 1994, <https://www.latimes.com/archives/la-xpm-1994-05-23-me-61195-story.html>.

30. Brinkley, Alan, *The Publisher: Henry Luce and His American Century*, Alfred A. Knopf, 2010, p. 195.

31. Peretz, Evgenia, 'La Dolce Viagra', *Vanity Fair*, 31 May 2011, <https://www.vanityfair.com/news/2011/07/silvio-berlusconi-201107>.

32. Barry, Paul, *The Rise and Rise of Kerry Packer Uncut*, Bantam, Sydney, 2007, p. 522.

The Moral Compass

1. Guthrie, Bruce, *Man Bites Murdoch: Four Decades in Print, Six Days in Court*, Melbourne University Pub, 2011, p. 101.
2. Ibid., p. 103.
3. Wickham, Alexander, 'Bullish but refreshing', *Prospect*, 9 January 2012, <https://www.prospectmagazine.co.uk/ideas/media/phone-hacking/49828/bullish-but-refreshing>.
4. Meade, Amanda, 'Stan Grant accuses the Australian newspaper of acting like a "racist hit squad"', *The Guardian*, 29 August, 2023, <https://www.theguardian.com/australia-news/2023/aug/29/nfbntw-stan-grant-accuses-the-australian-newspaper-of-acting-like-a-racist-hit-squad>.
5. Watkins, Emily, 'The War against Tim Flannery', *Crikey*, 24 October 2017, <https://www.crikey.com.au/2017/10/24/the-war-against-tim-flannery/>.
6. Abdel-Magied, Yassmin, 'What are they so afraid of? I'm just a young brown Muslim woman speaking my mind', *The Guardian*, 6 July 2017, <https://www.theguardian.com/australia-news/2017/jul/06/what-are-they-so-afraid-of-im-just-a-young-brown-muslim-woman-speaking-my-mind>.
7. Kazin, Michael, 'The Dual Defeat', *The Nation*, 12 November 2018, <https://www.thenation.com/article/archive/hubert-humphrey-and-the-unmaking-of-cold-war-liberalism/>.
8. Dover, Bruce, *Rupert's Adventures in China*, p. 155.
9. Anonymous, 'Confessions of a News of the World reporter: whistleblowing for Prince Harry', *Byline Investigates*, 12 October 2023, <https://bylineinvestigates.com/2023/10/12/confessions-of-a-news-of-the-world-reporter-whistleblowing-for-prince-harry/>.
10. Leslie Cannold, conversation with author, October 2023.
11. <https://handwiki.org/wiki/Philosophy:Moral_disengagement>, accessed October 2023.
12. 'Rupert Murdoch's resignation letter, in full', *Financial Review*, 22 September 2023, <https://www.afr.com/companies/media-and-marketing/rupert-murdoch-s-resignation-letter-in-full-20230922-p5e6qt>.
13. Hagerty, Bill, '"I don't do it for the money" – Rupert Murdoch', *British Journalism Review*, Vol. 10, Issue 4, 1999, <https://doi.org/10.1177/09564748990100402>.
14. <https://newscorp.com/news-corp-esg-report/#:~:text=There%20has%20always%20been%20a,our%20company's%20long%2Dterm%20success.>, accessed September 2023>.
15. Mahler, Jonathan & Rutenberg, Jim, 'How Rupert Murdoch's empire of influence remade the world', *New York Times Magazine*, 3 April

2019, <https://www.nytimes.com/interactive/2019/04/03/magazine/james-murdoch-lachlan-succession.html>.

16. Busby, Mattha, 'James Murdoch says US media "lies" unleashed "insidious forces"', *The Guardian*, 16 January 2021, <https://www.theguardian.com/media/2021/jan/16/james-murdoch-says-us-media-lies-unleashed-insidious-forces>.

17. Tifft, Susan E. & Jones, Alex S., *The Trust*, Little Brown, pp. 43, 658.

18. Kaiser, Charles, '"I figured I'd give it a year": Arthur Sulzberger Jr on how the New York Times turned around', *The Guardian*, 20 December 2020, <https://www.theguardian.com/media/2020/dec/20/arthur-sulzberger-jr-ag-new-york-times-retirement-interview>.

19. Swanberg, W.A., *Pulitzer*, Charles Scribner's Sons, New York, 1967, p. 76.

20. Pulitzer, Joseph, 'The College of Journalism', *North American Review*, Vol. 178, No. 570, May 1904, <https://www.jstor.org/stable/25119561>.

21. Callahan, Patricia; Bandler, James; Elliott, Justin; Burke, Doris and Ernsthausen, Jeff, 'The great inheritors: how three families shielded their fortunes from taxes for generations', *ProPublica*, 15 December 2021, <https://www.propublica.org/article/the-great-inheritors-how-three-families-shielded-their-fortunes-from-taxes-for-generations>.

22. Pizzigati, Sam, 'A media mogul's noble challenge to moguldom', *Institute for Policy Studies*, 15 March 2018, <https://ips-dc.org/media-moguls-noble-challenge-moguldom/>.

23. Callahan, Patricia: Bandler, James: Elliott, Justin: Burke, Doris and Ernsthausen, Jeff, 'The Great Inheritors'.

24. Brinkley, Alan, *The Publisher*, p. 268.

25. Kobler, John, *Luce, His Time, Life and Fortune*, p. 6.

26. Overholser, Geneva, 'A paper's purpose', *Washington Post*, 23 May 1998, <https://www.washingtonpost.com/archive/opinions/1998/05/24/a-papers-purpose/6877abea-5e0f-41b5-b35e-60ef77c28cdb/>.

27. Cooper, Gloria, 'The making of a publisher', *Columbia Journalism Review*, May/June 1997, <https://www.cjr.org/60th/the-making-of-a-publisher-katharine-graham-personal-history-washington-post-gloria-cooper.php/>.

28. Day, Peter, 'The life and times of a newspaper baron', BBC, 1 April 2016, <https://www.bbc.com/news/business-35924027>.

29. Evans, Harold, *My Paper Chase*, Little, Brown, 2009, p. 312.

30. Allsop, Jon, 'At *Le Monde*, journalists win a battle for editorial independence', *Columbia Journalism Review*, 8 October 2019, <https://www.cjr.org/the_media_today/le_monde_daniel_kretinsky.php>.

31. Rubio, Marthe, 'How France's Mediapart built a successful news model around investigative journalism', *Global Investigative Journalism*

Network, 16 March 2022, <https://gijn.org/stories/france-mediapart-successful-model-investigative-journalism/>.

32. Ibid.

33. Plenel, Edwy, 'French state sentenced over attempt to search Mediapart's offices', *Mediapart*, 7 July 2022, <https://www.mediapart.fr/en/journal/france/070722/french-state-sentenced-over-attempt-search-mediaparts-offices>.

34. 'Editorial standards and guidelines', *Rappler*, 22 February 2021, <https://www.rappler.com/about/policies/standards-guidelines-corrections-fact-check-content-comment-moderation/>.

35. Sheila Coronel, 'The triumph of Marcos dynasty disinformation is a warning to the U.S.', *New Yorker*, 17 May 2022, <https://www.newyorker.com/news/dispatch/the-triumph-of-marcos-dynasty-disinformation-is-a-warning-to-the-us>.

36. Lema Karen, 'Philippine Nobel winner Ressa calls Facebook "biased against facts"', Reuters, 9 October 2021, <https://www.reuters.com/world/philippine-nobel-winner-ressa-calls-facebook-biased-against-facts-2021-10-09/>.

37. O'Carroll, Lisa, 'EU warns Elon Musk over "disinformation" on X about Hamas attack', *The Guardian*, 11 October 2023, <https://www.theguardian.com/technology/2023/oct/10/eu-warns-elon-musk-over-disinformation-about-hamas-attack-on-x>.

38. Goldman, David, 'Elon Musk agrees with antisemitic X post that claims Jews "push hatred" against White people', CNN, 17 November 2023, <https://edition.cnn.com/2023/11/15/media/elon-musk-antisemitism-white-people/index.html>.

39. Frenkel, Sheera & Myers Steven Lee, 'Antisemitic and anti-Muslim hate speech surges across the internet', *New York Times*, 15 November 2023, <https://www.nytimes.com/2023/11/15/technology/hate-speech-israel-gaza-internet.html>.

40. Peers, Martin, 'Israel Gets Sensible and Thoughtful Musk', 27 November 2023, <https://www.theinformation.com/articles/israel-gets-sensible-and-thoughtful-musk>.

41. Lessin, Jessica, 'Don't fall for the Musk distraction machine', *The Information*, 15 August 2023, <https://www.theinformation.com/articles/dont-fall-for-the-musk-distraction-machinehttps://www.theinformation.com/articles/dont-fall-for-the-musk-distraction-machine>.

42. Callahan, Patricia; Bandler, James; Elliot, Justin; Burke, Doris & Ernsthausen, Jeff, 'The Great Inheritors'.

43. Nicks, Denver, 'Unsealed Clinton docs shed light on "vast right-wing conspiracy"', *Time*, 18 April 2014, <https://time.com/68537/unsealed-clinton-docs-shed-light-on-vast-right-wing-conspiracy/>.

44. Schwartz, Jason, 'The Weekly Standard, conservative outlet that criticized Trump, to shut down', *Politico*, 14 December 2018, <https://www.politico.com/story/2018/12/14/the-weekly-standard-to-shut-down-1064753>.

45. Ibid.

46. Grieve, Pete, '40 years later, reporters remember how they bought a bar to expose corruption', *Chicago Sun Times*, 27 January 2018, <https://chicago.suntimes.com/2018/1/26/18317254/40-years-later-reporters-remember-how-they-bought-a-bar-to-expose-corruption>.

47. 'Investigative works of Anas Aremeyaw Anas', *Wikipedia*, <https://en.wikipedia.org/wiki/Investigative_works_of_Anas_Aremeyaw_Anas>, accessed November 2023.

48. Brook, Stephen, 'Subterfuge is "justifiable", says press watchdog', *The Guardian*, 18 May, 2007, <https://www.theguardian.com/media/2007/may/18/pressandpublishing.uknews1>.

49. Carson, Andrea and Muller, Denis, 'Is it ok for journalists to lie to get a story?', LaTrobe University, 13 December 2022, <https://www.latrobe.edu.au/news/articles/2022/opinion/is-it-ok-for-journalists-to-lie-to-get-a-story>.

50. Rayner, Gordon, 'No expenses spared: the inside story of the Telegraph's MPs' expenses investigation', *The Telegraph*, 24 September 2009, <https://www.telegraph.co.uk/news/newstopics/mps-expenses/6226839/No-Expenses-Spared-the-inside-story-of-the-Telegraphs-MPs-expenses-investigation.html>.

51. Kobler, John, *Henry Luce*, p.149.

52. Baron, Martin, 'We want objective judges and doctors. Why not journalists too?', *Washington Post*, 24 March, 2023, <https://www.washingtonpost.com/opinions/2023/03/24/journalism-objectivity-trump-misinformation-marty-baron/>.

53. Rosen, Jay, 'The view from nowhere: questions and answers', *PressThink*, 10 November 2010, <https://pressthink.org/2010/11/the-view-from-nowhere-questions-and-answers/>.

54. Thompson, Hunter S., *Fear and Loathing on the Campaign Trail '72*, Harper Perennial Modern Classics, 2014, p. 44.

55. Gessen, Masha, 'One year after Trump's election, revisiting "autocracy: rules for survival"', *New Yorker*, 8 November, 2017, <https://www.newyorker.com/news/our-columnists/one-year-after-trumps-election-revisiting-autocracy-rules-for-survival>.

56. Remnick, David, 'Politico's new owner on the opportunity for "nonpartisan" media', *New Yorker*, 12 December 2022, <https://www.newyorker.com/podcast/political-scene/politicos-new-owner-on-the-opportunity-for-nonpartisan-media>.

57. <https://www.axelspringer.com/en/values>, accessed September 2023.

58. Pressman, Matthew, 'Journalistic objectivity evolved the way it did for a reason', *Time*, 5 November 2018, <https://time.com/5443351/journalism-objectivity-history/>.

59. 'How objectivity in journalism became a matter of opinion', *The Economist*, 16 July 2020, <https://www.economist.com/books-and-arts/2020/07/16/how-objectivity-in-journalism-became-a-matter-of-opinion>.

60. Dana, Frank, 'The Devil and Mr. Hearst', *The Nation*, 22 June, 2000, <https://www.thenation.com/article/archive/devil-and-mr-hearst/>.

61. Black, Conrad, *A life in progress*, Key Porter Books, 1993, pp. 15–16.

62. Ibid., p. 351.

63. Shawcross, William, 'Murdoch's New Life', *Vanity Fair*, October 1999, <https://archive.vanityfair.com/article/1999/10/murdochs-new-life>.

64. Deans, Jason, 'Phone hacking: NI confirms £2m for Dowlers and £1m charity donation', *The Guardian*, 22 October 2011, <https://www.theguardian.com/media/2011/oct/21/phone-hacking-dowlers>.

65. Martin, Roger, 'Rupert Murdoch and Rebekah Brooks scandal: management by wilful ignorance', *The Daily Beast*, 21 July 2011, <https://www.thedailybeast.com/rupert-murdoch-and-rebekah-brooks-scandal-management-by-willful-ignorance>.

66. Stelzer, Irwin, *The Murdoch Method: Notes on Running a Media Empire*, Atlantic Books, 2017, p. 36.

67. Saba, Jennifer and Lauria, Peter, 'Murdoch's tough guy Carlucci under pressure', Reuters, 1 September 2011, <https://jp.reuters.com/article/newscorp-carlucci-idCNN1E77N1JN20110901/>.

68. 'Time to shine for The Australian's top talents', *The Australian*, 25 November 2021.

Give 'em What They Want

1. Tucille, Jerome, *Rupert Murdoch*, 1989, Donald I. Fine Inc., p. 29.

2. Shawcross, William, *Rupert Murdoch*, p.109.

3. Bowman, David, *The Captive Press*, Penguin, 1988, p.87.

4. Fallows, James, 'The Age of Murdoch', *The Atlantic*, September 2003, <https://www.theatlantic.com/magazine/archive/2003/09/the-age-of-murdoch/302777/>.

5. Hoopes, Roy, 'The Forty-year Run', *American Heritage*, 1992, Vol. 43, Issue 7, <https://www.americanheritage.com/forty-year-run>.

6. Goldsmith, Bonnie Z., *William Randolph Hearst: Newspaper Magnate*, 2009, p. 28.

7. Bierce, Ambrose, *Imperial Hearst*, Kessinger Publishing, 2010, p. 23.

8. 'The press: the king is dead', *Time*, 20 August 1951, <https://content.time.com/time/subscriber/article/0,33009,859284-1,00.html>.

9. Kluger, Richard, *The Paper: The Life and Death of the New York Herald Tribune*, Knopf, 1986, p. 163.

10. Basso, Hamilton, 'From the stacks: "Mr. Hearst's Apostolic creed"', *The New Republic*, 8 May 1935, <https://newrepublic.com/article/114292/william-randolph-hearsts-dangerous-patriotism-stacks>.

11. Mencken, H.L., 'The Case of Hearst', July 1928, *The American Mercury*, <https://www.unz.com/print/AmMercury-1928jul-00379>.

12. Jack, Ian, 'The great age of Britain's popular press is drawing squalidly to its close', *The Guardian*, 9 July 2011, <https://www.theguardian.com/commentisfree/2011/jul/08/ian-jack-lord-northcliffe-popular-press>.

13. Sharman, Jon, 'Wikipedia bans the Daily Mail as a source for being "unreliable"', *The Independent*, 9 Februarn, 2017, <https://www.independent.co.uk/tech/wikipedia-editors-ban-daily-mail-source-citation-unreliable-mail-online-a7570856.html>.

14. Jolly, Nathan, 'Mumbrella360: is it time to reconsider The Daily Mail?', *Mumbrella*, 19 July 2023, <https://mumbrella.com.au/mumbrella360-is-it-time-to-reconsider-the-daily-mail-794629>.

15. Kiernan, Thomas, *Citizen Murdoch*, 1986, p. 52.

16. Ibid., p. 67.

17. Addley Esther, 'The News of the World's sensational history', *The Guardian*, 7 July 2007, <https://www.theguardian.com/media/2011/jul/07/news-of-the-world-history>.

18. Chippindale, Peter and Horrie, Chris, *Stick It Up Your Punter!: The Uncut Story of the Sun Newspaper*, Pocket Books, London, 2005, p. 32.

19. Munster, George, *Rupert Murdoch*, p. 135.

20. Chippindale, Peter and Horrie, Chris, *Stick it up Your Punter*, p. 29.

21. Ibid.

22. Munster, George, *Rupert Murdoch*, p. 135.

23. Lamb, Larry, *Sunrise*, Papermac, 1989, p. 110.

24. Snoddy, Raymond, *Good, the Bad and the Unacceptable: Hard News About the British Press*, Faber & Faber, 1992, p. 123.

25. Ibid., p124.

26. Smith, Griffin Jr., 'Weirdo Paper Plagues S.A.', *Texas Monthly*, November 1976, <https://www.texasmonthly.com/arts-entertainment/weirdo-paper-plagues-s-a/>.

27. Greenslade, Roy, 'Do these people have a right to privacy?', *The Guardian*, 26 January 2004, <https://www.theguardian.com/media/2004/jan/26/mondaymediasection.privacy>.

28. 'The world according to Conrad Black', *Toronto Star*, 11 March 2007, <https://www.thestar.com/sponsored-sections/the-world-according-to-conrad-black/article_410d12b2-87c6-5151-a2fc-9f6e05540f18.html>.

29. Swanberg, W.A., *Pulitzer*, Charles Scribner's Sons, New York, 1967, p. 127.

30. Horrie, Chris and Chippindale, Peter, *Stick It Up Your Punter!*, p. 251.
31. Ibid., p. 257.
32. Elliot, Tim, 'Inside the Northern Territory News', *Sydney Morning Herald*, 30 April 2015, <https://www.smh.com.au/lifestyle/inside-the-northern-territory-news-20150120-12uig6.html>.
33. Paige, Bruce, *The Murdoch Archipelago*, Simon & Schuster, 2003, p. 135.
34. Chancellor, Alexander, 'Murdoch and Gays', *Slate Magazine*, 11 November 1998, <https://slate.com/news-and-politics/1998/11/murdoch-and-gays.html>.
35. Burden, Peter, *News of The World? Fake Sheikhs and Royal Trappings*, Eyer Books, 2009, p. 170.
36. Clark, Kevin, 'The Baronet, the call-girls and the cannabis – how a newspaper sting targeting Lord Lambton nearly brought down a Government', *Sunderland Echo*, 3 June 2019, <https://www.sunderlandecho.com/news/people/the-baronet-the-call-girls-and-the-cannabis-how-a-newspaper-sting-targeting-lord-lambton-nearly-brought-down-a-government-379585>.
37. Wolff, Michael, 'Tuesdays with Rupert', *Vanity Fair*, 2 September 2008, <https://www.vanityfair.com/news/2008/10/wolff200810>.
38. Regan, Simon, *Rupert Murdoch: A Business Biography*, Angus & Robertson, 1976, p. 30. Boyer Lectures, 'Lecture 3: The future of newspapers: moving beyond dead trees', *ABC*, 16 November 2008, <https://www.abc.net.au/listen/programs/boyerlectures/lecture-3-the-future-of-newspapers-moving-beyond/3192452>.
39. Ibid.
40. Cohen, Roger, 'The Cameron Collapse', *New York Times*, 18 July 2011, <https://www.nytimes.com/2011/07/19/opinion/19iht-edcohen19.html>.
41. Wolf, Martin, 'Media lies threaten the truth and decency on which democracy depends', 3 May 2023, *Financial Times*, <https://www.ft.com/content/85c9beac-ece2-4bbf-90b0-082b0ff55718>.

Meddling with History

1. Whyte, Kenneth, *The Uncrowned King*, Counterpoint, Berkeley, 2009, p. 413.
2. Overholser, Geneva and Jamieson, Kathleen Hall, *The Press*, Oxford University Press, p. 313.
3. 'Cuba War: The War of the Yellow Papers', *News Museum*, <https://www.newsmuseum.pt/en/na-frente/war-yellow-papers>.
4. Egan, Timothy, 'The American Century's Opening Shot', *New York Times*, 6 June 1998, <https://www.nytimes.com/1998/06/06/arts/the-american-century-s-opening-shot.html>.

5. Hearst, William Randolph Jr. and Casserly, Jack, *The Hearsts: Father and Son*, Roberts Rinehart, 1991, p. 37.
6. Nasaw, David, *The Chief*, p. 136.
7. Swanberg, W.A., *Citizen Hearst*, pp. 174–75.
8. Heren, Louis, *The Power of the Press*, Orbis, 1985, p. 70.
9. Nasaw, David, *The Chief*, p. 125.
10. Rauchway, Eric, 'How "America First" got its nationalistic edge', *The Atlantic*, 6 May 2016, <https://www.theatlantic.com/politics/archive/2016/05/william-randolph-hearst-gave-america-first-its-nationalist-edge/481497/>.
11. Nasaw, David, *The Chief*, p. 268.
12. Ibid., pp. 470–77.
13. Ibid., p. 497.
14. Sklar, Dusty, 'Koch was not alone in aiding the Nazi war machine', *Jewish Currents*, 11 February 2016, <https://jewishcurrents.org/doing-business-with-hitler>.
15. Nasaw, David, *The Chief*, p. 494.
16. Mansky, Jackie, 'This Hollywood titan foresaw the horrors of Nazi Germany', *The Smithsonian*, 17 January 2017, <https://www.smithsonianmag.com/arts-culture/this-hollywood-titan-foresaw-horrors-nazi-germany-180961828/>.
17. Swanberg, W.A., *Citizen Hearst*, p. 580.
18. Nasaw, David, *The Chief*, pp. 553–54.
19. Price, G. Ward, *I Know These Dictators*, George Harrap, London, 1938, p. 103.
20. Philpot, Robert, 'How Britain's Nazi-loving press baron made the case for Hitler', *Times of Israel*, 5 August 2018, <https://www.timesofisrael.com/how-britains-nazi-loving-press-baron-made-the-case-for-hitler/>.
21. Simpson, John, *Unreliable Sources: How the Twentieth Century Was Reported*, Macmillan, 2011, ch. 9.
22. Greenslade, Roy, 'Historian fears Daily Mail used his website to traduce Ralph Miliband', *The Guardian*, 4 October 2013, <https://www.theguardian.com/media/greenslade/2013/oct/04/viscount-rothermere-edmiliband>.
23. Rothermere, 'Hurrah for the Blackshirts!', *The Daily Mail*, 15 January 1934, <https://go.gale.com/ps/i.do?p=GDCS&u=webdemo&v=2.1&it=r&id=GALE%7CEE1865176558&asid=1707109200000~a0faeb75>.
24. Ibid.
25. Lovell, Mary, *The Churchills: In Love and War*, W.W. Norton, 2011, p. 371.
26. Taylor, S.J., *The Great Outsiders: Northcliffe, Rothermere and The Daily Mail*, Weidenfeld & Nicholson, 1996, p. 298.

27. Simpson, John, *We Chose to Speak of War and Strife*, Bloomsbury, 2016, p. 171.
28. Ibid., p. 167.
29. Taylor, S.J., *The Great Outsiders*, p. 297.
30. Ibid.
31. Ibid., p. 301.
32. Norton-Taylor, Richard, 'Months before war, Rothermere said Hitler's work was superhuman', *The Guardian*, 1 April 2005, <https://www.theguardian.com/media/2005/apr/01/pressandpublishing.secondworldwar>.
33. Collins, Laurel, 'Mail Supremacy', *New Yorker*, 26 March 2012, <https://www.newyorker.com/magazine/2012/04/02/mail-supremacy>.
34. Brinkley, Alan, *The Publisher*, pp. 249–50.
35. Ibid., p. 261.
36. Herzstein, Robert, *Henry R Luce: A Political Portrait of the Man Who Created the American Century*, Scribner, 1994, p. 15.
37. 'The case against American isolationism during the second world war', *The Guardian*, 7 September 2009, <https://www.theguardian.com/world/2009/sep/07/american-isolationism-henry-luce-ww2>.
38. Kobler, John, *Luce*, p. 8.
39. Chisolm, Anne and Davie Michael, *Lord Beaverbrook: A Life*, Knopf, 1993, pp. 335–342.
40. Wintour, Charles, *The Rise and Fall of Fleet Street*, Hutchinson, 1989, p. 94.
41. Zwar, Desmond, *In Search of Keith Murdoch*, Macmillan, Australia, 1980, p. 22.
42. Murdoch, Keith Arthur, 'Gallipoli letter from Keith Arthur Murdoch to Andrew Fisher 1915', (1885–1952), *National Library of Australia* <https://www.nla.gov.au/sites/default/files/gallipoli_letter_0.pdf>.
43. Roberts, Tom, D.C., *Before Rupert: Keith Murdoch and the birth of a dynasty*, University of Queensland Press, 2015, p. 47.
44. Zwar, Desmond, *In Search of Keith Murdoch*, Macmillan, 1980, p. 42.
45. Carlyon, Les, *The Great War*, Macmillan, 2014, p. 526.
46. Wollaston, Sam, 'Gallipoli review: tragedy, scandal and the rise and fall of empires', *The Guardian*, 27 April 2015, <https://www.theguardian.com/tv-and-radio/2015/apr/27/gallipoli-review-tragedy-scandal-rise-fall-empires>.
47. Zwar, Desmond, *In Search of Keith Murdoch*.
48. Media, 'A new Britain, a new kind of newspaper', *The Guardian*, 25 February 2002, <https://www.theguardian.com/media/2002/feb/25/pressandpublishing.falklands>.
49. Ibid.

50. Simpson, John, *Unreliable Sources: How the Twentieth Century Was Reported*, Macmillan, 2011, ch. 18.

51. Manne, Robert, 'Murdoch's War', *The Monthly*, July 2005, <https://www.themonthly.com.au/node/62/wrap-xhr#mtr>.

52. Deans, Jason, 'Murdoch: US must ditch 'inferiority complex'', *The Guardian*, 3 April 2003, <https://www.theguardian.com/media/2003/apr/03/Iraqandthemedia.rupertmurdoch>. The italics in this quote and those on page 196 are mine.

53. Tiffen, Rodney, 'Can we talk about the weather, Mr Murdoch?', *Sydney Morning Herald*, 30 October 2013, <https://www.smh.com.au/opinion/can-we-talk-about-the-weather-mr-murdoch-20131030-2wgaw.html>.

54. Murdoch, Rupert, 'Immigration reform can't wait', *Wall Street Journal*, 18 June 2014, <https://www.wsj.com/articles/rupert-murdoch-immigration-reform-cant-wait-1403134311>.

55. Murdoch, Rupert, 'Rupert Murdoch's inaugural Margaret Thatcher lecture', *The Guardian*, 22 October 2010, <https://www.theguardian.com/media/2010/oct/21/rupert-murdoch-inaugural-margaret-thatcher-lecture>.

56. Page, Bruce, *The Murdoch Archipelago*, Pocket, 2004, p. 307.

57. Media Matters Staff, 'Tucker Carlson tells idiotic lie that "no one really believes in global warming"', *Media Matters for America*, 20 July 2022, <https://www.mediamatters.org/fox-news/tucker-carlson-tells-idiotic-lie-no-one-really-believes-global-warming>.

58. Fisher, Alison, 'Fox's "War on Earth Day"', *Media Matters for America*, 23 April 2021, <https://www.mediamatters.org/fox-news/foxs-war-earth-day>.

59. D'Angelo, Chris, 'A Fox News climate disinformation channel is the last thing we need', *Huffington Post*, 8 July 2021, <https://www.huffpost.com/entry/fox-news-weather-channel-climate-disinformation_n_60e71972e4b0787790104425>.

60. Kenny Chris, 'Bushfires blind alarmists in media to climate reality', *The Australian*, 24 November, 2019.

61. Ellison, Sarah, 'Murdoch family discord plays out publicly', *Washington Post*, 15 January 2020, <https://www.washingtonpost.com/lifestyle/style/murdoch-family-discord-plays-out-publicly/2020/01/15/ab4d177e-37c1-11ea-9541-9107303481a4_story.html>.

62. Cartwright, Lachlan, 'James Murdoch Slams Fox News and News Corp over climate change denial', *The Daily Beast*, 14 January 2020, <https://www.thedailybeast.com/james-murdoch-slams-fox-news-and-news-corp-over-climate-change-denial>.

63. Mason, Max, 'News Corp employee lashes bushfire coverage in reply-all email', *Financial Review*, 10 January 2020, <https://www.afr.com/

companies/media-and-marketing/news-corp-employee-lashes-company-s-bushfire-coverage-20200110-p53qfh>.

'We Go Out and Destroy Other People's Lives'

1. Greenslade, Roy, 'Do these people have a right to privacy?', *The Guardian*, 26 January 2004, <https://www.theguardian.com/media/2004/jan/26/mondaymediasection.privacy#:~:text=They%20have%20wealth%20and%20fame,positive%2C%20upbeat%2C%20happy%20stories.>.

2. Frankel, Glenn, 'Exclusive! Brash paper exposed!', *The Washington Post*, 29 October 1989, <https://www.washingtonpost.com/archive/lifestyle/1989/10/29/exclusive-brash-paper-exposed/d8a26c38-15c2-4cc2-b3f5-fa7b7dee95f7/>.

3. Mediawatch, ABC TV (Australia), 23 Mar 2009, <https://www.abc.net.au/mediawatch/episodes/tabloid-trading/9975016>.

4. Ibid.

5. Toynbee, Polly, 'If the Sun on Sunday soars Rupert Murdoch will also rise again', *The Guardian*, 24 February 2012, <https://www.theguardian.com/commentisfree/2012/feb/23/sun-on-sunday-rupert-murdoch>.

6. Casciani, Dominic, 'Sienna Miller says Sun illegally sought medical records of pregnancy', BBC News, 9 December 2021, <https://www.bbc.com/news/uk-59595458>.

7. Khan, Jemima, 'Sienna Miller: hacking's heroine', *The Independent*, 23 September 2011, <https://www.independent.co.uk/news/people/profiles/sienna-miller-hacking-s-heroine-2359415.html>.

8. Watson, Tom and Hickman, Martin, *Dial M for Murdoch*, Allen Lane, London, 2012, p. 306.

9. Greene, Richard Allen, 'Murdoch pays Charlotte Church nearly $1 million over hacking', CNN, 27 February 2012, <https://edition.cnn.com/2012/02/27/world/europe/uk-phone-hacking-church/index.html>.

10. Jones, Steve, '"I have watched him be destroyed" wife of Geoffrey Rush tells defamation trial', *Mumbrella*, 24 October 2018, <https://mumbrella.com.au/i-have-watched-him-be-destroyed-wife-of-geoffrey-rush-tells-defamation-trial-548244>.

11. McKinnell, Jamie, 'Geoffrey Rush wins defamation case against Nationwide News, publisher of The Daily Telegraph', ABC, 11 April 2019, <https://www.abc.net.au/news/2019-04-11/geoffrey-rush-wins-defamation-case-against-nationwide-news/10991756>.

12. Shawcross, William, *Rupert Murdoch*, p. 416.

13. AP, 'Princes caught off guard and an editor is sacked', *New York Times*, 21 November 1989, <https://www.nytimes.com/1989/11/21/world/princes-caught-off-guard-and-an-editor-is-sacked.html>.

14. Hagler, Tom, 'How News Corp sacrificed journalists' sources to save the company', *Press Gazette*, 19 October 2022, <https://pressgazette.co.uk/news/how-news-corp-sacrificed-journalists-sources-to-save-the-company/>.

15. Solove, Daniel J and Schwartz, Paul M, *Privacy and the Media*, 4th ed., Aspen Publishers, 2020, p. 107.

16. Editors' Code of Practice, *Independent Press Standards Organisation*, 2021, <https://www.ipso.co.uk/editors-code-of-practice/#:~:text=i)%20Everyone%20is%20entitled%20to,individual's%20private%20life%20without%20consent>, accessed 30 November 2023.

17. Dahn, Julia, 'What I learned about journalism at the *New York Post*', *Columbia Journalism Review*, 31 July 2017, <https://www.cjr.org/first_person/new-york-post-reporting-lessons.php>.

18. Watkins, Emily & Khalik, Jennine, 'The Perpetrators: how the media "hunts down" their "talent"', *Crikey*, 30 July 2019, <https://www.crikey.com.au/2019/07/30/media-roadkill-the-perpetrators/>.

19. Bernstein, Carl, 'Murdoch's Watergate?', *Newsweek*, 9 July 2011, <https://www.carlbernstein.com/murdochs-watergate>.

20. Watkins, Emily and Khalik, Jennine, 'The Perpetrators'.

21. Davoudi, Salamander and Warrell, Helen, 'Fresh arrest in phone hacking probe', *Financial Times*, 11 August 2011, <https://www.ft.com/content/ecbeb63c-c357-11e0-9109-00144feabdc0>.

22. Van Natta Jr., Don; Becker, Jo and Bowley, Graham, 'Tabloid hack attack on Royals, and beyond', *New York Times Magazine*, 1 September 2010, <https://www.nytimes.com/2010/09/05/magazine/05hacking-t.html>.

23. Davies, Nick, 'Trail of hacking and deceit under nose of Tory PR chief', *The Guardian*, 9 July 2009, <https://www.theguardian.com/media/2009/jul/08/murdoch-newspapers-phone-hacking>.

24. Oliver, Laura, 'PCC finds no evidence of further phone hacking at News Group', *Journalism,co.uk*, 9 November 2009, <https://www.journalism.co.uk/news/pcc-finds-no-evidence-of-further-phone-hacking-at-news-group/s2/a536419/>.

25. Fenton, Ben, 'Latest papers put pressure on James Murdoch', *Financial Times*, 2 November 2011, <https://www.ft.com/content/ac76927e-04a3-11e1-b309-00144feabdc0>.

26. Frost, Chris, *Journalism, Ethics and Regulation*, 3rd ed., Routledge, Taylor and Francis, London, p.247.

27. Davies, Nick & Hill Amelia, 'Missing Milly Dowler's voicemail was hacked by News of the World', *The Guardian*, 5 July 2011, <https://www.theguardian.com/uk/2011/jul/04/milly-dowler-voicemail-hacked-news-of-world>.

28. Ellison, Sarah, 'Murdoch and the vicious circle'
29. Ibid.
30. Leveson, Lord Justice, 'Leveson Inquiry – Report into the culture, practices and ethics of the press', Department for Culture, Media and Sport, 29 November 2012, <https://www.gov.uk/government/publications/leveson-inquiry-report-into-the-culture-practices-and-ethics-of-the-press>.
31. Nick Davies, *Hack Attack*, p. 154.
32. Van Natta Jr., Don: Becker, Jo and Bowley, Graham, 'Tabloid hack attack on Royals, and beyond'.
33. Sabbagh, Dan and MacAskill, Ewen, '"I was nothing more than a common thief": master of Fleet Street's dark arts reveals trade secrets', *The Guardian*, 7 March 2018, <https://www.theguardian.com/media/2018/mar/07/i-was-nothing-more-than-a-common-thief-master-of-fleet-streets-dark-arts-reveals-trade-secrets>.
34. Waterson, Jim, 'News of the World: 10 years since phone-hacking scandal brought down tabloid'.
35. Davies, Nick, *Hack Attack*, p. 135.
36. Allen, Gavin and Allen, Vanessa, '"Fine papers for lying to the PCC", former Sun editor Kelvin MacKenzie tells Leveson Inquiry', *Daily Mail*, 10 January 2012, <https://www.dailymail.co.uk/news/article-2084176/Leveson-Inquiry-Sun-editor-Kelvin-MacKenzie-says-fine-papers-lying-PCC.html>.
37. Thomas, Daniel, 'Rupert Murdoch's UK empire hit by a further £51m in costs over phone hacking', *Financial Times*, 10 April 2024, <https://www.ft.com/content/8026315c-6eb1-41a9-8cec-b0294a85ea7a>.
38. Newscorp Annual Report 2023.
39. Rayner, Gordon, 'Leveson: Murdoch hints that hacking crisis could spread to US', *The Telegraph*, 25 April 2012, <https://www.telegraph.co.uk/news/uknews/leveson-inquiry/9225890/Leveson-Murdoch-hints-that-hacking-crisis-could-spread-to-US.html>.
40. Epstein, Reid J., 'Murdoch: News Corp only made "minor mistake"', *Politico*, 14 July 2011, <https://www.politico.com/story/2011/07/murdoch-news-corp-only-made-minor-mistake-059031>.
41. 'Transcript of meeting with Sun staff: Rupert Murdoch', 3 July 2013, <https://genius.com/Rupert-murdoch-transcript-of-meeting-with-sun-staff-july-3-2013-annotated>.
42. Ibid.
43. Lamont, Tom, 'Prince Harry vs the press', *Prospect*, 9 May 2023, <https://www.prospectmagazine.co.uk/ideas/media/phone-hacking/61255/prince-harry-vs-the-press>.
44. Quinn, Ben & Waterson, Jim, '"Grotesque and sadistic": Prince Harry's key phone-hacking claims', *The Guardian*, 26 April 2023, <https://

www.theguardian.com/uk-news/2023/apr/25/prince-harry-key-phone-hacking-claims-charles-queen-murdoch>.

Fox News

1. Kurtz, Howard, 'Fox News chief Roger Ailes blasts National Public Radio brass as "Nazis"', *Daily Beast*, 14 July 2017, <https://www.thedailybeast.com/fox-news-chief-roger-ailes-blasts-national-public-radio-brass-as-nazis>.
2. Ibid.
3. Arendt, Hannah, *The Origins of Totalitarianism*, Harcourt, Brace, Jovanovich, 1994, p. 80.
4. Byers, Dylan, 'Fox News will be "loyal opposition" to Biden, Fox CEO says', NBC News, 5 March 2021, <https://www.nbcnews.com/media/fox-news-will-loyal-opposition-biden-fox-ceo-says-rcna355>.
5. Peters, Charles, *We Do Our Part: Toward a Fairer and More Equal America*, Random House, New York, 2017, p. 113.
6. Frum, David, 'Republicans originally thought that Fox worked for us, and now we are discovering we work for Fox', *Media Matters*, 23 March 2010, <https://www.mediamatters.org/abc/frum-republicans-originally-thought-fox-worked-us-and-now-we-are-discovering-we-work-fox>.
7. Chozick, Amy, 'Rupert Murdoch and President Trump'.
8. Meyer, Jane, 'The Making of the Fox News White House', *New Yorker*, 4 March 2019, <https://www.newyorker.com/magazine/2019/03/11/the-making-of-the-fox-news-white-house>.
9. Gertz, Matt, 'Two years of Trump's Fox live-tweeting obsession, by the numbers', *Media Matters*, 9 October 2020, <https://www.mediamatters.org/donald-trump/study-two-years-trumps-live-tweeting-obsession-numbers>.
10. Goggin, Benjamin, 'White House communications chief Bill Shine will reportedly receive $7 million from Fox while working for Trump', *Business Insider*, 25 November 2018, <https://www.businessinsider.com/bill-shine-to-receive-7-million-from-fox-while-working-in-white-house-2018-11>.
11. Mayer, Jane, 'The Making of the Fox News White House', *New Yorker*, 4 March 2019, <https://www.newyorker.com/magazine/2019/03/11/the-making-of-the-fox-news-white-house>.
12. Ibid.
13. 'Rupert Murdoch prepares to hand over his media empire', *The Economist*, 13 March 2021, <https://www.economist.com/business/2021/03/13/rupert-murdoch-prepares-to-hand-over-his-media-empire>.
14. French, David, 'Why Fox News lied to the viewers it 'respects", *New York Times*, 26 February 2023, <https://www.nytimes.com/2023/02/26/opinion/fox-news-lies-dominion.html>.

15. Thompson, Stuart A., 'How Russian media uses Fox News to make its case', *New York Times*, 15 April 2022, <https://www.nytimes.com/2022/04/15/technology/russia-media-fox-news.html>.

16. Sargent, Greg, 'Tucker Carlson's rage at Zelensky caps a year of getting things wrong', *Washington Post*, 23 December 2022, <https://www.washingtonpost.com/opinions/2022/12/23/tucker-carlson-zelensky-speech-congress-2022-elections/>.

17. Levine, Sam, 'Fox News to defend its on-air lies as blockbuster Dominion trial to kick off', *The Guardian*, 17 April 2023, <https://www.theguardian.com/us-news/2023/apr/16/fox-news-lawsuit-dominion-trial-rupert-murdoch>.

18. Levenson, Eric & Cohen, Marshall, 'Here are the 20 specific Fox broadcasts and tweets Dominion says were defamatory', CNN, 17 April 2023, <https://edition.cnn.com/2023/04/17/media/dominion-fox-news-allegations/index.html>.

19. Ibid.

20. Ibid.

21. Cohen, Marshall & Darcy, Oliver, 'Fox News settles with Dominion at the last second, pays more than $787 million to avert defamation trial over its 2020 election lies', CNN, 19 April 2023, <https://edition.cnn.com/2023/04/18/media/fox-dominion-settlement/index.html>.

22. Gerstein, Josh & Cheney, Kyle, 'Judge sends Dominion lawsuit against Fox News to trial', *Politico*, 31 March, 2023, <https://www.politico.com/news/2023/03/31/dominion-lawsuit-fox-trial-00090034>.

23. Smith, David, 'Murdoch feared Fox News hosts went "too far" on Trump election lie, files show', *The Guardian*, 9 March 2023, <https://www.theguardian.com/media/2023/mar/08/rupert-murdoch-fox-news-hosts-2020-voter-fraud-claims-dominion-voting-systems-court-filing>.

24. Blake, Aaron, 'Fox News-Dominion lawsuit: a timeline of major revelations', *Washington Post*, 19 April 2023, <https://www.washingtonpost.com/politics/2023/03/14/timeline-all-major-events-fox-news-dominion-case/>.

25. Darcy, Oliver, 'Fair and Balanced? Murdoch's private messages show Fox News was instructed to help Republicans', CNN, 2 March 2023, <https://edition.cnn.com/2023/03/02/media/rupert-murdoch-fox-news-reliable-sources/index.html>.

26. Kleefeld, Eric, 'Here are the Fox News executives Rupert Murdoch needs to fire, according to and starting with Rupert Murdoch', *Media Matters*, 11 August 2023, <https://www.mediamatters.org/2020-election-lawsuits/here-are-fox-news-executives-rupert-murdoch-needs-fire-according-and>.

27. Porter, Tom, 'Rupert Murdoch's son Lachlan ordered Fox News host to rein in "smug and obnoxious" anti-Trump comments about the 2020 election, court docs show', *Business Insider*, 1 March 2023, <https://www.businessinsider.com/lachlan-murdoch-son-rupert-fox-news-host-trump-criticism-lawsuit-2023-2>.

28. Klein, Charlotte, '"Our viewers ... believe it": what Fox News execs and stars were really thinking while the network boosted Donald Trump's election lies', 17 February 2023, <https://www.vanityfair.com/news/2023/02/fox-news-dominion-lawsuit>.

29. Narea, Nicole, 'Sean Hannity's damning deposition in the Fox News defamation lawsuit explained', *Vox*, 22 December 2022, <https://www.vox.com/policy-and-politics/2022/12/22/23523385/sean-hannity-fox-news-defamation-dominion-lawsuit>.

30. Wolff, Michael, *Landslide: The Final Days of the Trump Presidency*, The Bridge Street Press, 2021, pp. 56–57.

31. Ford, Matt, 'The Fox News text messages prove the hosts all know they're craven liars', *The New Republic*, 18 February 2023, <https://newrepublic.com/article/170666/fox-news-carlson-hannity-dominion>.

32. Ibid.

33. Stelter, Brian, 'I never truly understood Fox News until now', *The Atlantic*, 17 February 2023, <https://www.theatlantic.com/ideas/archive/2023/02/fox-news-dominion-voting-lawsuit-2020-election-conspiracy/673111/>.

34. Rutenberg, Jim, 'How Fox chased its audience down the rabbit hole', *New York Times Magazine*, 6 April 2023, <https://www.nytimes.com/2023/04/06/magazine/fox-dominion-jan-6.html>.

35. Windolf, Jim & Koblin, John, 'Fox News hosts sent texts to Meadows urging Trump to act as Jan. 6 attack unfolded', *New York Times*, 13 December 2021, <https://www.nytimes.com/2021/12/13/business/media/fox-news-trump-jan-6-meadows.html>.

36. Serwer, Adam, 'The Fox lawsuit was never going to save America,' *The Atlantic*, 19 April 2023, <https://www.theatlantic.com/ideas/archive/2023/04/dominion-lawsuit-smartmatic-fox-news-misinformation/673767/>.

37. Garber, Megan, 'Do you speak Fox? How Donald Trump's favorite news source became a language', *The Atlantic*, 16 September 2020, <https://www.theatlantic.com/culture/archive/2020/09/fox-news-trump-language-stelter-hoax/616309/>.

38. Zengerle, Jason, 'The rise of the Tucker Carlson politician', *New York Times Magazine*, 22 March 2022, <https://www.nytimes.com/2022/03/22/magazine/tucker-carlson-politician.html>.

39. Bruni, Frank, 'The marketing of a massacre', *New York Times*, 19 October 2023, <https://www.nytimes.com/2023/10/19/opinion/israel-hamas-attacks-palestinians.html>.

40. Dickinson, Tim, 'How Roger Ailes built the Fox News fear factory', *Rolling Stone*, 25 May 2011, <https://www.rollingstone.com/politics/politics-news/how-roger-ailes-built-the-fox-news-fear-factory-244652/>.

41. Grove, Lloyd, 'The Reliable Source', *Washington Post*, 19 November 2002, <https://www.washingtonpost.com/archive/lifestyle/2002/11/19/the-reliable-source/78c9570b-e972-47b8-a825-60d2c306499c/>.

42. Farhi, Paul, 'How chyrons took on a life of their own', *Washington Post*, 31 July 2018, <https://www.washingtonpost.com/graphics/2018/lifestyle/style/how-cable-news-chyrons-have-adapted-to-the-trump-era/>.

43. Mast, Nina, 'Sean Hannity's history of race-baiting and promoting Trump's Attacks on minorities', *Media Matters*, 20 September 2016, <https://www.mediamatters.org/sean-hannity/sean-hannitys-history-race-baiting-and-promoting-trumps-attacks-minorities>.

44. Heim, Joe, 'Recounting a day of rage, hate, violence and death', *Washington Post*, 14 August 14, 2017, <https://www.washingtonpost.com/graphics/2017/local/charlottesville-timeline/>.

45. Horton, Alex, 'Tucker Carlson suggested immigrants make the U.S. "dirtier"–and it cost Fox News an advertiser', *Washington Post*, 15 December 2018, <https://www.washingtonpost.com/business/2018/12/15/tucker-carlson-suggested-immigrants-make-us-dirtier-it-cost-fox-news-an-advertiser/>. Mastrangelo, Dominick, 'Critics blast Tucker Carlson's immigration remarks amid border surge', *The Hill*, 23 September 2021, <https://thehill.com/homenews/media/573690-critics-blast-tucker-carlson-over-immigration-remarks/>.

46. Confessore, Nicholas, 'How Tucker Carlson stoked white fear to conquer cable', *New York Times*, 30 April 2022, <https://www.nytimes.com/2022/04/30/us/tucker-carlson-gop-republican-party.html#:~:text=Carlson%20warns%20his%20viewers%20that,label%20them%20racist%2C%20if%20they>.

47. Confessore, Nicholas, 'Schumer calls on Murdoch and Fox News executives to stop amplifying replacement theory', *New York Times*, 17 May 2022, <https://www.nytimes.com/2022/05/17/nyregion/schumer-fox-news-replacement-theory-murdoch.html>.

48. Darcy, Oliver, 'Fox has no problem with Tucker Carlson's "replacement theory" remarks, says Lachlan Murdoch', CNN, 12 April 2021, <https://edition.cnn.com/2021/04/12/media/murdoch-response-adl-tucker-carlson/index.html>.

49. Garber, Megan, 'Do you speak Fox?'

50. Kilander, Gustaf, 'Tucker Carlson likens vaccine mandates to Nazi medical experiments', *Independent*, 22 January 2022, <https://www.independent.co.uk/news/world/americas/tucker-carlson-nazi-experiments-vaccine-b1998651.html>.

51. Waldman, Paul, 'Right-wing anti-vaccine hysteria is increasing. We'll all pay the price', *Washington Post*, 8 July 2021, <https://www.washingtonpost.com/opinions/2021/07/08/right-wing-anti-vaccine-hysteria-is-increasing-well-all-pay-price/>.

52. Porter, Tom, 'Tucker Carlson contradicted his Fox colleagues, telling viewers to ignore "medical advice on television" after hosts promoted COVID-19 vaccines', *Business Insider*, 20 July 2021, <https://www.businessinsider.com/tucker-carlson-continues-to-question-vaccine-break-with-other-hosts-2021-7#>.

53. Shephard, Alex, 'Fox News is killing its viewers again', *New Republic*, 13 July 2021, <https://newrepublic.com/article/162971/fox-news-vaccine-hesitancy-tucker-carlson-ingraham>.

54. Amore, Samson, 'Fox Corp boss Lachlan Murdoch says Tucker Carlson's vaccine misinformation is "brave"', *The Wrap*, 19 May 2021, <https://www.thewrap.com/fox-corp-boss-lachlan-murdoch-says-tucker-carlsons-vaccine-misinformation-is-brave/>.

55. Media Matters staff, 'Conservative former Australian prime minister: Murdoch news outlets are "contributing to death and disease"', *Media Matters*, 23 July 2021, <https://www.mediamatters.org/coronavirus-covid-19/conservative-former-australian-prime-minister-murdoch-news-outlets-are>.

56. Ingraham, Duffy and Carlson quoted in Fisher, Allison, 'In 2021, Fox News is still spreading dangerous climate denial', *Media* Matters, 12 May 2021,<https://www.mediamatters.org/fox-news/2021-fox-news-still-spreading-dangerous-climate-denial>. Gutfeld quoted in 'Fox News host claims climate change "improves people's lives"', *Media Matters*, 12 April 2023, <https://www.mediamatters.org/greg-gutfeld/fox-news-host-claims-climate-change-improves-peoples-lives>.

57. Cable News Fact Sheet, *Pew Research Center*, 14 September 2023, <https://www.pewresearch.org/journalism/fact-sheet/cable-news/>.

58. Clark, Jeffrey, 'Washington Post set to lose "$100 million in 2023" one decade after Jeff Bezos bought the paper: Report', *Fox News*, 22 July 2023, <https://www.foxnews.com/media/washington-post-lose-100-million-2023-one-decade-after-jeff-bezos-bought-paper-report>.

59. Hiltzik, Michael, 'Hate Fox News? Too bad – you still have to pay for it', *Los Angeles Times*, 17 April 2023, <https://www.latimes.com/

business/story/2023-04-17/hate-fox-news-too-bad-you-still-have-to-pay-for-it>.

60. Tim Dickinson, 'How Roger Ailes Built the Fox News Fear Factory'.

61. Redden, Molly, 'Fox settles with Gretchen Carlson over Roger Ailes sexual harassment claims', *The Guardian*, 7 September 2016, <https://www.theguardian.com/media/2016/sep/06/fox-news-gretchen-carlson-settlement-roger-ailes#>.

62. 'Former Fox News booker says she was sexually harassed and "psychologically tortured" by Roger Ailes for more than 20 years', *New York Magazine*, 29 July 2016, <https://nymag.com/intelligencer/2016/07/fmr-fox-booker-harassed-by-ailes-for-20-years.html>.

63. Steel, Emily and Schmidt, Michael S., 'Bill O'Reilly settled new harassment claim, then Fox renewed his contract', *New York Times*, 21 October 2017, <https://www.nytimes.com/2017/10/21/business/media/bill-oreilly-sexual-harassment.html>.

64. Darcy, Oliver, 'Fox News paid Kimberly Guilfoyle's former assistant $4 million after sexual harassment accusations, New Yorker reports', CNN, 1 October 2020, <https://edition.cnn.com/2020/10/01/media/kimberly-guilfoyle-fox-allegations/index.html>.

65. Fearnow, Benjamin, 'O'Reilly harassment accuser Andrea Mackris Breaks NDA: "Bill wasn't a victim"', *Newsweek*, 13 July 2021, <https://www.newsweek.com/oreilly-harassment-accuser-andrea-mackris-breaks-nda-bill-wasnt-victim-1609359>.

66. Steel, Emily, 'Fox is said to settle with former contributor over sexual assault claims', *New York Times*, 8 March 2017, <https://www.nytimes.com/2017/03/08/business/fox-news-roger-ailes-sexual-assault-settlement.html?_r=3&mtrref=undefined>.

67. Reuters, 'Bill O'Reilly sexual harassment suit settled by Fox News, report says', *The Guardian*, 11 January 2017, <https://www.theguardian.com/media/2017/jan/10/bill-oreilly-sexual-harassment-juliet-huddy-fox-news>.

68. Steel, Emily and Schmidt, Michael, S., 'Bill O'Reilly Thrives at Fox News, Even as Harassment Settlements Add Up', *The New York Times*, 1 April 2017, <https://www.nytimes.com/2017/04/01/business/media/bill-oreilly-sexual-harassment-fox-news.html?smid=nytcore-ios-share&referringSource=articleShare>.

69. Weprin, Alex, 'Fox News fined $1M by New York City Human Rights Commission', *Hollywood Reporter*, 29 June 2021, <https://www.hollywoodreporter.com/business/business-news/fox-news-fine-harassment-human-rights-1234975396/>.

70. Robertson, Katie, 'Fox News agrees to pay $12 million to settle hostile workplace suit', *New York Times*, 30 June 2023, <https://www.

nytimes.com/2023/06/30/business/media/abby-grossberg-fox-news-settlement.html>.

71. Ellison, Sarah, 'Fox News paid $15 million to former host who filed pay disparity claim', *Washington Post*, 19 June 2022, <https://www.washingtonpost.com/media/2022/06/19/fox-news-melissa-francis-gender-pay-gap-settlement/>.

72. Bond, Shannon, '$90 million in settlement of "derivative" shareholder claims against Fox officers and directors, including Rupert Murdoch, over the sexual harassment scandals that cost the jobs of Ailes and O'Reilly', *Financial Times*, 21 November 2017, <https://www.ft.com/content/09770cd0-ce63-11e7-b781-794ce08b24dc>.

73. Farhi, Paul, 'Fox News commentator exits with a searing attack on Fox News', *Washington Post*, 20 March 2018, <https://www.washingtonpost.com/lifestyle/style/fox-news-commentator-exits-with-a-searing-attack-on-fox-news/2018/03/20/fc876fc4-2c81-11e8-8ad6-fbc50284fce8_story.html>.

74. Goldberg, Jonah, 'Donald Trump's megaphone', *The Dispatch*, 16 December 2021, <https://thedispatch.com/newsletter/gfile/donald-trumps-megaphone/>.

The Ends Justify the Means

1. Cohen Roger, 'Rupert Murdoch's biggest gamble', *New York Times*, 21 October 1990, <https://www.nytimes.com/1990/10/21/magazine/rupert-murdoch-s-biggest-gamble.html>.

2. Carr, David, 'News Corp paid out $655m for corporate wrongs', *Sydney Morning Herald*, 20 July 2011, <https://www.smh.com.au/national/news-corp-paid-out-655m-for-corporate-wrongs-20110719-1hn87.html>.

3. Sweeney, Mark, 'News Corporation reaches $139m settlement with shareholders', *The Guardian*, 23 April 2013, <https://www.theguardian.com/media/2013/apr/22/news-corporation-settlement-shareholders>.

4. Fallows, James, 'The Age of Murdoch, *The Atlantic*, September 2003, <https://www.theatlantic.com/magazine/archive/2003/09/the-age-of-murdoch/302777/>.

5. Wintour, Charles, *The Rise and Fall of Fleet Street*, Hutchinson, 1989, p.87.

6. Chenoweth, Neil, *Virtual Murdoch: Reality Wars on the Information Highway*, Vintage, 2002, p.290.

7. Fari, Paul. 'Murdoch empire finds business not so taxing', *Washington Post*, 6 December 1997, <https://www.washingtonpost.com/archive/politics/1997/12/07/murdoch-empire-finds-business-not-so-taxing/752dde25-7634-4550-acdb-fa7af20c1544/>.

8. Chenoweth, Neil, *Virtual Murdoch*, p.289.

9. Chenoweth, Neil, 'Rupert Murdoch's News Corp is ATO's top tax risk', *Australian Financial Review*, 11 May 2015, <https://www.afr.com/policy/tax-and-super/rupert-murdochs-news-corp-is-atos-top-tax-risk-20150510-ggy6cf>.

10. Keane, Bernard, 'Tax dodging News Corp continues to rip Australia off—and is subsidised by taxpayers to do so', *Crikey*, 11 December 2020, <https://www.crikey.com.au/2020/12/11/news-corp-tax-dodging/>.

11. Chenoweth, Neil, 'News Corp's $882m blew the budget', *Australian Financial Review*, 17 February 2014, <https://www.afr.com/companies/media-and-marketing/news-corp-s-882m-blew-the-budget-20140217-ixs2c>.

12. Felsenthal, Carol, *Citizen Newhouse*, p. 331.

13. Ibid., pp. 332–35.

14. Lundberg, Ferdinand, *Imperial Hearst*, The Modern Library, 1936, p. 325.

15. McNish, Jacquie and Sinclair, Stewart, *Wrong Way: The Fall of Conrad Black*, Overlook Press, 2004, p. 10.

16. <https://projects.iq.harvard.edu/files/futureofmedia/files/us_media_ownership_may_2021.pdf>.

17. Kohler, Alan, 'Shock! News screws punters', *The Age*, 13 August 2005.

18. Horrie, Chris and Chippindale, Peter, *Stick It Up Your Punter!*, p. 5.

19. Curtis, Bryan, 'The great NFL heist: how Fox paid for and changed football forever', *The Ringer*, 13 December 2018, <https://www.theringer.com/nfl/2018/12/13/18137938/nfl-fox-deal-rupert-murdoch-1993-john-madden-terry-bradshaw-howie-long-jimmy-johnson-cbs-nbc>.

20. Ibid.

21. Plotz, David, 'The newspaper mogul thinks like an American and writes like a Brit. No wonder he's leaving Canada', *Slate*, 31 August 2001, <https://slate.com/news-and-politics/2001/09/conrad-black.html>.

22. Pearlstein, Steven, 'Black ink: Canada's media baron is basking in his success', *Washington Post*, 30 November 1998, <https://www.washingtonpost.com/archive/lifestyle/1998/12/01/black-ink/acob5f90-5e64-4bcd-9ba5-134b3de7517b/>.

23. Hastings, Max, *Editor: An Inside Story of Newspapers*, Macmillan, 2002, p. 240

24. Ibid.

25. Maeder, Jay, 'The story of media mogul William Randolph Hearst's run for New York City mayor', *Daily News*, 14 August 2017, <https://www.nydailynews.com/2017/08/14/the-story-of-media-mogul-william-randolph-hearsts-run-for-new-york-city-mayor/>.

26. Kenneth White, *The Uncrowned King*, Counterpoint, Berkeley, 2009, p. 71.

27. Tifft, Susan and Jones, Alex, *The Trust: The Private and Powerful Family Behind the New York Times*, Little Brown, 1999, p. 71.

28. Greenslade, Roy, *Press Gang: How Newspapers Make Profits from Propaganda*, Macmillan, 2003, p. 587.

29. Teather, David, 'CNN founder repeats Hitler jibe over Fox's rise to the top', *The Guardian*, 27 January 2005, <https://www.theguardian.com/media/2005/jan/27/business.rupertmurdoch>.

30. Bennett, Alan, *Writing Home*, Faber & Faber, 2008, p. 10.

31. 'Citizen Murdoch: the making of a media magnate', *Washington Post*, 27 July 1985, <https://www.washingtonpost.com/archive/entertainment/books/1985/07/28/citizen-murdochthe-making-of-a-media-magnate/d90d025a-a876-4370-b7a1-209ec83fe423/>.

32. Prince Harry, Duke of Sussex, *Spare*, Bantam, London, 2022, p. 194.

33. Tuccille, Jerome, *Rupert Murdoch*, Donald I. Fine, New York, 1989, p. 18.

34. McNight, David, *Rupert Murdoch: An Investigation of Political Power*, Allen & Unwin, 2012, pp. 84, 101.

35. Hickman, Martin, 'News International "tried to blackmail select committee"', *The Independent*, 28 May 2012, <https://www.independent.co.uk/news/uk/crime/news-international-tried-to-blackmail-select-committee-7792687.html>.

36. Hastings, Max, *Editor*, p. 248.

37. Brendon, Piers, *The Life & Death of the Press Barons*, p. 154.

38. Neil, Andrew, *Full Disclosure*, Macmillan, 1996, p. 167.

39. Black, Conrad, *A Matter of Principle*, p. 21.

40. Ibid., p. 509.

41. Hastings, Max, *Editor*, p. 249.

42. Ellison, Sarah, *War at the Wall Street Journal*, p. 44.

43. Nasaw, David, *The Chief*, pp. 567–70.

44. Glover, Stephen, 'Media Studies, *The Spectator*, 5 January 1999, p. 28.

45. Newman, Peter. C., *Here Be Dragons*, McLelland and Stewart, 2004, p. 416.

46. Black, Conrad, *A Matter of Principle*, p. 315.

47. Bower, Tom, *Outrageous Fortune*, pp. 1–2.

48. Taylor, A.J.P., *Beaverbrook*, Hamish Hamilton, 1972, p. 617.

49. Hinton, Les, 'Life with Murdoch', *British Journalism Review*, vol. 26, no. 3, 2015, <https://journals.sagepub.com/doi/10.1177/0956474815604292>.

'I Didn't Know that Hitler Kept a Diary'

1. Kosner, Edward, *It's News to Me: The Making and Unmaking of an Editor*, Thunder's Mouth Press, 2006, pp. 220–22.

2. Harris, Robert, *The Media Trilogy*, Faber & Faber, 1994, p. 482.

3. Ibid., p. 204.

4. Ibid., p. 566.
5. Ibid., pp. 510–11.
6. Ibid., p. 518.
7. Ibid., pp. 553–54.
8. Ibid., pp. 566–67.
9. Ibid., pp. 584–85.
10. Ibid., p. 397.
11. Ibid., pp. 354–55.
12. Ibid., p. 585.
13. Giles, Frank, *Sundry Times*, John Murray, 1986, pp. 246–47.
14. Greenslade, Roy, 'Murdoch "a megalomaniac twister"', *The Guardian*, 26 July 2010, <https://www.theguardian.com/media/greenslade/2010/jul/26/rupert-murdoch-hugh-trevor-roper>.
15. Harris, Robert, *The Media Trilogy*, pp. 483–85.
16. The Letter, *Time*, 26 March 1951, <https://content.time.com/time/subscriber/article/0,33009,805950,00.html>.

The New Moguls

1. 'Media oligarchs go shopping', Reporters Without Borders, 2015, <https://rsf.org/sites/default/files/2016-rsf-report-media-oligarchs-gpo-shopping.pdf>.
2. Trippenbach, Ivanne, 'Storm brews in Eric Zemmour's far-right party after crushing defeats', *Le Monde*, 21 July 2022, <https://www.lemonde.fr/en/politics/article/2022/07/21/storm-brews-in-eric-zemmour-s-far-right-party-after-crushing-defeats_5990860_5.html>.
3. Chrisafis, Angelique, 'New Sunday paper launches in France amid spotlight on media ownership', *The Guardian*, 7 October 2023, <https://www.theguardian.com/world/2023/oct/07/tribune-dimanche-new-sunday-paper-france-spotlight-media-ownership#>.
4. Vohra, Anchal, 'India's free press just became less free', *Foreign Policy*, 22 December 2022, <https://foreignpolicy.com/2022/12/22/the-new-goliath-of-indias-media-meets-his-david/>.
5. Ibid.
6. Sweeney, John, 'The Lebedev File', JohnSweeneyRoars, 14 July 2022, <https://johnsweeney.substack.com/p/the-lebedev-file>.
7. Hyde, Marina, 'Links to the KGB? Come on, guys. Lord Lebedev just wants to be a public servant', *The Guardian*, 27 June 2023, <https://www.theguardian.com/commentisfree/2023/jun/27/kgb-lord-evgeny-lebedev-boris-johnson-politicians>.
8. Lebedev, Evgeny, 'President Putin, please stop this war', *Evening Standard*, 1 March 2022, <https://www.standard.co.uk/news/world/president-vladimir-putin-please-stop-ukraine-war-evgeny-lebedev-b985076.html>.

9. 'Striking Back, *The Statesman*, 29 July 2023, <https://www.thestates man.com/opinion/striking-back-2-1503205767.html>.

10. Warren, James, 'Is *The New York Times* vs. *The Washington Post* vs. Trump the last great newspaper war?', *Vanity Fair*, 30 July 2017, <https://www.vanityfair.com/news/2017/07/new-york-times-washington-post-donald-trump>.

11. '*The Washington Post* has a Bezos problem', 27 September 2022, <https://www.cjr.org/special_report/washington-post-jeff-bezos.php>.

12. Fallows, James, 'Marty Baron's time at the Washington Post', *Breaking the News*, 6 October 2023, <https://fallows.substack.com/p/marty-barons-time-at-the-washington>.

13. Fisher, Marc, 'Why Trump went after Bezos: two billionaires across a cultural divide', *Washington Post*, 5 April 2018, <https://www.washingtonpost.com/politics/why-trump-went-after-bezos-two-billionaires-across-a-cultural-divide/2018/04/05/22bb94c2-3763-11e8-acd5-35eac230e514_story.html>.

14. Pompeo, Joe, 'Marty Baron, lionized and lambasted at *The Washington Post*, has a Story to Tell', *Vanity Fair*, 3 October 2023, <https://www.vanityfair.com/news/2023/10/marty-baron-book-hot-seat-interview-donald-trump-jeff-bezos#>.

15. Hoskins, Peter and Nanji, Noor, 'Elon Musk says Twitter blue tick to be revamped', BBC, 31 October 2022, <https://www.bbc.com/news/business-63451979>.

16. Berlinski, Claire, 'Twitter gave us an indispensable real-time news platform. X took it away', *Politico*, 8 November 2023, <https://www.politico.com/news/magazine/2023/11/08/twitter-news-global-conflicts-00123806>.

17. Calia, Mike, CNBC, 16 May 2023, <https://www.cnbc.com/2023/05/16/elon-musk-defends-inflammatory-tweets-ill-say-what-i-want.html>.

18. 'Russia tells media to delete stories mentioning Ukraine "invasion"', *Newsweek*, 26 February 2022, <https://www.newsweek.com/russia-tells-media-delete-stories-mentioning-ukraine-invasion-1682973>.

19. Van Sant, Shannon, 'Russia criminalizes the spread of online news which "disrespects" the government', *NPR*, 18 March 2019, <https://www.npr.org/2019/03/18/704600310/russia-criminalizes-the-spread-of-online-news-which-disrespects-the-government>.

20. Yaffa, Joshua, 'A Russian journalist's pained love for her country', *New Yorker*, 16 October 2023, <https://www.newyorker.com/news/persons-of-interest/a-russian-journalists-pained-love-for-her-country>.

21. Politkovskaya, Anna, *Is Journalism Worth Dying For? Final Dispatches*, Melville House, 2011, p. 3.

22. Baydar, Yavuz, 'In Turkey, media bosses are undermining democracy', *New York Times*, 19 July 2013, <https://www.nytimes.com/2013/07/21/

opinion/sunday/in-turkey-media-bosses-are-undermining-democracy. html>.

23. 'Turkey: 25 journalists imprisoned in half a year', Reporters Without Borders, 16 December 2022, <https://rsf.org/en/turkey-25-journalists-imprisoned-half-year#>.

24. 'Ten years of power for Sisi: Egypt has become one of the world's biggest jailers of journalists', Reporters Without Borders, 30 June 2023, <https://rsf.org/en/ten-years-power-sisi-egypt-has-become-one-world-s-biggest-jailers-journalists>.

25. Ahmed Azam, 'Using billions in government cash, Mexico controls news media', *New York Times*, 25 December 2017, <https://www.nytimes.com/2017/12/25/world/americas/mexico-press-government-advertising.html>.

26. Kitroeff, Natalie, 'Gunmen tried to kill a famous TV anchor. Mexico's leader suggested it was staged', *New York Times*, 21 December 2022, <https://www.nytimes.com/2022/12/21/world/americas/mexico-journalist-attack-ciro-gomez-leyva.html>.

27. 'Media oligarchs go shopping', Reporters Without Borders.

28. Gupta, Surbhi, 'In a nation-by-nation rating of press freedom, the country is edging closer to the bottom of the list', *New Lines Magazine*, 24 July 2023, <https://newlinesmag.com/spotlight/indian-media-icon-ravish-kumar-warns-about-the-future-of-journalism-in-his-country/#:~:text=%E2%80%9CIn%20India%2C%20there%20are%20hundreds,will%20be%20a%20herculean%20task.>.

29. Vohra, Anchal, 'India's free press just became less free'.

30. McLaughlin, Timothy, 'A newsroom at the edge of autocracy', *The Atlantic*, 1 August 2020, <https://www.theatlantic.com/international/archive/2020/08/scmp-hong-kong-china-media/614719/>.

31. Clifford, Mark, L., 'Hong Kong authorities should not underestimate Jimmy Lai', *Nikkei Asia*, 14 December 2023, <https://asia.nikkei.com/Opinion/Hong-Kong-authorities-should-not-underestimate-Jimmy-Lai>.

32. Fan, Jiayang, 'Why Beijing shut down Hong Kong's leading pro-democracy newspaper', *New Yorker*, 30 June 2021, <https://www.newyorker.com/news/daily-comment/why-beijing-shut-down-hong-kongs-leading-pro-democracy-newspaper>.

33. <https://rsf.org/en/country/vietnam>.

34. Schlein, Lisa, 'UN agency warns of Cambodian threats to journalists', *Voice of America*, 6 August 2022, <https://www.voanews.com/a/un-agency-warns-of-cambodian-threats-to-journalists-/6689847.html>.

The Media is Broken

1. Shirky, Clay, 'Newspapers and thinking the unthinkable', *The Edge*, 16 March 2008, <https://www.edge.org/conversation/clay_shirky-newspapers-and-thinking-the-unthinkable>.

2. 'Paul Dacre', *The Guardian*, 14 July 2008, <https://www.theguardian.com/media/2008/jul/14/mediatop1002008>.

3. Bradt, George, 'Wanamaker was wrong – the vast majority of advertising is wasted', *Forbes*, 14 September 2016, <https://www.forbes.com/sites/georgebradt/2016/09/14/wanamaker-was-wrong-the-vast-majority-of-advertising-is-wasted/?sh=107f9edb483b>.

4. Sadowski, Jathan, 'Google-eye view: Eric Schmidt and Jared Cohen's "The New Digital Age"', *Los Angeles Review of Books*, 5 July 2013, <https://lareviewofbooks.org/article/google-eye-view-eric-schmidt-and-jared-cohens-the-new-digital-age/>.

5. Hagey, Keach; Kruppa, Miles and Bruell, Alexandra, 'News publishers see Google's AI search tool as a traffic-destroying nightmare', *Wall Street Journal*, 14 December 2023, <https://www.wsj.com/tech/ai/news-publishers-see-googles-ai-search-tool-as-a-traffic-destroying-nightmare-52154074>.

6. Dopfner, Mathias, 'You don't have to be a conspiracy theorist to find Google alarming', *The Guardian*, 18 April 2014, <https://www.theguardian.com/commentisfree/2014/apr/18/google-alarming-no-conspiracy-theorist>.

7. Harris, Tristan, 'How technology is hijacking your mind – from a magician and Google design ethicist', *Medium*, 19 May 2016, <https://medium.com/thrive-global/how-technology-hijacks-peoples-minds-from-a-magician-and-google-s-design-ethicist-56d62ef5edf3>.

8. Patel, Nilay, 'Harvard professor Lawrence Lessig on why AI and social media are causing a free speech crisis for the internet', *The Verge*, 25 October 2023, <https://www.theverge.com/23929233/lawrence-lessig-free-speech-first-amendment-ai-content-moderation-decoder-interview>.

9. Ibid.

10. Beyond Borders, 'Elon Musk probably more valuable than gold', *New York Times* Deal Book Summit, <https://www.youtube.com/watch?v=io8cHZ_5fbE>.

11. Harari, Yuval Noah, *21 Lessons for the 21st Century*, Vintage, Australia, 2018, p. 283.

12. Sullivan, Margaret, 'Vice is going bankrupt, BuzzFeed News is dead. What does it mean?', *The Guardian*, 16 May 2023, <https://www.theguardian.com/commentisfree/2023/may/16/vice-bankruptcy-buzzfeed-news-dead-digital-age-revenue>.

13. Smith, Ben, 'We're watching the end of a digital media age. it all started with Jezebel', *New York Times*, 3 May 2023, <https://www.nytimes.com/2023/05/03/opinion/jezebel-gawker-buzzfeed-ben-smith.html>.

14. Timberg, Scott, 'Nick Denton isn't sorry: new interview reveals more about Gawker founder's ethics', *Salon*, 22 June 2016, <https://www.salon.com/2016/06/22/nick_denton_isnt_sorry_new_interview_reveals_more_about_gawker_founders_ethics/>.

15. Sorkin, Andrew Ross, 'Peter Thiel, tech billionaire, reveals secret war with Gawker', *New York Times*, 25 May 2016, <https://www.nytimes.com/2016/05/26/business/dealbook/peter-thiel-tech-billionaire-reveals-secret-war-with-gawker.html>.

16. Nicolaou, Anna & Indap, Sujeet, 'The fall of vice: private equity's ill-fated bet on media's future', *Financial Times*, 25 May 2023, <https://www.ft.com/content/b8010767-8fe8-4ec0-aa40-676440b90f8d>.

17. Shafer, Jack, 'SEO Speedwagon', *Slate*, 7 February 2011, <https://slate.com/news-and-politics/2011/02/aol-and-huffington-post-merger-the-rapid-rise-and-sale-of-arianna-huffington-s-post.html>.

18. Cohan, William D., 'The inside story of why Arianna Huffington left the Huffington Post', *Vanity Fair*, 8 September 2016, <https://www.vanityfair.com/news/2016/09/why-arianna-huffington-left-the-huffington-post>.

19. 'Huffington Post Italy launching: Arianna Huffington speaks to La Repubblica about new site', *HuffPost*, 24 September 2012, <https://www.huffpost.com/entry/huffington-post-italia-la_n_1908934>.

20. Pappas, Gregory, 'The "ultimate homecoming" for Arianna Huffington as she launches Huffington Post Greece', *Pappaspost*, 20 November 2014, <https://pappaspost.com/ultimate-homecoming-arianna-huffington-launches-huffington-post-greece/>.

21. Cohan, William D., 'The Inside Story of Why Arianna Huffington Left the Huffington Post'.

22. Elkins, Kathleen, 'How a fight with Nike led Buzzfeed's Jonah Peretti to create a billion-dollar media empire', CNBC, 3 August 2017, <https://www.cnbc.com/2017/08/02/how-jonah-peretti-created-buzzfeed-a-billion-dollar-media-empire.html>.

23. Rice, Andrew, 'Does BuzzFeed know the Secret?', *New York Magazine*, 5 April 2013, <https://nymag.com/news/features/buzzfeed-2013-4/>.

24. Smith, Ben, *Traffic: Genius, Rivalry, and Delusion in the Billion-Dollar Race to Go Viral*, Penguin Press, 2023.

25. Warzel, Charlie, 'The internet of the 2010s ended today', *The Atlantic*, 20 April 2023, <https://www.theatlantic.com/technology/archive/2023/04/buzzfeed-news-end-political-influence-cultural-impact/673803/>.

26. Kessler, Glenn, 'The Steele dossier: a guide to the latest allegations', *Washington Post*, 17 November 2021, <https://www.washingtonpost.com/politics/2021/11/17/steele-dossier-guide-latest-allegations>.

27. Nelson, Louis, 'Trump: BuzzFeed is a "failing pile of garbage"', *Politico*, 1 November 2017, <https://www.politico.com/story/2017/01/trump-presser-slams-buzzfeed-233483>.

28. Smith, Ben, *Traffic*.

29. Ibid.

30. Frey, Hilary, 'BuzzFeed News is dead: who is really to blame?', *Slate*, 20 April 2023, <https://slate.com/business/2023/04/buzzfeed-news-demise-blame-facebook.html>.

31. Hennessy, James, 'BuzzFeed News' business model turned to dust because they were always at the whim of mercurial tech titans', *The Guardian*, 26 April 2023, <https://www.theguardian.com/commentisfree/2023/apr/26/buzzfeed-news-business-model-turned-to-dust-because-they-were-always-at-the-whim-of-mercurial-tech-titans>.

32. Davidson, Adam, 'The rise and fall of podcasting', 22 November 2023, <https://adamjdavidson.com/the-rise-and-fall-of-podcasting/#>.

33. Ingram, Mathew, 'The Facebook armageddon', *Columbia Journalism Review*, 19 February 2018, <https://www.cjr.org/special_report/facebook-media-buzzfeed.php>.

34. Carson, Nicholas, 'Well, these new Zuckerberg IMs won't help Facebook's privacy problems', *Business Insider*, 14 May 2010, <https://www.businessinsider.com/well-these-new-zuckerberg-ims-wont-help-facebooks-privacy-problems-2010-5>.

35. Hughes, Chris, 'Facebook's Mark Zuckerberg is the most powerful unelected man in America', *New York Times*, 3 September 2020, <https://www.nytimes.com/2020/09/03/opinion/facebook-zuckerberg-2020-election.html>.

36. 'You are the product', *London Review of Books*, Vol. 39, No. 16, 16 August 2017, <https://www.lrb.co.uk/the-paper/v39/n16/john-lanchester/you-are-the-product>.

37. Lepore, Jill, 'Facebook's broken vows', *New Yorker*, 26 July 2021, <https://www.newyorker.com/magazine/2021/08/02/facebooks-broken-vows#>.

38. LaFrance, Adrienne, 'The largest autocracy on earth', *The Atlantic*, 27 September 2021, <https://www.theatlantic.com/magazine/archive/2021/11/facebook-authoritarian-hostile-foreign-power/620168/>.

39. Ibid.

40. Read, Max, 'Does even Mark Zuckerberg know what Facebook is?', *Intelligencer*, October 2017, <https://nymag.com/intelligencer/2017/10/does-even-mark-zuckerberg-know-what-facebook-is.html>.

41. Seetharaman, Deepa and Glazer, Emily, 'How Mark Zuckerberg learned politics', *Wall Street Journal*, 16 October 2020, <https://www.wsj.com/articles/how-mark-zuckerberg-learned-politics-11602853200>.

42. Silverman, Craig; Timberg, Craig; Kao, Jeff and Merrill, Jeremy B., 'Facebook groups topped 10,000 daily attacks on election before Jan. 6, analysis shows', *Washington Post*, 4 January 2022, <https://www.washingtonpost.com/technology/2022/01/04/facebook-election-misinformation-capitol-riot/>.

Reimagining Journalism

1. VandeHei, Jim, 'Axios finish line: the future of media', Axios, 25 May 2023, <https://www.axios.com/2023/05/26/future-of-media>.

2. 'Mathias Döpfner: the role of AI in journalism', *Axel Springer*, 20 September 2023, <https://www.axelspringer.com/en/inside/mathias-doepfner-the-role-of-ai-in-journalism>.

3. Maher, Bron, 'News execs fear "end of our business model" from AI unless publishers "get control" of their IP', *PressGazette*, 24 May 2023, <https://pressgazette.co.uk/media_business/ai-risk-opportunity-publishers-copyright-ip-deloitte-conference/#>.

4. Cheng, Michelle, '"I do a lot less Googling": Software developers share how ChatGPT is changing work', *Quartz*, 3 January 2024, <https://qz.com/what-software-developers-using-chatgpt-can-tell-us-abou-1851116767>.

5. Mullin, Benjamin, 'Inside the news industry's uneasy negotiations with OpenAI', *New York Times*, 29 December 2023, <https://www.nytimes.com/2023/12/29/business/media/media-openai-chatgpt.html>.

6. Maher, Bron, 'News execs fear "end of our business model" from AI unless publishers "get control" of their IP'.

7. Verma Pranshu, 'The rise of AI fake news is creating a "misinformation superspreader"', *Washington Post*, 17 December 2023, <https://www.washingtonpost.com/technology/2023/12/17/ai-fake-news-misinformation/>.

8. Grynbaum, Michael and Mac, Ryan, 'The Times sues OpenAI and Microsoft over A.I. use of copyrighted work', *New York Times*, 27 December 2023, <https://www.nytimes.com/2023/12/27/business/media/new-york-times-open-ai-microsoft-lawsuit.html>.

9. 'Axel Springer makes an AI deal', *Axel Springer*, 19 December 2023, <https://www.amediaoperator.com/newsletter/axel-springer-makes-an-ai-deal/>.

10. Naprys, Ernestas, 'German publisher cuts hundreds of jobs, will rely on AI', *cybernews*, 5 July 2023, <https://cybernews.com/tech/ai-replace-jobs-bild-german-publisher/>.

11. 'The New York Times' first director of AI signals key role the technology will play in news production', 13 December 2023, <https://edition.cnn.com/2023/12/13/media/new-york-times-first-director-ai/index.html>.

12. Khalaf, Roula, 'Letter from the editor on generative AI and the FT', *Financial Times*, 27 May 2023, <https://www.ft.com/content/18337836-7c5f-42bd-a57a-24cdbd06ec51>.

13. Barber, Lionel, *The Powerful and the Damned: Private Diaries in Turbulent Times*, W.H. Allen, 2021.

14. Brian Morrisey *The Rebooting*, December 2023, <https://www.therebooting.com/>.

15. Thompson, Ben, 'Business models of the future, *Stratechery*, March 2014, <https://stratechery.com/>.

16. Shafer, Jack, 'Pierre Omidyar and the bottomless optimism of billionaire publishers', Reuters, 18 October 2013, <https://www.reuters.com/article/idUSBRE99G1CW/>.

17. Kennedy, Dan, *The Return of the Moguls: How Jeff Bezos and John Henry are Remaking Newspapers for the Twenty-First Century*, ForeEdge, 2018, p. 1.

18. Shafer, Jack, 'Pierre Omidyar and the bottomless optimism of billionaire publishers'.

19. Miller, Jonathan, 'Subsidies have defanged the French media', *The Spectator*, 8 October 2023, <https://www.spectator.co.uk/article/subsidies-have-defanged-the-french-media/>.

20. Masnick, Mike, 'Why link taxes like Canada's C-18 represent an end to an open web', *Techdirt*, 21 March 2023, <https://www.techdirt.com/2023/03/21/why-link-taxes-like-canadas-c-18-represent-an-end-to-an-open-web/>.

21. Gallup poll reported in <https://www.poynter.org/commentary/2023/american-trust-in-media-is-near-a-record-low-study-finds/>.

22. Edelman Trust Barometer, <https://www.edelman.com/sites/g/files/aatuss191/files/2023-03/2023%20Edelman%20Trust%20Barometer%20Global%20Report%20FINAL.pdf>.

23. World Values Survey, <https://pressgazette.co.uk/media-audience-and-business-data/trust-news-media-uk-egypt/>.

24. Kovach, Bill and Rosenstiel, Tom, *The Elements of Journalism: What Newspeople Should Know and the Public Should Expect*, Three Rivers Press, 2001, p. 68.

25. Sulzberger, A.G., 'Journalism's essential value', *Columbia Journalism Review*, 15 May 2023, <https://www.cjr.org/special_report/ag-sulzberger-new-york-times-journalisms-essential-value-objectivity-independence.php>.

26. Ibid.

27. Gueta, Jasmin, 'Israel's communications minister threatens Haaretz, suggests penalizing its Gaza war coverage', *Haaretz*, 23 November 2023, <https://www.haaretz.com/israel-news/2023-11-23/ty-article/israels-communications-minister-threatens-haaretz-suggests-penalizing-its-war-coverage/0000018b-fdoc-de73-a9bb-ffefb9f10000>.

28. Froomkin, Dan, '*The Washington Post* has a Bezos problem'.

29. 'A New Chapter', *The Economist*, 15 August 2015, <https://www.economist.com/leaders/2015/08/15/a-new-chapter>.

30. Szalai, Jennifer, 'The problem of misinformation in an era without trust', *New York Times*, 31 December 2023, <https://www.nytimes.com/2023/12/31/books/review/elon-musk-trust-misinformation-disinformation.html>.

31. Wilson, Cam, 'Israel-Palestine is the final nail in the coffin – social media can no longer inform us', *Crikey*, 25 October 2023, <https://www.crikey.com.au/2023/10/25/israel-palestine-social-media-misinformation-propaganda-scams/>.

32. 'James Davison Hunter interviewed by Le Figaro', *Institute for Advanced Studies in Culture*, 10 October 2022, <https://iasculture.org/news/le-figaro-interviews-james>.

33. Moore, Suzanne, 'I've seen what happens when a liberal newspaper loses the plot', *Financial Review*, 12 January 2024, <https://www.afr.com/companies/media-and-marketing/i-ve-seen-what-happens-when-a-liberal-newspaper-loses-the-plot-20240109-p5ew54>.

34. Bennet, James, 'When the New York Times lost its way', 14 December 2023, <https://www.economist.com/1843/2023/12/14/when-the-new-york-times-lost-its-way>.

35. Ibid.

36. Jefferson, Thomas, 'Newspapers and its optimum organization, 1807', *M.Y.Z.*, 3 May 2022, <https://mzuo.ca/2022/05/03/thomas-jefferson-on-newspapers-and-its-optimum-organization-1807>.

37. 'Jefferson, Thomas, 'The College of Journalism', *North American Review*, May 1904, <https://www.jstor.org/stable/pdf/25119561.pdf>.

38. Stelter, Brian, 'This infamous Steve Bannon quote is key to understanding America's crazy politics', CNN, 16 September 2021, <https://edition.cnn.com/2021/11/16/media/steve-bannon-reliable-sources/index.html>.

39. Remnick, David, 'Trump and the enemies of the people, *New Yorker*, 15 August 2018, <https://www.newyorker.com/news/daily-comment/trump-and-the-enemies-of-the-people>.

40. 'Young people are abandoning news websites – new research reveals scale of challenge to media', *The Conversation*, 14 June 2023, <https://

theconversation.com/young-people-are-abandoning-news-websites-new-research-reveals-scale-of-challenge-to-media-207659#>.

41. Collins, Eliza, 'Les Moonves: Trump's run is "damn good for CBS"', *Politico*, 29 February 2016, <https://www.politico.com/blogs/on-media/2016/02/les-moonves-trump-cbs-220001>.

Afterword

1. Brewster, Jack, 'How I built an AI-powered, self-running propaganda machine for $105', *Wall Street Journal*, 12 April 2014, <https://www.wsj.com/politics/how-i-built-an-ai-powered-self-running-propaganda-machine-for-105-e9888705>.

2. Fox Standards of Business Conduct, <https://www.foxcorporation.com/corporate-governance/sobc/business-ethics/>.

3. VandeHei, Jim and Allen, Mike, 'Shards of glass: Inside media's 12 splintering realities', *Axios*, 25 March 2024, <https://www.axios.com/2024/03/25/news-media-filter-bubble-different-realities>.

4. Liebling, A.J., *The Press*, Ballantine Books, 1964, p. 7.

5. Rogoway, Mike, 'A.G. Sulzberger, New York Times' publisher and former Oregonian reporter, talks journalism in the digital age', *The Oregonian*, 9 February 2018, <https://www.oregonlive.com/business/2018/02/ag_sulzberger_new_york_times_p.html>.

Acknowledgements

This book was encouraged, inspired and nurtured by my two partners in life: Sue, my late wife, who passionately supported my career and idiosyncrasies, and Lynda, my partner, who collaborated in, and cajoled, this project. I am so grateful to them.

In a very real sense, the material in this book has been researched, observed and absorbed throughout a lifetime in journalism and publishing. It is also the culmination of a long, fascinating journey through the corridors and alleyways of media power. I would like to thank some of the many people who have provided, or offered, advice, counsel, feedback, perspective and assistance along those journeys: John Addis, Chris Anderson, Paul Barry, Peter Bartlett, Thomas Beecher, Michael Bradley, Julian Burnside, James Button, Jennifer Byrne, Leslie Cannold, Les Carlyon, Mark Carnegie, Rod Carnegie, Pilita Clark, John Dahlsen, Glyn Davis, Andrew Denton, Anna Draffin, Jon Faine, John Fairfax, Nick Fairfax, Allan Fels, Peter Fray, Nick Gaynor, Ray Gill, Sandy Grant, Michael and Diana Georgeff, Archie Glenn, Anna Gribble, Bridget Griffin-Foley, Bruce Guthrie, Will Hayward, Rose Herceg, Andrew Jaspan, Patrick Joyce, Bernard Keane, Alan Kohler, Bernie Leser, David Leser, Ranald Macdonald, Ian Macphee, Jan McGuinness, Stephen Mayne, Terry Moran, Bernard Murphy, Joanna Murray-Smith, Cameron O'Reilly, Matthew Ricketson, Morry Schwartz, Bob Sessions, Margaret Simons, Max Suich, Jonathan Swan, Malcolm Turnbull, Bradley Vann, Darrell Wade, Lindsay Wakefield, Christopher Warren, Max Webberley, Chong Weng Ho, Maureen and Tony Wheeler, Jo Wiles, Peter Wilson and Sally Young.

My gratitude goes to my daughters, Kate, Joanna and Sophie; my son Tom; and to my late business partner and indefatigable sounding board, Diana Gribble.

Thanks also to my publisher Ben Ball and editor Meredith Rose at Simon & Schuster, for their professionalism and tolerance.

Index

innovation grants scheme for small
    publishers 88–9
    News Corp as the negotiator 89
Instagram 285, 287
Isaacson, Walter 80

Jagannathan, R.
    Firstpost 49
Jagger, Mick 208
Jain family xi, 48
Jain, Samir 48, 49
Jain, Vineet 48
James, Clive 248
Jefferson, Thomas vii, 24, 26
Jenkins, Simon 171
Jobs, Laurene Powell 153, 273
John, Sir Elton 101, 200–1
Johnson, Boris 87, 270
Johnson, Lyndon 94, 139
Jones, Alex
    The Trust 142
Jordan, Chris 241
Journal
    provoking and interference in
        Spanish-American War 179–80
journalism
    accountability journalism 306
    AI and 301–5
    chequebook journalism 157
    concepts to reinvent in the AI age
        309
    democracy, power to manipulate
        24
    distrust of 26, 283, 312–13, 318–19,
        320
    funding of, as advertising revenue
        declines 309
    future of 301–21
    government, ownership/control of
        274–84
    government subsidising of 309–10
    independent publications 147–50
    journalism that interests the public
        166

moral justification for unethical
    139, 140
Murdochian journalism 170
objectivity in 157–9
protection of 24
public interest journalism 166
public service role v. business
    function 27, 142–3
undercover journalism 154–7
wealthy benefactors and
    self-interest 307–8
journalists
    ethical dilemmas faced by 139–40,
        153
    informants and sources 102
    privileged status of 24
Jowell, Tessa 102
Junor, Sir John 80

Kay, John 204
Keane, Bernard 10, 21
Keating, Paul 96
Keeler, Christine 170
Kelly, Paul 75–6
Keltner, Dacher 131
Kemp, Jack 98
Kennedy, John F. (JFK) 81, 108
Kenny, Chris 198
Khalaf, Roula 305
Kiernan, Thomas 83, 170
Kilmeade, Brian 225
King Edward VIII
    Beaverbrook's role in abdication of
        188–90, 240
Kluger, Richard
    The Paper 167
Knightley, Phillip 81, 263
Kobler, John 145
Kohler, Alan 244
Kosner, Ed 256
Kovach, Bill
    The Elements of Journalism 27,
        312–13
Kristol, Bill 152

Eric Beecher has had a long career in journalism, media and publishing. He started as a reporter on the Melbourne *Age*, and spent periods at *The Sunday Times* and *The Observer* in London, and at *The Washington Post*. He was appointed as the youngest-ever editor of *The Sydney Morning Herald*, and later as editor-in-chief of the Melbourne *Herald*. He subsequently became an independent media owner, launching several start-up companies, initially in print and then in digital news publishing. He is currently the chair and largest shareholder of Private Media, which owns several Australian news websites, including *Crikey*.